For Mum and Dad with love.

MATCH OF THE DAY
365

GOALS, MATCHES AND MEMORIES
FOR EVERY DAY OF THE YEAR

STEVE WILSON

BOOKS

1 3 5 7 9 10 8 6 4 2

BBC Books, an imprint of Ebury Publishing
20 Vauxhall Bridge Road,
London SW1V 2SA

BBC Books is part of the Penguin Random House group of companies
whose addresses can be found at global.penguinrandomhouse.com

Copyright © Steve Wilson 2015

Steve Wilson has asserted his right to be identified as the author of this Work
in accordance with the Copyright, Designs and Patents Act 1988

First published by BBC Books in 2015

www.eburypublishing.co.uk

A CIP catalogue record for this book is available from the British Library

ISBN 9781849909884

Illustrations © Ben Mounsey 2015

Printed and bound in Great Britain by Clays Ltd, St Ives PLC

Penguin Random House is committed to a sustainable future for our business, our readers
and our planet. This book is made from Forest Stewardship Council® certified paper.

Contents

Foreword

The summer of 1992 was an important one for me. I was 21 and made the first move of my career, from Southampton to Blackburn Rovers. It was also an important summer for football, with the creation of the new FA Premier League.

Little did I know in 1992 that within three years I'd be celebrating winning a Premier League title under Kenny Dalglish; or that the new league would grow into the cosmopolitan, world-renowned competition that we all enjoy today. I feel proud to have been part of those formative years and of scoring the odd goal along the way ... well 260 if you're asking!

I was fortunate enough to play with and against some of the world's best players: they have graced the league, and many feature here in *Match of the Day 365*. From Ronaldo to Rooney, Henry to Terry, Gascoigne to Giggs, Gerrard to Lampard, Cantona to Kane, Asprilla to Zola – they've all earned their place in the history of the Premier League (no not Gary Lineker – he really is that old!). Then there are those who have patrolled the technical area from Sir Alex Ferguson to 'The Special One' and Arsène to Rafa, along with Kevin Keegan and King Kenny who both taught me so much.

Match of the Day 365 charts all the biggest stories and best games played by the teams who have been good enough to perform at the very pinnacle of English football since the Premier League's birth more than two decades ago. It not only tells the story of the battle for domestic honours, but recalls how the Premier League's finest clubs have sought to conquer Europe. It also covers the highs and lows of all the Home Nations as generations of the very best players from the British Isles have tried to bring international success to our shores. Alas that search still goes on ...

My journey from Southampton's Dell to the BBC *Match of the Day* sofa took me to Ewood Park, St James' and Wembley; to a World Cup and three European Championships. Anyone who has followed this great league and our great game over those years will find incredible memories being stirred in the pages of this book.

These days I enjoy analysing goals alongside Gary almost as much as I enjoyed scoring them for Southampton, Blackburn, Newcastle and England – I said almost! Like the Premier League itself, *Match of the Day* has grown and evolved, but maintained its place at the heart of the game and we do our best to keep setting the agenda every Saturday night.

Match of the Day 365 is the perfect way to remember – especially for us Newcastle fans who have fallen on slightly harder times in recent years. I'm sure that – like me – you'll enjoy the chance to look back on an extraordinary era for football as our Premier League goes from strength to strength.

Alan Shearer

January

1 JANUARY
2015 – Kane and able

Harry Kane became a Premier League phenomenon in early 2015, but he had made his debut for Spurs more than three years earlier. Harry Redknapp gave Kane his debut in August 2011 in a Europa League qualifying game against Hearts at White Hart Lane. It was the first of six Europa League appearances for the striker that season, in which he scored his first Spurs goal in a 4–0 win at Shamrock Rovers.

Kane, then aged 18, had already benefited from a five-month loan spell at Leyton Orient and would go on to have more periods on loan at Millwall, Norwich and Leicester.

Managerial changes at Spurs saw Redknapp replaced by André Villas-Boas, who in turn made way for Tim Sherwood. Sherwood, determined to give the younger players at White Hart Lane an opportunity, gave Kane his first Premier League start in April 2014. The young striker rewarded his manager by scoring in a 5–1 win over Sunderland.

Goals against West Bromwich Albion and Fulham followed in successive games, but Sherwood was replaced by Mauricio Pochettino in the summer of 2014 and, under the Argentine, Emmanuel Adebayor started the Premier League season in the team, with Kane on the bench.

In the cups it was different; Kane played in eight Europa League and League Cup ties between August and November 2014, scoring nine goals. Spurs fans were clamouring for him to start in the league games too.

Finally, at home to Stoke, Kane got his chance. Spurs lost 2–1 and Kane didn't score – but he kept his place in the side for the next game and scored in a 2–1 win at Hull.

By the end of December Kane was undroppable and unstoppable. He scored in successive matches against Swansea, Newcastle, Burnley and Leicester. Tottenham fans were eager to see him play against rivals Chelsea on New Year's Day.

Kane scored twice as Chelsea were blown away by four Tottenham goals in 22 minutes either side of half-time. Spurs won 5–3, only their fifth home win over Chelsea in the last 30 meetings, and Kane was the talk of the Premier League.

Also on this day

1996 At 17 years and 3 days old Neil Finn became the youngest Premier League player. He played in goal for West Ham United against Manchester City when Luděk Mikloško was suspended and Les Sealey injured. It was Finn's only match in full-time professional football.

1997 Middlesbrough player-manager Bryan Robson played for the last time, in a 2–0 defeat at Arsenal just ten days before his 40th birthday.

2007 Playing their first season in the Premier League, Reading beat West Ham 6–0.

2015 Tony Pulis was appointed manager of West Bromwich Albion.

2 JANUARY
2015 – Gerrard's Liverpool exit

At his peak Steven Gerrard could have had his pick of clubs, almost joining Chelsea on two occasions and turning down both Real Madrid and AC Milan. He can certainly be considered one of Liverpool's all-time best players.

When Liverpool narrowly missed out on the Premier League crown in 2014, and Luis Suárez then left for Barcelona, it seemed that his last chance of winning a Premier League title had gone. Liverpool started the following season in poor form and with Gerrard's future unresolved.

Gerrard, who had joined Liverpool at the age of nine, was only contracted to the end of the 2014/15 season, and in October he told the *Daily Mail* and *Daily Telegraph* that, 'I won't be retiring this summer. I will play beyond this season. We will have to wait and see if that's at Liverpool or somewhere else. That's Liverpool's decision.'

Five days later, when manager Brendan Rodgers left Gerrard on the substitutes' bench for their Champions League game at Real Madrid, it seemed more likely that Gerrard's future lay elsewhere.

At the end of November Liverpool did offer Gerrard a new contract. But by then LA Galaxy, of America's Major League Soccer, had begun what they later described themselves as an 'aggressive' pursuit of Gerrard. The club that had lured David Beckham wanted Gerrard as their newest star name.

On 2 January, a day after scoring twice in a 2–2 draw at home to Leicester, Gerrard announced he would be leaving Liverpool at the end of his contract.

A week later, and with Gerrard having scored two more goals, this time at AFC Wimbledon to stave off an FA Cup embarrassment, Los Angeles was confirmed as his destination. Gerrard said, 'They told me what I wanted to hear, and I want to win some more medals and trophies and to end my career there. It's time for a new challenge.'

Also on this day

1999 Seventeen-year-old Joe Cole made his West Ham debut in a 1–1 draw with Swansea in the FA Cup third round.

2011 There were three goals in the last six minutes as Gérard Houllier's Aston Villa came from behind three times to draw 3–3 at Chelsea.

2013 Liverpool signed Daniel Sturridge for £12m from Chelsea.

2014 Ole Gunnar Solskjaer was appointed manager at Cardiff City.

3 JANUARY
2010 – Manchester United's cup KO

Apart from the 1999/2000 season, when Manchester United didn't enter the FA Cup, they hadn't failed to get beyond the third round of the competition since 1984. Then, managed by Ron Atkinson and as cup-holders, they had lost to Harry Redknapp's third-tier Bournemouth at Dean Court.

Twenty-six years later, and with six more FA Cup Final wins under their belts, Manchester United were drawn at home to Leeds United in the third round of the competition.

As representatives of Lancashire and Yorkshire, Manchester United and Leeds had always been geographical rivals, and had once been bitter rivals in the chase for major honours. But the two clubs had not met for almost seven years, since Leeds's relegation from the Premier League in 2004.

By 2009/10 Leeds were playing in the third tier – games at Stockport County and Oldham Athletic had been as close as they'd got to a trip to Old Trafford. Leeds were top of League One, unbeaten since October, but Manchester United had not lost any of their last 17 home games against Leeds – a run stretching back to 1981.

It was just like the old days when Leeds and Manchester United had been rivals for the game's top trophies; Old Trafford was full to the brim, including 9000 Leeds fans, as rivalries were revived. Sir Alex Ferguson, picking a strong team including Rooney, Berbatov and Welbeck, was in no mood to lose.

Even so, Leeds played marvellously well and their striker Jermaine Beckford scored the only goal of the game, his 20th of a memorable season. Leeds might even have won by more, Robert Snodgrass smashing a free-kick onto the crossbar.

Afterwards Leeds's manager Simon Grayson said how proud he was of becoming the first manager of a lower-division side to knock Ferguson's team out of the FA Cup: 'We knew we could hurt them today and this signalled how well we've been playing all season. This win is for the fans, who have stuck by us in every game.'

Leeds were promoted into the Championship at the end of the season, but Grayson was sacked two years later despite the club being ninth in the table. Jermaine Beckford moved to Everton at the end of the 2009/10 season, where he scored eight Premier League goals before being sold to Leicester a year later.

Manchester United are still waiting to win their next FA Cup.

Also on this day

2009 **Wayne Bridge moved from Chelsea to Manchester City for £10m.**

2013 **Mario Balotelli and manager Roberto Mancini were photographed apparently fighting at Manchester City's training ground.**

2015 **Alan Pardew was announced as the new manager of Crystal Palace, replacing Neil Warnock.**

4 JANUARY
2005 – Carroll and the Mendes mix-up

Spurs hadn't won at Old Trafford for 16 years but, after taking 18 points from their last seven games, they were hopeful of ending that sequence against a Manchester United side lagging well behind Chelsea in the title race.

The game seemed to be heading for an entertaining 0–0 draw when, in the 89th minute, Pedro Mendes tried a spectacular volleyed lob from only just inside the Manchester United half. As the ball fell

from a great height, United goalkeeper Roy Carroll back-pedalled towards his net. Carroll tried to catch the ball in front of his chest, but it bounced out of his grasp and landed about a yard over the goal line.

Carroll's reactions were quick; rather than watch in horror he dived after the ball and scooped it back out of the goal. To everybody's disbelief the referee Mark Clattenburg waved 'play on'. His assistant on the touchline had been sprinting back from where Mendes had hit the shot and failed to spot the ball crossing the line.

The Tottenham players were horrified, but the game finished 0–0. Afterwards assistant referee Rob Lewis argued, 'There was nothing I could have done differently apart from run faster than Linford Christie.'

Both managers, Sir Alex Ferguson and Martin Jol, agreed that the time had come for the use of goal-line technology. The following day FIFA's director of communications Markus Siegler said, 'FIFA is strongly against the use of video evidence to decide the referees' decisions. We just have to accept the decision last night of the referee and his assistant. There is no point arguing about that. It's part of football.'

Luckily, the mistake didn't prove too costly in the final league table; without the extra point United would still have finished third and with an extra two

Spurs would only have moved from ninth to eighth.

It was almost eight more years before Tottenham finally won at Old Trafford in September 2012, and nine years before goal-line technology was introduced.

Also on this day

1994 Liverpool came from 3–0 down to draw 3–3 with Manchester United at Anfield, Neil Ruddock scoring the equalizer with ten minutes to go.

2003 Managed by former Everton captain Kevin Radcliffe, Shrewsbury Town knocked Everton out of the FA Cup, 2–1 at Gay Meadow. It was Wayne Rooney's first ever game in the competition.

2012 On a windy night at Goodison Park, Everton goalkeeper Tim Howard scored against Bolton with a clearance from 93 metres – the longest-range goal in Premier League history.

5 JANUARY
2011 – Rock bottom for Roy

Following in the footsteps of Rafa Benítez at Liverpool was never going to be easy. In six seasons the popular Spaniard had taken Liverpool to Champions League and FA Cup success, but left in the summer of 2010 with the club in turmoil.

The relationship between Benítez and Liverpool's American owners Tom Hicks and George Gillett hadn't recovered from their attempt to line up Jürgen Klinsmann as a possible replacement for the Spaniard in 2007. By the time Roy Hodgson was appointed Liverpool manager, the two owners had fallen out with each other, plans for a new stadium looked like a pipe-dream and Liverpool were estimated to be £350m in debt.

Hodgson's time in charge started badly: their star summer signing, Joe Cole, was sent off on his league debut in a draw with Arsenal. Fernando Torres looked uninterested, Hodgson signings Slaviša Jokanović, Paul Konchesky and Christian Poulsen made little or no impact and, in a seven-game winless streak, Liverpool were knocked out of the League Cup at home to Northampton Town, beaten at Anfield by Blackpool and lost to Everton 2–0.

In December Premier League defeats to Spurs and Newcastle were followed by a home defeat to bottom of the table Wolves. Liverpool were booed off the pitch.

Their next home game, against Bolton, was a 2–1 win, but only 35,400 were there – Anfield's lowest league crowd for seven years.

Liverpool's next game was on 5 January at one of Hodgson's former clubs, Blackburn Rovers, and he must have suspected that it was one he couldn't afford to lose.

At half-time Liverpool had created little and were 2–0 down, Martin Olsson and Benjani with a goal each. Benjani added his second and Blackburn's third on the hour and although Steven Gerrard pulled one goal back, Liverpool's gloom was compounded when he missed a late penalty.

Liverpool had dropped to 12th in the table, and they were only four points above the relegation zone.

'I'm very, very dejected,' said Hodgson after the game. 'We didn't defend well enough. It's a bitter blow for us and we're all very frustrated. It'll take a day or two before we can get over it.'

Three days later, Hodgson was sacked.

Also on this day

1995 Tony Yeboah signed for Leeds from Eintracht Frankfurt for £3.4m.

2006 Manchester United saw off interest from Liverpool and completed the £7m signing of Nemanja Vidić from Spartak Moscow, United's first signing under the ownership of the Glazer family.

6 JANUARY
2010 – Coyle leaves Burnley

Owen Coyle was appointed manager of Burnley in 2007 having enjoyed some notable successes at St Johnstone. In his last season there Coyle had taken the Scottish second-tier club to the semi-finals of both the Scottish Cup and League Cup, enjoying an away win over Rangers for the first time in 35 years along the way.

At Burnley he won promotion to the Premier League in his second season, the club's first taste of the top flight since 1976.

Coyle's reputation as an emerging young manager was underlined by a win over reigning champions Manchester United in their first home game in the Premier League, Robbie Blake slamming home a memorable winner in front of a delirious Turf Moor crowd.

Burnley won their first four home games of that season, adding Everton, Sunderland and Birmingham to their list of scalps. They also drew at Manchester City and at home to Arsenal.

Meanwhile, 30 miles away in Bolton things were not going so well. They had won only one of their last ten games, and in late December manager Gary Megson was sacked. Bolton chairman Phil Gartside was casting envious glances at Turf Moor and Bolton's former player Coyle.

On 2 January Burnley beat MK Dons in the FA Cup. Then Coyle told the Burnley board that he intended to move to Bolton. A bitter few days of negotiation between the two Lancashire clubs ended when Coyle resigned from

Burnley. When he swapped clubs Burnley were 14th and Bolton 18th in the table.

Coyle's fourth match in charge of Bolton was at home to his former club, now managed by Brian Laws. Coyle got the treatment he would have expected from the travelling Burnley fans. The chants of 'Judas' barely stopped, but Bolton had the upper hand and won 1–0.

When the season ended in May, the clubs' positions in the table had been exactly reversed – Bolton stayed up in 14th place and Burnley were relegated in 18th.

Also on this day

2000 **Manchester United had David Beckham sent off and Sir Alex Ferguson sent from the dugout as they drew 1–1 with Necaxa in the Club World Championship in Brazil.**

2001 **Charlton came within four minutes of becoming the first Premier League side to lose to non-league opposition in the FA Cup. A late John Salako equalizer spared their blushes and sealed a 1–1 draw against Dagenham and Redbridge at the Valley.**

2009 **After one year at Portsmouth, Jermain Defoe returned to Tottenham Hotspur.**

2012 **Thierry Henry returned to Arsenal in a loan deal from New York Red Bulls. He played seven games, all**

as a substitute, and scored goals against Leeds, Blackburn and Sunderland.

7 JANUARY
2007 – Manchester United 2 Aston Villa 1: Larsson's debut

Henrik Larsson only played 13 games in English football, and he was 36 when he arrived, but the Swede did enough in those few games to enhance his reputation as one of the great strikers of his generation.

Larsson joined Celtic from Feyenoord for £650,000 in July 1997, and few players have ever provided better value for money. He stayed at Celtic for seven seasons, scoring 242 goals in 315 games, winning the Scottish Premier League four times, the Scottish Cup twice and the Scottish League Cup three times.

Impressive though Larsson's goal record was, his standing as a great of European football was questioned by critics who pointed out that Celtic were a strong club in a weak league. His supporters pointed to goals for Sweden in five major tournament finals from 1994 to 2006.

In 2004, Larsson moved to Barcelona and won the Champions League in 2006 before moving to his home-town team in Sweden, Helsingborgs.

When the Swedish league season finished in December 2006, Larsson got

an unexpected offer. Manchester United, top of the Premier League, were looking to add some impetus to their campaign and offered him the chance to join them for the three months of the Swedish off-season.

Larsson made his debut in the FA Cup third round against Aston Villa, scoring soon after half-time with a neat volley as United won 2–1.

He scored his first Premier League goal in a 4–0 win over Watford later that month and scored against Lille in the Champions League in March.

Sir Alex Ferguson tried everything he could to get Larsson to extend his stay in England, but the Swede was as good as his word to his club back home: 'I have signed a contract with Helsingborgs and it's a contract I intend to honour. Their season

starts in the first week in April and I will be there. Manchester United has been a wonderful experience at a great club. It is something I'll always be grateful for.'

United won the Premier League and so grateful were they to their Swede that they got special dispensation to give Larsson a medal, even though he had played only seven league games rather than the ten normally needed. It was a brief but brilliant encounter.

Also on this day

1994 Mike Walker resigned as manager of Norwich to take over as Everton manager.

2003 After his positive drugs test for cocaine, Mark Bosnich was sacked by Chelsea.

2004 Liverpool won against Chelsea for the first time since 1989, Bruno Cheyrou scoring their goal in a 1–0 win.

2011 Edin Džeko signed for Manchester City for £27m from Wolfsburg.

8 JANUARY
1997 – Kevin Keegan resigns

'I feel I have taken the club as far as I can.'

It was not much of an explanation for one of the most shocking resignations in Premier League history. Kevin Keegan, the man who wore his heart on his sleeve, had resigned with barely a word.

They called Keegan 'The Messiah' on Tyneside, and no wonder. The club had been close to sinking into the third tier when he became manager in 1992, and had been agonizingly close to being champions in 1996.

With Alan Shearer in the side, it seemed that Newcastle might finally end their 70-year wait for the title in 1997. They had smashed Manchester United, their nemesis of the previous season, 5–0 at St James' Park. Having beaten Spurs 7–1 and Leeds 3–0 in their last two league games, Newcastle were fourth in the table, only five points behind leaders Liverpool.

On Sunday 5 January, Brian McNally had written in the *Sunday Mirror* that Keegan had been close to resigning before the win over Spurs: 'The simple truth is that Keegan hasn't mentally recovered from the choking disappointment of blowing the title seven months ago.'

That afternoon Newcastle drew 1–1 at Charlton in the FA Cup and afterwards Keegan was annoyed at being asked about the *Sunday Mirror*'s story: 'I'm here to talk about the game. You know the guy who wrote that. End of story.'

Three days later, to the dismay and bewilderment of the fans who idolized him, Keegan did resign. The club offered Bobby Robson the manager's job the next day. Robson, who had only been in charge at Barcelona for seven months, declined, describing the offer as 'the right job at the wrong time'.

Also on this day

2005 Manchester United were held 0–0 at home by Conference side Exeter City in the FA Cup third round. United won the replay 2–0.

2006 In the FA Cup third round, Manchester United were held by a Conference side for the second season running. This time they drew 0–0 at Burton Albion. United won the replay 5–0.

2010 The national team of Togo, including Manchester City's Emmanuel Adebayor, was targeted by armed terrorists as they travelled to Cabinda province in Angola. Three of the Togolese party were killed and nine others injured.

2011 Kenny Dalglish took over from Roy Hodgson, starting his second spell as Liverpool manager.

2012 Neil Warnock was sacked as manager of Queens Park Rangers.

2014 Having lost 5–0 at Nottingham Forest in the FA Cup three days earlier, West Ham lost the first leg of their League Cup semi-final 6–0 at Manchester City.

9 JANUARY
2009 – Facts about Ferguson

Liverpool were top of the league having lost only once all season. Chelsea were second, three points behind, with Manchester United a further four points adrift. Almost 19 years after their last title, it seemed Liverpool might soon be crowned champions.

Sir Alex Ferguson had tried to plant some seeds of doubt in Liverpool minds by suggesting that nerves might get the better of Rafael Benítez's team. Asked for his response, the Liverpool manager launched into a premeditated attack on his United rival.

'Maybe they are nervous because we are at the top of the table,' he said. Then, pulling out a piece of paper, he began to read. 'But I want to talk about facts … During the Respect campaign – and this is a fact – Mr Ferguson was charged by the FA for improper conduct after comments made about Martin Atkinson and Keith Hackett. He was not punished. He is the only manager in the league that cannot be punished for these things.

'Then he was talking about the fixtures. Now he is complaining about everything, that everybody is against United. But the second half of the season will see them playing at home against all the teams at the top of the table, it is a fantastic advantage.

'And about his behaviour with referees … I am not playing mind games, just facts … We know what happens every time we go to Old Trafford. They are always going man-to-man with the referees, especially at half-time when they walk close to the referees and they are talking and talking. All managers need to know is that only Mr Ferguson can talk about the fixtures, can talk about referees and nothing happens. We need to know that I am talking about facts, not my impression. There are things that everyone can see every single week.'

Benítez, in trying to stand up to Ferguson, gave the impression of a man being tormented by his opposite number. It seemed Ferguson's arrows had hit their mark. Despite losing only one more league game that season, Liverpool couldn't finish the job and Manchester United revelled in winning the Premier League title with four more points than their Merseyside rivals.

Also on this day

1993 Manchester United went to the top of the Premier League table for the first time after Éric Cantona inspired a 4–1 win over Spurs.

2001 Sven-Göran Eriksson resigned from his job at Lazio to take over as England manager earlier than expected.

2007 Julio Baptista became the first player to score four times against

Liverpool at Anfield since 1945, as Arsenal won 6–3 there in the League Cup. It was also the first time a team had scored six against Liverpool at Anfield since 1930.

2008 After 2 wins in 13 games Sam Allardyce left his job as manager of Newcastle 'by mutual consent'.

2014 Pepe Mel was appointed manager of West Bromwich Albion.

10 JANUARY
1995 – Taking Cole from Newcastle

Kevin Keegan had signed Andy Cole for Newcastle from Bristol City for £1.75m in March 1993. His impact was huge and immediate, scoring 12 goals in his first 12 games to help seal promotion to the Premier League.

In the top flight Cole, who had failed to make the grade at Arsenal, was a sensation. He hit 41 goals in the 1993/94 season, including four hat-tricks. His total of 34 Premier League goals that season was equalled by Alan Shearer for Blackburn in 1994/95, but has never been beaten.

Newcastle finished third in 1993/94, and then won their first eight matches of 1994/95, with Cole scoring seven times. His tally was 15 goals by the end of November, and he had a new strike partner in Paul Kitson. But Newcastle won only one game out of 12 from early November to 8 January, and when they drew with Blackburn in the FA Cup, Cole had gone nine games without scoring.

On 9 January Keegan and Newcastle's chief executive Freddie Fletcher met with Manchester United officials at Bramall Lane, where Alex Ferguson's side were playing Sheffield United in the FA Cup. United offered a British record £6m plus teenage winger Keith Gillespie in return for Cole. The deal, which was completed the next day, stunned both sets of supporters.

Keegan stood on the steps of St James' Park that afternoon trying to explain to angry fans what they had done, pleading for their trust and patience.

At least Newcastle had the good sense to ensure that Cole couldn't play against them when Manchester United played at St James' Park five days later and they would have found some consolation when Kitson scored their goal in a 1–1 draw. But the transfer was pivotal to the season of both clubs; Cole scored 12 goals in 18 games for Manchester United that season as they battled with Blackburn for the title. Newcastle faded to finish sixth.

Also on this day

1996 Terry Venables announced that he would stand down as England manager after Euro 96.

2006 Patrice Evra joined Manchester United from Monaco for £5.5m.

2007 Walter Smith resigned as manager of Scotland.

2007 Clint Dempsey joined Fulham from New England Revolution.

2012 Mark Hughes was appointed manager of Queens Park Rangers.

2015 With a 2–1 defeat at Burnley, QPR set a new Premier League record by losing their tenth consecutive away game from the start of the season.

11 JANUARY
2007 – Beckham to LA

David Beckham could have signed for Inter Milan, Lyon or Marseille. In England there were offers from Newcastle, West Ham and Bolton – but none from Manchester United.

Instead of leaving Real Madrid to wind down his career at a smaller European club, Beckham chose to start afresh in MLS with LA Galaxy. He said he wanted 'a new challenge of growing the world's most popular game in a country that is as passionate about its sport as my own. I didn't want to go to LA at 34 and for people to turn around and say, "He's only going there to get the money". It's not what I'm going out there to do. I'm going to, hopefully, build a club and a team that

has a lot of potential. I think that is what excites me.'

There was also money though – lots of it. Beckham, it was reported, might earn as much as £128m over the five years of his contract if all the bonuses and clauses were triggered. In 2007 the next highest earner in the MLS was Juan Francisco Palencia of Chivas USA, who was paid £700,000 a year. LA Galaxy's lowest earner was paid a salary of just £5,650.

The eye-watering figures had become possible because of an MLS rule change the previous November. The change allowed each club to have a 'designated player' whose salary could exceed the usual cap in place for everybody else. It was nicknamed 'The Beckham Rule'.

America loved Beckham, and he loved America. He played for Galaxy from 2007 to 2012, also fitting in two loan spells at AC Milan in the MLS off-season, and won the US championship twice. Beckham's impact hugely increased the profile of football in the States as well as making it an attractive, and credible, place to play for those like Thierry Henry, Robbie Keane, Juan Pablo Ángel, Frank Lampard and Steven Gerrard.

Even having left Galaxy at the end of the 2012 MLS season, Beckham had one last ace up his sleeve. He signed a five-month deal with Paris Saint-Germain, winning the hearts of even the most sceptical Parisian by helping them to the championship and donating his entire salary to charity.

Also on this day

2003 Liverpool drew 1–1 at home to Aston Villa, their 11th league game without a win and their worst run in 48 years.

2005 Norwich City signed striker Dean Ashton from Crewe for a club record £3m.

2008 Chelsea signed Nicolas Anelka from Bolton for £15m.

12 JANUARY
2000 – Weah to Chelsea

George Weah was one of the greatest African footballers of all time. In 1995 he was voted World, European and African Footballer of the Year. Five years later, at 34, Weah was in his fifth year at AC Milan, but had played only 14 times in Italy in the first half of the season.

When Chelsea manager Gianluca Vialli gave him the opportunity to move to London on a six-month loan deal, Weah grabbed it.

On 12 January 2000, Weah woke up in Milan, still waiting for his international clearance to join Chelsea. In the early afternoon he stepped off his flight from Milan to Heathrow and went straight to Chelsea's Harlington training ground – which was only a few minutes away, sandwiched between the airport and the M4 motorway.

Late in the afternoon, Weah got his clearance to play for Chelsea confirmed by the Foreign Office and Vialli named him as one of his substitutes for the home game with Spurs that evening. He got a hero's ovation when he was introduced to the crowd before kick-off, and another when he came on for Tore André Flo with half an hour to play.

A busy day for the Liberian had the perfect ending when he headed home the only goal of the game from a Dennis Wise cross with three minutes to go. 'It's a good beginning,' said Weah. 'I feel welcome. I'm hoping to do great things in London and I'm very happy that Gianluca believes in me.'

Weah played 15 games in his loan spell, scoring five goals and starting the FA Cup Final in which Chelsea beat Aston Villa 1–0.

That was his last game for Chelsea, and Weah signed for Manchester City in the summer. There he scored four goals in nine games before falling out with manager Joe Royle after being dropped for a game against Bradford. City cancelled his contract and Weah joined Marseille.

Also on this day

1999 The FA secured the purchase of Wembley Stadium and the surrounding land and set a budget of £320m to rebuild the stadium. The final cost of the rebuild was later estimated to be £798m.

2003 Thierry Henry scored his 100th goal for Arsenal in his 180th game as they beat Birmingham 4–0.

2008 Cristiano Ronaldo scored his first hat-trick for Manchester United in a 6–0 win over Newcastle.

2009 Cristiano Ronaldo became the first Premier League player to be voted World Player of the Year.

13 JANUARY
2001 – Villa's Angel delight

Aston Villa's pursuit of the Colombian Juan Pablo Ángel had been long and tortuous. The 25-year-old striker, who had successfully replaced Hernán Crespo at River Plate, was a wanted man – the next big thing from South America. Villa thought they'd pulled off a major coup by agreeing a fee with his Argentine club.

At £9.5m Ángel was set to become Villa's record signing when the FA pulled the rug out from under Villa's feet. They said the deal broke FIFA regulations and couldn't go ahead. The problem was that half of Ángel's registration was held by his agent, Gustavo Mascardi, and half by River Plate. It was the first time most

people in England had heard of the issue of third-party ownership.

Villa, who were having an indifferent season, were desperate for a goalscorer and tried to persuade Liverpool to sell them Robbie Fowler, who was being kept out of Gérard Houllier's side by Michael Owen and Emile Heskey.

Finding that Liverpool didn't want to sell Fowler, Doug Ellis, the Villa chairman, had one last attempt to untangle the web surrounding Ángel – and this time got his man. 'It has undoubtedly been a difficult week, but ultimately we all feel it has been worth it,' said Ellis.

Villa were playing Liverpool on the day Ángel signed, and were 2–0 down when the Colombian was introduced to the crowd at half-time. They lost 3–0, and Fowler wasn't even on the Liverpool bench.

Ángel stayed with Villa for six-and-a-half years, scoring 62 goals in 205 games. In his best season, 2003/04, he scored 23 goals – but never quite lived up to his billing as a world-class striker.

Ángel lost his place in the side when Martin O'Neill bought the muscular Norwegian John Carew and soon the Colombian crossed the Atlantic again to join New York Red Bulls, where he scored over 60 goals. Ángel's career ended where it had begun, scoring goals for Atlético Nacional in Medellín.

Also on this day

1993 Bolton, then playing in the third tier, won their FA Cup replay against Liverpool 2–0 at Anfield.

1995 John Hartson left Luton for Arsenal in a £2.5m deal, a British record for a teenager.

2006 Steve Staunton was appointed manager of the Republic of Ireland.

2010 Brian Laws was named as the new manager of Burnley.

2012 Chelsea signed Gary Cahill from Bolton for £7m.

14 JANUARY
2008 – Liverpool try to Kop Klinsmann

Even a popular and successful manager is seldom under more threat than when his club has a new owner.

Less than a year after the Americans Tom Hicks and George Gillett had bought Liverpool, their relationship with Rafa Benítez seemed irreparably damaged. With Benítez untouchable in the eyes of most Liverpool fans, Hicks and Gillett were inevitably cast as the bad guys.

Benítez was not accustomed to managing a team on a limited budget, but with grand promises to build a new stadium, £350m of debt to restructure and Fernando Torres having been signed the previous summer, there wasn't much left for the manager to spend. In fact, daunted by the mounting cost of his involvement, Gillett was already looking for a way out of his co-ownership of the club and sounding out Dubai International Capital as a possible buyer – something Hicks would block, contributing to a breakdown in the relationship between the two owners.

Benítez, it was reported, was being courted by Real Madrid, where he'd worked as youth coach. The Spaniard didn't distance himself from reports that he might be a natural replacement for Real's coach Bernd Schuster.

Against this backdrop of a highly political power-struggle it was reported on 14 January that Liverpool's owners had attempted to hire Jürgen Klinsmann to replace Benítez at Anfield.

Confirming stories of a meeting, but denying the offer of a job to Klinsmann, George Hicks explained, 'In November, when it appeared we were in danger of not advancing in the Champions League, weren't playing well in our Premier League matches, and Rafa and we were having communication issues over the January transfer window, George and I met with Jürgen to learn as much as we could about English and European football. He is a very impressive man.'

Twenty-four hours later Liverpool played Luton at Anfield in the FA Cup, and their fans made it clear who they wanted in charge of the team – Benítez was cheered throughout a 5–0 win. Klinsmann went to Bayern Munich and Benítez kept his job – but the impression of an unhealthy stand-off between the manager and the owners of Liverpool never went away.

Also on this day

1997 **Kenny Dalglish, who had replaced Kevin Keegan as a player at Liverpool in 1977, was appointed Keegan's successor as Newcastle manager.**

1999 **Wimbledon spent £7.5m on John Hartson from West Ham, almost quadrupling their record outlay on a player.**

2006 **Patrice Evra suffered a nightmare Manchester United debut, being substituted at half-time as United, with Cristiano Ronaldo sent off, lost 3–1 to Manchester City.**

15 JANUARY
2006 – Sven and the Fake Sheikh

As well as making the back pages of the newspapers with some notable successes on the pitch, England manager Sven-Göran Eriksson's had frequently featured on the front pages too.

One of the victims of the newspaper phone-hacking scandal, Eriksson was reported in 2002 to have had an affair with TV presenter Ulrika Jonsson, and in 2004 there were allegations of an affair with Faria Alam, the personal assistant to FA executive director David Davies.

Eriksson also reportedly agreed to take over at Manchester United when Sir Alex Ferguson had intended to retire in 2002, and he'd been photographed leaving the flat of Chelsea chief executive Peter Kenyon when they were looking to replace Claudio Ranieri in 2004.

But the most damaging story came in 2006, when Eriksson fell for a sting organized by the *News of the World* reporter Mazher Mahmood, better known as the Fake Sheikh.

Posing as a rich Arab businessman, Mahmood had lunch with Eriksson in Dubai on the pretext of discussing a consultancy for a sports project in the city. During conversations over two days the newspaper reported that Eriksson was happy to discuss the possibility of managing Aston Villa after the 2006 World Cup – even suggesting that he could persuade David Beckham to leave Real Madrid to join him.

The *News of the World* also reported that Eriksson had discussed Wayne Rooney having a 'temper' and said that Rio Ferdinand could be 'lazy sometimes'. Eriksson, they reported, had also claimed that Michael Owen had told him he only joined Newcastle because of the 'incredible' salary they were paying him.

In the frenzy that followed publication Eriksson initially got the backing of the FA, but eight days later he announced that he would leave his job after the World Cup finals.

A year later Eriksson still sounded angry when he recalled, 'The real reason I was sacked was because of a newspaper story about Dubai. And of course what was written in those stories was not true – or a lot of it. It's very easy for a newspaper if they want to hurt you to do it. The FA knew why I went to Dubai and I didn't go there to listen for a new job. I went to listen about football in Dubai. They tried to set me up and they were lucky. I was sacked because this time the FA had had enough, and they didn't check if it was true or not.'

Also on this day

1998 **Newcastle sold Faustino Asprilla to Parma for £6.1m.**

1999 **Terry Venables left Crystal Palace after only six months in charge.**

1999 **Arsenal signed Kanu from Inter Milan for £4.5m.**

2004 **Leeds faced the possibility of going into administration and admitted they needed to sell Mark Viduka, Alan**

Smith and possibly their Elland Road stadium.

2013 **Gordon Strachan was appointed manager of Scotland.**

16 JANUARY
2001 – Ferguson's retirement plan

It was going to be a long goodbye. Sir Alex Ferguson had made it clear that he would not be renewing his Manchester United contract that expired in the summer of 2002.

Despite Martin Edwards, with whom Ferguson had a difficult relationship, being replaced as chief executive by Peter Kenyon, Ferguson confirmed that there would be no about-turn.

After winning the Premier League six times, the FA Cup four times, the League Cup, the Cup Winners' Cup and the Champions League, he was going after the final game of 2001/02 and would then have some vague role, possibly in setting up academies for the club in the Far East. With Hampden Park in his native Glasgow to be the venue for the 2002 Champions League Final, perhaps Ferguson envisaged a fairy-tale farewell on Scottish soil.

Ferguson was keen to get his future role 'upstairs' clarified, but United seemed unhurried. They remembered how the

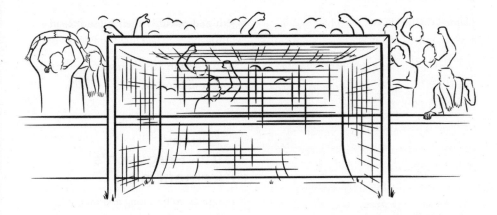

presence of Sir Matt Busby after his Old Trafford retirement had undermined successor Wilf McGuinness, and seemed wary of having Ferguson around.

United won the Premier League title in 2001 with five games to spare and there were rumours that the success might lure the manager into staying. On the contrary, angered by the board's unwillingness to find him a future position with the club, Ferguson said, 'I will definitely be working somewhere after next season but, as far as United are concerned, the door is closed now.'

United started the 2001/02 season looking like a side lacking direction, losing six Premier League games before Christmas and slumping to ninth in the table. They lost home and away to Deportivo La Coruña in the group stage of the Champions League, lost 4–0 at Arsenal in the League Cup and 2–0 at Middlesbrough, now managed by Ferguson's former assistant Steve McLaren, in the FA Cup.

Ferguson's early announcement seemed to have undermined his authority. With Sven-Göran Eriksson, Ottmar Hitzfeld, Martin O'Neill, Marcello Lippi and David O'Leary all being touted as possible successors, the club were in limbo.

Suddenly, in February 2002, Ferguson performed a U-turn. He would stay and sign a three-year deal, he said, later revealing that his wife Cathy had persuaded him to stay, pointing out that, 'One, your health is good. Two, I'm not having you in the house. And three, you're too young anyway.'

United lost only two more league games that season but missed out on the title, which was won by Arsenal. Ferguson didn't take his team to Hampden either, losing to Bayer Leverkusen in the Champions League semi-final.

Also on this day

1999 Robbie Fowler scored a hat-trick, including his 100th league goal, for Liverpool as they beat Southampton 7–1 at Anfield.

2008 Eleven years after resigning, Kevin Keegan returned to Newcastle for a second spell as manager.

2010 Chelsea scored seven in a top-flight game for the first time in 49 years as they beat Sunderland 7–2 at Stamford Bridge.

2015 After only 11 months playing for Toronto FC in America, Jermain Defoe returned to the Premier League, joining Sunderland.

17 JANUARY
2001 – Mancini the fox

There wasn't much Roberto Mancini hadn't done as player in 15 seasons at Sampdoria and three at Lazio.

He'd won the Serie A title twice, the Italian Cup six times and played in four European finals, winning the Cup Winners' Cup twice. He'd also played 36 times for Italy and been to the 1998 European Championship and the 1990 World Cup.

At Lazio, aged 36, Mancini had been elevated to the position of player-coach by manager Sven-Göran Eriksson. When the Swede left Rome to take up his position as England manager, Mancini decided it was time to move on too.

Eriksson was taking over England from the caretaker manager Peter Taylor, who was also managing Leicester. A word from the Swede convinced Taylor to offer a contract to Mancini. A recommendation from his old strike-partner at Sampdoria, Gianluca Vialli, convinced Mancini that Leicester could be good for him.

Mancini made his debut playing alongside Dean Sturridge in a 0–0 draw with Arsenal at Filbert Street. He stayed in the side for the next three games – against Aston Villa, Southampton and Chelsea – before coming on as a substitute in a defeat at Everton.

With an FA Cup tie against Bristol City looming, Taylor intended putting his Italian back in the side, but two days before that game Mancini was offered the manager's job at Fiorentina, and Leicester didn't stand in his way.

'It's obviously a big blow because we were expecting him to be playing on Saturday,' said Taylor. 'But I can't praise Roberto enough for what he did while he was with us.'

Mancini's spell was short, but he later said that it had been enough to convince him that one day he would like to return to England as a manager.

Also on this day

1998 Newcastle's Georgian midfielder Temuri Ketsbaia scored a last-minute winner in their 2–1 win against Bolton and celebrated by taking off his shirt, throwing it into the Gallowgate End and then aiming several kicks at the advertising hoardings around the pitch. He said his celebration was out of frustration born of spending most of his time as a substitute.

2004 Rio Ferdinand played his last game before starting an eight-month suspension for missing a drugs test. Manchester United and Ferdinand lost 1–0 at Wolves.

2015 José Mourinho described his Chelsea team's performance at Swansea as 'the perfect game'; Chelsea won 5–0.

18 JANUARY
2009 – Mrs Redknapp

Darren Bent had been signed by Martin Jol for Spurs for £16.5m in June 2007, an addition to a squad already boasting strikers Dimitar Berbatov, Jermain Defoe and Robbie Keane.

Berbatov and Keane seemed to be Jol's preferred partnership, but after Juande Ramos replaced Jol as manager and Jermain Defoe moved to Portsmouth, Bent started getting more opportunities.

His chances of being Tottenham's main striker increased dramatically when first Keane joined Liverpool and then Berbatov moved to Manchester United. Bent partnered Russian signing Roman Pavlyuchenko at the start of the 2008/09 season – but goals were in short supply and Ramos was sacked in October to be replaced by Harry Redknapp.

Bent scored seven goals in Redknapp's first five games in charge. Pavlyuchenko had got over his slow start too, so both strikers might have been surprised when Redknapp spent £15m on bringing Defoe back to Spurs from Portsmouth, especially as they had sold him for £9m only a year earlier.

Two days after Defoe's return, a disgruntled Bent was on the substitutes' bench as the new signing started with Pavlyuchenko in their game at Wigan.

It was the same story a week later against Portsmouth at White Hart Lane. But when Pavlyuchenko was injured after only half an hour, Bent got the chance to prove his worth.

With Spurs losing 1–0, Defoe equalized with 20 minutes to play. The opportunity for Bent to impress came in injury-time. David Bentley crossed and somehow Bent missed the target with his header from almost in front of an open goal. After the game Redknapp took aim with rather more accuracy than his striker had done. 'You can't miss chances like that,' he grumbled. 'I was off my seat waiting to see the ball in the back of the net. You get paid to put those away. My missus could have scored that one.'

Redknapp later revealed that Bent was so furious about his comment that he asked for a transfer. The final indignity for Bent came two weeks later when Tottenham brought Robbie Keane back to White Hart Lane from Liverpool. In the summer Bent was sold for a £6.5m loss to Sunderland, where he answered his critics by scoring 25 goals in his first season.

Also on this day

2008 Fulham signed Brede Hangeland from Viking Stavanger for £2.5m.

2010 David Sullivan and David Gold took control of West Ham United.

2013 After sacking Nigel Adkins, Southampton appointed Mauricio Pochettino as manager.

2015 Arsenal won 2–0 at Manchester City, their first away win against reigning league champions since they beat Manchester United at Old Trafford in 2002.

19 JANUARY
2004 – Chelsea's Cech mate

Petr Čech was singled out for great things from an early age. His first impact outside Prague came when he saved two French penalties in a shoot-out to help his side win the final of the European Under-21 Championships in Switzerland.

His saves had followed a man-of-the-match performance, and caught the eye of scouts from London; Arsenal were the club who first tried to bring him to England. Čech later said, 'I was watched by Arsenal but when I couldn't get a work permit the situation was missed. At the last minute I think the person who was the chief scout at Arsenal didn't think I was good enough for the English league. So in the end it didn't happen.'

Čech went to Rennes instead and, although still only 20, he excelled in two outstanding seasons in France, also establishing himself as the first-choice goalkeeper for the senior Czech Republic side.

Chelsea's four goalkeepers in the 2003/04 season were Carlo Cudicini, Neil Sullivan, Marco Ambrosio and Jürgen Macho – aged 30, 33, 30 and 36 respectively. In the opinion of Claudio Ranieri, none were good enough to be first choice for a club with new horizons being set by the Abramovich takeover. With Real Madrid and Inter Milan also having taken an interest in Čech, Chelsea had to move fast.

Rennes put up a fight, and at least persuaded Chelsea to allow Čech to stay with them until the end of the season, but a bid of £8.5m was too good to turn down for a club battling against relegation.

When Čech arrived at Chelsea in the summer, Ranieri had been sacked, but José Mourinho inherited one of the best goalkeepers the Premier League has seen.

Also on this day

1999 **Gary Mabbutt, who had enjoyed a 21-year career starting at Bristol Rovers and who appeared 668 times for Spurs, announced his retirement at the age of 37.**

2009 **Brazilian Kaká was reported to have rejected the chance to earn £500,000 a week at Manchester City, who were said to be offering AC Milan a £107m transfer fee.**

2010 **Carlos Tévez continued his feud with Gary Neville as Manchester City beat Manchester United 2–1 in the first leg of the League Cup semi-final. Tévez scored twice and afterwards told ESPN Argentina that, 'My celebration was directed at Gary Neville. He acted like a complete boot-licker when he said I wasn't worth £25m, just to suck up to the manager.**

I don't know what the hell that moron is talking about me for. I never said anything about him.'

2012 **The FAW announced that Chris Coleman would be Gary Speed's successor as manager of Wales.**

20 JANUARY
2006 – Arsenal's boy wonder

It was Harry Redknapp who gave Theo Walcott his debut. At 16 years and 143 days old, Walcott became the youngest ever Southampton player when he came on for Kenwyne Jones with 17 minutes to go in a home game against Wolves in the Championship in August 2005. Six more substitute appearances followed before Walcott made his first start, at Elland Road against Leeds.

Redknapp recalled in his autobiography: 'He was on the right track even then, a smashing kid from a lovely family. I had no worries at all introducing him to first-team football at such a young age. Theo was so good it was frightening. He scored after 25 minutes and could have had five. I haven't seen such a confident debut from a young man.'

That goal made him Southampton's youngest goalscorer too. Blessed with pace, skill and intelligence it was clear that Walcott was a special talent. He stayed in the Southampton team for their next ten games, scoring a further three goals, during which time Redknapp was replaced as manager by George Burley. At Queens Park Rangers in mid-January he was back in the Southampton side.

Still two months short of his 17th birthday, Chelsea and Arsenal tried to prise him from St Mary's. Walcott had only a pre-contract agreement with Southampton, with full terms to be signed on his next birthday – so he could, if Southampton blocked a move, wait to leave on his 17th birthday for almost nothing.

Burley, ignoring the inevitable, said, 'He is in the best place and doing tremendously well. He is playing regularly, which is fantastic at his age.'

Arsenal's bid was for £5m straight away with the fee rising to £12m – Chelsea's bid was thought to be bigger. Walcott rejected the higher wages on offer at Chelsea and moved to Arsenal on 20 January, making him the most expensive 16-year-old in history.

Wenger tucked the teenager into his reserves, and Walcott had to wait until the end of May for his next senior game. That wasn't for Arsenal, but for England – in a friendly match against Hungary. The 17-year-old Walcott was off to Germany for the World Cup.

Also on this day

1994 Alan Ball was appointed manager of relegation-threatened Southampton; at the end of the season they stayed up by one point.

1995 Calum Chambers was born.

2001 After winning 66 caps for England, Tony Adams announced his retirement from international football.

2010 Aston Villa recovered from 2–0 down to beat Blackburn 6–4 in the second leg of the League Cup semi-final, sealing a 7–4 aggregate win.

21 JANUARY
2004 – Northern Ireland turn to Sanchez

When Steve Lomas scored for Northern Ireland in the 18th minute of their friendly against Poland played in Limassol, Cyprus, in February 2002, it's unlikely that many in the crowd of just 221 got too excited.

Northern Ireland were already 2–0 down when Lomas scored, and eventually lost 4–1, but his goal was the last scored by the team before what became one of the worst goal droughts ever suffered by a European nation.

Sammy McIlroy had been Northern Ireland's manager since January 2000, and had just presided over two of his better results, a 3–0 win over Iceland and a 1–0 win in Malta. The match against the Poles in Cyprus was the beginning of McIlroy's preparations for the European Championship qualifying campaign.

Over the next two years Northern Ireland played 13 games. They drew 0–0 in Liechtenstein, then lost 5–0 at home to Spain. A 0–0 home draw with Cyprus was followed by a 3–0 defeat in Spain. Then came a 0–0 draw at home to Ukraine and a 1–0 defeat at home to Finland, a 1–0 loss in Armenia, a 2–0 defeat at home to Greece and a 2–0 defeat in Italy. A 0–0 draw at home to Spain was followed by a 0–0 draw in Ukraine and a 1–0 defeat at home to Armenia and then a 1–0 defeat in Greece.

Thirteen games, five draws, eight defeats; 16 goals had been conceded and none had been scored. Northern Ireland were 124th in the FIFA rankings, only just above the Faroe Islands. McIlroy resigned.

Lawrie Sanchez, who'd won three caps with Northern Ireland as a player, had taken Wycombe Wanderers to the FA Cup semi-final in 2001. He had been out of work for four months after his sacking at Wycombe, and took the job.

His first game was at home to Norway and they were 3–0 down at half-time. But when David Healy nodded in a Keith Gillespie cross after 56 minutes Norway's goals didn't seem to matter – Northern Ireland had scored their first goal for 1298 minutes.

Also on this day

2005 Arsenal announced that they would wear redcurrant-coloured shirts for the 2005/06 season, their last at Highbury. Arsenal wore the colour in their first season at the stadium in 1913.

2009 Spurs recovered from 3–0 down at Turf Moor against Burnley to lose 3–2 in the second leg of their League Cup semi-final. It was enough to give Harry Redknapp's side a 6–4 aggregate win.

22 JANUARY
2006 – Neville's dash

'I can't stand Liverpool, I can't stand the people. I can't stand anything to do with them.' So said Gary Neville.

Geography, music and football have all conspired over decades to make the cities of Manchester and Liverpool the bitterest of rivals. The clearest indication of that mutual dislike comes whenever the red teams meet.

In January 2006 Liverpool were European Champions, a fact that was hard to stomach in Manchester. After 8 titles in 13 years, United were only 3 short of Liverpool's record of 18 championships, a fact that was unpalatable on Merseyside.

Chelsea might have been runaway leaders at the top of the Premier League, but Manchester United were second and Liverpool third, adding an edge to the game at Old Trafford – as if it were needed.

It was a tetchy affair, low on quality and chances, Liverpool edging possession and missing the best opportunity through Djibril Cissé.

A goalless draw would have seemed about right, the same outcome as the Anfield meeting four months earlier. Then Ryan Giggs took a 90th-minute free-kick and Rio Ferdinand headed a winner.

As the other United players celebrated in front of the Stretford End, Gary Neville set off on a length-of-the-field run to taunt the Liverpool fans at the other end. 'There's a line and Neville crossed it,' said Jamie Carragher afterwards.

Neville was fined £5000 by the FA but said, 'You are caught up in the moment and for a few seconds you can go bananas. What are you meant to do? Smile sweetly and jog back to the halfway line?'

Also on this day

2002 Diego Forlán signed for Manchester United from Independiente of Argentina for £7m. He had flown to England expecting to sign for Middlesbrough, but Alex Ferguson stepped in with a last-minute offer.

2008 Spurs hammered Arsenal 5–1 in the second leg of their League Cup semi-final to win 6–2 on aggregate.

It was Spurs's biggest win over Arsenal for 25 years.

2012 Mario Balotelli scored a last-minute winner for Manchester City in their 3–2 win over Spurs. Balotelli was later given a four-match ban for a stamp on Scott Parker that the referee had failed to spot.

2013 Bradford City became the first fourth-tier side to reach the League Cup Final in more than 50 years, despite losing the second leg of their League Cup semi-final 2–1 at Aston Villa. Bradford had won the first leg 3–1 and went through 4–3 on aggregate.

23 JANUARY
2013 – Swansea's hazardous route to Wembley

With the rise of Swansea City and Cardiff City, a race was on to be the first Welsh club to play in the Premier League. Swansea narrowly won that race in 2011, beating Reading in the Championship play-off final at Wembley. Cardiff had lost in the same fixture to Blackpool 12 months earlier.

But Swansea had seen their arch rivals reach two cup finals: Cardiff had been beaten by Portsmouth in the 2008 FA Cup Final and by Liverpool in the League Cup Final four years later.

In late January 2013, Cardiff were top of the Championship and looking certain to join Swansea in the top flight the following season. Swansea, under Michael Laudrup's management, were sitting comfortably in the top half of the Premier League table and playing with style.

Laudrup had also taken his side to the last four of the League Cup, beating Liverpool on the way. They drew Chelsea in the semi-final with the first leg away.

Swansea stunned Rafa Benítez's side with a 2–0 win in London, goals from Michu and Danny Graham securing a first win at Stamford Bridge for 89 years. In their centenary season, Swansea were one game away from their first major final.

In the return game Swansea stood firm as Chelsea created little. With 13 minutes to go a misplaced pass from César Azpilicueta went for a Swansea goal-kick. The ball boy behind the goal was so slow in returning it to the goalkeeper that Eden Hazard went to get it from him – in the tussle that followed the ball boy ended up lying on top of the ball with Hazard trying to kick it out from under his stomach.

It transpired later that before the game tweets had been posted from the ball boy's account saying: 'The king of all ball boys is back making his final appearance #needed #for #timewasting.'

Hazard was shown a red card by referee Chris Foy for violent conduct; no action was taken against Swansea or the ball boy.

Also on this day

2004 Louis Saha signed for Manchester United from Fulham for £12.85m.

2006 Embarrassed by the revelations made to the 'Fake Sheikh' by England manager Sven-Göran Eriksson, the FA announced he would leave his job after the World Cup.

2007 Aston Villa signed Ashley Young from Watford for a club record £9.65m.

2010 Wayne Rooney scored four goals in a match for the first time, getting all Manchester United's goals against Hull City.

2012 Harry Redknapp's trial on charges of tax evasion began. Redknapp and co-defendant Milan Mandarić were cleared.

24 JANUARY
2015 – The cup shocks runneth over

The fourth round of the FA Cup in 2015 provided a remarkable afternoon, as the top three sides in the Premier League were all knocked out at home.

Least surprising was third-placed Southampton's exit at the hands of Crystal Palace, who made it four wins in four under new boss Alan Pardew by twice coming from behind to win 3–2 at St Mary's.

Second in the Premier League were Manchester City. They flew back into the wintry northwest from a training trip in Abu Dhabi only the evening before their match at home to the Championship's second-placed team, Middlesbrough.

At first City dominated but failed to score, and soon Middlesbrough grew in confidence to take the lead with a goal from Chelsea loan player Patrick Bamford. Lampard hit a post for City, but Kike sealed the win with a late second goal.

At Stamford Bridge, Chelsea took a 2–0 lead after 40 minutes against third-tier Bradford City, and seemed certain to win their 13th consecutive home game. Then Jon Stead, a striker with three Premier League clubs on his CV, scored just before half-time.

Six-thousand Bradford fans watched in astonishment as Filipe Morais, a former Chelsea reserve, scored the equalizer with 15 minutes to go. With Bradford on a roll, Andy Halliday fired them in front before Mark Yeates's 90th-minute goal finished the Premier League leaders off.

Afterwards Chelsea boss José Mourinho went into the Bradford dressing room to congratulate the winners, but told the media that he was 'ashamed' and 'embarrassed' to lose,

growling, 'It's a disgrace for a big team to lose to a small team from a lower league.'

Bradford manager Phil Parkinson said the result would 'take some beating' and former Liverpool striker Robbie Fowler agreed, telling viewers of the BBC's *Final Score* that this was 'the biggest FA Cup shock ever'.

In the next round Middlesbrough went out to Arsenal, Crystal Palace lost to Liverpool and Bradford beat Premier League Sunderland to reach the quarter-final, where they lost in a replay to Reading.

Also on this day

1995 Faustino Asprilla agreed a £7.5m move from Parma to Newcastle.

1999 Dwight Yorke and Ole Gunnar Solskjaer scored in the last two minutes as Manchester United beat Liverpool 2–1 in the FA Cup fourth round.

2002 With Aston Villa seventh in the Premier League, John Gregory resigned as manager.

2008 George Burley was appointed manager of Scotland.

25 JANUARY
1995 – Cantona kung-fu kicks the fan

Éric Cantona had been Manchester United's hero three days previously, scoring the winner against Premier League leaders Blackburn. If they could beat Crystal Palace at Selhurst Park the following Wednesday, United would go top, albeit having played two extra games. The stakes were high.

Palace boss Alan Smith had given his defender Richard Shaw the job of man-marking Cantona, and he did it well. Throughout the first half Shaw stuck to the Frenchman, irritating him with his tackles and eventually, it seemed, irritating him just by his presence. Cantona complained about Shaw's treatment to referee Alan Wilkie but was told to get on with the game.

Eleven minutes into the second half Cantona had had enough. As the pair chased a Peter Schmeichel clearance, Cantona kicked out at his marker under the linesman Eddie Walsh's nose. His flag went up immediately and the red card followed in a flash.

Leaving a melee of players surrounding the referee, Cantona stalked towards the tunnel at the other end of the pitch. That's when Crystal Palace fan Matthew Simmons ran from his seat to the front of the stand and allegedly shouted abuse at the United striker. In a second Cantona had flown spectacularly at Simmons, hurdling the advertising hoarding to plant a kick into the supporter's chest, following it up with a hail of punches.

United's kit man Norman Davies had to drag Cantona out of the crowd and Peter Schmeichel helped pull him towards the dressing rooms. The result, a 1–1 draw, was the last thing on anybody's mind.

Cantona was arrested and charged with assault for which he was later ordered to do community service. Manchester United initially suspended him until the end of the season and fined him two weeks' wages – the ban was extended to eight months by the FA with a further £10,000 fine.

Alex Ferguson's immediate reaction at full-time was, 'I'm devastated. This is a nightmare of the worst kind.'

But Ferguson's words from the previous summer came to mind. Then Cantona had been sent off in a pre-season tournament at Ibrox Stadium, and Ferguson had said, 'When he feels he's been done an injustice, he's got to prove to the world that he's going to correct it. But he can't control his temper. Love him or hate him, we have to live with it.'

Also on this day

1994 Liverpool lost 1–0 at home to Bristol City in an FA Cup third-round replay, heaping more pressure on manager Graeme Souness.

1997 Goal of the Season – Trevor Sinclair scored it for Queens Park Rangers against Barnsley at Loftus Road.

1998 Despite leading with an early goal from Alan Shearer, Newcastle could only draw 1–1 at non-league Stevenage Borough in the FA Cup.

2009 Saadi Gaddafi, son of the Libyan leader Muammar Gaddafi, was reported to be offering to buy cash-strapped Portsmouth.

26 JANUARY
1993 – A new low

Just getting a ticket for a Premier League game can be an achievement these days, they're often the hottest ticket in town – but it hasn't always been that way. When the Premier League started, many football grounds were unrecognizable from the spectacular, all-seated grounds of today. Stadia were being rebuilt according to the recommendations of the Taylor Report, which followed the Hillsborough disaster, and the game was reinventing itself after that tragedy as well as Heysel, Bradford and too many other dark days.

In 1992/93, the first ever Premier League season, only two clubs averaged more than 30,000 fans a game: they were Liverpool (37,004) and Manchester United (35,152). More than half of the top-flight clubs averaged fewer than 20,000 fans.

Villa Park (capacity 45,000) had only 16,180 people watching Villa play Southampton in November 1993. In December that year, 13,600 watched Everton play Southampton at Goodison Park (capacity 38,500). At Stamford Bridge (capacity 29,700) only 10,128 watched Chelsea play Manchester City in November 1993, and the following May just 8923 were there for a game against Coventry.

But Wimbledon struggled for a following more than anyone. The club, which had risen from the Southern League to the Premier League, were ground-sharing with Crystal Palace at the 30,000-capacity Selhurst Park. In 1992/93 they had seven attendances numbering fewer than 5000, and only six of more than 10,000 – even when Wimbledon played against their landlords Crystal Palace only 12,275 fans were there.

But the lowest ever crowd for a Premier League game came on 26 January 1993. Wimbledon were in the relegation zone and hosting mid-table Everton on a Tuesday night. Everton won 3–1 at Selhurst – the attendance was 3039.

Also on this day

1997 Mark Hughes came on as a substitute to inspire Chelsea into recovering from 2–0 down at home to Liverpool to win 4–2 in the FA Cup fourth round. Gianluca Vialli scored twice, Hughes and Gianfranco Zola once each.

2008 Havant and Waterlooville, of the Conference South, led 1–0 and 2–1 at Anfield against Liverpool before losing 5–2 in the FA Cup fourth round.

2014 Manchester United signed Juan Mata from Chelsea for £37.1m

27 JANUARY
2006 – Robbie's return

As an 18-year-old Robbie Fowler had burst on the scene at Liverpool with a flurry of goals. He was adored by the fans as one of their own, and nicknamed simply 'God'.

Gérard Houllier, who became Liverpool's manager in 1998, was less enamoured. The Frenchman preferred to play Emile Heskey with Michael Owen, and Fowler was too often injured to argue. After 170 goals in 330 games he left Liverpool, aged 26, for Leeds.

Fowler was at Elland Road for only a little over a year before the cash-strapped club sold him to Manchester City. In three years there Fowler played 92 games and scored 28 goals.

Halfway through the 2005/06 season, Fowler was 30 years old and struggling with a back injury. His limitations and abilities were both demonstrated by the fact that he'd started only one game all season – but he'd scored a hat-trick in it.

Fowler's old club, Liverpool, were looking for goals. Peter Crouch, Djibril Cissé and Fernando Morientes had scored only 25 goals between them, when Rafa Benítez decided his squad needed a lift.

Much to everybody's surprise the ever-pragmatic Benítez, the man who had refused to buy Michael Owen back from Real Madrid, decided it was time to bring Fowler back to Liverpool. Delighted, Fowler agreed a contract to the end of the season.

It took a while for his back injury to clear up and a while longer for the rustiness to disappear from his game, but having scored his first goal in a 5–1 win over Fulham, Fowler scored four more in his last six games of the season. He'd earned the right to stay another year.

Although he was used sparingly, he scored seven more goals before moving on to Cardiff City. In his second spell at Anfield he'd hit 12 goals in 37 games, and appeared to have loved it almost as much as Liverpool's Kop enjoyed having him back.

Also on this day

1999 West Ham completed the signing of both Paolo Di Canio from Sheffield Wednesday for £1.7m and Marc-Vivien Foé from Lens for £4.2m.

2001 Everton lost at home to Merseyside neighbours Tranmere Rovers 3–0 in the FA Cup.

2002 Three players were sent off in five minutes at Highbury as Arsenal beat Liverpool 1–0 in the FA Cup. Martin Keown and Dennis Bergkamp had already been dismissed for Arsenal when Liverpool's Jamie Carragher was hit by a coin thrown from the crowd. He was sent off for throwing it back.

2009 In a 5–0 win over West Bromwich Albion, Manchester United goalkeeper Edwin van der Sar set a new Premier League record by keeping his 11th consecutive clean sheet.

2010 Manchester United beat Manchester City 3–1 in the second leg of the League Cup semi-final to win 4–3 on aggregate.

28 JANUARY
1994 – TV at the FA

England were at a low ebb at the end of 1993. The failure to reach the World Cup under the management of Graham Taylor had left the relationship between the national team and the country's fans at breaking point.

The FA were preparing to host Euro 96, and as host nation England would qualify automatically – but that brought its own problems. How, without the cut and thrust of competitive qualifying matches, could a failing England side be turned into a team of which the nation could be proud in two years' time?

The options were limited. Nobody at the FA was ready to contemplate hiring a foreign coach to lead out an England team in an English tournament, and how many managers would want the inevitable expectation to win a home tournament?

The former England captain, and respected BBC summarizer, Jimmy Armfield was given the job of head-hunter. In his autobiography, *Right Back to the Beginning*, Armfield recalls that Bryan Robson, Ray Wilkins, Peter Reid and Trevor Francis were considered too young. He interviewed QPR manager Gerry Francis twice, but he'd implied that he 'could live without all the pressure'. One by one Howard Kendall, Joe Royle and Howard Wilkinson were ruled out and, according to Armfield: 'Just one name stayed in the frame – Terry Venables.'

Venables had impressed as an up-and-coming manager with Crystal Palace and QPR. He'd been bold enough to manage Barcelona at the age of 41. In Catalonia he'd ended Barcelona's 11-year wait for the title and taken them to the European Cup Final of 1986. Back in England he'd won the FA Cup with Spurs in 1991.

Venables's coaching credentials seemed ideal. At the FA's headquarters there were some who were less keen.

Chairman Sir Bert Millichip was reported to have said 'over my dead body' when the idea was mooted.

Venables was too colourful for many of the old guard at the FA. He'd tried his hand as an author, released a record, co-created the TV detective series *Hazell* and owned a Kensington club. Most of all, the FA were wary of Venables's spell as chief executive of Spurs, which had resulted in a tangled web of legal disputes with Tottenham's chairman Alan Sugar – disputes that the courts were trying to unravel.

Despite the misgivings of Millichip, and FA board members Noel White and Peter Swales, Armfield got his way: 'My brief is to find the best coach for the England football team and, right now, Terry is that man.'

Also on this day

1994 Graeme Souness resigned as manager of Liverpool.

1999 Glenn Hoddle was appointed caretaker manager of Southampton, replacing Dave Jones.

2005 Manchester City sold Nicolas Anelka to Fenerbahçe for £7m.

2010 Ajax Amsterdam agreed to sell Luis Suárez to Liverpool for £23m.

29 JANUARY
1999 – El Macca

Steve McManaman almost left Liverpool in 1997. Managed by Louis van Gaal with Bobby Robson as general manager, Barcelona offered Liverpool £12m for McManaman, a fee the club accepted. But no sooner had McManaman arrived in Barcelona to discuss the terms of the deal than he discovered that the Spanish club had signed Rivaldo from Deportivo La Coruña instead.

Barcelona's bid to sign McManaman, it seemed, had been part of a plan to convince Rivaldo's agent that he should agree to a deal that had been stalling over personal terms. Bobby Robson would later say, 'Rivaldo wasn't known then as he is now, but I could see what a player he was. I said, "He'll get you 18 goals a year, and stick in seven free-kicks. McManaman won't score you 18 goals a season and make another 25."'

The saga must have given McManaman plenty of food for thought. Not only had he begun to imagine life in Spain with one of its giant clubs, he'd realized, to his surprise, that Liverpool were willing to let him go. Later he recalled, 'I was surprised when Liverpool said they would let Barcelona talk to me because I didn't want to join them. Liverpool could have simply rejected the deal.'

Just over a year later, with his contract at Liverpool into its final season,

McManaman got the chance to resurrect a move to Spain. Real Madrid were interested, and offering to make the Liverpool man the highest-paid English footballer anywhere, so long as he joined them on a Bosman free transfer.

Nothing Liverpool could offer came close to matching the contract on the table in Madrid and, after all, they'd been willing to see McManaman leave when it suited them.

In January 1999, McManaman announced he was leaving Anfield – the first high-profile Englishman to take advantage of the Bosman ruling.

Also on this day

2000 Manchester United players were criticized for haranguing referee Andy D'Urso after he awarded the first penalty against them at Old Trafford for six years. Juninho missed it and United beat Middlesbrough 1–0.

2004 Scott Parker joined Chelsea from Charlton for £10m.

2005 Goal of the Season – Wayne Rooney scored it for Manchester United against Middlesbrough at Old Trafford.

2007 Alex McLeish was appointed manager of Scotland.

2014 Newcastle sold Yohan Cabaye to Paris Saint-Germain.

30 JANUARY
1999 – Hoddle's own-goal

Glenn Hoddle's England won the Tournoi de France in 1997. It was no mean feat – the Tournoi was a four-team tournament held in France the summer before they hosted World Cup Finals. England beat Italy 2–0 and France 1–0, before losing 1–0 to Brazil. England came home in high spirits and with a trophy.

Nobody could deny that England's exit at the World Cup next summer had been gallant. David Beckham, rather than Hoddle, carried the bulk of the blame from the public for the loss to Argentina. But for Beckham's flick at Diego Simeone, who could say how far in the tournament England might have gone? Even so, the manager's book, *Glenn Hoddle – My World Cup Story*, was not well received. Surely an England manager in the midst of a World Cup campaign should have more important things on his mind than writing a book?

The other question mark – and it was a big one – was Hoddle's reliance on Eileen Drewery. She was a faith-healer who enjoyed the unfailing confidence of the England manager. Hoddle encouraged his players to see her – many did, some in order to take the mickey. The FA's David Davies in his autobiography *FA Confidential* recalls that when Drewery laid hands on Ray

Parlour's head he said, 'Short back and sides, please.'

Hoddle certainly didn't appease the sceptics when he revealed he considered that his biggest mistake at the World Cup had been not taking Drewery.

When results began to tail off at the beginning of the campaign to qualify for Euro 2000, Drewery became an obvious stick with which to beat Hoddle. To build bridges with the media a select band of journalists were invited to conduct one-on-one interviews with the England manager.

On 30 January *The Times* printed Hoddle's interview with their chief football correspondent, Matt Dickinson. In it Hoddle strayed from football to faith, from reinvigorating England to reincarnation.

Hoddle said, 'You and I have been physically given two hands and two legs and half-decent brains. Some people have not been born like that for a reason. The karma is working from another lifetime. I have nothing to hide about that. It is not only people with disabilities. What you sow, you have to reap.'

There were immediate calls for Hoddle to resign. When Prime Minister Tony Blair added his voice to the clamour, there was no saving the England boss.

Also on this day

2002 Matt Holland played his 200th consecutive game for Ipswich Town in a 1–0 win over Fulham. He had played in every Ipswich game since joining the club four-and-a-half years earlier from Bournemouth.

2008 Cristiano Ronaldo scored both goals in a 2–0 win over Portsmouth at Old Trafford. His second goal, a free-kick, was described by Sir Alex Ferguson as 'The best free-kick in the history of the Premier League.'

31 JANUARY
2011 – Deadline headlines

Chelsea had already tried, without success, to sign Fernando Torres from Liverpool. But when the Spanish striker returned to England after Spain's successful World Cup campaign in South Africa, things had changed. Here was a striker, with European Championship and World Cup winner's medals, returning to a club who were not in the Champions League, whose owners were bickering with the board and with each other, whose best players were leaving and whose popular Spanish manager had been sacked.

Although new boss Roy Hodgson said he expected Torres to stay, his statement that 'His beef is with the club and not with me' sounded like a man preparing to wash his hands of any blame.

The transfer window passed and Torres got back to work. But it was nearly the end of October before the Spaniard scored his first league goal of the season, and by the time Hodgson was sacked in early January Liverpool were 12th in the table, nowhere near the title race.

The return as manager of Kenny Dalglish lifted the gloom a little, and Torres scored three goals in the manager's first four games. But the day after an unconvincing 1–0 win over Fulham, Liverpool received another bid from Chelsea, this time of £40m. Liverpool rejected it, but the following evening Torres submitted a transfer request.

The time for refusal had passed, the time for negotiating had come. On deadline day Liverpool, who had just completed the signing of Luis Suárez from Ajax, talked Chelsea's bid up to a record £50m.

Torres wasn't the only player on his way to London. It seemed that Andy Carroll was packing his bags for a move from Newcastle to Spurs for £25m. Desperate for a good-news story and suddenly cash-rich, Liverpool blew Tottenham away with a £35m offer.

Torres, Carroll and £85m – two stunning deals dramatically completed in the final hours of the transfer window.

Also on this day

1994 Roy Evans was appointed Liverpool manager.

2002 Despite manager Terry Venables having threatened to resign if Jonathan Woodgate was sold, the Leeds defender moved to Newcastle for £9m.

2006 Duncan Ferguson was sent off for punching Wigan's Paul Scharner. The FA banned the Everton striker for seven matches.

2008 New England manager Fabio Capello left David Beckham, on 99 caps, out of the squad for his first match in charge.

2010 Wayne Rooney marked Manchester United's 3–1 win over Arsenal with his 100th Premier League goal.

2013 West Bromwich Albion striker Peter Odemwingie drove himself to Queens Park Rangers's Loftus Road stadium in the hope of sealing a deadline-day transfer. The move didn't happen.

February

1 FEBRUARY
2003 – Sunderland's unwanted hat-trick

Given that Sunderland had failed to score more than twice in any of their 25 league games in season 2002/03 – and that they failed to score at all in 12 of them – conceding as few goals as possible was imperative for a side needing points to get out of the relegation zone.

Howard Wilkinson had been Sunderland manager for four months, having replaced Peter Reid in October, but there had been no upturn in form. Their opponents at the beginning of February, Alan Curbishley's Charlton, were in great shape – happily mid-table after losing only one of their last 12 league games. A win for the Londoners at the Stadium of Light was widely predicted: the manner of it wasn't.

The first goal, after 24 minutes, was credited to Sunderland defender Stephen Wright. Charlton's Mark Fish hit a bobbling shot that deflected off two Sunderland players, the last of which was Wright, before flashing past Thomas Sørensen in the Sunderland goal.

The second goal came five minutes later. Charlton defender Chris Powell had his shot well saved by Sørensen low to his left-hand side, but the unlucky goalkeeper saw the ball rebound onto the shin of Sunderland defender Michael Proctor and into the net.

Charlton's third goal followed just three minutes later. A left-wing corner bounced through a crowd of bodies before hitting Proctor – him again – and flying into the corner of the net.

Sunderland had scored three own-goals in seven minutes. A late penalty from their striker Kevin Phillips was no consolation. The defeat sent Sunderland to the bottom of the Premier League table with a dozen games to play. They lost all 12 of them.

Also on this day

2005 Patrick Vieira and Roy Keane had to be separated in the players' tunnel at Highbury before the game between Arsenal and Manchester United. Manchester United won 4–2 despite the sending-off of Mikaël Silvestre.

2006 After an error-strewn first-half performance Sol Campbell was substituted in Arsenal's game against West Ham at Highbury with the visitors winning 2–0. Campbell left the stadium with the game still in progress and wasn't seen at Arsenal for five days. He didn't play again until mid-April.

2009 After 12 years at Newcastle, goalkeeper Shay Given joined Manchester City.

2014 Craig Bellamy scored for Cardiff in their 2–1 win over Norwich to become the first player to score for seven different Premier League clubs. Bellamy had previously scored for Coventry, Newcastle, Blackburn, Liverpool, West Ham and Manchester City.

2 FEBRUARY
2009 – Keane's comeback

When Liverpool signed Robbie Keane from Spurs for £20m it brought to an end an exceptional six-year spell at White Hart Lane in which he scored over 100 goals.

Liverpool worked hard to get Keane. Not only did they pay a £20m transfer fee, but also made a donation to the club's charity, the Tottenham Hotspur Foundation, as an apology for what Spurs had complained bitterly was a pursuit of their player that breached Premier League rules.

Keane arrived at Anfield as a new strike partner for Fernando Torres, and immediately announced that he'd always been a Liverpool fan. It seemed a marriage made in heaven.

Despite having worked so hard to sign him, Rafa Benítez seemed to go off Keane surprisingly quickly. He was dropped from the starting 11 to the bench in only Liverpool's seventh game of the season, and had played the full 90 minutes in only two of the first six

matches. Keane, who made scoring for Spurs look so easy, didn't score his first league goal for Liverpool until November.

A rare highlight was a spectacular equalizer at Arsenal in December, but by then Keane was already missing as many games as he played. Benítez, it seemed, had decided the partnership with Torres was an expensive mistake.

Back at Spurs Jermain Defoe, who had just returned to the club from Portsmouth, faced a long recovery after fracturing his foot. Manager Harry Redknapp found himself short of strikers and took a chance that Liverpool might be willing to cut their losses on Keane.

Redknapp was right; Liverpool sold him back to Tottenham on 2 February 2009 for £7m less than they'd paid for him only six months earlier. In total Keane played 29 games for Liverpool and scored seven goals.

Redknapp said, 'I don't think he got a great crack of the whip there but that's up to Rafa Benítez. He picks the team and he obviously didn't see Robbie as a player who fitted into his system, or a player that he particularly wanted.'

When Liverpool played Spurs at Anfield on the final day of the season, Keane and Torres scored in the same game for the first time – but by then on opposite sides.

Also on this day

1999 Glenn Hoddle was sacked as England manager. In his 28 games in charge England had 17 wins, 4 draws and 7 defeats.

2004 Jermain Defoe signed for Spurs from West Ham for £7m.

2006 Graeme Souness was sacked as manager of Newcastle with Glenn Roeder made caretaker manager.

3 FEBRUARY
2015 – Redknapp's Rangers farewell

When Queens Park Rangers won promotion to the Premier League by beating Derby County in the 2014 Championship play-off final, it was with a last-minute goal by Bobby Zamora. A week later Rangers's manager Harry Redknapp admitted that had they lost the match, he would probably have stood down from his job: 'I think maybe I'd have called it a day. But I'm looking forward to the Premier League, I can't wait now.'

So, at 67 years old, Redknapp was the oldest manager in the Premier League when the 2014/15 season kicked off. Rangers had invested £30m on six players in the summer transfer window, but the signs weren't good when they lost at home to Hull on the opening day of the season.

Their first away game was at one of Redknapp's former clubs, Spurs. They were outclassed and lost 4–0 at White Hart Lane, beginning an almost unprecedented sequence of miserable trips away from home for their players and fans.

The next away match was at Manchester United; it was no surprise that they lost, and again the score was 4–0. At least the 2–1 defeat at Southampton, which came next, saw Rangers score their first goal away from home that season. Next, those long-suffering supporters went to West Ham (a 2–0 defeat), to Chelsea (2–1) and the long haul to Newcastle where they lost 1–0.

The next trip, in early December, was to Swansea, who beat them 1–0. A 3–1 loss at Everton was followed by a 2–1 defeat at Arsenal and another by the same score at Burnley. More in hope than expectation they went to Stoke and lost 3–1.

Redknapp's team had played 11 away games in the season and lost them all, something no top-flight side had suffered since Liverpool did the same in season 1953/54.

Three days later Harry Redknapp resigned, saying that his need for an operation on his knee meant that he could no longer face the physical demands of the job.

The change for Rangers seemed to be as good as a rest. A week later caretaker manager Chris Ramsey took QPR to Sunderland, where they won 2–0.

Also on this day

2007 After Liverpool and Everton drew 0–0 at Anfield, Liverpool manager Rafa Benítez whipped up a storm on the Mersey by describing Everton as a 'small club'.

2009 The transfer window was extended by 24 hours as bad weather hampered players and agents trying to travel around the country. One beneficiary was Andrey Arshavin, whose much-delayed move from Zenit Saint Petersburg to Arsenal was completed for £16.9m.

4 FEBRUARY
2006 – The History Boys

Sometimes stars collide. On the afternoon of Saturday 4 February 2006, two of the Premier League's greatest goalscoring stars reached personal milestones within a few seconds of each other, but miles apart.

At Birmingham City's St Andrew's stadium Arsenal were the visitors, while at St James' Park Newcastle were playing Portsmouth in what was Glenn Roeder's first game in charge of the home side after the sacking of Graeme Souness.

Both Newcastle and Arsenal led 1–0 at half-time. At St James' Park Charles

N'Zogbia had put Newcastle in front, firing home a rebound after Portsmouth keeper Dean Kiely had saved from Alan Shearer. In Birmingham, Abou Diaby's shot had been saved by Birmingham goalkeeper Maik Taylor, but Emmanuel Adebayor headed home the loose ball to score on his Arsenal debut.

In the 63rd minute of the game in Newcastle Shola Ameobi's back-heel set up Shearer who, playing his 394th game for the club, fired low past Kiely into the net. It was Shearer's 201st goal for Newcastle, beating the club record set by the great Jackie Milburn that had stood since 1957. The celebrations even included a handshake from referee Mark Halsey.

In the 64th minute at St Andrew's Thierry Henry, playing his 322nd game for Arsenal and already their all-time record goalscorer having surpassed Ian Wright, latched on to a pass from Cesc Fàbregas to score. It was the Frenchman's 200th Arsenal goal. The headline writers didn't know who to salute – Shearer or Henry.

Also on this day

1993 Martin Keown rejoined Arsenal from Everton for £2m.

1996 Mick McCarthy was appointed manager of the Republic of Ireland.

2002 Newcastle spent £5m on Jermaine Jenas from Nottingham Forest.

2004 Despite being 3–0 down and reduced to ten men after the sending-off of Joey Barton, Manchester City came back to win 4–3 at Spurs in the FA Cup.

2009 An unscheduled advertising break meant that TV viewers missed Dan Gosling's extra-time winner for Everton against Liverpool in their FA Cup fourth-round replay.

2012 Thierry Henry scored in his final home game for Arsenal, a 7–1 win over Blackburn.

2014 Michael Laudrup was sacked as manager of Swansea, with Gary Monk put in temporary charge.

5 FEBRUARY
2010 – Terry stripped of the captaincy

The newspapers had been having a field day. The allegations against the England captain mixed football, sex, infidelity and deceit.

The allegation was that Terry conducted an affair with Vanessa Perroncel, the ex-partner of his former Chelsea teammate Wayne Bridge. Perroncel denied the relationship, and has received apologies from the newspapers concerned; but at the time the spotlight on all the parties involved was unrelenting. Bridge had subsequently moved to Manchester City, but the defenders were still England colleagues and the World Cup Finals in South Africa were looming. The stories were the last thing manager Fabio Capello needed to read in his morning paper as he recovered from knee surgery in Switzerland.

In Capello's absence the FA's chairman Lord Triesman, chief executive Ian Watmore, director of communications Adrian Bevington and head of development Trevor Brooking had met with the team's general manager Franco Baldini and agreed that, as manager, Capello alone should make the decision on what to do.

The Italian flew into London and Terry was summoned to a meeting at the FA's Wembley headquarters. The meeting lasted 12 minutes, after which the FA released a statement on Capello's behalf. It said, 'After much thought I have made the decision that it will be best for me to take the captaincy away from John Terry.'

Terry also released a statement saying, 'I fully respect Fabio Capello's decision and I will continue to give everything for England.'

Rio Ferdinand was appointed England's new captain, but with Terry still certain to be a part of the World Cup squad, Bridge decided to retire from international football.

Also on this day

1995 Adnan Januzaj was born.

2000 Bradford City stunned title-chasing Arsenal at Valley Parade, beating them 2–1 with goals from Dean Windass and Dean Saunders.

2002 Sir Alex Ferguson made public his decision to change his mind about retiring as manager at the end of the season. Ferguson agreed a new three-year contract, but said that 'once this contract is up that will be it. I have no intention of staying at the club in any capacity whatsoever.'

2011 Newcastle came from 4–0 down at half-time to draw 4–4 with Arsenal at St James' Park. Arsenal led 4–0 after 26 minutes but, after Abou Diaby was sent-off, conceded four times, the last of which was scored by Cheick Tioté with three minutes to play.

6 FEBRUARY
2007 – Hicks and Gillett buy Liverpool

The Moores family, whose fortune came from the Littlewoods business empire, had owned Liverpool Football Club for more than 50 years. David Moores had been chairman for 15 years, during which time the club's dominance of English and European football had been slowly eroded.

On the pitch a revival had been under way since the appointment of Rafa Benítez, but keeping pace financially with the biggest clubs in England and abroad was becoming impossible. Moores needed outside investment, but had baulked at selling completely. Steve Morgan, the founder of the Redrow building company and later the owner of Wolves, and Thaksin Shinawatra, the former Thai prime minister who would later buy Manchester City, had both failed with takeover bids.

In 2006 two new suitors for Liverpool emerged. The first was Sheikh Mohammed, the ruler of Dubai, the founder of Emirates Airlines and owner of the Godolphin racing stables. The second were the American investors and sports tycoons Tom Hicks and George Gillett. Gillett owned the National Hockey League franchise the Montréal Canadiens and Hicks owned both the Dallas Stars NHL team and Major League Baseball's Texas Rangers.

After much soul-searching, Moores decided to take the American bid. Hicks and Gillett took control for £174m, and with a promise to get a new stadium built as soon as possible.

In a statement the new owners said, 'We fully acknowledge and appreciate the unique heritage and rich history of Liverpool and intend to respect this heritage in the future.'

By May 2010 Moores was bitterly regretting his decision to take the Americans' offer. After four years of bad management and bad results the club was in disarray, burdened by spiralling debts and with no sign of the promised new stadium. In a letter to *The Times*, Moores pleaded with Hicks and Gillett to 'accept their limitations as joint owners, acknowledge their role in the club's current demise, and stand aside, with dignity, to allow someone else to take up the challenge. Don't punish the club's supporters any more – God knows they've taken enough.'

Also on this day

1997 West Ham signed Paul Kitson from Newcastle for £2.3m.

1998 Gary Speed joined Newcastle from Everton for £5.5m.

1999 Ole Gunnar Solskjaer became the first Premier League substitute to come on and score four goals. The occasion was Manchester United's 8–1 win at Nottingham Forest, the biggest margin of victory by an away team in Premier League history.

2010 Portsmouth scored three own-goals as they lost 5–0 at Manchester United.

2011 West Bromwich Albion sacked manager Roberto Di Matteo.

2013 Ashley Cole won his 100th England cap in a 2–1 win over Brazil at Wembley.

7 FEBRUARY
2008 – The 39th game

When, in October 2005, the Arizona Cardinals beat the San Francisco 49ers 31–14 in the Azteca Stadium in Mexico City, it was the first American football National Football League regular-season game to be played outside the USA and the attendance of 103,467 was a record.

Fans of the sport soon accepted the 'International Series', and in May 2007 the NFL were discussing the possibility of all teams playing an extra 17th regular-season game on foreign soil, with each host city around the world being given 4 matches.

In 2007, Wembley Stadium hosted the NFL's international game for the first time, with 81,000 watching the Miami Dolphins play the New York Giants. The event was such a success that the league's commissioner Roger Goodell said, 'There's a great deal of interest in holding a Super Bowl in London, so we'll be looking at that.'

Four months later the Premier League came up with their own international plan – the 39th game. All 20 Premier League clubs met and agreed to explore the idea of playing one extra match a season in venues around the globe. Premier League chief executive Richard Scudamore emerged from the meeting on 7 February saying, 'It's an extra game, it's not taking anybody's game away, and it includes all 20 clubs, which is very important. All 20 clubs will benefit and there is a huge element of solidarity about it.'

The response elsewhere was hostile. UEFA president Michel Platini said, 'It will never be received by FIFA, by the fans or the national associations. It's a nonsense idea, it's not good for football. In England, you already have no English coach, no English players and maybe now you will have no clubs playing in England. It's a joke.'

FA chairman Lord Triesman was dismissive: 'We haven't got what I would call a sustainable plan in front of us.' FIFA president Sepp Blatter bluntly said, 'This idea to play a 39th round outside the country does not work.'

Facing such a storm, the idea was dropped – but not forgotten. In August 2014 Scudamore said, 'The clubs wanted it then and they all would still probably want it now. It will happen at some point. Whether it is on my watch, who knows?'

Also on this day

1993 Spurs scored four goals in five minutes to come from behind and beat Southampton 4–2 at White Hart Lane. Teddy Sheringham got their first after 54 minutes, quickly followed by goals from Nick Barmby (56 minutes), Darren Anderton (57 minutes) and Sheringham again (59 minutes).

1996 A UEFA summit in Geneva agreed to increase the number of clubs eligible to play in the Champions League from the top-eight nations from one to two.

2007 The Republic of Ireland saved themselves from embarrassment when a 95th-minute goal from Stephen Ireland secured a 2–1 win in San Marino in a European Championship qualifier.

8 FEBRUARY
2012 – Capello quits and Redknapp waits

Having made the decision to strip John Terry of the England captaincy in 2010 Fabio Capello reinstated Terry to the role in 2011. Then Capello had said, 'I think one year's punishment is enough.'

In both 2010 and 2011, those decisions on the captaincy had been taken by Capello alone, without input from his bosses at the FA.

When, in 2012, there were allegations that Terry had racially abused Anton Ferdinand, the FA had a new chairman in David Bernstein. Unlike his predecessor, Bernstein didn't leave Capello to decide what stance the FA should take. Despite Capello's objections, the FA decided to strip Terry of the England captaincy.

Capello gave his thoughts on that decision to the Italian broadcaster RAI. 'I thought it was right that Terry should keep the captain's armband,' he said. 'I have spoken to the chairman and I have said that in my opinion one cannot be punished until it is official and the court had made a decision to decide if John Terry has done what he is accused of.'

Capello's open disagreement meant a crisis point at the FA with the European Championship Finals only four months away. At a meeting with Bernstein and FA general secretary Alex Horne, Capello refused to back down and offered his resignation.

An FA statement revealed that, 'The discussions focused on the FA Board's decision to remove the England team captaincy from John Terry, and Fabio Capello's response through an Italian broadcast interview. In a meeting for over an hour, Fabio's resignation was accepted and he will leave the post of England manager with immediate effect.'

By coincidence, the resignation of Capello came on the same day that Harry Redknapp was cleared of tax evasion after a trial at Southwark Crown Court. Former England manager Sven-Göran Eriksson declared that Redknapp would be 'a very, very good choice to succeed Capello'.

Also on this day

1998 Stephen Hughes scored both goals for Arsenal in a 2–0 win over Chelsea at Highbury.

2003 Teddy Sheringham scored the 300th goal of his career as Spurs beat Sunderland 4–1 at the Stadium of Light.

2009 Tony Adams was sacked as manager of Portsmouth.

2014 Premier League leaders Arsenal conceded four goals in the first 20 minutes of their game against Liverpool at Anfield. Arsène Wenger's side lost 5–1. 'We had a very poor day,' said Wenger.

9 FEBRUARY
2009 – Scolari's sacking

In 2009 Luiz Felipe Scolari's reputation in England was almost as high as it was in Portugal or his native Brazil; after all, he had the knack of beating England every time it mattered. In 2002 Scolari had masterminded Brazil's World Cup win, which included a quarter-final victory over England. Then, in 2004, England had fallen to Scolari's Portugal side in the last eight of the European Championship, and in the 2006 World Cup Portugal and Scolari had done it again – beating England in the quarter-final.

No wonder the FA had offered him the England manager's job. The timing of that offer, just before the World Cup Finals of 2006, had been terrible and Scolari turned England down. Two years later, when he was managing Portugal at Euro 2008, Scolari announced that he had accepted an offer to join Chelsea.

Scolari's time at Stamford Bridge started well enough, Chelsea won 9 and drew 3 of their first 12 games of the season. Then Liverpool won 1–0 at Stamford Bridge, ending Chelsea's remarkable run of 86 home league games without defeat.

A 3–1 loss at Roma in the Champions League was quickly followed by defeat in a penalty shoot-out to Burnley in the League Cup, and a home defeat to Arsenal in the league. When Chelsea needed a replay to knock Southend out of the FA Cup and were beaten 3–0 at Manchester United in the league, there were serious questions being asked of Scolari.

In February Chelsea lost to Liverpool again, so in five games against their main title rivals – Liverpool, Manchester United and Arsenal – Chelsea had managed only one point.

The following weekend Chelsea could only draw at home to relegation-threatened Hull City and Roman Abramovich had seen enough. After the Brazilian was sacked a Chelsea statement read: 'In order to maintain a challenge for the trophies we are still competing for we felt the only option was to make the change now. The search for a new manager has already started and we hope to have someone in place as soon as possible.'

That someone was Guus Hiddink, who was appointed manager the following day.

Also on this day

1994 Arsenal were knocked out of the FA Cup by Bruce Rioch's Bolton Wanderers, who won their fourth-round replay 3–1 after extra-time at Highbury.

2002 Liverpool's new signing from Everton, Abel Xavier, scored on his debut as Liverpool beat Ipswich 6–0 at Portman Road.

2013 Mauricio Pochettino recorded his first win as manager of Southampton: 3–1 against Manchester City at St Mary's Stadium.

10 FEBRUARY
2008 – Munich remembered

On 6 February 1958 the Munich air disaster claimed the lives of 23 people including 8 members of Matt Busby's Manchester United team and the former Manchester City goalkeeper Frank Swift, who was on the flight as a journalist reporting on Manchester United's game.

Fifty years later, the game which fell nearest to the anniversary of the crash was against Manchester City at Old Trafford. Theoretically it was the perfect fixture to remember the dead; however, some feared that the reality might be different if local rivalries couldn't be set aside.

Manchester United's chief executive David Gill was wary: 'We've been working closely with City and discussed it with them. Frank Swift was one of their greatest goalkeepers and we're working to ensure they remember that it wasn't just Manchester United, it was the city of Manchester that was affected. We hope and believe that the minute's silence will be observed appropriately.'

A lone piper led the two teams onto the Old Trafford pitch, the Manchester United players wearing a replica of the 1958 kit – no sponsors, no logos, no squad numbers or players' names – just red with a white V-neck.

The two managers, Sir Alex Ferguson and Sven-Göran Eriksson, each laid a wreath in their respective club colours on either side of the centre spot and, watched by Munich survivors Sir Bobby Charlton, Harry Gregg, Albert Scanlon, Bill Foulkes and Kenny Morgans, the referee Howard Webb blew his whistle for silence.

Silence, total respectful silence, is what there was. There were 75,970 people inside Old Trafford, each stood and raised a scarf above their heads – sky blue in the City end, red elsewhere – and not a sound could be heard.

Manchester, a city – united.

Also on this day

1996 Just hours after arriving in Newcastle to complete his move from Parma, Faustino Asprilla made a surprise debut as a substitute in Newcastle's 2–1 win at Middlesbrough.

1999 After six years out of the side, caretaker manager Howard Wilkinson recalled Lee Dixon to win his 22nd England cap in a 2–0 defeat against France at Wembley. It was Dixon's last cap. Dixon's daughter was reported to have asked, 'Does that mean you won't play for Arsenal any more?'

2011 West Ham beat Spurs to the right to take over the Olympic Stadium in Stratford.

11 FEBRUARY
2012 – Cry God for Harry, England and Saint George

Harry Redknapp's acquittal on charges of tax evasion had come just hours after the resignation of England manager Fabio Capello. Almost immediately it seemed that the England job was Redknapp's for the taking.

At Spurs Redknapp had improved his CV, taking them into the Champions League for the first time in their history, and they had hopes of qualifying again as well as continuing their run in the FA Cup. As the list of football's great and good recommending Redknapp for the manager's job grew by the day, it seemed his time had come.

Sir Alex Ferguson's view was typical: 'There is no doubt Harry Redknapp is the best man. He has the experience and personality and the knowledge of the game. He has changed the fortunes of every club he has been at.'

Redknapp himself was coy: 'It is nice that people put me in a position where they think I've got a chance of the job. It's flattering. Other managers have come out and said nice things, and I appreciate everybody's support.'

With the clamour to offer the job to Redknapp becoming deafening, Spurs had a game at home to Newcastle on 11 February. There were more photographers, more press and more TV cameras than ever as Redknapp emerged to a rapturous ovation from the Tottenham crowd.

As a job application the next 90 minutes could not have gone any better. Spurs sped into a 3–0 lead with Redknapp's newest signing, Louis Saha, scoring twice on his debut. Tottenham won 5–0 and afterwards Redknapp was diplomacy itself: 'I've just got to focus on what's happening here. There's been no approach and I've not heard from anybody.'

As top managers ruled themselves out of the job, probably suspecting that they would be flattened by the unstoppable Redknapp steamroller, one voice struck a slightly different tone: 'Harry's receiving the backing from virtually all quarters – he's had a very good period of time now with Tottenham and he's got a lot of backing from a lot of people in the country.' Stating facts, but no opinion, was the voice of Roy Hodgson.

Also on this day

1995 Tommy Johnson scored his first Aston Villa goals, a hat-trick in a 7–1 win over Wimbledon with all three goals scored inside 16 minutes.

1998 Aged 18 years and 59 days, Michael Owen became the youngest England player of the twentieth century when he made his debut in the 2–0 defeat against Chile at Wembley.

2011 Roy Hodgson was appointed manager at West Bromwich Albion.

2012 In his second game back from serving a ban for racially abusing Patrice Evra, Luis Suárez refused to shake Evra's hand before kick-off. Suárez scored in Liverpool's 2–1 defeat.

2015 After five consecutive Premier League defeats Aston Villa sacked manager Paul Lambert.

12 FEBRUARY
2012 – Odemwingie dances with Wolves

As 2 of the 12 founder members of the Football League, West Bromwich Albion and Wolves can claim that there is no older rivalry in English football than the Black Country derby. In fact, the clubs' first meeting pre-dates the foundation of the Football League by two years – an FA Cup tie on 2 January 1886.

Some 126 years later they met in the Premier League, their 160th meeting. Both were in relegation trouble: Wolves were 17th in the table and out of the relegation zone only on goal difference and West Bromwich Albion were 15th, just five points better off.

Wolves, banking on becoming Premier League regulars, had announced an ambitious redevelopment plan for their Molineux home, intended to take capacity to almost 40,000 – but only if they stayed up.

Wolves were fortunate to be level at half-time, Peter Odemwingie's opener for Albion being cancelled out by Steven Fletcher's equalizer. In the second half there was no reprieve for the home side as West Brom scored four times in the last 25 minutes, with Odemwingie completing a hat-trick – the first in this fixture since 1996.

West Brom's 5–1 win equalled their biggest winning margin over Wolves since 1893. Afterwards Wolves boss Mick McCarthy was embarrassed: 'I apologize for the performance. I've never done that before but I feel it's warranted because we were awful. We capitulated, which is not something you can associate with me or my team. An apology is as much as I can do at the moment. All I can do is keep my dignity and carry on with my job.'

The next day McCarthy was sacked and assistant manager Terry Connor put in charge. They took only four points from their remaining 14 games and were relegated.

Also on this day

1997 England suffered their first ever Wembley defeat in a World Cup match, losing a qualifying game against Italy 1–0 with Gianfranco Zola scoring the goal.

1998 Chelsea unexpectedly sacked Ruud Gullit as manager and replaced him with Gianluca Vialli.

2000 West Ham scored three times in the last 25 minutes to come from 4–2 down and beat Bradford 5–4.

2003 Wayne Rooney became England's youngest ever player, aged 17 years and 111 days, but finished on the losing side as they were beaten 3–1 by Australia at Upton Park.

2011 Goal of the Season – Wayne Rooney scored it for Manchester United against Manchester City at Old Trafford.

13 FEBRUARY
1999 – Play it again

Arsenal were expected to beat second-tier Sheffield United in their FA Cup fifth-round tie on 13 February 1999, and they did – but in a manner that manager Arsène Wenger described as 'sport-wise, not right'.

The score was 1–1 with 14 minutes to play, Patrick Vieira and Marcelo each scoring with a header. When Sheffield United's Lee Morris went down injured, their goalkeeper Alan Kelly kicked the ball out of play so that his teammate could get treatment. Once Morris was fit to continue, Arsenal's Ray Parlour followed the sporting convention by throwing the ball back towards Kelly so that Sheffield United had possession.

Then Arsenal's Kanu, who was making his debut for the club and had only come on 12 minutes earlier, made sure that everyone in England knew his name. The Nigerian raced on to Parlour's throw before it could reach the goalkeeper and passed the ball to Marc Overmars, who scored. Referee Peter Jones had no choice but to award the goal as Kanu had broken only a convention, not a law of the game.

Sheffield United were incensed and their manager, Steve Bruce, threatened to call his players off the pitch in protest. During a seven-minute stoppage Arsenal goalkeeper Dave Seaman offered to let a goal in deliberately if that would help, but eventually order was restored and the game completed. Immediately afterwards Arsène Wenger offered Sheffield United a rematch at Highbury, and the FA agreed.

After the game Wenger immediately jumped to the defence of his new striker:

'Kanu is new to English football, and he didn't want to cheat. He didn't know why the goalkeeper had kicked the ball out of play.'

The FA spokesman Steve Double heaped praise on Arsenal's manager: 'Everybody in football will welcome Arsène Wenger's sporting gesture and he should be congratulated for it.'

Sheffield United boss Steve Bruce didn't see it that way: 'I think what's been overlooked is that we were a few minutes away from a replay anyway, back at Bramall Lane (not Highbury). My players deserve that replay.'

Arsenal won the rematch by the same scoreline, 2–1, with Overmars

again getting a goal. Referee Peter Jones was rewarded for his handling of an unprecedented situation when he was put in charge of the FA Cup Final three months later.

Also on this day

2002 **French World Cup winner Youri Djorkaeff joined Bolton from Kaiserslautern.**

2004 **Wanting a break from management, Gordon Strachan resigned as boss of Southampton.**

2008 **A month short of his 70th birthday, Giovanni Trapattoni agreed to become the new manager of the Republic of Ireland, replacing Steve Staunton.**

14 FEBRUARY
2014 – Thirteen: unlucky for Fulham

When Shahid Khan, the owner of American football franchise the Jacksonville Jaguars, bought Fulham Football Club from Mohamed Al-Fayed in 2013, they were about to embark on their 13th consecutive Premier League season.

With Martin Jol at the helm Fulham had finished in the top half of the Premier League in three of the last five seasons – not spectacular but very solid. While Al-Fayed had often been portrayed as an eccentric and occasionally controversial owner, who had never managed to achieve his stated dream of turning Fulham into 'the Manchester United of the south', there was no doubt that they had been a well-run club.

Now Khan was promising even better things, calling his purchase 'the passing of the baton, taking it to the next level'.

Fulham seemed to drop that baton almost straight away. The new owner gave Jol only 13 league games in charge, from which Fulham had three wins and ten points, before he sacked him. Jol's replacement was René Meulensteen, another Dutchman, who had been first-team coach at Manchester United.

Khan allowed Meulensteen to bring in five new players, spending a club record £11m on striker Kostas Mitroglou from Olympiakos. But with none of the five having made an impact, and Mitroglou yet to even play for the club, Meulensteen was sacked. He was in charge for 13 league games too; and again Fulham had won 3 and earned ten points.

Meulensteen's replacement, on 14 February 2014, was Felix Magath. A German, Magath had scored the winning goal for Hamburg in the 1983 European Cup Final and had managed eight different Bundesliga clubs, winning the title three times and never being relegated.

With the expensive Mitroglou playing just one full game, Fulham managed only three more wins and 12 more points from the remainder of the season, and were relegated with a whimper in a 4–1 defeat at Stoke.

Magath never got a 13th game in charge – he was sacked after 12.

Also on this day

1994 Southampton's Matt Le Tissier scored a hat-trick in their 4–2 win over Liverpool.

1997 West Ham signed John Hartson from Arsenal for £3.2m. Hartson's partnership with fellow new signing Paul Kitson brought 13 goals from West Ham's last 14 games, helping them avoid relegation.

2005 Arsenal beat Crystal Palace 5–1, making history by not having a British player in their starting 11 or among the substitutes.

2007 Tim Howard turned his loan move from Manchester United to Everton into a permanent deal.

2015 Aston Villa appointed Tim Sherwood as manager.

15 FEBRUARY
2003 – One in the eye for Beckham

It was the FA Cup fifth round and Manchester United had lost at home – to make matters worse, they'd lost at home to Arsenal. Sir Alex Ferguson was furious.

Ferguson launched into one of his infamous 'hairdryers' in the United dressing room after the game and David Beckham, who had been substituted with a leg injury, found himself sitting in the wrong place at the wrong time.

In his autobiography Ferguson described what became known, predictably, as 'bootgate'. 'He was around 12 feet from me. Between us on the floor lay a row of boots. David swore. I moved towards him, and as I approached I kicked a boot. It hit him right above the eye. Of course he rose to have a go at me and the players stopped him. "Sit down," I said. "You've let your team down. You can argue as much as you like."'

Beckham, who was restrained from retaliating by Ryan Giggs and Gary Neville, needed two stitches on his left eyebrow. Beckham later said that as he left the dressing room he ignored Ferguson's apology.

Rumours of a bust-up circulated quickly and, as he arrived for training the next day, Beckham wore his hair scraped back in a band to make sure that the waiting photographers could see exactly what damage had been done.

Ferguson and Manchester United were aware that Real Madrid had been in touch with Beckham's agents indicating that they'd like to sign him. But it was

Manchester United, not Beckham, who decided to end their relationship.

Ferguson had made his mind up to sell his biggest star: 'We were aware that David's work rate was dropping and we had heard rumours of a flirtation between Real Madrid and David's camp. It was in those days that I told the board David had to go.'

Also on this day

1993 The first manager to be sacked in Premier League history was Chelsea's Ian Porterfield. He was replaced at Stamford Bridge by Dave Webb.

1995 The friendly international between the Republic of Ireland and England was abandoned after 27 minutes because of rioting England supporters.

2001 The National Football Museum was opened at Preston's Deepdale Stadium.

2011 In the Champions League, Spurs won 1–0 in the San Siro against AC Milan with Peter Crouch scoring the goal. After the game Milan's Gennaro Gattuso seemed to aim a head-butt at Tottenham's first-team coach, and former Milan player, Joe Jordan.

16 FEBRUARY
2000 – Collymore fired up

Liverpool broke the English transfer record when they signed Stan Collymore from Nottingham Forest for £8.5m. He could be brilliant, but also unpredictable. After two seasons Liverpool were happy to sell at a loss to Aston Villa who, three seasons later, allowed him to join Leicester for nothing when, at 29, he should still have been at his peak.

By the time Collymore moved to Filbert Street he had scored 114 career goals in 281 games, a record most strikers would be proud of. He'd also suffered from depression at a time when mental illness in football was a taboo subject, and gained notoriety after an altercation with his then girlfriend Ulrika Jonsson in a Paris bar.

Collymore had been at Leicester barely a week, and played only one game, when the club's players went on a team-building exercise and training break at La Manga resort in Spain. The trip was designed to help them prepare for the upcoming League Cup Final against Tranmere Rovers.

On the first night of the planned four-day break, Collymore let off a fire extinguisher in the bar of the hotel where the players had been drinking heavily. The manager of the resort asked Leicester to leave, complaining: 'Their behaviour was totally and utterly unacceptable. We have major concerns about looking after all our clients and we can't expose them to this sort of behaviour.'

Leicester's manager, Martin O'Neill, had been due to join his team the following day. On 16 February he said threateningly, 'They have misbehaved, the football club has been let down and because of that they are coming back home. Rest assured that the guilty parties will be punished – regardless of who they are.'

Collymore apologised, but was fined two weeks wages. Despite, or maybe because of, a major telling-off Leicester won the League Cup Final 2–1 and Collymore scored a hat-trick in their next league game, a 5–2 win over Sunderland. The headlines said he was on fire.

Also on this day

1999 Marian Pahars became the first Latvian to play in the Premier League, joining Southampton from Skonto Riga.

2008 Barnsley knocked Liverpool out of the FA Cup with a last-minute Brian Howard goal securing a 2–1 win at Anfield.

2011 Arsenal scored two late goals to come from behind and beat Barcelona 2–1 at the Emirates in the first leg of their Champions League tie.

2013 Arsène Wenger lost to a lower-division side for the first time as

Championship team Blackburn won 1–0 at the Emirates Stadium in the FA Cup.

17 FEBRUARY
1999 – Keegan's four-match agreement

Kevin Keegan's job title at Fulham was a strange one – 'chief operating officer'. But since the sacking of head coach Ray Wilkins, he had been the club's manager in all but name.

When Glenn Hoddle resigned as England manager, Keegan was immediately the number one choice to replace him. As Newcastle boss Keegan had assembled a thrilling and popular side that had come within an ace of winning the Premier League. His resignation from Newcastle and subsequent appointment at third-tier Fulham had revealed a capacity for springing a surprise, but the FA assumed that installing him as England's new boss would be straightforward.

The FA's assumption was wrong. Keegan was insisting on continuing to work for Fulham until the end of his contract in June 2000. He was willing to be England manager, but only on a part-time basis. There were other complications: Fulham were scheduled to play Walsall on 27 March, the same day England were playing Poland in a European Championship qualifier. Then there was talk of Keegan wanting to miss the scheduled friendly against Hungary in April, if Fulham were embroiled in a battle for promotion.

For England to be squabbling with a club in the third tier of English football over their manager must have been difficult to swallow at the FA. After some skilful negotiating, Keegan agreed to manage England for the next four games against Poland, Hungary, Sweden and Bulgaria.

Keegan began his high-profile secondary job with a dig at his predecessor Glenn Hoddle: 'I know I need people to help me but I don't need a faith-healer.'

The FA's David Davies recalls in his autobiography that the FA hoped that Keegan would want the job permanently once he'd had a taste of it. They were right – Keegan loved his new role and gave up his job at Fulham at the beginning of May to become England's boss full-time.

Also on this day

1993 John Barnes was booed by England fans as David Platt scored four goals in a 6–0 World Cup qualifying win over San Marino at Wembley.

1999 Struggling Everton ended a seven-game winless streak with a 5–0 win over Middlesbrough to climb away from the relegation zone.

2012 Newcastle owner Mike Ashley branded St James' Park as the Sports Direct Arena.

18 FEBRUARY
2009 – Van der Sar's saves

Edwin van der Sar was certainly the best goalkeeper Manchester United had had since Peter Schmeichel, and seemed to be evidence of the old adage that, like a good red wine, goalkeepers improve with age.

The Dutchman had just turned 38 when Manchester United lost 2–1 at Arsenal on 8 November 2008 to drop to fourth in the Premier League table. It was the last time he conceded a Premier League goal until March.

His first clean sheet came in United's 5–0 win over Stoke at Old Trafford. Then came a 0–0 draw at Villa Park and a 1–0 win at neighbours Manchester City. United beat Sunderland 1–0, drew 0–0 at Spurs, won 1–0 at Stoke and 1–0 at home to Middlesbrough. A 3–0 win over Chelsea and a 1–0 win at Bolton took van der Sar to within one game of Petr Čech's record of ten consecutive clean sheets. He equalled that in Manchester United's 5–0 win at West Bromwich Albion and surpassed it in the 1–0 victory over Everton, setting a new record of 1120 minutes without conceding a single goal.

But he didn't finish there – a 1–0 win at West Ham was followed by a 3–0 victory over Fulham at Old Trafford on 18 February – a 14th consecutive league game without conceding.

United's next match was a 2–1 win at home to Blackburn – but van der Sar missed the match with a slight injury, Tomasz Kuszczak conceding the goal.

When the record ended, it ended with a mistake. Nine minutes into United's next league game at Newcastle, van der Sar spilled a Jonás Gutiérrez shot into the path of Peter Lovenkrands, who scored. In all, a British record of 1311 minutes had gone by since van der Sar had last been beaten. Manchester United came back to win the game at Newcastle 2–1, and moved seven points clear at the top of the table.

Also on this day

1994 Coventry's Mick Quinn scored the Premier League's 200th goal in their 4–0 win over Manchester City.

2003 Bobby Robson celebrated his 70th birthday by managing Newcastle to a 3–1 win over Bayer Leverkusen in the Champions League.

2006 Manchester United's Alan Smith broke his leg and dislocated his ankle in his club's FA Cup defeat against Liverpool at Anfield.

19 FEBRUARY
1997 – Schmeichel and Wright

The intense rivalry between Manchester United and Arsenal pre-dates the formation of the Premier League. During Arsenal's 1–0 win at Old Trafford in October 1990 there had been a mass brawl involving 21 players, which was so serious that Arsenal were deducted two points and Manchester United one.

The arrival of Arsène Wenger at Arsenal did nothing to lessen the ill feeling. As early as 1997, only a few months into Wenger's time at Arsenal, Ferguson snarled, 'Wenger doesn't know anything about English football. He's at a big club – well, Arsenal used to be big. He should keep his mouth shut, firmly shut. He's a novice and should keep his opinions to Japanese football.'

Those comments were made in the light of a high-profile feud between United goalkeeper Peter Schmeichel and Arsenal striker Ian Wright.

In the first meeting of 1996/97, the pair had clashed and Wright claimed that Schmeichel had racially abused him after the goalkeeper had been hurt by an ill-timed challenge from the Arsenal striker.

While conducting their investigations the FA asked Schmeichel to be the focal point of their anti-racism campaign. Schmeichel refused on the basis that, while he supported the aims of the campaign, for him to be involved might give the impression that he had been guilty of abusing Ian Wright.

When the two sides met again at Highbury in February, the affair was in the hands of the Crown Prosecution Service, who were considering whether to press charges.

Inevitably there was a spark: when a through ball sent Wright running towards Schmeichel's goal, the offside flag went up against the Arsenal striker. Either Wright wasn't aware that he was offside, or couldn't stop, or didn't stop, but he lunged at Schmeichel with a two-footed challenge for which he was booked, and which left Schmeichel bruised and furious. At the end of the game the pair clashed again in the tunnel and had to be kept apart by stewards and police.

Wright was given a two-match ban for an accumulation of bookings and soon the CPS decided that Schmeichel had no case to answer. But the problems between Manchester United and Arsenal were just beginning.

Also on this day

2001 In a poll organized by Manchester United's official magazine Éric Cantona was voted the club's best ever player. George Best was second, Ryan Giggs third and Bobby Charlton fourth.

2004 Roy Keane revealed that he was considering a return to playing international football for the Republic of Ireland after a self-imposed exile lasting almost two years since he walked out of the 2002 World Cup.

2011 Chelsea were knocked out of the FA Cup in a fourth-round replay by Everton in a penalty shoot-out. It was Chelsea's first defeat in the competition since March 2008.

20 FEBRUARY
1992 – The Premier League becomes a reality

As the 1980s moved into the 1990s there was only one place any aspiring footballer wanted to play – Italy. The 1990 World Cup had showcased Italy, where everything from the football grounds to the salaries were bigger and better. The world's best players all wanted to be in Serie A.

Ruud Gullit, Marco van Basten and Frank Rijkaard were at AC Milan; Andreas Brehme, Lothar Matthäus and Jürgen Klinsmann were at Inter; Thomas Hässler and Júlio César were at Juventus, there was Rudi Völler at Roma and – the greatest of them all – Diego Maradona at Napoli. Soon England's World Cup stars were moving too: Paul Gascoigne to Lazio, David Platt to Bari and Des Walker to Sampdoria.

Despite the good performance of the England team at the World Cup, English club football was in a mess. The five-year ban on English clubs playing in European competition that followed the 1985 Heysel Stadium disaster had taken its toll on the quality of the league.

Clubs were calculating the cost of the Taylor Report into Hillsborough and its recommendation that crumbling stadia should be modernized and made all-seater. With the Bradford fire, the Millwall riot at Luton Town, dwindling attendances and the continuing bad behaviour of some England fans abroad, the national game had never been in worse shape.

Without the money from European matches, the 'big five' clubs (Liverpool, Everton, Manchester United, Tottenham and Arsenal) had been grumbling about the way the Football League distributed the revenue earned by their deal with TV to all 92 clubs. Without more money to offer their best players, those clubs knew the trickle of talent to Italy would become a torrent.

There was an uneasy relationship between the FA and the Football League. Based at opposite ends of the country, they often seemed to be working against each other. Aware of the clubs' dissatisfaction with the League, and encouraged by Greg Dyke, the head of London Weekend Television, the FA produced a document – 'The Blueprint for Football' – suggesting a breakaway league that would keep the money it generated to itself. This, they argued, should stop the best players leaving and put the national team at the top of a pyramid of excellence.

The First Division clubs loved it. A Founder Agreement was signed, and in the summer of 1991 the 22 top-flight teams gave notice of their intention to resign from the Football League.

On 20 February 1992 the FA Council gave its approval. The FA Premier League was born and raring to go.

Also on this day

2001 Leading 3–0 at half-time, Southampton were stunned by a second-half comeback and lost 4–3 at Tranmere Rovers in their FA Cup fifth-round replay.

2007 Liverpool signed Javier Mascherano from West Ham.

2010 Everton stormed back from 1–0 down to beat Manchester United 3–1 at Goodison Park.

21 FEBRUARY
1995 – George Graham sacked

George Graham had taken Arsenal back to the top. With the Scot in charge, the club enjoyed one of its finest periods of success – winning the league title in 1989 and 1991, the FA Cup in 1993, the League Cup in 1987 and 1993 and the European Cup Winners' Cup in 1994. He seemed untouchable.

On 22 April 1994 a letter was sent to Arsenal's accountants by the Inland Revenue; it shook the club to the core. In it the Inland Revenue said it had evidence that 'coaching staff have received payments or monies … which have emanated from transfer fees paid by your client'.

The Inland Revenue's trail led to Norway and a football agent called Rune Hauge, who had facilitated Arsenal's purchase of two Scandinavian players, John Jensen from Brøndby and Pål Lydersen from IK Start.

George Graham didn't deny that he had received £425,000 from Hauge – £140,000 in cash in a hotel bar and £285,000 by banker's draft through the post – and he repaid it to Arsenal in full with interest added. In his defence, Graham claimed that the money had been 'unsolicited gifts'.

An FA disciplinary commission claimed a different version of events to Graham's. They contested that, in the case of the Lydersen deal, Rune Hauge had informed Graham that IK Start were willing to sell to Arsenal for £500,000, and that Graham then got the authorization to pay that amount from the Arsenal board of directors.

The commission's version of events said that, when Graham went to Oslo to meet Hauge and officials from IK Start to discuss the deal, he discovered that the club were willing to sell for £215,000. They said that, once £25,000 had been deducted as a signing-on payment to Lydersen, the difference between what Arsenal paid and what IK Start received – around £260,000 – had been divided between Graham and Hauge. The Jensen deal, they ruled, had worked in a similar way.

Graham protested his innocence but to no avail. Arsenal chairman Peter Hill-Wood said, 'I cannot recall a sadder day.'

Also on this day

1997 Sampdoria coach Sven-Göran Eriksson went back on an agreement to become the new manager of Blackburn Rovers.

2004 Blackburn goalkeeper Brad Friedel scored a last-minute equalizer for Blackburn at Charlton. Seconds later Friedel conceded a goal as Charlton won 3–2.

2004 Arsenal won 2–1 at Stamford Bridge, Chelsea's last home league defeat for 86 matches over the next four-and-a-half-years.

2006 Thierry Henry scored the only goal as Arsenal beat Real Madrid in Spain in their Champions League tie.

2007 Craig Bellamy, who had been accused of attacking teammate John Arne Riise with a golf club at a team-bonding session, scored in Liverpool's 2–1 Champions League win over Barcelona in Spain. Bellamy celebrated with a swing of an imaginary golf club.

22 FEBRUARY
1997 – Anelka to Arsenal

Nicolas Anelka may well be the only player who will ever be able to say that he played for Arsenal, Chelsea, Liverpool and Manchester City.

Anelka was 17 and had played just 11 games for Paris Saint-Germain when Arsène Wenger spent £500,000 to take him to Arsenal. Once there Anelka seemed to have a knack of saving his best for the big occasion, making his debut as a substitute against Chelsea and scoring his first goal in Arsenal's 3–2 win over Manchester United.

When Ian Wright suffered an injury at the beginning of 1998 a door opened for Anelka, and he didn't look back. He completed a brilliant season with a goal in the FA Cup victory over Newcastle.

But Anelka stayed with Arsène Wenger for only one more season, scoring 18 goals and being named the PFA's Young Player of the Year. The summer of 1999 was dominated by stories linking Anelka with a move to either Lazio or Real Madrid. Anelka's single-minded determination to leave Arsenal earned him the tabloid nickname 'Le Sulk'.

With Anelka's move to Madrid imminent, Arsenal fans hoped that their new French signing might be as good – his name was Thierry Henry.

Also on this day

2001 **Michael Owen missed a penalty as Liverpool were beaten 1–0 at Anfield by Fabio Capello's Roma in their UEFA Cup fourth-round tie but went through 2–1 on aggregate. The Italians were furious after the referee clearly awarded them a penalty for handball by Markus Babbel at the Kop end, only to change his mind.**

2005 **There were mixed Champions League fortunes for the Premier League against the Bundesliga as Bayern Munich beat Arsenal 3–1 in Bavaria but Liverpool beat Bayer Leverkusen by the same score at Anfield.**

2006 **Chelsea lost at home to Barcelona 2–1 in the first leg of their Champions League second-round tie. Chelsea played most of the match with ten men after Asier del Horno was sent off for a challenge on Lionel**

Messi. Afterwards Chelsea manager José Mourinho asked, 'How do you say cheating in Catalan?' Norwegian referee Terje Hauge reported receiving death threats in the days after the match.

23 FEBRUARY
2013 – Giggs's last goal

When 39-year-old Ryan Giggs collected a pass from Nani and drove a shot past Júlio César to seal Manchester United's 2–0 win at Queens Park Rangers, it was his 168th – and last – goal for the club. Giggs played on the following season, making a dozen more appearances in the Premier League, but couldn't extend his record of having scored in 23 consecutive seasons.

Ryan Giggs's remarkable playing career for Manchester United began in earnest with his debut on 2 March 1991 and ended on 6 May 2014. He was the last playing link between the Premier League and the old First Division of the Football League, and no player in English football has ever won more honours.

When Giggs retired he had played 963 times for United, won the Premier League title 13 times, the FA Cup four times, the League Cup three times and the Champions League twice. He had been voted the PFA Young Player of the Year, the PFA Player of the Year, the BBC Sports Personality of the Year and been made an OBE. He had also become the oldest player to score in the Champions League and in the Olympic Games.

From a flying winger to a probing midfielder, Giggs's ability to reinvent himself was the key to his longevity. His appointment as caretaker manager following the sacking of David Moyes stabilized a club in crisis in April 2014, and as Louis van Gaal's assistant he has become an important link to the best traditions of the club. There's also every chance that, if he wants to be, Ryan Giggs will be a Manchester United manager of the future.

Also on this day

2004 Arsenal got permission to go ahead with construction of their new stadium.

2005 Didier Drogba was sent off as Chelsea were beaten 2–1 in Barcelona in the first leg of a Champions League second-round tie. Afterwards José Mourinho criticized referee Anders Frisk and accused him of inviting Barcelona manager Frank Rijkaard into his dressing room at half-time. UEFA banned Mourinho for two matches. Anders Frisk retired from refereeing three weeks later after receiving death threats. UEFA's referee assessor Volker Roth later described Mourinho as 'an enemy of football'.

2008 Arsenal's Eduardo suffered a broken leg and dislocated ankle after a tackle by Birmingham's Martin Taylor at St Andrew's. It was almost 12 months before he played for Arsenal again.

24 FEBRUARY
2002 – Cole's goal as Rovers return

In 1998 the England manager Glenn Hoddle had decided not take Andy Cole to the World Cup Finals, despite the striker having scored 25 times for Manchester United that season. Hoddle's reasoning was that, in his opinion, Cole needed 'five chances to score a goal'.

In 2002 Cole was playing for Blackburn Rovers, who had reached their first major cup final since 1960. Blackburn's opponents in that League Cup Final were Spurs – now managed by Hoddle.

Rovers's manager Graeme Souness was without injured midfielders Tugay and Garry Flitcroft, so played 38-year-old Mark Hughes in the centre of midfield. Hughes played brilliantly, seemingly inspired by playing in Cardiff's Millennium Stadium – the home of the Welsh national team that Hughes had been managing for two years, at the same time as playing for Rovers.

Matt Jansen gave Blackburn the lead after 25 minutes, only for Christian Ziege to equalize for Tottenham eight minutes later; it was 1–1 at half-time. The second half was tense and the two sides seemed evenly matched, until a piece of opportunism from Cole settled the game.

Henning Berg lofted a long ball towards the Tottenham penalty area, Ledley King misjudged it and his header went across his own penalty area to Andy Cole, who lifted a shot beyond Neil Sullivan into the Tottenham net.

Blackburn had their first ever League Cup win and Cole had his revenge on Hoddle. 'That made it feel really good,' he said after the match. 'I'm not prepared to hold grudges as I'm too old for that. It's water under the bridge. But the way he went about dropping me for England, in telling the press before he told me, well, that just shows his style.'

Also on this day

1998 After four years in charge, Brian Little resigned as manager of Aston Villa.

2008 Spurs, managed by Juande Ramos, came from behind to win their first trophy for nine years, beating Chelsea 2–1 in the League Cup Final. A Dimitar Berbatov penalty for Spurs equalized Didier Drogba's first-half goal, and Jonathan Woodgate

scored the winner four minutes into extra-time.

2013 Swansea City won the League Cup with a 5–0 victory over fourth-tier Bradford City, the first major trophy in their history. Bradford played the last half-hour with ten men after goalkeeper Matt Duke was sent off. It was the biggest margin of victory ever in the League Cup Final but Swansea manager Michael Laudrup paid tribute to Bradford: 'I think what they have done this year is incredible.'

25 FEBRUARY
2000 – The end of the crazy days

The first most people knew about Wimbledon FC was their FA Cup run of 1975. As a Southern League club they beat top-tier Burnley at Turf Moor and then, in the fourth round, drew at Elland Road against mighty Leeds, before being unlucky to lose the replay 1–0.

In 1977 the club was elected into the Football League and, after five seasons of consolidation, were then sensationally promoted from the fourth tier to the first in only four years, guided by manager Dave Bassett and the owner Sam Hammam.

In the top flight Wimbledon became notorious for a direct, physical style of play – epitomized by Vinnie Jones – and for their practical jokes, which included burning the clothes of new players as an initiation ceremony. This boisterous behaviour earned them the nickname 'The Crazy Gang'.

In 1988, a year after Bobby Gould had taken over from Bassett, they won the FA Cup against Liverpool. After the formation of the Premier League, despite having to ground-share with Crystal Palace and having by far the smallest fan base in the top flight, they continued to thrive.

In 1992 Joe Kinnear was appointed manager and two years later they finished sixth – a club record high. Under Kinnear, Wimbledon either produced or developed players such as John Scales, Warren Barton, Dean Holdsworth, Keith Curle and Terry Phelan – who were sold on for huge profits. But even so, financing the club was hard work, and in 1997 Hammam sold some of his stake in it to Norwegian investors Bjørn Rune Gjelsten and Kjell Inge Røkke.

A slow decline began, and in 1999 Joe Kinnear suffered a heart attack and stood down as manager. He was replaced by Egil Olsen, the former boss of the Norwegian national team. On 25 February 2000 the final link with the club's glory days and the Crazy Gang was severed when Gjelsten and Røkke bought the last of Sam Hammam's stake in the club.

Three months later Wimbledon were relegated out of the Premier League.

Also on this day

2001 Dwight Yorke scored a hat-trick as Manchester United beat Arsenal 6–1 at Old Trafford to go 16 points clear at the top of the Premier League.

2001 Liverpool won the League Cup with a penalty shoot-out against Birmingham City after a 1–1 draw. It was the first cup final to be played at Cardiff's Millennium Stadium and the first to be decided on penalties.

2004 Roy Keane was sent off for stamping as Manchester United lost 2–1 at FC Porto in Sir Alex Ferguson's 100th Champions League game.

2007 John Obi Mikel, Emmanuel Adebayor and Kolo Touré were all sent off in the closing moments of Chelsea's 2–1 win over Arsenal in the League Cup Final.

2014 The pressure increased on David Moyes as Manchester United lost 2–0 at Olympiakos in the Champions League.

26 FEBRUARY

2010 – Portsmouth into administration

It was Portsmouth's seventh season in the Premier League. They'd won the FA

Cup in 2008, they'd played in Europe, beaten some of the best teams and bought some of the best players – and it had all been done on borrowed money. In 2010 Portsmouth discovered they were on borrowed time as the debts were called in.

Portsmouth had gone through owners almost as quickly as some clubs go through managers. Alexandre Gaydamak had been in charge since 2006, but when his father Arcadi was convicted of arms dealing in October 2009, Gaydamak junior found his access to funds drying up. Gaydamak senior later had his conviction overturned, but by then his son had sold the club.

Sulaiman Al-Fahim owned Portsmouth for 40 days before selling it to Ali Al-Faraj. Al-Faraj was a man who kept such a low profile that some Portsmouth fans believed he didn't actually exist, but had been invented as a cover for Balram Chainrai, a Hong Kong businessman who was the next to take over just four months later.

Portsmouth were estimated to be £135m in debt. As cash haemorrhaged, players were sold as quickly as possible and the team slumped to the bottom of the table; wages were unpaid and the Inland Revenue issued a winding-up order. With the possibility that the club might be unable to fulfil its fixtures, Portsmouth went into administration,

accepting the resulting nine-point penalty from the Premier League and certain relegation.

Even without the points deduction Portsmouth would have finished bottom of the Premier League in 2010, but extraordinarily they managed to reach the FA Cup Final again, where they lost 1–0 to Chelsea.

By the time the Pompey Supporters' Trust bought the club in 2013 it had been through another owner, another administration, a ten-point penalty and two more relegations. However, in September 2014 the trust announced that Portsmouth was finally a debt-free club.

Also on this day

2000 **Alan Shearer announced that he would retire from international football after the European Championship Finals.**

2006 **Playing in their first ever major final, Wigan Athletic were beaten 4–0 by Manchester United in the League Cup.**

2012 **Arsenal recovered from 2–0 down to beat Spurs 5–2 at the Emirates in the north London derby.**

2012 **With Kenny Dalglish as manager, Liverpool won the League Cup Final in a penalty shoot-out against Cardiff City.**

27 FEBRUARY
2004 – Ferguson's Cheltenham plea

Through his love of horseracing, Sir Alex Ferguson had become close friends with John Magnier, the boss of the famous Coolmore racing stud, and his business partner J.P. McManus. Just as Ferguson loved racing, so McManus loved football – and Manchester United in particular – and along with Magnier they became majority shareholders in Ferguson's club.

There wouldn't have been a problem had they not given Ferguson 50 per cent ownership in the outstanding horse Rock of Gibraltar in 2001. Ferguson would later write, 'My understanding was that I had a half-share in the ownership of the horse; theirs was that I would be entitled to half the prize money.'

The difference might seem slight, but as an owner of a half-share in the horse, Ferguson would be entitled to 50 per cent of stud fees, maybe as much as £50m; his share of the prize money alone would be a fraction of that amount.

In early 2004, with Ferguson having launched legal action to claim the money he considered he was entitled to, Magnier and McManus hit back with a series of 99 questions that they put to the Old Trafford board, which probed Ferguson's influence over the club's finances and transfer dealings. The relationship had ruptured completely and both the wellbeing of Manchester United and Ferguson's future were on the line.

Manchester United fans didn't need persuading to see Magnier and McManus as the bad guys. Fans' groups organized protests at racecourses and threatened to cause chaos at the upcoming Cheltenham Festival.

On 27 February 2004, Ferguson stood outside Old Trafford and read a statement: 'The reputation of Manchester United is paramount to my thinking. The private dispute I have is just that and I don't want to exacerbate the whole thing. Cheltenham is such a great festival and I don't want it marred in any way.'

Ferguson's plea not only pacified the fans but smoothed the path to a resolution in the dispute. Within a month he had agreed a settlement of £2.5m with Magnier and dropped all future claims to ownership of the horse in return.

Magnier and McManus didn't lose out though: a year later they were reported to have sold their stake in Manchester United to the Glazers for an estimated profit of £80m.

Also on this day

1999 Robbie Fowler and Graeme Le Saux clashed in Chelsea's 2–1 win over Liverpool at Stamford Bridge. Le Saux was later banned for one match for elbowing Fowler, who got a two-match ban for an offensive gesture made towards Le Saux.

2000 Leicester City won the League Cup for the second time in four years, beating Tranmere Rovers 2–1 in the final.

2005 José Mourinho won his first trophy in English football, beating Liverpool 3–2 in the League Cup Final.

2010 Arsenal's Aaron Ramsey suffered a double-fracture of his leg in a challenge with Stoke's Ryan Shawcross. It would be more than 12 months before Ramsey played for Arsenal again.

2010 Wayne Bridge refused to shake John Terry's hand before Manchester City's 4–2 win at Chelsea.

2011 Birmingham City won the League Cup, their first major honour since 1963, with a 2–1 win over Arsenal in the final.

28 FEBRUARY
2005 – Norwich's half-time entertainment

After nine years out of the Premier League, Norwich City had found life in the top flight difficult. Under Nigel Worthington they had been forced to wait until their 14th game of the 2004/05 season for their first win. They were in the relegation zone with 20 points from 27 games, when Manchester City went to Carrow Road in February.

The game started brilliantly for Norwich, with Dean Ashton and Leon McKenzie goals putting them 2–0 up inside 20 minutes. Then Norwich began to lose their grip; first Antoine Sibierski headed in to make it 2–1 and then Robbie Fowler converted Shaun Wright-Phillip's pass to equalize with eight minutes of the first half still to play.

After such a psychological blow the next 45 minutes felt like they could be pivotal to Norwich's season. Sensing the mood of the crowd, director Delia Smith went onto the pitch, grabbed the microphone and attempted to give the fans a gee-up.

There was something about the famous and normally decorous TV cook almost snarling into the microphone that caught the imagination of the country. 'A message for the best football supporters in the world: we need a twelfth man here. Where are you? Where are you? Let's be 'avin' you! Come on!'

Soon her call-to-arms was being replayed on news programmes across the country. Later Smith admitted, 'You forget you are on television. We had had a two-goal lead and lost it. I was desperate. I know what was in my heart. It was the heart of a football supporter and I am not in any way putting any blame on the fans. It was just a plea. If I was there among them I'd have said it and no-one would have batted an eyelid.'

Perhaps she should have delivered her message to the players rather than the fans? In the second half Norwich had Mattias Jonson sent off, and lost 3–2.

Also on this day

2001 England beat Spain 3–0 at Villa Park in Sven-Göran Eriksson's first match as England manager.

2010 Manchester United won the League Cup with a 2–1 win over Aston Villa, who claimed that Nemanja Vidić should have been shown a red card.

2015 Seventeen months after beginning treatment for testicular cancer, Jonás Gutiérrez returned to Newcastle's squad for a 1–0 win over Aston Villa.

29 FEBRUARY
2004 – Middlesbrough's cup at last

When members of the Middlesbrough cricket club decided to give themselves something to do in the winter months by forming a football team in 1875, they must have hoped that a trophy might have come their way a bit sooner than 2004.

Middlesbrough had come close to winning something. In the 1997 League Cup Final they were leading 1–0 against Leicester with two minutes of extra-time to play, but Emile Heskey had equalized and Leicester won the replay 1–0, also in extra-time.

Six weeks later Middlesbrough had lost the FA Cup Final 2–0 to Chelsea, a heart-breaking defeat that came just six days after the club had been relegated out of the Premier League.

Chelsea were the opponents again the following March when Middlesbrough again lost the League Cup Final in extra-time, this time 2–0. In 13 months Middlesbrough had played in three cup finals and lost them all. Maybe that trophy would never come?

In 2004 their luck seemed to be changing. In the League Cup Middlesbrough had won penalty shoot-outs against both Everton and Spurs and they'd beaten Arsenal home and away in the semi-final. At the Millennium Stadium Bolton Wanderers stood between them and that first major trophy.

Middlesbrough blew Bolton away almost from the kick-off. They were 2–0 up after only seven minutes through Joseph-Désiré Job and a Boudewijn Zenden penalty. Kevin Davies pulled a goal back for Bolton when his shot squirmed through Mark Schwarzer's grasp, but Middlesbrough held out – and their 129-year wait was finally over.

Afterwards Middlesbrough's Juninho, nicknamed 'The Little Fella' and playing his third spell with the club, said his medal with them meant as much as his 2002 World Cup winner's medal with Brazil.

Also on this day

2000 In a match marred by crowd trouble, Chelsea lost 1–0 at Marseille in the Champions League.

2012 Stuart Pearce's only match as England's caretaker manager ended in a 3–2 defeat to the Netherlands at Wembley. England, with Scott Parker as captain for the only time in his career, came from 2–0 down thanks to goals from Gary Cahill and Ashley Young, only for Arjen Robben to win it for the Dutch. By the time of England's next game, Roy Hodgson was the manager.

March

1 MARCH
2009 – Foster's homework

In 1970 Gordon Banks became one of the first goalkeepers to wear anything resembling what we would call goalkeepers' gloves. He was ahead of his time; most other goalkeepers either used their bare hands or wore the kind of gloves you might buy in a garden centre.

Soon gloves were standard, but in 2009 Ben Foster took technology to the next step. Foster was 25, highly rated, but on the fringes of the action for both club and country. Having been signed by Manchester United for £1m before he'd even made his debut for Stoke, Foster was then loaned to Watford for two seasons before returning to join the ranks at Old Trafford.

With Edwin van der Sar untouchable, Foster had played only six first-team games for the club when Sir Alex Ferguson decided to use him in the League Cup Final of 2009 against Tottenham Hotspur.

Foster had already made one superb save from Aaron Lennon when, with the game goalless, extra-time began. There was only one real goalscoring opportunity in the added half-hour, and again Foster was needed to save well from Darren Bent.

For only the second time the League Cup Final would be decided on penalties. As the two teams prepared themselves, Foster took out his iPod. On it Foster and goalkeeping coach Eric Steele had stored information about all Tottenham's preferred penalty takers, including which side of the goal they liked to send their kicks.

Ryan Giggs took the first penalty and scored for United. Jamie O'Hara stepped up for Tottenham, but Foster had O'Hara's preferred technique fresh in his mind and saved. The next three penalties were scored, then David Bentley shot wide for Spurs, allowing Anderson to win the cup for United.

Later that month Foster was back at Wembley making his first England appearance for two years, but never quite became Ferguson's first-choice goalkeeper and was sold to Birmingham at the end of the following season.

Also on this day

1995 Ronny Rosenthal scored a hat-trick for Spurs as they came from 2–0 down at half-time to win 6–2 after extra-time at Southampton in an FA Cup fifth-round replay.

2004 Arjen Robben, who had turned down the chance to join Manchester United, signed for Chelsea for £13.5m from PSV Eindhoven.

2014 Newcastle manager Alan Pardew was sent off for head-butting Hull

City's David Meyler in Newcastle's 4–1 win at the KC Stadium. Pardew was fined £100,000 by Newcastle and a further £60,000 by the FA. He was also banned from attending Newcastle's next three games and banned from the dugout for four more after that.

2015 José Mourinho won the first trophy of his second spell as Chelsea manager with a 2–0 win over Spurs in the League Cup Final.

2 MARCH
1993 – Gory, gory Tottenham Hotspur

In 1993 Spurs had an unusual management structure. Terry Venables, their manager from 1987 to 1991, had become the club's chief executive under chairman Alan Sugar while coaches Doug Livermore and Ray Clemence had taken over managing the team from the sacked Peter Shreeves.

In early spring of 1993 the arrangement seemed to be working well, new signing Teddy Sheringham was thriving and Spurs travelled to Bramall Lane knowing that a win over relegation-threatened Sheffield United would take them into fourth place in the Premier League. Spurs's best run of the season, six consecutive wins, had taken them up the table and into the FA Cup quarter-final.

Tottenham's performance was dismal, with Sheffield United leading 4–0 at half-time. Franz Carr, the tricky winger of Nottingham Forest's excellent team of the late 1980s, scored the first, followed by three goals in eight minutes: Andy Gray scored an own-goal, then Ian Bryson hit two in two minutes, trebling his tally for the entire season.

Spurs steadied the ship after half-time and put on forward John Hendry in the hope of at least reducing the arrears. It only served to reinvigorate United, who scored two more late goals through Brian Deane and Paul Rogers, whose goal was his first since joining from non-league Sutton United.

The 6–0 thrashing was Tottenham's heaviest defeat since being beaten 7–0 at Liverpool in 1978. Sheffield United boss Dave Bassett steered his side to safety by winning their last three games of the season while Spurs finished eighth, not enough to save Livermore and Clemence from the sack. Venables was also dismissed – a decision which triggered his bitter feud with Alan Sugar.

Also on this day

2002 Goal of the Season – Dennis Bergkamp scored it for Arsenal against Newcastle at St James' Park.

2003 Liverpool beat Manchester United 2–0 to win the League Cup

Final with goals from Michael Owen and Steven Gerrard.

2014 Manchester City came from 1–0 down to beat Sunderland 3–1 and win the League Cup for the first time since 1976.

3 MARCH
2010 – England 3 Egypt 1: Crouch's double

England were labouring at Wembley against Egypt, who had recently been crowned African champions at the Nations Cup in Angola. Mohamed Zidan had given the Egyptians the lead in the 20th minute and England had rarely looked like equalizing – until Peter Crouch came on for Jermain Defoe at half-time.

It took Crouch ten minutes to score, sweeping home a Gareth Barry pass, and suddenly England were on the front foot. With 15 minutes to go Shaun Wright-Phillips fired England in front and the winger then set up Crouch for England's third with five minutes to play.

Crouch, with his 19th and 20th international goals from 37 caps, had surely done enough to ensure a place on the plane to South Africa for the World Cup Finals. 'There's always pressure playing for England, especially in a World Cup year, but I've always been very proud of my record for England,' said Crouch afterwards. 'I always feel very confident in this team that I'm going to get chances.'

The plaudits for Crouch were a far cry from his early days in the England side. Crouch had been booed when he came on to win his third cap in a game against Poland in 2005 – using a six-foot-seven striker was seen as a retrograde step. At that time Joe Cole, the player Crouch had replaced, had felt the need to come to Crouch's defence: 'It was ridiculous, he is a great player. Peter is an important member of the squad and he is going to have some great moments in an England shirt.'

Within three months of being a target for boos, Crouch had changed people's perceptions with a first international goal against Uruguay, a hat-trick against Jamaica, but perhaps most of all with his robot-dance goal celebration, which endeared him to fans for its carefree silliness.

Crouch went to two World Cups for England and scored 22 goals in 42 games for his country. His last appearance came in November 2010 when he came on with five minutes to go against France, and scored 60 seconds later. Despite that, he was never selected again.

No wonder the dedication in his autobiography reads: 'To those who have unfashionably believed in me.'

Also on this day

1995 Crystal Palace striker Chris Armstrong was offered counselling after failing a random drugs test for cannabis.

2011 It was revealed that Manchester City defender Kolo Touré had failed a drugs test for a substance present in a weight-control treatment used by his wife. He served a six-month suspension.

4 MARCH
1995 – Ipswich's Old Trafford ordeal

George Burley's Ipswich were one place off the bottom of the Premier League table, seven points adrift of safety with 12 games to play. In contrast, Manchester United were involved in a two-horse title race with Blackburn Rovers, who held a three-point advantage.

Blackburn's goal difference was also superior – but not for long. While Rovers were winning a tight game 1–0 at Aston Villa, Manchester United were ripping Ipswich to shreds at Old Trafford.

Roy Keane hit United's first goal after 15 minutes – a bobbling 20-yard shot that deceived Ipswich goalkeeper Craig Forrest – but Ipswich's main tormentor was Andy Cole.

Cole was playing his seventh game for United after his shock £7m move from Newcastle and had two goals from his first six games – a reasonable return but not a stunning start to life in Manchester.

Four minutes after Keane had opened the scoring, Cole touched in a Ryan Giggs cross to make it 2–0. Cole's second goal, after 37 minutes, was a tap-in after Mark Hughes's overhead kick had come back off the crossbar. It was 3–0 at half-time but United, with an eye on Blackburn's goal difference, were in no mood to stop scoring and added four more in the first 20 minutes of the second half.

First Cole completed his hat-trick on 53 minutes, heading in an Andrei Kanchelskis cross, then Mark Hughes added two more goals in the next five minutes to make it 6–0. Cole's fourth came six minutes later – another close-range shot after Forrest had saved from Brian McClair.

After 72 minutes Paul Ince chipped Forrest with a quickly taken free-kick and Cole got his fifth to make it 9–0 with a half-volley from close range.

It was Manchester United's biggest win since they beat Anderlecht 10–0 in 1956, the biggest win in Premier League history and the first time a player had scored five goals in a Premier League game.

When he was told the result, Blackburn boss Kenny Dalglish – on his 44th birthday – responded with a growl, 'You only get three points whether you win 9–0 or 1–0.'

Also on this day

1996 An Éric Cantona goal for Manchester United ended Newcastle's 100 per cent home record. The win brought United to within one point of Newcastle at the top of the table.

2012 André Villas-Boas was sacked by Chelsea and Roberto Di Matteo named as caretaker manager.

2015 Manchester United's Jonny Evans and Newcastle's Papiss Cissé were seen spitting at each other during a game at St James' Park. Evans was banned for six matches and Cissé for seven.

5 MARCH
2013 – Nani sent off and Ferguson sees red

The 2012/13 Champions League Final was to be played at Wembley and, although it was still a closely guarded secret, Sir Alex Ferguson had decided that it was to be his last season at Manchester United, and his last chance to join Bob Paisley as the only manager to have won the European Cup three times.

United had easily won a group containing Galatasaray, Cluj and Braga and knew they would face one of the group runners-up – either FC Porto, Shakhtar Donetsk, Valencia, Celtic, AC Milan or Real Madrid – in the second round. Ferguson must have been cursing his luck when they drew José Mourinho's Madrid.

United took the lead in Spain in the first leg and, even though Danny Welbeck's goal was equalized by Cristiano Ronaldo, a 1–1 draw meant United were favourites to go through at Old Trafford.

United looked set for victory when Sergio Ramos scored an own-goal early in the second half. Ten minutes later United cleared a Real attack and a high ball fell between Nani and Madrid's Álvaro Arbeloa. The United winger raised his foot in an attempt to control the high ball, but it caught Arbeloa in the chest at the same time. Both players went down injured, but when Nani got up he was sent off by Turkish referee Cüneyt Çakır.

It was an extremely harsh decision and Ferguson raced from his seat in disgust while United's players protested, but they had more than half an hour to play with ten men.

Luka Modrić scored Real's first with a brilliant shot that went in off the post and soon Cristiano Ronaldo's hands were raised in apology to the United fans who had once adored him after he'd scored the winning goal. It was the first time Ronaldo had been back to Old Trafford in the four years since he'd left for Madrid. Afterwards he seemed overcome at having knocked out his former side: 'It was emotional, unbelievable. I don't have words to explain what I feel.'

That was no consolation to Sir Alex Ferguson, and nor was it when José Mourinho addressed the media afterwards and admitted his team's good fortune: 'In my opinion the best team lost, but that's football. We played well for ten minutes against ten men – but the man of the match was our goalkeeper Diego López.'

Ferguson sent his assistant Mike Phelan out to talk to the press: 'It's a distraught dressing room and a distraught manager – that's why I am sitting here now. I don't think the manager is in any fit state to talk to the referee about the decision.'

Ferguson knew that his last chance of a treble of Champions League titles had gone.

Also on this day

1997 Fabrizio Ravanelli scored a second-half hat-trick as bottom of the table Middlesbrough beat Derby 6–1.

2004 Paul Sturrock was appointed manager of Southampton.

6 MARCH
1993 – Norwich hit the rocks at Rangers

Norwich City, who had finished 18th in the last season of the Football League's First Division in 1992, won 4–2 against Arsenal at Highbury on the first ever weekend of Premier League football.

It was the shock of the day, and soon Norwich were the surprise package of the season and came close to being the first champions of the Premier League.

Under new manager Mike Walker, who had been promoted from his job as youth team manager, Norwich won seven of their first nine Premier League games to go four points clear at the top of the table.

In October the high-flying Canaries were brought down to earth with a 7–1 defeat at Blackburn and a 4–1 loss at Liverpool. But those who assumed a title challenge had been derailed were wrong; four consecutive wins in November and early December saw Norwich go back to the top and build an eight-point lead over nearest rivals Blackburn, Aston Villa and Chelsea.

A resurgent Manchester United had cut that lead to three points by the end of 1992, and with Aston Villa also involved it was a three-way title race in the spring of 1993.

Norwich's defeat at Southampton and draws at home to Blackburn and Arsenal allowed Manchester United and Aston Villa to go above them and when Mike Walker took his team to QPR on 6 March they were six points off the lead.

Les Ferdinand's two goals inside the first 15 minutes gave Norwich too much to do. They lost 3–1 at Loftus Road while United were winning 2–1 at Anfield.

Although Norwich enjoyed memorable wins over Villa, Leeds and Liverpool before the end of the season, the damage had been done. Norwich finished third while Manchester United beat Villa to the title.

Third was, and still is, Norwich's highest ever league finish.

Also on this day

2006 **After winning only 2 of their first 28 league games of the season Sunderland sacked Mick McCarthy and replaced him with caretaker boss Kevin Ball. They won only one more game that season and were relegated.**

2011 **Ryan Giggs beat Sir Bobby Charlton's record of 606 league games for Manchester United, but finished on the losing side at Anfield as Dirk Kuyt scored a hat-trick in Liverpool's 3–1 win.**

7 MARCH
1999 – Vinnie calls it a day

Vinnie Jones was the hod-carrier from Wealdstone who made it to Hollywood via Wimbledon and Wembley.

A central midfielder signed from non-league football for just £10,000, Jones seemed a perfect fit for Wimbledon, playing up to his hard-man image and embracing the Crazy Gang

culture. He was credited by teammate John Fashanu for intimidating Steve McMahon in the first few seconds of Wimbledon's famous 1988 FA Cup Final win over Liverpool, Fashanu saying, 'At 3.01 p.m. Vinnie went in for a tackle with Steve McMahon and that was the key moment. The tackle started at his throat and ended at his ankle. That was the game won; psychologically we had made our mark.'

Jones was soon revelling in his notoriety. In 1992 he was fined £20,000 for taking part in a video called *Soccer's Hard Men* in which he gave instruction on how to 'follow through with your studs down his Achilles, and if you're cute the ref won't see you'.

In the video he also said, 'If their top geezer gets sorted out early doors, you win.' He was as good as his word in 1992 when he was booked after a world-record three seconds for a foul on Sheffield United's Dane Whitehouse. 'I must have been too high, too wild, too strong or too early, because, after three seconds, I could hardly have been too bloody late!' he remembered in his autobiography.

Gary Lineker once said, 'We don't need people like Vinnie Jones who is just a self-hyped personality – fine for him, but he isn't a good player and no benefit to the game.' Nevertheless Jones earned transfers to Leeds, Sheffield United and Chelsea.

Having a grandfather from Ruthin allowed Jones to play 9 times for Wales, but in spring 1999 when he was player-coach of Queens Park Rangers – and after 477 games, 40 goals and 12 red cards – Jones retired to concentrate on an acting career that began with a role playing a violent debt-collector in Guy Ritchie's *Lock, Stock and Two Smoking Barrels*.

Also on this day

1993 Manager Terry Venables named David Platt as England captain, replacing Stuart Pearce.

2006 Ronaldinho and Frank Lampard scored as Chelsea drew 1–1 at Barcelona in the second leg of the Champions League second-round tie, José Mourinho's side losing 3–2 on aggregate.

2015 Aston Villa beat local rivals West Bromwich Albion 2–0 in the FA Cup quarter-final at Villa Park, a win soured by a pitch invasion before the final whistle.

8 MARCH

2005 – Chelsea and Barcelona, the six-goal classic

Chelsea had been beaten 2–1 in the Nou Camp, a result that José Mourinho had claimed was 'adulterated' by the referee Anders Frisk. The Swedish official had sent off Didier Drogba when Chelsea were leading 1–0 and Mourinho claimed that Frisk had been seen talking suspiciously to Barcelona coach Frank Rijkaard at half-time. In fact Frisk had ordered the Barcelona manager to leave him alone during the break, and

Mourinho was later banned for two matches for his accusation.

With Drogba suspended and Arjen Robben injured, Chelsea were not given much hope of going through and Barcelona striker Samuel Eto'o dismissed Chelsea's chances of scoring more than once in the second leg.

He was probably regretting having said that when Chelsea raced into a 3–0 lead after only 19 minutes, Eidur Gudjohnsen, Frank Lampard and Damien Duff ripping through the Spanish defences in front of a jubilant Stamford Bridge.

Then Ronaldinho showed why he was World Player of the Year, first converting a penalty awarded for handball and then scoring with an outrageous shot that had left Petr Čech motionless – all this before half-time.

With the tie level at 4–4 on aggregate, Barcelona held the advantage of the extra away goal. With less than 20 minutes to go, they almost put it beyond Chelsea's reach but somehow Čech turned a shot from Andrés Iniesta onto the post and Eto'o missed from the rebound.

Three minutes later John Terry climbed to head home a Damien Duff corner and an exultant Chelsea had recorded one of their most famous victories.

In the midst of the celebrations Mourinho purred, 'It was a fantastic result. We have beaten the team that is – according to some – the best in the world. The football was magnificent.'

Also on this day

2008 There were two FA Cup quarter-final shocks as Barnsley won 1–0 against Chelsea at Oakwell and Manchester United lost by the same score at home to Portsmouth, Pompey's first win at Old Trafford since 1957.

2010 Hugo Rodallega scored the only goal in relegation-threatened Wigan's 1–0 win over Liverpool, their first league win for two months.

2011 Arsenal went out of the Champions League to Barcelona after a 3–1 defeat in Spain. Arsenal were drawing 1–1, and winning 3–2 on aggregate, when Robin van Persie was controversially sent off for not stopping play when the referee Massimo Busacca blew his whistle. Van Persie claimed he couldn't hear the whistle above the noise of the crowd and Arsène Wenger said, 'I think two kinds of people will be unhappy – those who love Arsenal, and those who love the game.'

9 MARCH
2004 – Mourinho's touchline dash

Manchester United had been careless in the first leg in Portugal. Playing José Mourinho's UEFA Cup holders FC Porto in the Estádio do Dragão, Alex Ferguson's side had taken the lead through Quinton

Fortune, but conceded two goals to Benni McCarthy before having Roy Keane sent off for a stamp on Porto goalkeeper Vítor Baía.

United took the lead in the second leg of the Champions League second-round tie too, Paul Scholes heading home after half an hour to give United a slender advantage on away goals. Just before half-time Scholes thought he'd scored again, only for a linesman to rule him offside – replays showed that the goal should have counted.

United fans were holding their breath when Porto were awarded a free-kick for a foul by Phil Neville just outside their penalty area in the 90th minute. Benni McCarthy curled it towards goal, United keeper Tim Howard saved it, but could only push the ball into the path of the onrushing Costinha, who pounced to send Porto through and United out. On the touchline a delirious, mad Mourinho was sprinting and leaping with joy to celebrate with his players.

Later Porto's captain Jorge Costa would recall, 'When Costinha scored, I was going crazy. Mourinho was going crazy, everybody was going crazy. In that season it didn't matter who we played – United, Real Madrid, Lazio – we went to the game and thought "Can we win? Yes, we can."'

Porto went on to beat Lyon and Deportivo La Coruña before overcoming Monaco 3–0 in the Champions League Final in Gelsenkirchen – but the enduring moment is of Mourinho's explosive celebration in Manchester.

Also on this day

2005 Arsenal beat Bayern Munich 1–0 at Highbury in the Champions League but went out 3–2 on aggregate.

2011 Harry Redknapp became the first English manager to take an English club to the quarter-finals of the Champions League as Spurs drew 0–0 at home to AC Milan in the second leg of their second-round tie to go through 1–0 on aggregate. 'This is an impossible dream that we have achieved so far,' said Redknapp.

2015 Manchester United lost 2–1 at home to Arsenal in the FA Cup quarter-final and had British record signing Ángel Di María sent off when he grabbed the shirt of referee Michael Oliver. Arsenal's winning goal was scored by former United striker Danny Welbeck.

10 MARCH
2001 – Wycombe's Ceefax striker

Managed by Lawrie Sanchez, Wycombe Wanderers were playing in the third tier but had beaten Millwall, Grimsby,

Wolves and Wimbledon to get into the quarter-final of the FA Cup, where they were drawn away to Premier League Leicester City.

Two weeks before the match Sanchez had a serious problem – injuries meant that he was running out of strikers. The club put an appeal on their website for any fit forwards who were without a club to make themselves known.

Roy Essandoh was a 25-year-old Belfast-born, Ghana-raised striker who had played non-league football in Scotland with Cumbernauld United before brief spells at Motherwell and East Fife and two seasons playing in Finland.

Back in England he had made two substitute appearances for Rushden and Diamonds in the Conference, but had not done enough to earn a contract.

A keen-eyed Ceefax journalist had reprinted Wycombe's appeal for a striker on the pages of the BBC text service, and Essandoh's agent responded on his behalf.

Wycombe gave him a two-week deal, and a debut in a 1–0 home defeat to Port Vale in which Essandoh played 76 minutes before being taken off.

Against Leicester Sanchez brought Essandoh on for the last 15 minutes with the score at 1–1. In injury-time their Ceefax striker found himself in the Leicester box when a high cross was headed back across goal, he rose and sent a perfect header powering into the roof of the Leicester net. Essandoh, who said he didn't know the names of all his own teammates, had become a household name in an instant.

Wycombe played Liverpool in the FA Cup semi-final and lost 2–1, with Essandoh coming on for the last 25 minutes but unable to repeat his headline-grabbing goal. He played 15 games in all for Wycombe, but never scored again, before dropping down the divisions once more to become one of non-league football's best-known names.

Also on this day

1997 For the second successive season Newcastle were beaten 4–3 at Anfield by Liverpool as Robbie Fowler scored an injury-time winner.

2000 Liverpool bought Emile Heskey from Leicester for £11m.

2003 After just 2 wins in 20 Premier League games Howard Wilkinson was sacked by Sunderland.

2005 Kevin Keegan resigned as manager of Manchester City.

2009 Liverpool beat Real Madrid 4–0 in the second leg of their Champions League second-round tie.

2010 David Beckham came on to play for AC Milan in their 4–0 defeat at Manchester United. Beckham left the pitch wearing one of the green and gold scarves produced by United fans in protest at the Glazer family.

11 MARCH
2006 – Portsmouth's Great Escape

When Portsmouth lost 1–0 at Aston Villa in early March 2006 it left Harry Redknapp's side deep in the relegation zone, eight points from safety with only ten games to play.

Not all Pompey fans were behind Redknapp – who had left them to take over at rivals Southampton, only to return again late in 2005. Some had dressed as pirates at Villa Park and at the end of the game they unfurled a banner reading 'Judas – walk the plank'. Portsmouth had taken just one point from their last eight games.

All this despite Redknapp having acquired half a new team in the January transfer window. He'd brought in Noé Pamarot, Sean Davis, Wayne Routledge and Pedro Mendes from Spurs, Benjani from Auxerre, goalkeeper Dean Kiely from Charlton and Andrés D'Alessandro on loan from Wolfsburg. All seven had gone straight into Redknapp's team – and they were still losing.

Portsmouth's next match on 11 March was at Fratton Park against mid-table Manchester City. For an hour Portsmouth were the better side but couldn't score as the atmosphere became more and more frantic. Then Pedro Mendes, a Champions League winner with FC Porto, smashed home a 25-yard drive to give Portsmouth a precious lead. Rather than protect it with their lives, they threw it away, Richard Dunne equalizing with a header from a corner with seven minutes to go.

In desperation the home side poured forward. Three minutes into injury-time, a corner was cleared to Mendes on the edge of the box – his shot ripped into the roof of the Manchester City net and Fratton Park erupted. It was Portsmouth's first win since December.

Afterwards Redknapp said, 'If we didn't win today we were dead and buried. It has given the players a lift and the fans a lift. Pedro hits balls like that in training. He's been doing it all week and we said, "Save one for Saturday, Pedro," well, he saved two!'

Incredibly, Portsmouth won five and drew two of their next eight games and in May they were safe with a game to spare.

Also on this day

2008 A Fernando Torres goal gave a Liverpool a 1–0 win over Inter Milan in the San Siro and a 3–0 aggregate win.

2009 Manchester United knocked José Mourinho's Inter Milan out of the Champions League with a 2–0 win at Old Trafford.

2013 Brian McDermott was sacked by Reading, who named Nigel Adkins as their new manager.

2015 Chelsea went out of the Champions League on away goals against Paris Saint-Germain after a 2–2 draw at Stamford Bridge, despite the French club having Zlatan Ibrahimović sent off.

12 MARCH
2008 – Lampard hits four

Frank Lampard's goalscoring record places him with some of the very best the Premier League has ever seen – scoring more league goals than Michael Owen, Thierry Henry, Les Ferdinand and Robbie Fowler. And all those goals came with Lampard playing in midfield.

In March 2008 Lampard became the first midfielder ever to score four times in a Premier League game. He converted a penalty, a two-yard tap-in, a shot from distance and another from just inside the penalty area after a clever one-two, as Derby were crushed 6–1 at Stamford Bridge. Lampard had also hit the post when the score was 0–0.

After the game Chelsea manager Avram Grant said, 'He scored his 100th goal for Chelsea earlier this season and I think he'll get 150 goals for this club.' Grant was being conservative – in fact Lampard scored 211 Chelsea goals in 648 games.

Although Lampard's Premier League career was bookended by spells at West Ham and Manchester City, it's the 13 seasons he spent at Stamford Bridge which defined his career. Lampard won the Premier League three times, the FA Cup four times, the League Cup twice and both the Champions League and Europa League with Chelsea. In May 2013, with 2 goals at Aston Villa, he became the club's highest ever goalscorer, surpassing Bobby Tambling's 43-year-old record of 202 for the club. He also set a Premier League record for an outfield player of appearing in 164 consecutive games from August 2001 until December 2005.

Lampard scored 12 or more goals for Chelsea in ten consecutive seasons from 2003 to 2013. His most prolific season came in 2009/10, scoring 22 in the league – 27 in all competitions – and also providing 17 assists.

No wonder Bobby Tambling, the man whose scoring record he beat, described Lampard as Chelsea's greatest ever player.

Also on this day

1998 Unable to further expand their Highbury home, Arsenal made a £120m offer to buy Wembley Stadium.

2002 Everton sacked manager Walter Smith.

2003 Mick McCarthy was appointed manager at Sunderland, their third of the season after Peter Reid and Howard Wilkinson.

2014 Pablo Zabaleta was sent off for Manchester City as they went out of the Champions League following a 2–1 defeat to Barcelona in Spain, completing a 4–1 aggregate defeat.

13 MARCH
2003 – Diouf's Celtic spit

The UEFA Cup quarter-final between Celtic and Liverpool in 2003 was as eagerly anticipated as any so-called 'Battle of Britain', but was overshadowed by the actions of one of the most controversial players to have played in the Premier League.

The Senegalese striker El Hadji Diouf was signed by Liverpool during his country's historic run to the quarter-final of the World Cup in 2002. Diouf was already African Footballer of the Year and Liverpool manager Gérard Houllier decided that spending £10m on him was a better bet than turning Nicolas Anelka's loan move from Paris Saint-Germain into a permanent deal.

That was already looking like a questionable decision when Liverpool travelled to Glasgow for the first leg of the tie with Celtic in mid-March. Diouf had

scored only six goals that season, and only three of them in the Premier League.

The score was 1–1, but the headlines were made by Diouf. With three minutes to go, chasing a wayward pass, Diouf collided with the advertising hoardings and almost fell into the Celtic fans. As he got up a fan ruffled his head – Diouf turned, looked at the supporter and spat at him. The reaction was so visible, and the response to it from the Celtic fans so furious, that Diouf had to be substituted and taken down the tunnel by a police escort for his own protection.

Liverpool immediately fined him two weeks' wages and made a £60,000 donation to a charity of Celtic's choice. He was also later fined £5000 by the Glasgow Sheriff Court.

Manager Gérard Houllier told reporters after the game that, 'He did not understand how much spitting is frowned on in this country. He does now, though. I can tell you one thing. It will not happen again. He will not repeat the same mistake.'

Houllier was wrong about Diouf: when he was playing for Bolton he was fined £500 for spitting water at Middlesbrough fans and two weeks' wages for spitting in Portsmouth's Arjan de Zeeuw's face. In 2012, by which time Diouf was at Doncaster, he was accused by Blackpool goalkeeper Matt Gilks of spitting at him.

Liverpool lost the second leg of the tie against Celtic 2–0 at Anfield, and Diouf never scored another goal for the club.

Also on this day

2008 Bolton went out of the UEFA Cup 2–1 on aggregate after a 1–0 defeat in Portugal against Sporting Lisbon.

2012 Steven Gerrard scored a hat-trick as Liverpool beat Everton 3–0 at Anfield.

2013 Goals from Olivier Giroud and Laurent Koscielny gave Arsenal a 2–0 Champions League victory against Bayern Munich in Germany, but Arsène Wenger's side went out on away goals having lost the first leg 3–1 in London.

14 MARCH
2009 – Torres tears into United

It was arguably one of Fernando Torres's best games for Liverpool and one of Nemanja Vidić's worst for Manchester United, as Sir Alex Ferguson's side suffered their biggest home defeat for 17 years.

United were seven points clear of both Chelsea and Liverpool in the title race, but a record-equalling 18th title looked far from certain after Liverpool's 4–1 win in front of the Stretford End.

Having beaten Real Madrid 4–0 at Anfield four days earlier Liverpool were entitled to be confident, but fell behind to a Cristiano Ronaldo penalty midway through the first half. Liverpool were level five minutes later. Vidić, with Torres hounding him in pursuit, chased a Martin Škrtel pass and hesitated for a fraction of a second, which was all the Liverpool striker needed to steal the ball and race through to score past Edwin van der Sar.

In the last seconds of the first half Torres linked with Steven Gerrard, who was tripped by Patrice Evra. Having converted the penalty, Gerrard's sense of drama took him to run and kiss the lens of the nearest TV camera.

Liverpool's third and fourth goals came from the most unlikely of sources. With barely 15 minutes to go Vidić, who had been tormented by Torres throughout, found himself beaten by Steven Gerrard; he pulled the Liverpool captain down and was sent off. Liverpool's Brazilian left back Fábio Aurélio curled home the free-kick brilliantly – only his second goal of the season.

Andrea Dossena, an Italian defender who had scored his first Liverpool goal in the win over Madrid, calmly lobbed the fourth – the only Premier League goal he ever scored for the club. Van der Sar in the United goal had conceded more in one match than in the previous 23 games combined.

A shell-shocked Alex Ferguson said, 'As always at this club, when you lose a game you have to respond. And that's what we'll do.' Ferguson was right – they dropped only four points from their last ten games and won the Premier League again.

Also on this day

1998 A Marc Overmars goal gave Arsenal a 1–0 win at Old Trafford, putting them to within six points of leaders Manchester United with three games in hand. Arsenal went on to pip United to the title by one point.

2000 Graeme Souness was named manager of Blackburn Rovers.

2015 After scoring only four Premier League goals in their last 14 away games and none in their last 6 games, Aston Villa scored four times in 21 minutes at Sunderland. Villa won 4–0 and Sunderland manager Guy Poyet was sacked two days later.

15 MARCH
2001 – FIFA's African promise

By 2001 there had been 16 World Cups, and the only time the tournament had not been played in either Europe or South and Central America was in 1994 when the United States had been hosts.

FIFA, and President Sepp Blatter in particular, were keen to send the tournament to new frontiers. Asia had won the right to host in 2002 with South

Korea and Japan's joint bid, but Germany had prevailed over South Africa for the 2006 Finals in puzzling circumstances that had left the South Africans feeling they had been manoeuvred unfairly out of a winning position.

Germany had won the 2006 Finals by one vote when Charles Dempsey, FIFA's Oceania delegate, had controversially decided to abstain in the final round of voting, later saying that he was under intolerable pressure. Dempsey had supported England's bid in the first two voting rounds and his instructions from the federations he was representing were that should England's bid be eliminated, he was to vote for South Africa – instead he didn't vote at all.

Had the ballot been split 12–12, rather than 12–11 in Germany's favour, then Sepp Blatter would have had the casting vote – and that would certainly have gone to South Africa. South Africa's president Thabo Mbeki declared the outcome 'a tragedy for Africa'.

So in March 2001 FIFA decreed that the 2010 World Cup would be held in Africa for the first time. South Africa bid again, joined by Morocco, Egypt, Tunisia and Libya. After three years of canvassing the Tunisian and Libyan bids were withdrawn, Egypt won no votes at all, Morocco got 10 votes and South Africa won with 14.

Although South Africa's World Cup was a success in 2010, the manner in which it had been awarded to the country became part of the FBI's investigations into FIFA corruption.

In 2015 it was claimed that the South African government had paid $10m to ensure the support of key FIFA executives in the ballot. It was even suggested that Morocco might actually have won the vote, but that FIFA awarded the tournament to South Africa anyway. The South African government admitted a payment to help fund football development in the Caribbean, but denied that it was a bribe.

Also on this day

2006 Middlesbrough progressed to the quarter-finals of the UEFA Cup after a 2–1 defeat at AS Roma. Middlesbrough had won the first leg 1–0 and went through thanks to Jimmy Floyd Hasselbaink's away goal in Italy.

2008 Fernando Torres became the first Liverpool player to score 20 league goals in a season since Robbie Fowler in 1996 as Liverpool beat Reading 2–1.

2010 Phil Brown was sacked by Hull City.

2012 Manchester United and Manchester City went out of the Europa League on the same night. United were beaten 2–1 in Spain by Athletic Bilbao to go out 5–3 on aggregate; City won 3–2 at home to Sporting Lisbon but went out on away goals.

16 MARCH
2002 – Moyes's Goodison start

'Remember this date, 16 March 2002, because the good times are coming back to Goodison Park.' So said the public address announcer at Everton as their new manager, David Moyes, was introduced before his first game in charge of the club.

With 9 games of the season to go Everton were in dire straits, out of the relegation zone only on goal difference and with one win in their last 13 league games, in which they'd scored only six goals. They had also just been beaten

3–0 at Middlesbrough in the FA Cup quarter-final. Walter Smith had been sacked and Everton had turned to Moyes, who had impressed in his four years in charge of Preston.

Moyes would later recall meeting the Everton squad for the first time: 'Everybody in the dressing room was hanging on my words. I was thinking, "These guys probably don't know who I am." But you get on with your work, try to get on with it. It started very well for me.'

It could hardly have started better; the new man's first press conference had been a storming success, Moyes describing Everton as 'Merseyside's People's Club' – a dig at Liverpool that went down very well with Evertonians. His first big decision had come quickly, allowing Paul Gascoigne to leave the club on a free transfer for Burnley, and his first match was at home to Fulham.

It was a dream start as Everton took the lead through David Unsworth after 27 seconds – their first goal at Goodison for six weeks. Twelve minutes later Goodison hero Duncan Ferguson, back after seven games out injured, made it 2–0.

Thomas Gravesen's red card after 28 minutes left Everton hanging on grimly, particularly after Steed Malbranque's goal for Fulham, but they showed the kind of grit and spirit that became an Everton trademark under Moyes, and won.

It was the beginning of Moyes's 11-year stay at Goodison, during which they were regulars in the Premier League's top eight.

Also on this day

2001 Spurs sacked manager George Graham.

2010 José Mourinho's Inter Milan knocked Chelsea out of the Champions League with a 1–0 win at Stamford Bridge, completing a 3–1 aggregate victory. Afterwards Mourinho said, 'I am very, very happy because we won and not because Chelsea and my ex-players and Roman [Abramovich] lost. We were the better team from the first minute to the last minute. Roman is intelligent, he knows Inter were the best team.'

2015 Sunderland replaced sacked manager Gus Poyet with Dick Advocaat.

17 MARCH
2012 – The Muamba miracle

Five minutes before half-time in an FA Cup match between Spurs and Bolton at White Hart Lane, Bolton midfielder Fabrice Muamba fell to the floor. Within seconds it was clear that this was no ordinary injury, but a 23-year-old fighting for his life.

Muamba had suffered a cardiac arrest and was fortunate that Dr Jonathan Tobin, Bolton's club doctor, was by his side within seconds and that Dr Andrew Deaner, a consultant cardiologist at the London Chest Hospital who was at the game as a fan, had persuaded a steward to allow him to run onto the pitch to help.

In seven minutes of treatment on the pitch doctors made attempts at mouth-to-mouth resuscitation and two defibrillator shocks were given – but to no avail. Players and fans from both clubs prayed and some cried as they stood and watched in horror.

Muamba received 12 more unsuccessful defibrillator shocks in an ambulance on the way to the London Chest Hospital. It took 48 minutes from the moment of collapse to get Muamba there and a further 30 minutes in the hospital before paramedics managed to start his heart beating. 'There was no heartbeat for 78 minutes and he was not breathing – he was effectively dead in that time,' said Dr Tobin.

Incredibly, only six weeks later an emotional Muamba was back at Bolton's Reebok Stadium as they played Spurs to receive the acclaim of both clubs' fans.

Unable to play again, Muamba began a degree in sports journalism and later said, 'I wish things could have been different, but it's something I can't control. I'm just more grateful and thankful that I have my life. Would you prefer to be dead forever, or not play football?'

Also on this day

2003 Sir Alex Ferguson coined the phrase 'squeaky-bum time'. Talking about Arsenal's bid to win the title and FA Cup, the Manchester United boss said, 'They have a replay against Chelsea and if they win it they would face a semi-final three days before playing us in the league. It's squeaky-bum time and we've got the experience now to cope.'

2004 Goal of the Season – Dietmar Hamann scored it for Liverpool against Portsmouth at Anfield.

2007 Goal of the Season – Wayne Rooney scored it for Manchester United against Bolton at Old Trafford.

2007 Tottenham goalkeeper Paul Robinson scored in their 3–1 win over Watford.

2010 Iain Dowie was appointed manager of Hull City.

2015 Arsenal won 2–0 in Monaco in the Champions League but went out on away goals having lost 3–1 at home.

18 MARCH
2010 – Fulham thrash Juventus

Fulham's Europa League campaign had begun in July 2009 with a match in Lithuania against FK Vetra. They had played a dozen more games when tournament favourites Juventus came to Craven Cottage for the second leg of the round of 16 match.

Fulham had been beaten 3–1 in the first match in Turin, a daunting deficit to overturn, though Dixon Etuhu's away goal did give Roy Hodgson's side some hope for the second leg.

That hope seemed to have been extinguished after only two minutes when David Trezeguet put Juventus in front in London and ahead 4–1 on aggregate. 'We couldn't have had a worse start,' Hodgson admitted afterwards.

Crucially Fulham scored only seven minutes later, Bobby Zamora holding off Fabio Cannavaro to score from Paul Konchesky's cross – it changed the mood among the fans and sowed some seeds of doubt in Juventus minds.

If Cannavaro, World Player of the Year in 2006, had been at fault for Zamora's goal then his tackle on Zoltán Gera after 26 minutes handed Fulham the initiative. When Gera got goal-side of Cannavaro and onto a Zamora pass, he was fouled by the defender; referee Björn Kuipers sent Cannavaro off and suddenly Juventus were hanging on.

Simon Davies hit the bar and Etuhu hit the post before Gera made it 2–1 on the night five minutes before half-time. Fulham knew that one more goal would send the tie to extra-time and two more would win it – so long as Juventus didn't score.

Only four minutes into the second half Fulham were awarded a penalty for handball by Diego and Gera stepped up to score – Fulham led 3–1 on the night and it was now 4–4 on aggregate.

The goal that won the tie for Fulham was memorable for its quality as well its importance, Clint Dempsey floating a perfectly judged chip over the goalkeeper from a tight angle into the far corner of the Juventus net. The celebrations were wild and Jonathan Zebina's late red card for Juventus snuffed out any hope for them.

Afterwards Hodgson glowed, 'It's a remarkable achievement that the boys have done so well. I don't know if it is the biggest night in the club's history but it must come close.'

Also on this day

1998 Manchester United's Champions League hopes were ended by Monaco at the quarter-final stage. The French side drew 1–1 at Old Trafford after a goalless draw in the first leg to go through on away goals.

1999 Holders Chelsea reached the semi-finals of the European Cup Winners' Cup with a 3–2 win in Oslo against Vålerenga, for a 6–2 aggregate win.

2015 Despite Joe Hart's heroics, Manchester City lost 1–0 in Barcelona to go out of the Champions League 3–1 on aggregate.

19 MARCH
2015 – Everton, and England, over and out

The Premier League started the 2014/15 season with seven representatives in the two European competitions: after Everton were beaten in Ukraine by Dynamo Kiev on 19 March all seven had been knocked out. It was the first time in 20 years that there would be no English club playing in the quarter-finals in Europe.

The first side to go were Hull City. They had booked their place in the Europa League as runners-up to Arsenal in the FA Cup. Their first ever season in Europe didn't last long, a win over Slovakia's AS Trenčín being followed by defeat in late August to Lokeren of Belgium.

Next to exit were Liverpool and Spurs on the same night in February. Spurs, who had got through their Europa League group, were beaten 3–1 over two legs by Fiorentina in the first knockout round. Liverpool had finished third in their Champions League group, so were placed into the Europa League, where they were beaten by Turkey's Beşiktaş on penalties.

Arsenal, Manchester City and Chelsea, unlike Brendan Rodger's side, all qualified from their Champions League groups – but none got past the first knockout stage.

First Chelsea lost against Paris Saint-Germain on away goals, a 1–1 draw in Paris having been followed by a 2–2 draw at Stamford Bridge.

The following week Arsenal were eliminated by Monaco, also on away goals. Monaco had won 3–1 at the Emirates in the first leg, and although Arsenal won 2–0 away, it was not enough.

The next night, 18 March, Manchester City failed to produce a Nou Camp miracle and were beaten 1–0 at Barcelona, who had won the first leg 2–1 in Manchester.

Everton were the last club standing. They had won the first leg of their Europa League tie against Dynamo Kiev 2–1 at Goodison Park, but were swept aside 5–2 in Kiev.

Also on this day

1996 Nottingham Forest were knocked out of the UEFA Cup quarter-finals by Bayern Munich, who won the second leg of their tie at the City Ground 5–1.

2002 Five months after life-saving heart surgery, Gérard Houllier returned to the dugout for Liverpool as they beat AS Roma 2–0 to reach the quarter-finals of the Champions League.

2008 Chelsea lost the lead three times in a thrilling 4–4 draw against Spurs at White Hart Lane.

2014 A hat-trick from Robin van Persie helped Manchester United overcome a two-goal first-leg deficit to beat Olympiakos 3–0 and reach the

Champions League quarter-finals, easing the pressure on manager David Moyes.

20 MARCH
2002 – Arsenal's treble dream ends in Turin

In 2002 Arsenal had high hopes of being able to emulate Manchester United's 1999 treble of Premier League, Champions League and FA Cup.

Arsène Wenger's side were second in the Premier League, only one point behind Manchester United and with a game in hand after a 13-match unbeaten run. They had drawn at Newcastle in the FA Cup quarter-final and were favourites to go through in the Highbury replay, and were in contention to reach the last eight of the Champions League despite a damaging 2–0 home defeat to Deportivo La Coruña in the second group stage.

Arsenal's final Champions League group game was away to Juventus. Deportivo led the group on ten points, Arsenal and Bayer Leverkusen were joint second on seven points and Juventus on four points were already eliminated. Arsenal knew that to progress they had to get a better result in Turin than Leverkusen could achieve in La Coruña.

The omens for Arsenal were good when the teams were announced: Juventus coach Marcello Lippi picked practically a reserve side with no Buffon,

Thuram, Nedvěd, Del Piero or Trezeguet. The atmosphere in the Stadio delle Alpi was funereal. Juventus fans disliked the stadium that had been built for the 1990 World Cup Finals and, with their side unable to progress whatever the result, they stayed away. There were over 60,000 empty seats as the game kicked off.

The match was a stalemate, the Juventus fringe players determined not to lose, while Arsenal's seemed to be waiting for news from La Coruña as to whether a draw would be enough.

Soon after half-time Arsenal knew they had to win – Michael Ballack and Bernd Schneider had put Leverkusen 2–0 up in Spain. But Juventus were stubborn and stand-in goalkeeper Fabián Carini saved from Thierry Henry.

Just as Arsenal were given hope by a Deportivo goal in La Coruña, Juventus's Uruguayan Marcelo Zalayeta headed a corner beyond David Seaman and into the corner of the net. Leverkusen's third goal in Spain sealed Arsenal's elimination.

Arsène Wenger's side went on to win both the Premier League and FA Cup, but a wonderful treble had eluded them.

Also on this day

2003 **Alan Thompson and John Hartson scored as Celtic reached the semi-finals of the UEFA Cup with a 2–0 win at Anfield against Liverpool.**

2007 The FA rejected an idea from Rafa Benítez to follow the Spanish model and allow Premier League reserve sides to play in the lower leagues.

2015 FIFA confirmed that the Qatar World Cup Finals would be played in the northern hemisphere winter for the first time, with the final to be played on 18 December 2022.

21 MARCH
2012 – Fortress City

It took almost three years, but in 2011 the massive investment into Manchester City started paying off when the club won the FA Cup, its first trophy for 35 years. Building on that success, manager Roberto Mancini then raided Arsenal to sign both Gaël Clichy and Samir Nasri and spent £35m on Sergio Agüero from Atlético Madrid.

City started the 2011/12 campaign with a squad to match any in England, and playing against them at their Etihad home became almost a mission impossible. Swansea were the first side to be swept away in Manchester, beaten 4–0 in what was their first ever Premier League match. Northwest rivals Wigan and Everton then made fruitless trips to City's home, losing 3–0 and 2–0 respectively.

City brushed aside challenges from Aston Villa, Wolves and Newcastle before Norwich were crushed 5–1 to make it seven home wins in seven.

The next visitors were Arsenal, who were made of sterner stuff, but still lost 1–0. On Boxing Day Stoke put up little resistance and lost 3–0, and early in the New Year of 2013 Liverpool were beaten by the same score.

At last a visiting team threatened to damage City's record, but despite a superb display Spurs were beaten 3–2 by a last-minute Mario Balotelli penalty. Fulham provided less resistance and were crushed 3–0.

Once Blackburn and Bolton had been beaten, City had won all 14 of their home league games that season – something last achieved in the top flight by Newcastle in 1907.

City's 15th opponents at the Etihad were Chelsea, managed by Roberto Di Matteo, who had just replaced André Villas-Boas. Gary Cahill's deflected shot put Chelsea in front with half an hour to go. Almost immediately Mancini sent on Carlos Tévez for City – the Argentine's first appearance since his apparent refusal to play against Bayern Munich almost six months earlier.

Ten minutes later City were level, Agüero crashing home a penalty after a handball by Essien. City poured forward looking for a winner. With five minutes to go Tévez picked out Nasri, who beat Čech with a clever finish.

Not only were City still on course for the title, they had won that record-breaking 15th consecutive home game from the start of the season.

The run ended there – Sunderland surprised their hosts with a 3–3 draw at the Etihad ten days later.

Also on this day

1995 Liverpool paid Millwall £2m for 18-year-old Mark Kennedy.

1999 George Graham's Tottenham Hotspur won the League Cup for the third time with a 1–0 win over Leicester thanks to a last-minute goal from Allan Nielsen.

2003 Terry Venables was sacked as manager of Leeds, with Peter Reid taking temporary charge.

22 MARCH
2014 – Wenger's not so grand day out

All week Arsène Wenger had been playing down the significance of his personal milestone in favour of concentrating on the importance of the game. Having been top of the Premier League in late January, Arsenal had lost to Liverpool and Stoke and slipped to third place in the most competitive Premier League title race in years.

Chelsea were top of the table with a four-point advantage over Liverpool and Arsenal but had played one game more. Manchester City were a further two points behind but had two more games in hand. The outcome of Arsenal's match at Stamford Bridge would be of much more significance than the mere fact of it being Arsène Wenger's 1000th in charge of Arsenal. Nevertheless, the Arsenal manager had remarked that 'every defeat leaves a scar in your heart that you never forget' so he would have recalled that his 500th game had been spoiled by a 1–0 defeat to Mourinho's Chelsea in 2005.

For the 1000th game that margin of defeat was eclipsed within 20 minutes in which Arsenal conceded three goals. First Samuel Eto'o and André Schürrle found the Arsenal net and then Eden Hazard converted a penalty after the referee had mistakenly sent off Kieran Gibbs when it was Alex Oxlade-Chamberlain who had handled the ball. Arsenal did what they could with ten men, but conceded further goals to Oscar, who got two, and Mohamed Salah.

The 6–0 loss equalled the heaviest margin of defeat ever suffered by Arsenal under Arsène Wenger and was only the tenth time in those 1000 games that his side had lost by four goals or more.

'I take full responsibility for that defeat today. After 20 minutes it was game over and that becomes a nightmare with no chance to come back. Despite the vast experience that you have, if your team doesn't turn up like that then it's your responsibility.'

Also on this day

1994 Manchester United's Éric Cantona was sent off for the second time in four days. Having been sent off in a draw at Swindon, Cantona was dismissed again in a 2–2 draw with Arsenal at Highbury.

2000 Chelsea lost a home match in European competition for the first time as Lazio won 2–1 in the Champions League at Stamford Bridge.

2003 Ruud van Nistelrooy scored a hat-trick in Manchester United's 3–0 win over Fulham, the first game in the Dutch striker's Premier League record-breaking ten-match scoring streak.

2014 David Beckham was in the crowd at West Ham as Wayne Rooney scored a goal from near the halfway line for Manchester United that echoed Beckham's 1996 effort against Wimbledon.

2015 Steven Gerrard was sent off 38 seconds after coming on as a substitute in Liverpool's 2–1 home defeat to Manchester United.

23 MARCH
1998 – Toongate

When Newcastle beat Barnsley in an FA Cup quarter-final in 1998 the chairman Freddie Shepherd and vice-chairman Douglas Hall were in the mood to celebrate.

Luckily for them, the pair were expected in Spain where they were to be entertained by a wealthy Arabic businessman hoping to foster good relations with the pair for future deals. Unluckily for them, the businessman was actually the *News of the World* reporter Mazher Mahmood, otherwise known as the Fake Sheikh. Mahmood was renowned for his stings on celebrities; though some cases involving evidence gathered by Mahmood became the subject of a Crown Prosecution Service review in 2014.

In a long night Shepherd and Hall were reported by the newspaper to have revealed that they considered women from Newcastle to be 'dogs' and that they thought Newcastle fans were being charged excessive prices for replica shirts.

When the story was printed on 15 March there was an outcry, with the *Newcastle Evening Chronicle* calling for the pair to resign immediately. Gerrard Tyrrell, a solicitor acting on behalf of Douglas Hall, said there would be no resignations and that the pair couldn't remember what they'd said to the reporter. 'They had been celebrating the win over Barnsley,' he said. 'If they did say these things, they totally apologize and it was totally out of character. They don't remember what was said.'

A week later, and under intense pressure, Shepherd and Hall did stand down. Ten months after their resignation, but still as majority shareholders, they voted themselves back on to the board at St James' Park, and in 2007 Shepherd sold his shares in Newcastle to Mike Ashley, the sportswear tycoon, for a reported £37.6m.

Also on this day

2000 Thierry Henry was sent off for Arsenal in the UEFA Cup quarter-final against Werder Bremen, but a Ray Parlour hat-trick in a 4–2 win put them through.

2002 Alen Bokšić scored the only goal as Middlesbrough won 1–0 at Manchester United, a result that allowed Liverpool to go top of the Premier League table with Arsenal in third.

2008 The top four teams in the Premier League table played each other. First-placed Manchester United had a 3–0 win over fourth-placed Liverpool, who had Javier Mascherano sent off at Old Trafford, and Chelsea went above Arsenal into third place with a 2–1 victory at Stamford Bridge.

24 MARCH
1993 – Le Tiss and the miss

Matt Le Tissier was a supremely talented footballer who stayed at Southampton for the whole of his professional career, playing 540 games for the club and scoring 210 goals. While managers elsewhere tried to tempt him away from the club who had found him as a boy in Guernsey, Le Tissier always turned them down, later saying, 'My ties with Southampton were very strong, not too many from Guernsey have had that opportunity. I knew that at Southampton I could play football the way I liked to play football, and that was important to me.'

Despite his ability, Le Tissier only won eight caps for England. His international career was probably damaged in 1997 when he was selected by Glenn Hoddle to play in a crucial World Cup qualifier against Italy at Wembley. Le Tissier told his brother that he was in the team and playing in a free role behind striker Alan Shearer – his brother then told his local radio station, from where news spread rapidly.

Le Tissier never played for England again, although Hoddle did select him for a 'B' international just before the 1998 World Cup and Le Tissier scored a hat-trick against Russia. Still he was not selected for the senior squad.

Le Tissier was known for his goals. He scored 20 or more in four different seasons, was the first midfielder to reach 100 Premier League goals and scored his best tally, 30, in season 1994/95. With either foot he could score spectacular volleys, perfectly executed chips or wickedly curling free-kicks.

Le Tissier was also considered to be a master from the penalty spot. He took 48 penalties in his career and scored 47 of them. The one exception came in March 1993 when Southampton lost 2–1 at home to Nottingham Forest, and their goalkeeper Mark Crossley saved Le Tissier's kick.

Also on this day

1994 **Everton signed Anders Limpar from Arsenal for £1.6m.**

1996 **Aston Villa won the League Cup for the second time in three seasons with a 3–0 win over Leeds.**

1997 **Robbie Fowler unsuccessfully tried to convince referee Gerald Ashby not to award him a penalty after a challenge from David Seaman in a match between Arsenal and Liverpool at Highbury. Seaman saved Fowler's kick, but Jason McAteer scored from the rebound and Liverpool won 2–1.**

1998 **Paul Gascoigne joined Middlesbrough from Rangers for £3.45m.**

2007 **The first game was played at the rebuilt Wembley Stadium.**

Giampaolo Pazzini scored the first goal as England's Under-21 side lost to Italy's Under-21s 3–2.

2007 **The first ever football match was played at Dublin's Croke Park, home of Gaelic sports. A crowd of 72,539 watched the Republic of Ireland beat Wales 1–0 with a goal from Stephen Ireland.**

25 MARCH
2009 – Redknapp's King-sized complaint

When Fabio Capello named Ledley King in his squad for England's friendly match against Slovakia and a World Cup qualifying game against Ukraine in March 2009, he caused quite a stir.

King, who had not played for England for almost two years, suffered from a chronic injury to his right knee that meant that he was only able to play once a week, that he never trained with his teammates at Spurs and kept fit alone.

Tottenham's manager was Harry Redknapp, and he was not happy: 'He could overdo it for England and with Spurs and in eight months' time be on the scrapheap. I'd love to see him play for England, but he simply cannot play two games in a week. I had the Spurs physios on the phone, panicking, when Ledley was picked.'

King travelled to meet up with the England squad at their training ground and saw the England doctors, who examined his knee and sent him home. 'I'm relieved they've seen sense,' said Redknapp.

King's injury problems had begun two months before the 2006 World Cup, leading to his exclusion from Sven-Göran Eriksson's squad. He was then injured again in December 2006 and played only six games in the next 12 months; even when fit he rarely played consecutive games until the spring of 2010. Four back-to-back games for Tottenham at the end of that season encouraged Capello to call up King for the World Cup Finals in South Africa, and he was in the starting line-up for the opening game against the USA – only to get injured and be taken off at half-time.

King played on, when he could, for two more seasons at Spurs, where he was immensely popular, but announced his retirement at the end of the 2011/12 season after playing 268 games for the club – injuries having caused him to miss almost as many.

Also on this day

1993 Graeme Le Saux moved from Chelsea to Blackburn Rovers for £700,000.

1998 With new manager Lawrie McMenemy in charge, Northern Ireland won their first match in over a year, 1–0 against Slovakia.

2003 Wimbledon won 1–0 at Norwich in a match played on a Tuesday night. There were just ten travelling Wimbledon fans at Carrow Road to watch the match.

2006 Liverpool's Steven Gerrard and Everton's Andy van der Meyde were sent off as Liverpool won the Merseyside derby 3–1 at Anfield.

2014 Nine days after losing 3–0 at home to Liverpool in the Premier League, David Moyes's Manchester United team lost by the same score at home to Manchester City.

26 MARCH
2004 – Eriksson for Chelsea?

Before Chelsea had even kicked a ball in anger under the new regime of Roman Abramovich, England manager Sven-Göran Eriksson had been seen attending a meeting with Chelsea's new owner, leading to speculation that the Swede was considering ditching England for Stamford Bridge, where Claudio Ranieri's future was uncertain.

By the following March, Chelsea were nine points behind Arsenal at the top of the Premier League and had just been held 1–1 by Arsène Wenger's side at

Stamford Bridge in the first leg of their Champions League quarter-final.

When, on 26 March, the *Sun* published pictures of Eriksson attending another meeting, this time at the home of Chelsea's chief executive Peter Kenyon, it seemed only a matter of time before Ranieri would be leaving Chelsea, with Eriksson ready to replace him.

Eriksson's employers at the FA acted quickly to avoid losing their man to Stamford Bridge; two days after the publication of the photographs, Eriksson signed a two-year contract extension with the FA worth £4m a year.

The Swede would later reveal that within two years of being named England manager he had agreed to leave the job for something he considered better – and Peter Kenyon was involved then too.

It was the 2001/02 season and Kenyon was chief executive of Manchester United. Sir Alex Ferguson had announced his intention to retire and, as Eriksson recalled in his autobiography, Kenyon called him to a breakfast meeting in London without any indication of what the meeting was about. 'Straight off the bat,' Eriksson wrote, 'Kenyon asked me did I want the job as manager of Manchester United as of next season. I didn't think about it. "Yes," I said. "I do."'

According to Eriksson a contract with United was agreed and signed, before Ferguson changed his mind. 'I know that he was made aware that the club had picked me as his successor. Had he vetoed my appointment? It did not matter. He kept his job and I kept mine.'

Claudio Ranieri was not so lucky, and was replaced at Chelsea by José Mourinho.

Also on this day

2000 Goal of the Season – Paolo Di Canio scored it for West Ham against Wimbledon at Upton Park.

2008 David Beckham won his 100th cap for England and Michael Owen his 89th (and, as it turned out, last) cap. England lost the match 1–0 to France at Wembley.

2011 Goals from Frank Lampard and Darren Bent gave England a 2–0 win over Wales in Cardiff in a European Championship qualifier.

2013 Relegation-threatened Reading appointed Nigel Adkins as their new manager.

27 MARCH
1994 – Aston Villa's cup

Aston Villa's glory days were in the late nineteenth century when five league titles and three FA Cups were won between 1894 and 1900. Trophies came at irregular intervals over the next eight decades until Ron Saunders's Villa side won the league title in 1981 and, although Saunders was replaced by new manager Tony Barton, Villa followed it up with the European Cup in 1982.

More than a decade later it seemed as though Villa had a team with the potential to rival that of the early 1980s. Ron Atkinson had become their manager in 1991 after winning the FA Cup twice with Manchester United and the League Cup with Sheffield Wednesday.

Atkinson's impact was immediate. Under Dr Jozef Vengloš, their Czechoslovakian manager, Villa had finished 17th in 1991, under Atkinson they were 7th in 1992. With a team that included Steve Staunton, Paul McGrath, Ray Houghton, Garry Parker, Dalian Atkinson and Dean Saunders, Villa were then runners-up to Manchester United in the Premier League's inaugural 1992/93 season – only being knocked off top spot with six games to play.

Atkinson brought in Andy Townsend from Chelsea and Guy Whittingham from Portsmouth in the hope of being title contenders again in 1994. In fact the longed-for success came in the League Cup.

Villa knocked out local rivals Birmingham City, then Sunderland, Arsenal and Spurs before needing a penalty shoot-out to beat Tranmere Rovers over two matches in the semi-final.

At Wembley Villa faced Manchester United – Atkinson's old club and the team that had pipped them to the title the previous season. The tactical battle was won by Villa, their counter-attacking game working to perfection. Dalian Atkinson gave them a half-time lead that was doubled by Dean Saunders with 20 minutes to play. Mark Hughes's goal gave United hope of a comeback, but Andrei Kanchelskis handled in the last minute and was sent off, with Saunders scoring from the resulting penalty.

Villa's 12-year wait for a trophy was over, but Ron Atkinson was sacked eight months later as they won only two more league games that season, finishing tenth. Manchester United might have lost the League Cup – but they won the Premier League and FA Cup double.

Also on this day

1997 **Joe Royle left his job as manager of Everton after chairman Peter Johnson refused to sanction a bid to sign Tore André Flo from Brann Bergen. Flo later joined Chelsea instead.**

1997 **After scoring in a Cup Winners' Cup match against Brann Bergen at Anfield, Robbie Fowler revealed a T-shirt supporting the striking Liverpool dockworkers. UEFA later fined him 2000 Swiss francs.**

2002 **Peter Crouch signed for Aston Villa from Portsmouth for £5m.**

2015 Harry Kane scored 79 seconds after coming on for his England debut in a 4–0 win over Lithuania at Wembley.

28 MARCH
2010 – The Cotton Mill derby

The last time Burnley and Blackburn had been in the top flight in the same season was 1966. Only around 14 miles separate the Turf Moor and Ewood Park stadiums, but such was the antipathy between supporters of the two sides that fans were not allowed to travel independently from one town to the other. Police insisted that fans only be given their match ticket once they had taken their seat on a sanctioned supporters' coach. Away fans were escorted into the opposition's stadium two-and-a-half hours before kick-off for their own safety.

Owen Coyle's Burnley had lost 3–2 at Sam Allardyce's Blackburn in October, but by March Coyle had gone to Bolton, and Burnley were managed by Brian Laws. They were in desperate trouble, having taken only one point from their previous seven games, and were 19th in the table, ahead only of Portsmouth.

Blackburn won the game with a controversial penalty conceded by Burnley goalkeeper Brian Jensen, who was adjudged to have fouled Martin Olsson. 'He took a dive. He conned the referee – it's left us with a mountain to climb,' said Brian Laws. Even Rovers boss Allardyce had his doubts about the decision. 'In a big game like this, you need a little bit of luck and perhaps we've had it,' he said.

The win ensured that Blackburn were safe in the Premier League for another season while Laws set Burnley a target for survival from their last six games: 'It's going to be a huge task, but we need three or four wins. I believe that we can do that.'

Burnley did manage a 4–1 win at relegation rivals Hull two weeks later, but were sunk by the end of April. Twelve months later Blackburn followed them into the Championship.

Also on this day

2001 Ashley Cole made his England debut in a 3–1 World Cup qualifying win in Albania. As Cole celebrated England's third goal he was hit on the head by a lipstick thrown from the crowd.

2002 After 16 years at Southampton Matt Le Tissier retired.

2009 David Beckham beat Bobby Moore's record to become England's most capped outfield player when he made his 109th appearance in a 4–0 win over Slovakia.

2015 Wales continued their unbeaten start to their 2016 European Championship qualifying campaign with a 3–0 win at group leaders Israel. Gareth Bale with two and Aaron Ramsey were Wales's goalscorers.

29 MARCH
1998 – Gascoigne's Wembley return

It might partly have been because Middlesbrough were a second-tier side taking on a Premier League team; it might also have been because it was their third Wembley final in two seasons and a repeat of the FA Cup Final of the previous campaign; but the main reason that Middlesbrough got the lion's share of publicity prior to the 1998 League Cup Final against Chelsea was because they had just signed Paul Gascoigne.

Gascoigne had spent almost three years in Glasgow with Rangers, where he'd won four major titles. But the Scottish champions were willing to let him go after he'd contributed only three goals in 28 games in the 1997/98 season. Gascoigne's form had been poor enough for England manager Glenn Hoddle to leave him out of his squad for friendlies against Chile and Switzerland. With a World Cup coming up, Gascoigne needed to be playing – and playing well.

Crystal Palace had been first to agree a deal with Rangers, but Gascoigne preferred to move nearer his Newcastle roots, even if it meant not playing in the Premier League immediately. Middlesbrough's £3.45m bid was accepted and Gascoigne signed up with his new club battling for promotion and looking forward to that Wembley final.

Gascoigne was named as a substitute by manager Bryan Robson, who saw his side contain Chelsea in a game of very few chances. Gascoigne came on with 25 minutes to play but his only real contribution was to get booked for a foul on Gianfranco Zola.

The game went into extra-time with Gascoigne unable to provide any spark for his new side. After 95 minutes Frank Sinclair headed Chelsea in front and with time running out Roberto Di Matteo added a second goal to clinch the Londoners' victory.

Gascoigne, who was always generous – often to a fault – received his losers' medal and immediately gave it to Craig Hignett, whose place in the cup-final squad he had taken.

Middlesbrough had lost at Wembley again, but within a few weeks had won arguably the bigger prize of promotion back to the Premier League.

Also on this day

1994 Blackburn Rovers's title hopes were dealt a severe blow by a 4–1 defeat to Wimbledon.

1995 The Republic of Ireland drew their European Championship qualifying match 1–1 with Northern Ireland in Dublin.

2002 Newcastle came from behind to beat Everton 6–2 at St James' Park.

2011 Andy Carroll scored his first England goal as Fabio Capello's side drew 1–1 with Ghana at Wembley.

2015 Sunderland striker Steven Fletcher became Scotland's first hat-trick scorer for 46 years as they beat Gibraltar 6–1 at Hampden Park in a European Championship qualifier.

30 MARCH
2003 – Ridsdale resigns after living the dream

'Should we have spent so heavily in the past? Probably not. But we lived the dream.' Leeds chairman Peter Ridsdale coined the phrase that has stuck in the lexicon of football as a shorthand for creating a nightmare.

Ridsdale took over as Leeds chairman in 1997. In 1998 Leeds were fifth in the Premier League while Arsenal did the Premier League and FA Cup double. In 1999 Leeds were fourth while Manchester United did the Premier League, FA Cup and Champions League treble.

Watching enviously, Ridsdale decided the time had come to launch an assault on the elite clubs. In the two years from May 1999 to 2001 Leeds spent more than £70m on new players – in the same period Manchester United spent a little over £25m.

Danny Mills, Darren Huckerby, Michael Duberry, Michael Bridges, Jason Wilcox, Olivier Dacourt, Mark Viduka, Dominic Matteo, Rio Ferdinand, Robbie Keane, Seth Johnson and Robbie Fowler were all brought to the club for large fees and with wages to match. The money Leeds were spending was generated by taking out loans secured against future TV income and gate receipts. Being able to service those loans was a gamble that depended on success.

At first Ridsdale's spending plan worked. Leeds finished third in 2000, qualifying for the Champions League, where they played in Munich, Barcelona, Milan, Rome, Madrid and La Coruña before defeat to Valencia in the semi-final.

But in the league David O'Leary's side dropped to fourth – edged by Liverpool on the final day of the season to the last Champions League place.

The Premier League was awarded a fourth Champions League place for the top clubs in 2001/02, but Leeds missed out by one place again – finishing fifth behind Newcastle. The first casualty of that failure was manager David O'Leary, who was sacked and replaced by Terry Venables – but soon the financial pack of cards was falling around Venables's ears. Players had to be sacrificed: first out was Rio Ferdinand, quickly followed by Keane, Fowler, Dacourt, Lee Bowyer and Jonathan Woodgate.

With the club looking to sell both its training ground and stadium, and with the team battling relegation, Venables left. Soon after his departure Ridsdale resigned, leaving Leeds an estimated £80m in debt.

The club was relegated twice over the next four seasons and has never been back to the Premier League – the cruel price of big dreams.

Also on this day

1998 Leeds manager David O'Leary was praised for his calm in helping to evacuate his players after an engine blew up on their plane at Stansted airport as it was preparing to take off.

2001 Glenn Hoddle left Southampton to take over as manager at Spurs.

2012 Aston Villa midfielder Stilyan Petrov revealed that he had been diagnosed with acute leukaemia.

2013 Martin O'Neill was sacked as manager of Sunderland.

31 MARCH
1995 – Sardines

Two months after Éric Cantona's astonishing kung-fu kick at a Crystal Palace supporter, Croydon Magistrates' Court sentenced him to two weeks in prison for common assault. After spending three hours in a police cell below the courtroom Cantona was released on bail with the club intending to appeal.

Manchester United's then head of security, Ned Kelly, later told BBC Radio 5 Live that, 'I followed him down the stairs with the prison wardens. A warden said, "Don't take any food from here, I'll go down the road and get you some McDonald's and chips." We're eating away and having a chat about it, and he said, "I just can't be bothered with all of this, I'll just serve my sentence."'

But United's appeal did succeed in reducing that sentence to 120 hours of community service, which Cantona spent coaching football to youngsters in Manchester.

On hearing the news of their success, United quickly arranged a press conference at the Croydon Park Hotel to meet the frenzied demand for an opportunity to hear for the first time from Cantona himself. Flanked by his agent and Manchester United's solicitor Maurice Watkins, and immaculately dressed, Cantona had the attention of just about every media outlet in the world. He wasn't about to leave them disappointed.

'When the seagulls,' he said – before taking a long pause and a drink of water – 'follow the trawler, it's because they think sardines will be thrown into the sea. Thank you very much.'

With that he left the room.

Also on this day

1993 Ian Rush became Wales's all-time record goalscorer with his 24th goal for his country in a 2–0 win over Belgium, surpassing a record jointly held by Ivor Allchurch and Trevor Ford.

2001 Arsenal fans hoping to mark Arsène Wenger's 250th game in charge of the club, a 2–0 win over Spurs, were left shocked by the death of former player David Rocastle at the age of 33.

2004 Northern Ireland won their first match for 16 months as David Healy scored in a 1–0 win over Estonia.

2007 The Premier League's biggest ever crowd (76,098) watched Manchester United beat Blackburn 4–1 at Old Trafford.

2013 Sunderland appointed Paolo Di Canio as manager.

April

1 APRIL
2009 – Newcastle turn to Shearer

Just as in 1996, when he signed for Newcastle as a player, Alan Shearer's arrival at St James' Park as manager was greeted with delight. But in 1996 Newcastle had been serious title contenders; in 2009 they were haunted by the spectre of relegation.

Newcastle fans had endured a turbulent campaign, which had included the resignation of Kevin Keegan and the shock appointment of Joe Kinnear. In February, Kinnear discovered he needed urgent heart surgery and had been forced to stand down, leaving Chris Hughton to fill in as caretaker manager – just as he had for three games after Keegan's departure.

By the beginning of April, when Shearer took over for their last eight games, Newcastle's season had featured only six wins but four changes of manager. They were 18th in the Premier League table, two points off safety. On his first day Shearer said, 'It's a club I love and I don't want them to go down. I'll do everything I can to stop that. The supporters are well renowned and I know they won't let us down. They never do and I hope we can repay them with a performance.'

As Shearer moved in, Newcastle's director of football Dennis Wise, thought to be partly responsible for Keegan's resignation, moved out – a change which was also popular with the Geordie fans.

In 1996 buying Shearer had not quite made Newcastle's dream of winning the title a reality, and there were no fairy-tales in 2009 either. For a club that seemed to be in turmoil from top to bottom, there was something appropriate about the goal that relegated them being an own-goal in a 1–0 defeat at Aston Villa.

'It's painful and it hurts,' said Shearer. 'It's been a great experience for me and in a weird way I have enjoyed it, but big changes need to be made at this club.'

Also on this day

1995 Sheffield Wednesday suffered their heaviest ever home defeat, 7–1 to Nottingham Forest, for whom Brian Roy and Stan Collymore scored two goals each.

2000 Paul Scholes scored a hat-trick as Manchester United beat West Ham 7–1 at Old Trafford, the London club's heaviest Premier League defeat.

2001 Goal of the Season – Shaun Bartlett scored it for Charlton against Leicester at the Valley.

2009 John Terry's late goal gave England a 2–1 win over Ukraine at Wembley, preserving their 100 per cent record in qualifying for the 2010 World Cup.

2013 In a west London derby that included an own-goal, a missed penalty and a red card, Fulham beat relegation-threatened QPR 3–2 at Craven Cottage.

2 APRIL
2005 – Bowyer's Dyer warning

Newspaper coverage in the build-up to Newcastle's match against Aston Villa at St James' Park was dominated by Alan Shearer's decision to postpone his retirement to play on for one more season. The match, a mid-table affair between sides 10th and 11th in the table, seemed of little consequence. It was mid-table, but turned out to be anything but run-of-the-mill.

Villa's Juan Pablo Ángel fired them in front after only 5 minutes, and for the next 65 minutes there was little to discuss, other than a Gareth Barry shot that hit the post.

With just over a quarter of an hour to play a Newcastle mix-up allowed Darius Vassell to sprint clear and go round Newcastle goalkeeper Shay Given. Vassell's shot was handled on the line by Steven Taylor, who was sent off, and Gareth Barry converted the penalty.

Seven minutes later Vassell was judged to have been fouled by Stephen Carr, and Barry scored again from the spot to make it 3–0. So far, so good for Villa – but not the stuff of Sunday-morning headlines – not yet.

With Newcastle launching an attack, their midfielders Lee Bowyer and Kieron Dyer suddenly started trading punches with each other. Gareth Barry dragged the two Newcastle players apart but manager Graeme Souness could only watch in disgust as both were sent off, leaving the team with only eight men.

Dyer would later say, 'I didn't know you could get sent off for fighting your own teammate, so when the red card came out I thought, "What the hell!"'

Dyer was banned for three games and Bowyer for four, meaning that both missed the FA Cup semi-final against Manchester United – which Newcastle lost 4–1.

Also on this day

1995 Liverpool won the League Cup, with Steve McManaman scoring twice in a 2–1 win over Bolton Wanderers.

2000 David James saved two penalties in a shoot-out as Aston Villa won their FA Cup semi-final against Bolton 4–1 on spot-kicks, after a 0–0 draw.

2003 Police made 106 arrests as crowd trouble marred England's 2–0 win over Turkey at the Stadium of Light in a European Championship qualifier.

2008 Arsenal and Liverpool drew 1–1 at the Emirates Stadium in the first leg of their Champions League quarter-final tie.

2011 Wayne Rooney scored a hat-trick as Manchester United came from 2–0 down to win 4–2 at West Ham. Rooney was later banned for two matches for swearing into the lens of a TV camera.

2011 West Bromwich Albion beat Liverpool for the first time in 30 years as Roy Hodgson led them to a 2–1 win over his former club.

3 APRIL
1996 – Keegan's Anfield despair

On 20 January 1996 Newcastle had led the Premier League table by 12 points from both Liverpool and Manchester United. On the night of 3 April Newcastle found themselves three points behind Manchester United, who had played one game more.

Newcastle arrived at Anfield having suffered losses to West Ham, Manchester United and Arsenal in their last five games – the title that had seemed certain to be theirs for the first time in almost 70 years was slipping away. A win at third-placed Liverpool was imperative, but Roy Evans's side hoped they could still win the title too.

Liverpool, who had just booked their place in the FA Cup Final, took the lead after two minutes as Robbie Fowler headed home a Stan Collymore cross. Newcastle levelled eight minutes later, Les Ferdinand turning in a cross from Faustino Asprilla at the Kop end. After only 14 minutes Newcastle were in front, David Ginola racing on to Ferdinand's pass to beat David James in the Liverpool goal.

It stayed 2–1 until early in the second half, when the goalscorers exploded into life again, Robbie Fowler expertly finishing from Steve McManaman's pass only for Asprilla to run clear of Liverpool's defence and score two minutes later: 3–2 to Newcastle.

With just over 20 minutes to play, Liverpool's Jason McAteer curled a glorious pass to the waiting Collymore, who touched it past Newcastle's goalkeeper Pavel Srníček to make the score 3–3.

As the tension mounted with every second and with Liverpool fans baying and Newcastle fans praying, both sides pushed on for more goals, but none came until injury-time. John Barnes and Ian Rush combined on the edge of the Newcastle penalty area, then Barnes pushed a pass to the left-hand side where Collymore was arriving at full pace. His left-footed shot from ten yards gave Srníček no chance. As Liverpool fans exploded in celebration and their players chased a delirious Collymore, Kevin Keegan slumped behind an advertising hoarding in horror.

In winning what was perhaps the Premier League's greatest ever game, Liverpool had swung the title out of Newcastle's hands towards Alex Ferguson's grateful grasp.

Also on this day

1993 Mark Bright scored an extra-time winner as Sheffield Wednesday beat neighbours Sheffield United 2–1 in the FA Cup semi-final at Wembley.

1999 Robbie Fowler celebrated scoring a penalty in front of the Everton supporters by sniffing the white line of the six-yard box, a reference to unfounded allegations of drug use made against him by Evertonians. Sensing trouble, Liverpool's manager Gérard Houllier said it was a copy of a Cameroonian grass-eating ceremony Fowler had learned from full-back Rigobert Song. Nobody thought that was plausible and Fowler was fined £60,000.

2004 Southampton's Claus Lundekvam celebrated his 250th game for the club by scoring his first ever goal in a 4–1 win over Wolves.

4 APRIL
1993 – Adams's semi-final

For two clubs who had long been among the most successful in the FA Cup, Arsenal and Spurs had met each other in the competition surprisingly infrequently.

In 1949 Arsenal had won the first ever FA Cup meeting 3–0 in a third-round tie at Highbury, and in 1982 Spurs had won 1–0 at the same stage of the competition at White Hart Lane. Two meetings in over a century were followed by two more in two years.

The first semi-final ever to be staged at Wembley was won by Spurs in 1991, Gascoigne's majestic free-kick helping them to a 3–1 win against their biggest rivals. Two years later the clubs were drawn to meet again for a place in the 1993 FA Cup Final.

The FA decided that Wembley should be the venue once more, as it was for the other semi-final between Sheffield Wednesday and Sheffield United. Although Arsenal had already won the League Cup that season, neither club were in the running for league honours, so the FA Cup offered both a chance of glory.

In a tense game, Spurs were convinced they should have had a penalty when Darren Anderton was fouled by Andy Linighan. Tottenham players argued that Linighan might also be sent off, but referee Philip Don awarded only a free-kick, which was wasted, and the Arsenal defender stayed on.

The deadlock was broken with just 11 minutes left to play. Tottenham's Justin Edinburgh fouled Ray Parlour just outside the penalty area, Paul Merson swung in a cross and Arsenal captain Tony Adams was free at the back post to score with a powerful downward header.

For the first time in history the FA Cup Final would feature the same opponents as the League Cup Final – Arsenal against Sheffield Wednesday.

Also on this day

2001 Bowing to pressure from the Premier League, the Football League agreed that in future League Cup second-round ties would be played over one leg.

2006 The FA drew up a shortlist to replace Sven-Göran Eriksson as England manager after the World Cup Finals: the four contenders were Steve McLaren, Martin O'Neill, Alan Curbishley and Sam Allardyce.

2012 Chelsea set up a Champions League semi-final against Barcelona by beating Benfica 2–1 at Stamford Bridge (3–1 on aggregate) in their quarter-final tie.

2015 Stoke's Charlie Adam scored from 66 yards out against Chelsea at Stamford Bridge, but Chelsea won the game 2–1.

5 APRIL
2009 – Introducing Federico Macheda

There aren't many players who are almost completely unknown when they make their Premier League debuts, even fewer who play for Manchester United. Almost none make as big an impact as Federico Macheda.

Manchester United were involved in a three-way title race in 2009. Liverpool were top of the table, two points better off than United, with Chelsea a further point behind. Importantly, Sir Alex Ferguson's side, beaten in their previous two games, had two games in hand.

The first of those games in hand was at home to Aston Villa. Cristiano Ronaldo and John Carew scored in the first half to make it 1–1, but Villa were playing superbly and deserved the lead given them by Gabriel Agbonlahor after 58 minutes.

Ferguson's response was to put on 17-year-old Macheda. The Italian had signed from Lazio the previous summer and had scored a hat-trick for the reserves six days earlier, earning a surprise place on the substitutes' bench.

With ten minutes left United equalized thanks to a superb goal from Ronaldo. It was the catalyst for an onslaught of attacks aimed at the Villa goal, with Brad Friedel making great saves from Darren Fletcher and Danny Welbeck.

Then, in stoppage time, Macheda struck. He received a pass from Ryan Giggs, controlled it and with one touch turned inside Luke Young to curl a brilliant shot beyond Friedel into the net. It put United back on top of the table and was a hammer blow to Liverpool and Chelsea.

Ferguson's side won seven of their eight remaining league games to win the title by four points. Strangely, Macheda's career never hit such heights again; unsuccessful loan spells at Sampdoria, Queens Park Rangers, Stuttgart and Doncaster followed before he was given a free transfer to Cardiff City, having made United's starting line-up only 15 times.

For all that, his name is unlikely to be forgotten on the Stretford End.

Also on this day

1997 **Paulo Wanchope scored on his debut for Derby County in a 3–2 win at Manchester United.**

2000 **Chelsea scored three goals in eight minutes to beat Barcelona 3–1 at Stamford Bridge in the first leg of their Champions League quarter-final.**

2000 **Fans Christopher Loftus and Kevin Speight were killed during rioting in Istanbul the day before Leeds United's UEFA Cup semi-final first-leg defeat at Galatasaray.**

2005 **In the clubs' first meeting since the 1985 Heysel tragedy, Liverpool beat Juventus 2–1 at Anfield in the Champions League quarter-final first leg.**

2008 **Portsmouth reached their first FA Cup Final since 1939 with a 1–0 win over West Bromwich Albion.**

2011 **Spurs lost 4–0 at Real Madrid in the first leg of their Champions League quarter-final.**

6 APRIL
2005 – Mourinho the laundry man

Chelsea had beaten Barcelona to reach the last eight of the Champions League, but José Mourinho had caused a furious outcry when he'd accused referee Anders Frisk of being influenced by Barcelona manager Frank Rijkaard. UEFA had subsequently banned Mourinho from attending either leg of their quarter-final against Bayern Munich.

The first game at Stamford Bridge was sensational. Chelsea led through Lucio's own-goal, but Bastian Schweinsteiger equalized early in the second half. The last half-hour ranked alongside the most exciting seen at Stamford Bridge for years, as Frank Lampard restored Chelsea's lead before getting their third goal with a breathtaking volley.

With ten minutes to go Didier Drogba scored to make it 4–1, but just as Chelsea fans were pleading for the final whistle Michael Ballack converted a penalty to give his side hope for the second leg.

As if that wasn't dramatic enough, rumours soon began to spread that Mourinho had found a way to sidestep his ban from the stadium. Chelsea's fitness coach Rui Faria had been wearing a large woolly hat and seemed to be frequently scratching at his ear, while goalkeeping coach Silvino Louro was seen going to and from the dressing room carrying pieces of paper. Was Mourinho there after all, and speaking on the phone to Faria?

Soon it was whispered that Mourinho had been smuggled into the Chelsea dressing room, hidden inside a large skip used for transporting kit and laundry. Having given his pre-match and half-time team talks it was said that he had been wheeled out to the nearby Stamford Bridge Leisure Club, where he would claim to have spent the whole evening.

The story of Mourinho became something of an urban myth until it seemed to be confirmed when, four years later their former defender Nuno Morais said: 'I was on the bench for the home game,' he said. 'It was very different to go into the dressing room and see José hiding in the skip that night.'

Also on this day

2004 Chelsea beat Arsenal in the Champions League quarter-final with a 2–1 win at Highbury, their first win over Arsenal in 19 attempts.

2006 Middlesbrough beat FC Basel 4–1 at the Riverside to reach the last four of the UEFA Cup. They trailed 3–0 on aggregate with just under an hour to play, but won the tie with a last-minute goal from Massimo Maccarone.

2010 Lionel Messi scored all four goals for Barcelona as Arsenal were beaten 4–1 in the Nou Camp, and 6–3 on aggregate, in the Champions League quarter-final.

2011 Manchester United won 1–0 at Chelsea in the first leg of their Champions League quarter-final with a goal from Wayne Rooney.

2014 Norwich sacked manager Chris Hughton.

7 APRIL
2010 – Munich's Manchester revenge

Manchester United had played Bayern Munich eight times in their history and won only once – but it was the one that mattered most. Bayern had been United's opponents in 1999 when they came from behind in the last few seconds to win the Champions League Final.

That defeat had been avenged to some extent by Bayern's win in the quarter-final of the Champions League in 2000/01, while two draws in the group stage of 2001/02 had satisfied both sides.

United should have been approaching the second leg of their latest Champions League quarter-final against the Germans at least on level terms; they had led in Munich for over an hour before conceding twice in the last 15 minutes. United were narrow favourites to overcome that 2–1 deficit back at Old Trafford.

Louis van Gaal's Bayern were blown away by United's irresistible attacking football, which brought three goals in the first 40 minutes: Darron Gibson and Nani (twice) found the net to surge United into a 4–2 aggregate lead. Bayern knew they needed to score twice to go through – and only if they could prevent United from adding more goals.

Crucially Ivica Olić pulled one back for Bayern just before half-time. Franck Ribéry had been causing United's Rafael problems, which had already led to a yellow card for the United defender. When Rafael fouled him again soon after the break the Brazilian defender was sent off, giving the momentum to Bayern.

Suddenly the question was whether United could hang on. They couldn't – Arjen Robben scored a brilliant volley from a corner to put Bayern through on away goals.

'It's hard to digest something like that,' said Sir Alex Ferguson. 'In one way I could say we're unlucky, or I could say we threw it away. The Bayern players got Rafael sent off, there's no doubt about that – they forced the referee to get the card out. Until the sending-off we put in a fantastic performance.'

United also lost the Premier League title by one point to Chelsea, and had to content themselves with winning only the League Cup that season, while Bayern lost to Inter Milan in the Champions League Final.

Also on this day

1994 Paul Gascoigne broke his leg playing in a training game for Lazio.

1999 Ryan Giggs scored a last-minute equalizer as Manchester drew 1–1 at home to Juventus in the first leg of their Champions League semi-final at Old Trafford.

2005 Newcastle beat Sporting Lisbon 1–0 in the first leg of their UEFA Cup quarter-final at St James' Park.

8 APRIL
1996 – David Busst's injury

David Busst was a centre half with Coventry City who had been a latecomer to league football. He made his debut in January 1993 as a 25-year-old, after impressing in non-league football with Birmingham's Moor Green in the Southern League Premier Division.

Busst seemed finally to be establishing himself in the Premier League, and had earned good reviews for his performance in Coventry's 1–0 win over Liverpool just two days before he was selected to play at Old Trafford against Manchester United on Easter Monday. It was his 50th Premier League appearance.

The game was only two minutes old when Busst went forward for a Coventry corner, which was flicked on by Noel Whelan for Peter Schmeichel to save. Busst stretched for the rebound with United's Denis Irwin and Brian McClair and immediately crumpled in agony; Schmeichel was first to see the damage to Busst's leg and bolted from it in horror, his hands covering his face.

The match was held up for nine minutes, and sand was used to soak up the blood in the six-yard box as players from both sides were sickened by the injury. Busst had suffered a double compound fracture of the tibia and fibula in his right leg, which had snapped into an 'L' shape.

He underwent more than 20 operations on the leg, 10 in the first 12 days after the injury. Contracting MRSA in hospital caused further tissue damage and at one stage doctors feared they would have to amputate his leg.

Busst, who never played football again, continued to work for Coventry and became director of their Football in the Community programme. His injury is considered to be the worst of its kind ever seen on a football field and is a reminder of how fragile a professional footballer's future can be.

Also on this day

2001 **Arsenal and Liverpool booked their places in the FA Cup Final. Liverpool were held for almost 80 minutes by third-tier Wycombe Wanderers in the FA Cup semi-final before winning 2–1 at Villa Park. At Old Trafford, Arsenal came from behind to beat Spurs 2–1.**

2008 In a thrilling match Liverpool knocked Arsenal out of the Champions League quarter-finals with a 4–2 win at Anfield to go through 5–3 on aggregate. Arsenal had been leading on away goals with just four minutes to go.

2010 Manchester United agreed a £10m fee with Guadalajara for Javier Hernández.

2012 The Premier League title seemed to be slipping away from Manchester City as they were beaten 1–0 at Arsenal. It left City eight points behind Manchester United with six games to play. Mario Balotelli was sent off for City and manager Roberto Mancini said of the Italian, 'He needs to change; if not he can lose all his talent.'

9 APRIL
1995 – Amokachi's semi-final

Daniel Amokachi was a Nigerian striker who had scored twice at the 1994 World Cup Finals, and who was bought by Joe Royle at Everton for £3m from Club Brugge.

Amokachi's season had been a disappointment, scoring just one goal before suffering an injury in November that ruled him out of action for four months. When Everton went to Leeds United's Elland Road ground to face Tottenham Hotspur in the FA Cup semi-final, Amokachi still hadn't added to his goal tally for the club, and it was no surprise that he was only a substitute.

With Klinsmann, Anderton, Barmby and Sheringham in their team, Tottenham were hot favourites to go through; Everton were only one point above the relegation zone and had failed to win any of their last seven games against Tottenham.

But Everton played with power and pace from the start and were worth their lead at half-time, Matt Jackson's header from a corner putting them in front. That lead was doubled after the break when Ian Walker's poor goal-kick went to Everton striker Paul Rideout, and Graham Stuart tapped home after Walker had parried Rideout's shot.

Jürgen Klinsmann's penalty gave Spurs hope of a fightback. By now Rideout was struggling with an injury and Amokachi was desperate to get on the pitch. As soon as Rideout came near the touchline for treatment Amokachi took his chance; stripped and ready for action, he was practically on the pitch before Royle had even decided to take Rideout off. He later told the *Liverpool Echo*, 'I'd been sat there listening to the physio telling Joe that Paul Rideout was injured and needed to come off. The gaffer kept saying he wanted to give him five minutes, but he wasn't getting any better, so I decided to bring myself on. I just thought "I hope this works" and thank God it did, or it could have been my last game for Everton.'

Royle later said, 'What a good mistake!' First Amokachi headed home Stuart's right-wing cross, and then he side-footed in a Gary Ablett pass as Everton won 4–1 to reach their 12th FA Cup Final.

Also on this day

1994 **Matt Le Tissier scored a hat-trick as relegation-threatened Southampton beat Norwich 5–4 at Carrow Road.**

1994 **Two Gavin Peacock goals secured Chelsea their first FA Cup Final place since 1970 as they beat Luton Town 2–0 in the semi-final.**

1997 **Coventry City beat Chelsea 3–2 at Highfield Road. It was the end of a bad day for Chelsea, who had forgotten to take their change kit to the game and had to wear Coventry's away kit to avoid a clash of colours.**

2002 **Liverpool went out of the Champions League to Bayer Leverkusen after a 4–2 defeat in Germany in the quarter-final.**

2014 **Manchester United lost 3–1 at Bayern Munich to go out of the Champions League in their quarter-final tie.**

10 APRIL
1993 – Fergie time

Manchester United's wait to be crowned champions for the first time since 1967 probably should have ended in 1992. United had led the table after losing only one of their first 20 games but lost 3 consecutive games in April to hand the title to Leeds.

A year later, in the Premier League's inaugural season, United had been embroiled in a three-way title race with Norwich and Aston Villa. It was a race United looked like losing when they took just six points from five games in March, leaving Villa top of the table.

United couldn't afford to slip up again, but beating Sheffield Wednesday at Old Trafford was no foregone conclusion; Wednesday, who would play in both the League and FA Cup Finals that season, were battling for a European place.

The tension born of almost 26 years without the title was palpable around Old Trafford. The Stretford End, half rebuilt, ached for the win that might swing the championship their way.

After an hour, the game deadlocked at 0–0, referee Michael Peck was injured and replaced by linesman John Hilditch. Within five minutes Hilditch had awarded Sheffield Wednesday a penalty after Paul Ince fouled Chris Waddle – John Sheridan scored it and Old Trafford was engulfed by a feeling of déjà-vu.

With five minutes to go the mood changed as intense pressure was rewarded by a looping Steve Bruce header that cleared Chris Woods and nestled into the net.

Aston Villa's match against Coventry finished 0–0 while play continued at Old Trafford; United knew that one more goal would send them back to the top. In injury-time, first Gary Pallister, then Bruce, then Mark Hughes were denied as corner after corner rained in on Wednesday's goal.

Still they played on. United's Pallister crossed to Bruce once more and his perfect header arrowed into the corner of the Wednesday net – it was the 97th minute. Alex Ferguson and his assistant Brian Kidd gambolled on the pitch like schoolchildren in sheer joy.

The title they thought they had once again thrown away was back within touching distance.

Also on this day

2002 **David Beckham broke a metatarsal bone in his foot playing for Manchester United against Deportivo La Coruña, making him a doubt for the World Cup Finals.**

2005 **James Vaughan became the Premier League's youngest ever scorer when he found the net for Everton**

against Crystal Palace aged 16 years and 271 days.

2007 **Fulham sacked manager Chris Coleman.**

2007 **Manchester United beat AS Roma 7–1 in the second leg of their Champions League quarter-final to go through 8–3 on aggregate.**

11 APRIL
2010 – Portsmouth to Wembley

Portsmouth had enjoyed some of their happiest times with Harry Redknapp as their manager and with Jermain Defoe and Peter Crouch in their team. Season 2009/10 had been anything but happy, the chronic financial mismanagement of years had caught up with them and cost a devastating nine-point penalty when they went into administration.

Miserable off the pitch, they had been miserable on it too. Avram Grant's appointment as a replacement for Paul Hart in November had done nothing to halt a tide of defeats that never seemed to ebb. A cast of players had been assembled out of the few old-stagers who hadn't been sold and a loan market that offered cast-offs, wannabes and other flotsam and jetsam from the football world.

Somehow, through the devastation, Portsmouth had made it into the last four of the FA Cup, where they met Redknapp, Defoe and Crouch – all now representing red-hot favourites Spurs.

Portsmouth's preparation for the semi-final had included receiving confirmation of their relegation the previous afternoon, when Burnley had made their escape impossible with a 4–1 win at Hull. Defiant and undaunted, Portsmouth's mobile army of dedicated fans descended on Wembley hoping for the kind of improbable story that only the FA Cup seems capable of mustering.

For once Portsmouth's forward planning had been impeccable; Avram Grant's organized team smothered and stifled Tottemham's creativity, but were still grateful for a poor refereeing decision when Crouch's effort was wrongly disallowed.

By then Portsmouth had already stirred the Wembley pot to turn the incredible into the possible – Frédéric Piquionne, a striker loaned from Lyon, scored the first goal of the game nine minutes into extra-time.

Spurs roared forward against a Portsmouth defence that had conceded five times against Chelsea and four against Liverpool in the last month – but goalkeeper David James stood firm and saved at point-blank range from Vedran Ćorluka.

The ascent from despair to delight was completed with three minutes to go when Tottenham's Wilson Palacios fouled Aruna Dindane, and Portsmouth's Kevin-Prince Boateng – a former Spurs midfielder – converted the penalty.

Manager Grant revelled in the unexpected glory of it, the burden of battling impossible odds lifted for a day. 'We didn't take the easy solution,' he said. 'The easy solution is to give up. We have lived day by day. Despite this we're in the final. It is a crazy day.'

Also on this day

2007 Fulham appointed Lawrie Sanchez as manager.

2009 Federico Macheda came on to score Manchester United's winner for the second time in three games as they won 2–1 at Sunderland to stay top of the league.

2013 Spurs lost their Europa League quarter-final to FC Basel in a penalty shoot-out at White Hart Lane; both legs had finished 2–2.

12 APRIL
2011 – United beat Chelsea again

Roman Abramovich's dream of winning the Champions League seemed destined never to be realized. Chelsea had been beaten semi-finalists four times and beaten finalists once in the last eight seasons. Falling just short had become a habit.

In 2011, Chelsea once again harboured hopes of cracking the code to success. A group including Žilina, Marseille and Spartak Moscow had been easily negotiated with five wins and just one defeat. The draw in the first knockout round had been kind and FC Copenhagen had offered little resistance to Chelsea's progress. The prospect of playing a Champions League final in their home city of London at Wembley Stadium was edging ever nearer. Under manager Carlo Ancelotti's skilful guidance there was every reason to be confident – the Italian had lifted the European Cup twice in four years as manager of AC Milan.

The quarter-final draw paired Chelsea with Manchester United – a clash both clubs would have preferred to avoid – in a repeat of the final of 2008, a defeat that had left its scars on Stamford Bridge.

At home Chelsea had succumbed to a Wayne Rooney goal and travelled to Manchester in the knowledge that they would have to win to keep their season alive, as their Premier League title was already almost certainly on its way back to Old Trafford.

Chelsea came up short. United deservedly took the lead through Javier Hernández as Fernando Torres, a surprise starter ahead of Didier Drogba, laboured to no effect.

Ancelotti corrected his selection error at half-time by taking the Spaniard off, and Drogba equalized only moments after a red card for Ramires had left Chelsea with ten men and an even harder task.

Any United doubts didn't last long, Park Ji-Sung scoring from a cross supplied by the evergreen Ryan Giggs. Ancelotti had no answer as Chelsea went back to square one in their search for Abramovich's treasured prize.

Also on this day

1994 Arsenal reached their first European final for 14 years by beating Paris Saint-Germain 1–0 at Highbury in the second leg of their Cup Winners' Cup semi-final for a 2–1 aggregate win. The victory was tainted by a booking for Ian Wright that meant he would be suspended for the final.

1995 Manchester United's Roy Keane was sent off for stamping on Gareth Southgate in their 2–0 win over Crystal Palace in the FA Cup semi-final replay. Palace were also reduced to ten men when Darren Patterson was dismissed for fighting Keane.

1999 Michael Owen suffered the first of a series of hamstring injuries that would hamper his career. Owen pulled up in a 0–0 draw at Leeds and would not play again for four months.

13 APRIL
1997 – Chesterfield so near and yet so far

Chesterfield were playing in the third tier of English football in 1997, and had won only one of their previous 12 league games when they went to Old Trafford to play Middlesbrough in the FA Cup semi-final. John Duncan's side might not have been thriving in the league, but they contributed magnificently to one of the great FA Cup semi-finals.

Middlesbrough's Slovakian defender Vladimír Kinder was being given a torrid time by Kevin Davies, who would go on to enjoy a long Premier League career with Blackburn, Southampton and Bolton. Kinder got a yellow card for throwing the ball away from a free-kick and was then sent off when he pulled Davies back by the shirt having been beaten by him again.

Against ten men Chesterfield sensed a shock was a possibility. Early in the second half Andy Morris tapped home after a Davies shot had been saved to put Chesterfield in front. Middlesbrough were soon on the ropes again, goalkeeper Ben Roberts conceding a penalty and captain Sean Dyche holding his nerve to score, his first goal in four years. It

was an amazing scoreline: Chesterfield 2 Middlesbrough 0.

Chesterfield only held that two-goal lead for four minutes, Fabrizio Ravanelli finishing a clever move to put the Premier League side back in the game. Then came the moment that would haunt Chesterfield for years; in a melee inside the Middlesbrough penalty area Jonathan Howard saw his shot hit the underside of the Middlesbrough bar and bounce down before spinning clear. The linesman, Alan Sheffield, signalled a goal, but referee David Elleray overruled him – replays showed the linesman to be correct and the referee to be wrong, but Middlesbrough had escaped.

A few, frantic moments later Craig Hignett converted a Middlesbrough penalty that took the game to extra-time.

Middlesbrough looked to have won it when Gianluca Festa fired them in front for the first time – but Chesterfield still weren't beaten. In the last minute of extra-time a fantastic instinctive header from Jamie Hewitt made it 3–3 and earned Chesterfield a replay. Given the incorrectly disallowed goal it was the least they deserved. Nine days later there was considerably less drama as Middlesbrough won that replay 3–0.

Also on this day

1996 Manchester United changed out of their grey-coloured away kit at half-time as they were losing 3–0 at Southampton. United's players had complained that the kit made teammates difficult to see. The match finished 3–1.

2003 David Seaman kept a clean-sheet in his 1000th match as Arsenal beat Sheffield United 1–0 in the FA Cup semi-final.

2014 Hull City reached their first FA Cup Final with a 5–3 win over Sheffield United in the semi-final.

2014 Liverpool seemed to be edging nearer to the Premier League title with an epic 3–2 win over Manchester City at Anfield.

14 APRIL
1999 – Giggs's goal

In 1999 Arsenal pursued Manchester United and their lead at the top of the Premier League with a marvellous unbeaten run that had brought them to within a point of Sir Alex Ferguson's side. In the FA Cup both teams had progressed to the semi-finals, and with United also through to the semi-finals of the Champions League they were talking about a treble in Manchester. In London, Arsenal had their eye on repeating their league and cup double of the previous season.

In the FA Cup semi-final one of those dreams had to end. In the first meeting at Villa Park there were no goals after 90 minutes plus a period of extra-time in which Arsenal's Nelson Vivas had been sent off. United felt aggrieved after Roy Keane's volley had been ruled out for a debatable offside.

The replay, three days later, was football at its most dramatic. David Beckham swept United ahead with a curling shot that fooled David Seaman. Dennis Bergkamp equalized as his shot whipped past Schmeichel, and soon Nicolas Anelka was mobbed by teammates as he tucked away a rebound – but this time an offside decision favoured United.

When Roy Keane was sent off for a second bookable offence after a foul on Marc Overmars, it seemed likely to be decisive, and with ten men United were hanging on in the final seconds when Phil Neville tripped Ray Parlour and Arsenal were awarded a penalty.

Dennis Bergkamp took the responsibility of sending Arsenal to Wembley with what would be almost the last kick of the game. Schmeichel's save to his left was the stuff of legends – the game went to extra-time.

Refusing to allow Arsenal's numerical advantage to count, United clung grimly to the hope of survival and penalties – but did so much more.

It was a tired pass from Patrick Vieira that gave the ball to Ryan Giggs ten yards inside his own half. The Welshman immediately sensed an opportunity. Hurdling Vieira's attempt to make amends for his mistake, Giggs weaved his way past Lee Dixon, left Martin Keown on his backside, beat Dixon again and lashed an unstoppable shot over Seaman into the Arsenal net.

It was the only possible winner of the Goal of the Season award – and arguably the goal of Giggs's life.

Also on this day

2001 Manchester United sealed their 14th title, and 7th in nine years, as they beat Coventry 4–2 while rivals Arsenal were beaten 3–0 at home to Middlesbrough.

2005 Newcastle lost 4–1 at Sporting Lisbon to go out of the UEFA Cup at the quarter-final stage.

2006 Despite holding Manchester United to a 0–0 draw at Old Trafford, Sunderland were relegated.

2009 Chelsea and Liverpool drew 4–4 at Stamford Bridge in the second leg of their Champions League quarter-final, Chelsea going through 7–5 on aggregate.

2012 Liverpool beat Everton 2–1 in the FA Cup semi-final.

15 APRIL
2009 – Hillsborough and the cry for justice

On 15 April 1989 the Hillsborough disaster took the lives of 96 Liverpool fans attending the FA Cup semi-final against Nottingham Forest when they were crushed behind the goal at the Leppings Lane end of the stadium.

For two decades calls for justice from the families of the dead had fallen on deaf ears. In the immediate aftermath of the disaster there was a version of events, widely accepted in the media, which said drunkenness and hooliganism had been the root cause of the tragedy. This version of the truth dismissed fans' testimony of police mismanagement, errors of judgement and the unsuitability of the stadium.

Each year at Liverpool's Anfield stadium the people of the city congregated to remember. In 2009, the 20th anniversary of the disaster, Andy Burnham, the Secretary of State for Culture, Media and Sport, attended the memorial to speak for the government.

As he read his speech, there was a lone cry from the crowd – 'Justice!' Then another, again calling 'Justice!' It was a cry quickly taken up by the crowd of around 30,000: 'Justice for the 96.' Burnham stood, visibly moved and, for a while, speechless.

The next day Burnham attended a cabinet meeting and asked the Prime Minister Gordon Brown if he could take the issue of Hillsborough to Parliament. He got his permission, which led to the formation of the Hillsborough Independent Panel. This in turn led to new inquests, new evidence and finally the admission that a 'lack of police control' had been the prime cause of the disaster.

The real truth about Hillsborough was, in fact, that version which the families had been trying to get heard for more than 20 years. Stadium gates had been opened by the police and not forced by fans, police statements had been altered to implicate supporters and the stadium, which had no safety certificate, was both unfit and unsafe.

Five years later Andy Burnham spoke again at the memorial service and paid tribute to the man whose lone voice had begun the mass call for justice five years earlier, 'Wherever you are out there, Roy Dixon. Take a bow.'

Also on this day

2006 **Dennis Bergkamp scored his last Arsenal goal on what the club had called 'Bergkamp Day'. His goal helped Arsenal beat West Bromwich Albion 3–1 at Highbury and was the 120th of his career with the club.**

2009 **Manchester United and Arsenal reached the Champions League semi-finals with wins over FC Porto and Villarreal respectively.**

2012 **Chelsea thrashed Spurs 5–1 in the FA Cup semi-final at Wembley.**

16 APRIL
2012 – Wigan: the great escapologists

Wigan were promoted to the Premier League in 2005, and routinely tipped to be relegated in each of the next eight seasons.

In 2007 they had come close, a David Unsworth penalty against Sheffield United saving them on the last day of the season. In 2011 they finished 16th, again needing a final-day win – this time at Stoke – to ensure safety.

A year later it seemed there could be no escape. Roberto Martínez's side were bottom of the table with only 22 points from 29 games following a 1–1 draw at home to West Bromwich Albion. They had played a game more than all their relegation rivals and had a terrible run of fixtures to cope with, including Liverpool, Chelsea, Manchester United and Arsenal.

The first of those games brought a stunning 2–1 win at Liverpool, followed by a win at home to Stoke and a narrow loss at Chelsea. When Shaun Maloney scored the only goal in an astonishing

1–0 home win over leaders Manchester United, Wigan found themselves out of the bottom three for the first time since September.

Their next game, on 16 April, was at Arsenal – where they had never managed even a draw, let alone a win. For the first five minutes Arsenal peppered Wigan's goal with a flurry of goal attempts and corners, but when James McCarthy released Victor Moses after seven minutes a lightning-fast counter-attack finished with Franco Di Santo beating Wojciech Szczęsny. Arsenal had barely regrouped when Wigan scored again 94 seconds later, Moses beating Bacary Sagna to find Jordi Gómez, who bundled the ball home for 2–0.

Thomas Vermaelen headed one back for Arsenal, but despite applying persistent second-half pressure, they couldn't score again – Wigan's latest great escape was on. Their manager was desperate to take nothing for granted. 'I still think it will go to the end,' said Martínez. 'We need the same intensity in the last four games.'

He needn't have worried – they won three of those four matches and were safe with a game to spare.

Also on this day

1997 Leicester City won their first major honour for 33 years as they beat Middlesbrough 1–0 in the League Cup Final replay with an extra-time goal from Steve Claridge.

1998 Chelsea beat Vicenza 3–1 at Stamford Bridge to reach the final of the European Cup Winners' Cup 3–2 on aggregate.

2001 Liverpool won at Goodison Park for the first time since 1990 as they beat Everton 3–2 with a last-minute free-kick from Gary McAllister.

2011 Yaya Touré scored as Manchester City beat Manchester United 1–0 in the FA Cup semi-final. Paul Scholes was sent off for United.

17 APRIL
2011 – Stoke's Wembley high-five

Stoke City had first entered the FA Cup in 1883, five years before they became one of the founder members of the Football League. Their record in the knockout competition was therefore very long, but very undistinguished.

There had been a catalogue of cup calamities. In 1885 they had been eliminated for failing to show up for a match against Queen's Park in Glasgow. In 1890 they'd been granted a rematch against Wolves after a 4–0 defeat because of the poor state of the pitch – only to lose the second game 8–0. There had been defeats to Rhyl, to Bury after a marathon four replays, to Blyth Spartans, Telford and Nuneaton Borough. There had been three semi-finals, all lost – Stoke City fans had never experienced the final itself.

In 2011 Stoke tried yet again. First they needed extra-time to defeat Cardiff in a third-round replay, then managed a single-goal victory over Wolves. A home tie against Brighton in round five was favourable, and Tony Pulis's side duly won 3–0 to reach the last eight.

Against West Ham at the Britannia Stadium Stoke shrugged off a penalty miss by Matthew Etherington to win 2–1. With the two Manchester giants also into the last four, Bolton were the team Stoke were hoping to be paired against in the semi-final draw – and luck was with them.

At Wembley Stoke ripped Bolton to shreds to record the biggest margin of victory in an FA Cup semi-final since 1939; they were 3–0 up after only 30 minutes. First, Etherington had latched on to a mistake to shoot left-footed past Jussi Jääskeläinen. Six minutes later Robert Huth beat the Bolton goalkeeper from a similar distance, and then Kenwyne Jones clipped in a third.

In the second half Stoke's Jonathan Walters, who had played six times for Bolton as a teenager before being sold to Hull, curled home a brilliant fourth and with ten minutes to go Walters scooped home a fifth with Bolton well beaten.

After almost 130 years, the club that could boast Stanley Matthews and Gordon Banks among its former players could finally look forward to an FA Cup Final.

Also on this day

1994 Goal of the Season – Rod Wallace scored it for Leeds against Spurs at Elland Road.

1996 Alan Shearer scored twice for Blackburn against Wimbledon, becoming the first player to score 30 goals in three consecutive top-flight seasons since Jimmy Dunne for Sheffield United in the 1930s.

2006 Alan Shearer scored his 409th – and last – career goal in Newcastle's 4–1 win at Sunderland. A knee injury sustained later in the match meant it was also his last career game.

2011 Arsenal took the lead in the ninth minute of injury-time against Liverpool at the Emirates Stadium thanks to a Robin van Persie penalty – only for Liverpool to equalize three minutes later with another penalty scored by Dirk Kuyt. The lengthy injury-time had been added after treatment to Jamie Carragher.

18 APRIL
1993 – Arsenal's hero and fall guy

Steve Morrow was a young defender or midfielder who was good enough to go on to captain his country, Northern Ireland, but never quite good enough to hold down a regular place in the side at Arsenal. When he left Highbury for Queens Park Rangers in 1997 in a £1m deal, Morrow had scored three goals in 85 appearances for Arsenal, many of them

as a substitute. He also had an enduring place in Arsenal's history and in the affections of the club's fans.

With John Jensen injured, Morrow found himself starting the 1993 League Cup Final against Sheffield Wednesday – the first occasion on which squad numbers and named shirts had ever been used in English football.

Wednesday had already hit the post through Paul Warhurst when John Harkes gave them an eighth-minute lead from a neatly worked free-kick. After 20 minutes Paul Merson equalized for Arsenal with a spectacular swerving shot that beat Chris Woods in the Wednesday goal.

Midway through the second half Morrow's big moment arrived. Merson broke down the Arsenal left and when his cross was only half-cleared by Carlton Palmer, Morrow reacted more quickly than anyone else to hammer the ball into the net from eight yards – his first ever goal in senior football, and it won the cup for Arsenal.

Within moments of the final whistle, the Arsenal captain Tony Adams lifted Morrow onto his shoulders in celebration – and promptly dropped him. Morrow fell awkwardly and needed oxygen as he was stretchered away with a broken arm. He didn't play for Arsenal again for seven months.

A few minutes after Morrow had been taken to hospital in an ambulance, Tony

Adams lifted the cup – and managed not to drop it.

Also on this day

2000 **Chelsea had Celestine Babayaro sent off as they went down 5–1 at Barcelona in extra-time to lose their Champions League quarter-final tie 6–4 on aggregate.**

2010 **Wigan boosted their survival chances by coming from 2–0 down to win 3–2 at home to Arsenal with three goals in the last ten minutes.**

2015 **Alexis Sanchez scored twice as Arsenal booked their place in a record 19th FA Cup Final with a 2–1 extra-time win over Reading at Wembley.**

19 APRIL
2014 – Sunderland's bridge to safety

Sunderland's 2013/14 season had been a chaotic mixture of highs and lows. They had revelled in a 3–0 win at St James' Park against rivals Newcastle, knocked Chelsea and Manchester United out of the League Cup on their way to a first major final in 22 years – and had taken the lead against Manchester City in that final before losing 3–1.

But Sunderland had also earned just one point from their first eight Premier League matches of the campaign, during which Paolo Di Canio had been replaced as manager by Gus Poyet. They had been stuck in the relegation zone all season, and by the time they went to Chelsea in mid-April they were bottom of the table, six points adrift of safety with only five games left to play.

Chelsea were the outsiders of three in a desperately close title race being led by Liverpool, with Manchester City hot on their heels – and with games in hand. Having taken only two points from their last nine league games, Sunderland were given no chance of avoiding defeat at Stamford Bridge, where Chelsea were unbeaten all season and had never lost a league game in two spells with José Mourinho as manager.

Sure enough, Samuel Eto'o put the home side in front after 12 minutes. The goal came from the fourth of 31 goalscoring chances created by the home side during the match – but it was the only one they converted.

Sunderland equalized when Connor Wickham turned home a rebound after Marcos Alonso's shot had been saved. Chelsea had a goal disallowed, hit the underside of the bar and found Sunderland goalkeeper Vito Mannone in unbeatable form.

With only eight minutes to go, Sunderland broke, and when Jozy Altidore was challenged by César Azpilicueta, referee Mike Dean pointed to the penalty spot. Fabio Borini, a former Chelsea striker who was on loan at Sunderland from Liverpool, scored to win the game.

Sunderland were still bottom but won their next three games, including one at Old Trafford, to finish 14th – their highest league position of the entire season.

Also on this day

2000 Despite fighting back from 3–0 down against Real Madrid in the second leg of their Champions League quarter-final at Old Trafford, a 3–2 defeat saw Manchester United eliminated.

2001 Liverpool reached their first European final since 1985 when a Gary McAllister penalty gave them a 1–0 win over Barcelona in the second leg of the UEFA Cup semi-final.

2009 Everton reached their first FA Cup Final since 1995 when they beat Manchester United in the semi-final. Former United goalkeeper Tim Howard saved penalties from Dimitar Berbatov and Rio Ferdinand to help Everton win 4–2 on spot-kicks.

2015 Aston Villa beat Liverpool 2–1 at Wembley to reach their first FA Cup Final since 2000.

2014 – Moyes's grim Goodison return

Having been chosen by Sir Alex Ferguson as his replacement, David Moyes had moved to Old Trafford with a lot of goodwill from fans of Manchester United. Everton supporters were less happy, feeling they'd been cast aside after a relationship that had lasted 11 years.

While Everton were prospering under Moyes's replacement, Roberto Martínez, Manchester United were labouring under Moyes. United had lost home and away to their bitterest rivals, Liverpool and Manchester City. They had also lost at home to West Bromwich Albion, Newcastle and Spurs, gone out of the FA Cup at home to Swansea, and been beaten by Bayern Munich in the Champions League.

David Moyes returned to Goodison Park with his United side seventh in the table and looking certain to miss out on Champions League qualification for the first time since 1995. Everton, who had won at Old Trafford four months earlier, were two places above United in the table and nine points better off. They could hardly wait to show how much they'd progressed without the man who had left them behind.

The irony of Leighton Baines scoring Everton's first goal was lost on no-one. Moyes had tried, unsuccessfully, to make Baines his first signing as Manchester United manager. Baines's goal was a penalty dispatched with typical calmness, but which sparked wild celebrations among the Everton fans, who taunted their former manager at every opportunity.

Everton's second goal was scored by Kevin Mirallas after a sweeping counter-attack close to half-time. United never looked likely to launch a comeback.

Amid the cacophony of celebrating Evertonians making the most of Moyes's discomfort, one Everton fan sat quietly just yards from the United manager. A keen-eyed photographer captured the image of the day: it was of Moyes, digesting defeat, with the fan sitting behind – dressed as the grim reaper, mask, scythe and all – his eyes fixed on the United boss.

Sure enough, the reaper came calling two days later when Moyes was sacked.

Also on this day

1995 Arsenal goalkeeper David Seaman saved three Sampdoria penalties as Arsenal reached the final of the European Cup Winners' Cup in a shoot-out after the tie had finished 5–5 on aggregate.

2002 Alan Shearer scored his 200th Premier League goal in Newcastle's 3–0 win over Charlton.

2004 Chelsea lost the first leg of their Champions League semi-final 3–1 in Monaco.

2008 Aston Villa beat local rivals Birmingham 5–1, their biggest win in the second-city derby since 1988.

2011 Gérard Houllier was admitted to hospital amid concerns about a recurrence of the heart problems he had suffered at Liverpool. He stood down as Villa manager at the end of the season.

21 APRIL
1999 – United's Italian job

'It was the most emphatic display of selflessness I have seen on a football field. Pounding over every blade of grass, competing as if he would rather die of exhaustion than lose, he inspired all around him. I felt it was an honour to be associated with such a player.'

Those were the words of Manchester United manager Alex Ferguson about his captain Roy Keane, after an immense individual display had helped United on their way to an epic victory and to their first European Cup final since 1968.

United had drawn 1–1 with Juventus in Manchester, and seemed out of the tie when Zinedine Zidane and Filippo Inzaghi conspired to tear through their defence twice within the first ten minutes of the return leg in Turin.

Needing two goals to go through, United scored their first only 15 minutes after Inzaghi's shot had made it 2–0 to the Italians. Keane arrived to meet a Beckham corner with a deft header that glanced inside the far post to give his side a toehold in a match that had seemed to be passing them by.

Moments later Keane was shown the yellow card for a foul on Zidane; it ensured that if United went through Keane would be suspended for the final. If he felt any personal disappointment, Keane refused to let it show as he propelled his side onwards. Dwight Yorke scored a brilliant header ten minutes before half-time and United had the slenderest of advantages courtesy of their extra away goal.

Both sides had chances to score again, before United sealed their place in the final with a breakaway goal converted by Andy Cole after Dwight Yorke's dazzling run.

As United celebrated their manager didn't forget the man who had been their inspiration – but who would be a spectator on the night of the final.

Also on this day

1993 Aston Villa's 3–0 defeat at Blackburn left Manchester United one win away from sealing the first Premier League title.

2001 Roy Keane was sent off for the eighth time in his career for a notorious tackle on Manchester City's Alf-Inge Haaland. Having fouled Haaland, Keane stood and shouted abuse into the stricken City player's face. Keane later admitted that he had not forgotten an incident in 1997, when Haaland had accused him of faking an injury. Two years later Haaland was forced to retire.

2003 Marc-Vivien Foé scored Manchester City's last ever goal at Maine Road as they beat Sunderland 3–0.

2009 Andrey Arshavin scored all four Arsenal goals in a remarkable 4–4 draw against Liverpool at Anfield that damaged Liverpool's hopes of winning the Premier League.

2013 Luis Suárez was universally condemned after he bit Branislav Ivanović in Liverpool's 2–2 draw with Chelsea at Anfield. Suárez, who had served a seven-match ban in the Netherlands for a similar offence when playing for Ajax, was later banned for ten matches.

22 APRIL
2013 – Three for RVP; 20 for MUFC

Robin van Persie was the big fish that both Manchester United and Manchester City wanted to catch in the summer of 2012. The Dutchman, who had scored 44 goals for club and country in 2011/12, announced in July that he wanted to leave Arsenal and the scramble between the two Manchester clubs began immediately.

With the two sides so evenly matched – City had won the title from United on goal difference in 2012 – many observers felt that the choice van Persie made could almost decide the destination of the title. After a month of negotiations, van Persie explained his decision to choose United. 'I always listen to the little boy inside of me in these situations,' he revealed. 'What does he want? That boy was screaming for Man United.'

It was no coincidence that United's much-prized new man was given the squad number 20: United were hoping he'd deliver their 20th league title.

Van Persie's first United goal came on his home debut against Fulham, and he scored a hat-trick at Southampton in his third game in United red. His last-minute winner at Manchester City in December served to underline the instinctive brilliance that City had missed out on.

In all competitions Van Persie had scored 25 goals for Manchester United when Aston Villa went to Old Trafford in April. United, with City trailing in second place, needed just one more win from their final five games of the season to win the league. Villa were in no shape to spoil the party, and fell behind to van Persie's first goal of the night after just 83 seconds.

Van Persie's second was special – even by his standards. Wayne Rooney delivered a long ball from the halfway line to the edge of the Villa penalty area and without even breaking stride van Persie volleyed it with his left foot past a startled Brad Guzan in the Villa goal. It was a worthy winner of the Goal of the Season award.

Van Persie's hat-trick was completed before half-time as he steered home a pass from Ryan Giggs. United had won the league and van Persie went on to be the Premier League's top scorer with 26 goals – more than Manchester City's Carlos Tévez and Sergio Agüero combined.

Also on this day

2000 Manchester United sealed their sixth Premier League title in eight seasons with a 3–1 win at Southampton.

2007 David James broke David Seaman's record with his 142nd Premier League clean sheet as Portsmouth drew 0–0 at James's former club Aston Villa.

2012 Manchester United missed the chance to go eight points clear of Manchester City as Everton scored twice in the last seven minutes to secure a 4–4 draw at Old Trafford.

23 APRIL
2003 – Real's *Galácticos* end United's Old Trafford dream

Real Madrid's collection of world superstars were nicknamed '*Los Galácticos*'. From the year 2000 it became the policy of Real's president Florentino Pérez to sign at least one of the world's elite players every year – whatever the cost. In 2000 it had been Luís Figo, in 2001 Zinedine Zidane and in 2002 the Brazilian Ronaldo.

Real were the reigning European champions when they were drawn against Manchester United in the quarter-final in 2003, but Sir Alex Ferguson's side were even more desperate than usual to progress because they knew the final of the competition would be played at their own Old Trafford stadium. If they could only reach the final, surely they would make that home advantage count?

Madrid against Manchester – one of the Spanish daily sports newspapers declared them the two greatest teams in the world. The reality in the first game in Madrid's Bernabéu was that there was a huge gulf between the two sides. Real were disappointed to win only 3–1, Ruud van Nistelrooy's goal reducing their

advantage and putting a rose-tinted hue on the result that United barely deserved.

Back in Manchester, Sir Alex Ferguson conjured a performance of such verve and bravery that, for all their genius, Madrid were shaken to the core.

Ferguson surprised Madrid by leaving David Beckham, the man they coveted as their next Galáctico, on the bench. They surprised Madrid even more by refusing to accept defeat even when the prospect of victory looked preposterous.

Real were in front after only 12 minutes, Ronaldo smacking a shot past Fabien Barthez. Now needing four goals to win, United decided that attack was the only policy; van Nistelrooy equalized before half-time, but at 4–2 on aggregate the odds still overwhelmingly favoured Madrid.

Again the sides exchanged goals, first Ronaldo for Real and then an own-goal by Helguera for United. When Ronaldo completed a sublime hat-trick with half an hour to play it left the home side needing a hero, and a miraculous four goals.

Enter substitute David Beckham. With 19 minutes to play he curled in a wicked free-kick, and with 6 minutes left he jabbed home a second. For a few moments United and their fans believed in Beckham's magical powers, and Real seemed haunted by the prospect of collapse. But time ran out on United and Real left Old Trafford relieved to be

through, and even more convinced that Beckham was a jewel worthy of a place in their crown.

Also on this day

1997 Borussia Dortmund beat Manchester United in the Champions League semi-final with a 1–0 win at Old Trafford.

2001 Having taken a year to recover from a knee injury, Ruud van Nistelrooy finally joined Manchester United in a £19m deal from PSV Eindhoven.

2011 After 14 games and 903 minutes of football, Fernando Torres scored in Chelsea's 3–0 win over West Ham – his first goal since joining for £50m.

24 APRIL
2012 – Chelsea's Nou Camp triumph

For Chelsea and Barcelona, familiarity had bred contempt. They had met eight times in five seasons from 2005 to 2009, with controversy never far away.

The absence of José Mourinho from the Chelsea dugout made for a less fractious build-up to the Champions League semi-final in 2012. Roberto Di Matteo's Chelsea won the home leg thanks to a Didier Drogba goal, but had relied on the strength of their defence, and some luck, as Barcelona hit the woodwork twice.

In the Nou Camp it was something of a miracle that Chelsea's slender one-goal advantage lasted 35 minutes. Barcelona savaged them from the start and a goal from Sergio Busquets only hinted at their dominance. Within 90 seconds of the goal, Chelsea captain John Terry seemed to have ended his side's chances as he planted his knee in the back of Alexis Sanchez – a red card was inevitable.

With Terry's defensive partner Gary Cahill having been injured early in the match, Di Matteo mustered a makeshift back four of Ramires, Ivanović, Bosingwa and Cole, in which only Cole was playing in his natural position.

With only two minutes of the first half to play, Barcelona made it 2–0 through Andrés Iniesta. Had it stayed 2–0 for those two remaining minutes, perhaps Barcelona would have cruised through? But it was a very different Chelsea dressing room after Ramires had chipped a goal back in the closing seconds to give them a slender advantage on away goals.

It was vital that Chelsea didn't concede again, but when Didier Drogba felled Cesc Fàbregas just after the break, Barcelona looked certain to restore their lead in the tie. Lionel Messi had already scored a staggering 63 goals that season, and one more would surely squeeze hope from Chelsea hearts. Messi's penalty hit the bar.

With 11 minutes to go, and with Chelsea defending for their lives, Di Matteo took Drogba off and sent on Fernando Torres. Torres – the butt of opposition jokes; Torres – the £50m striker with a paltry eight goals in 60 Chelsea appearances. But it was Torres who was the Chelsea hero, when, in injury-time, he showed the ice-cool finishing of a predator to kill off the mighty Barcelona.

Also on this day

2004 Danny Murphy became the first player to convert a penalty against Manchester United at Old Trafford in more than a decade since Ruel Fox had scored in December 1993. Liverpool won the match 1–0.

2005 Wayne Rooney scored a stunning volley in Manchester United's 2–1 win over Newcastle – and in the evening was named the Professional Footballers' Association Young Player of the Year.

2010 Scott Parker scored the winning goal after an inspirational display as relegation-threatened West Ham won 3–2 against Wigan at Upton Park.

25 APRIL
2004 – Arsenal's title at Tottenham

What could be better than revelling in trophy success at the home of one of your biggest rivals? Arsenal seemed to have made a habit of it, winning the league title at White Hart Lane in 1971, at Anfield in 1989 and at Old Trafford in 2002.

In 2004, as Arsenal travelled to Spurs, they were sitting nine points clear of Chelsea at the top of the table, unbeaten in all 33 games they had played. While Arsène Wenger and his side were making the short journey to White Hart Lane, Chelsea were suffering a 2–1 defeat at Newcastle. By the time Spurs and Arsenal kicked off, the visitors knew that a draw would be enough to be crowned champions for the 13th time.

Arsenal started as though they had only one game in which to earn that point rather than five; Patrick Vieira opening the scoring after only three minutes as he converted a pass from Dennis Bergkamp.

To the delight of their fans, Arsenal had the game under their control and added a second goal ten minutes before half-time as Vieira turned provider for Robert Pirès to score his 19th goal of the season – the celebrations could almost begin.

Spurs, who still needed points to be sure of staying in the top flight, took some of the shine off Arsenal's day by pulling a goal back through Jamie Redknapp midway through the second half. Then they earned a valuable point with a last-minute penalty converted by Robbie Keane after a foul by Arsenal's goalkeeper Jens Lehmann.

The loss of two points was quickly forgotten as Arsenal paraded round the home of their great rivals in celebration of the title. David Dein, the club's vice-chairman, was quick to set them a new target for the rest of the season. 'It's the most exciting and most talented Arsenal side, and this season has been a marvellous journey, they have been a joy to watch,' said Dein. 'To win the league is a tremendous achievement, but to go through it unbeaten has never been done before.'

Also on this day

2006 Arsenal reached the final of the Champions League with a 0–0 draw in Villarreal securing a 1–0 aggregate win. Arsenal goalkeeper Jens Lehmann ignored Thierry Henry's advice to dive to his right and went left to save a last-minute penalty from Juan Riquelme and preserve their slender advantage.

2007 Chelsea beat Liverpool 1–0 at Stamford Bridge in the first leg of the Champions League semi-final.

2009 Manchester United came back from 2–0 down at half-time to score five goals in 19 minutes and beat Spurs 5–2 at Old Trafford. The win maintained their three-point advantage over Liverpool in the title race.

2010 Stoke City suffered their heaviest ever Premier League defeat when they lost 7–0 at Chelsea.

26 APRIL
1993 – Brian Clough and the end of an era

When Brian Clough announced that he would retire after 18 years as manager of Nottingham Forest at the end of the 1992/93 season, it drew the curtain down on one of the most successful and colourful managerial careers English football had ever seen.

Clough made history at both Derby County and Nottingham Forest by making them each league champions for the first time in their history. At Forest he surpassed that achievement by winning the European Cup in 1979 and retaining it in 1980.

His outspoken nature, and 44-day spell as manager of Leeds in 1974, became the stuff of football legend, earned him the nickname 'Old Big 'Ead' and cost him serious consideration for the England manager's job. The FA, an inherently conservative organization in the 1970s and 1980s, appointed first Ron Greenwood and then Bobby Robson.

When Clough was given the freedom of the city of Nottingham in 1993 he joked, 'It's a beautiful place with lovely people. The River Trent is lovely too, I've walked on it for 18 years.'

But Forest were in terrible trouble, having lost 7 of their last 11 matches in the Premier League and staring almost certain relegation in the face. Clough's remarkable powers had been sadly diminished, and the strain of leading a failing team was etched into his familiar features.

When Clough, aged 58 but looking much older, announced his retirement his side had two more games to play. The first was at home to Sheffield United, a game they lost 2–0, confirming their relegation from the top flight after 17 years. Clough's last match was a 2–1 defeat at Ipswich in which his son Nigel scored Forest's goal.

Later Clough would famously say, 'I wouldn't say I was the best manager in the business. But I was in the top one.' Forest fans agreed – even as they were relegated the crowd at the City Ground sang, 'Brian Clough's a football genius.'

Also on this day

1995 Germany lost their 100 per cent record in the European Championship qualifying campaign as they were held to a 1–1 draw in Düsseldorf by Wales, for whom Dean Saunders scored.

2003 Michael Owen reached a century of Liverpool goals in his 185th game when he scored four times in a 6–0 win over West Bromwich Albion.

2008 Luka Modrić agreed a deal to join Tottenham Hotspur from Dinamo Zagreb at the end of the season for a club record-equalling £16.5m.

2008 Patrice Evra and a Chelsea groundsman had to be prevented from brawling after a row erupted while the Manchester United player was warming down after their 2–1 defeat at Stamford Bridge. Evra was later fined £15,000 and banned for four matches while Chelsea were fined £25,000.

27 APRIL
2014 – Gerrard's slip

Liverpool's title challenge seemed to be an irresistible force. In late January they had found an extra gear in a 4–0 win over Everton at Anfield, and had gone on to register big wins over Arsenal, Manchester United and Spurs in an 11-match winning streak, which had included a dramatic 3–2 success over title rivals Manchester City.

After a shock home defeat to Sunderland had ended Chelsea's hopes of winning the league, José Mourinho made their forthcoming Champions League semi-final against Atlético Madrid his priority. They drew 0–0 in the Spanish capital, and the second match at Stamford Bridge followed three days after their league fixture at Anfield.

Chelsea, wanting an extra day's preparation for the Atlético semi-final, had tried everything they could to get that game at Anfield moved from the Sunday to the Saturday. Having made enquiries to the Premier League and Sky TV, Mourinho believed that Liverpool's objections were the reason that their request was refused.

The Chelsea manager felt an injustice had been done, and used it to motivate his players. He later told the *Daily Telegraph*, 'I said to the players, "We are going to be the clowns, they want us to be the clowns in the circus. The circus is here. Liverpool are to be champions." I wasn't having that.'

Aware that Liverpool's success had been built on a high-tempo attacking game from the first whistle, Mourinho sent Chelsea out to frustrate, smother and slow the game down as much as possible.

Liverpool couldn't find a rhythm, and barely scratched the surface of Chelsea's defences. A draw would mean that the title race would still be in Liverpool's control – a defeat would put Manchester City in charge, thanks to their superior goal difference.

Liverpool decided to push for the win – and ended up losing.

The turning point was one that Liverpool's inspirational captain Steven Gerrard is unlikely ever to forget. Receiving a pass just inside his own half, Gerrard slipped, allowing Demba Ba to race clear and score in front of a horrified Kop. Once ahead, Chelsea's stranglehold was tighter than ever, and Willian added a second goal in injury-time.

The title, which seemed destined for Anfield, had been wrenched from Liverpool's grasp.

Also on this day

1994 Newcastle's Andy Cole scored a club record 40th goal of the season in their 5–0 win over Aston Villa.

2003 Relegation-threatened West Ham won 1–0 at Manchester City, Trevor Brooking's first game as caretaker manager after Glenn Roeder was forced to step aside due to illness.

2006 Massimo Maccarone scored an 89th-minute winner as Middlesbrough came back from 3–0 down on aggregate

against Steaua Bucharest to win their UEFA Cup semi-final 4–3.

2007 The Premier League decided against deducting points from West Ham, instead fining them £5.5m for acting improperly and withholding documentation over the ownership of Carlos Tévez and Javier Mascherano.

28 APRIL
1993 – Gazza's cheek as England choke

England's qualifying campaign for the 1994 World Cup Finals had started reasonably well. A home draw to Norway had been disappointing, but then the Norwegians had beaten the Dutch. England had recovered to record 4–0 and 2–0 wins over Turkey, and a 6–0 thumping of San Marino.

When the Netherlands came to Wembley, three teams – Norway, England and the Dutch, were level on seven points.

England couldn't have asked for a better start when they were awarded a free-kick after only 30 seconds and John Barnes curled it brilliantly into the top corner of Ed de Goey's net. Over the next half-hour England played some of their best football in years and a second goal came midway through the first half, David Platt poaching after Les Ferdinand had hit the inside of the post. England were cruising against arguably their group's toughest opponent.

Ten minutes before half-time, and completely against the run of play, Dennis Bergkamp scored a wonderful goal. Jan Wouters found the Ajax striker with a chipped pass, and Bergkamp cushioned a volleyed lob over England's goalkeeper Chris Woods.

If Wouters's skill had been impressive in the build-up to the goal, his next act was born of sheer aggression. Climbing for a high ball with Paul Gascoigne, Wouters stabbed the point of his elbow into Gascoigne's face, breaking the cheekbone of England's best player. The referee was standing within five yards, but ignored England's furious calls for Wouters to be sent off. With Gascoigne replaced by Paul Merson, England lost their edge.

The equalizing goal came five minutes from time, as Marc Overmars showed an astonishing turn of pace to beat England's quickest defender, Des Walker. Walker pulled at his shirt and the Dutch were correctly awarded a penalty, which Peter van Vossen rolled past Woods.

Years later manager Graham Taylor admitted that it was the game which sent England's campaign into a downward spiral. 'I went home and for the first time thought that we might not qualify,' he said. 'It was the turning point in my career as England manager, and I try not to think about it.'

Also on this day

1999 After England's 1–1 draw in a friendly in Hungary, Kevin Keegan announced that he was ready to stop being England's part-time manager and commit himself fully to the role. Within hours Keegan was joining the country in mourning the death of the 1966 World Cup-winning manager Sir Alf Ramsey.

2001 After two seasons in the Premier League, Bradford City were relegated following a 2–1 defeat at Everton.

2004 Arsenal agreed a fee of £3m with Feyenoord for the purchase of Robin van Persie.

2006 Felipe Scolari rejected the chance to become England manager.

2013 A 0–0 draw between Reading and Queens Park Rangers at the Madejski Stadium meant that both clubs were relegated from the Premier League.

29 APRIL
1996 – Keegan's rant

In mid-April 1996, Leeds went to Old Trafford to play their traditional rivals Manchester United, who were locked in a thrilling title race with Newcastle.

After 17 minutes Leeds's goalkeeper Mark Beeney was sent off and, with no substitute keeper available, he was replaced in goal by defender Lucas Radebe. Despite the huge odds, Leeds battled magnificently to keep the game goalless for more than an hour, until Roy Keane's late United winner.

After the match a relieved Alex Ferguson, well aware that Leeds United's next game was against Newcastle, suggested that Howard Wilkinson's side had only tried so hard because they wanted Kevin Keegan's team to win the league. 'If they played like that every week they'd be near the top of the table,' he said. 'You wonder if it's just because they're playing Manchester United? Pathetic, I think.'

On 28 April Manchester United won their penultimate game of the season 5–0 against Nottingham Forest. Forest also still had a game at Newcastle to play, and again Ferguson had his say. This time United's manager inferred that, because Newcastle had agreed to play Forest in a testimonial for their captain Stuart Pearce in May, Forest would also prefer Newcastle to win the title.

The following night Newcastle kept their slender title hopes alive with a 1–0 win at Leeds. Facing the Sky TV cameras immediately after the match, Keegan let rip with one of the most impassioned and infamous managerial rants in history. With his finger jabbing as though Ferguson was standing in front of him, Keegan barked and spluttered down the lens: 'When you do that with footballers, like he said about Leeds – and when you do things like that about a man like Stuart Pearce: I've kept really quiet but I'll tell you something, he went down in my estimation when he said that. I'll tell you now, and he'll be watching it, we're still fighting for this title and he's got to go to Middlesbrough and get something. I'll tell you, honestly, I will love it if we beat them – love it.'

Four days later Nottingham Forest held Newcastle to a 1–1 draw, virtually ensuring that Manchester United would win the league.

Also on this day

2006 Chelsea retained the Premier League title with a 3–0 win over Manchester United at Stamford Bridge.

2006 Portsmouth completed their escape from almost certain relegation with their sixth win in nine games, 2–1 over Wigan.

2007 With Bolton Wanderers poised to qualify for the UEFA Cup, Sam Allardyce resigned as manager and was replaced by his assistant, Sammy Lee.

2008 Paul Scholes scored as Manchester United sealed a place in the Champions League Final, beating Barcelona 1–0 at Old Trafford.

2010 In the Europa League semi-finals Liverpool went out to Atlético Madrid on away goals after a 2–1 win at Anfield, but Fulham reached their first ever European final with a 2–1 win over Hamburg at Craven Cottage.

30 APRIL
2005 – The 50-year wait

Chelsea had been crowned champions of England only once – in 1955. In the five decades that followed they won the FA Cup and League Cup three times each and the European Cup Winners' Cup twice – but the title had eluded them, finishing third in 1965, 1970 and 1999 and second in 2004.

New manager José Mourinho had not only won the Champions League with FC Porto, he had won the Portuguese title in each of his two seasons in charge. Owner Roman Abramovich made sure that Mourinho had the tools to succeed – Chelsea spent over £90m in the summer of 2004 on Petr Čech, Paulo Ferreira, Ricardo Carvalho, Alex, Tiago, Arjen Robben, Mateja Kežman and Didier Drogba. The big question was whether so much change so quickly could hinder, rather than help, their title ambitions.

The first test was passed on the first day of the season, Chelsea beating Manchester United 1–0. Their new-look defence gelled instantly, conceding only two goals in their first ten Premier League games. In early November Chelsea knocked reigning champions Arsenal off the top of the table and by Christmas they were five points clear, and on a run of ten consecutive games without conceding a goal.

From his position lagging behind Chelsea, Arsenal's manager Arsène Wenger observed that, 'They are a bit like a matador, waiting for the bull to get weak. When the bull has lost enough blood, they just kill him off.'

On the last day of April, Mourinho took his side to the Reebok Stadium knowing that a win would seal the title with three games to spare. Bolton kept Chelsea at bay for an hour, then Frank Lampard controlled a Drogba flick, turned inside Vincent Candela and drove a shot past Jussi Jääskeläinen. Fifteen minutes later Chelsea broke from a corner and Lampard was left with a clear run on goal. His cool finish ended that long wait, and the celebrations began.

Also on this day

1994 Liverpool played their last game in front of the Kop terrace, losing 1–0 to Norwich.

2002 Manchester United missed out on reaching the Champions

League Final at Hampden Park when they drew 1–1 in Germany against Bayer Leverkusen, going out on away goals.

2008 Chelsea reached their first Champions League Final with a 3–2 win over Liverpool in extra-time at Stamford Bridge.

2012 With two games to play, Manchester City beat Manchester United 1–0 to go above their neighbours to the top of the Premier League on goal difference.

2014 Chelsea lost their Champions League semi-final to Atlético Madrid after a 3–1 defeat at Stamford Bridge.

May

1 MAY
2012 – Hodgson for England

Sometimes playing a quiet, patient game bears fruit. When Fabio Capello resigned as England manager in February 2012, it seemed that Harry Redknapp was almost certain to succeed him. The Tottenham manager made no secret of the fact that he wanted the job, and pundits everywhere formed a queue to support his appointment. But as weeks went by with no announcement, it became clear that the FA were unwilling to rush into Redknapp's open arms.

Later, in his autobiography, Redknapp pondered on what had gone wrong. 'I'll admit, I thought it was mine. Everyone seemed so certain, everyone I had met from all parts of the game seemed utterly convinced it was my job,' he wrote. 'I am still asked quite regularly about what went wrong. I wish I knew for certain. Nobody at the FA has ever explained why I was overlooked. I think with the FA there are certain managers who are considered a little rough around the edges.'

Whether he was considered too 'rough around the edges' or not, Redknapp wasn't even interviewed.

In the background, saying little and being diplomacy itself, was Roy Hodgson. He had the experience of having been an international manager with Switzerland, Finland and the UAE, he was hugely respected at former clubs Inter Milan and Fulham – whom he took to the Europa League final – but was remembered with horror at Liverpool, where his time in charge coincided with a rapid decline.

After Anfield came West Bromwich Albion, where Hodgson had done much to repair his reputation with a year of steady improvement. As the Redknapp rollercoaster lost momentum, Hodgson's safe pair of hands began to seem more appealing.

At the beginning of May – just six weeks before England's opening game at Euro 2012 – Roy Hodgson was confirmed as England boss.

Hodgson's words at his first England press conference might have offered a clue as to why he, not Redknapp, got the job. 'Given my CV, I had the right to hope and harbour the wish that the FA, after going through the process, would choose me. I didn't expect though. I've never expected, but always hoped – nobody should expect.'

Also on this day

2000 Wimbledon sacked manager Egil Olsen and named Terry Burton as caretaker manager.

2004 Leicester City were relegated from the Premier League despite a 2–2 draw at Charlton.

2007 Liverpool held their nerve in a penalty shoot-out to beat Chelsea in the

Champions League semi-final. After the tie finished 1–1 on aggregate, Liverpool won 4–1 on penalties at Anfield.

2 MAY
1993 – Champions at last

When Manchester United won the league title in 1967 it was the fifth time they had been crowned champions under Matt Busby, and the prelude to becoming the first English club to win the European Cup a year later.

Nobody could have envisaged that the 'holy trinity' of George Best, Denis Law and Bobby Charlton would never win another league title. Certainly nobody could have envisaged that the club would be relegated in 1974, and wait 26 years to be champions again.

United had won the FA Cup four times in the intervening years and had hinted at the glories to come with a win over Barcelona in the 1991 European Cup Winners' Cup Final. In those 26 years United had been forced to watch as their bitterest rivals Liverpool had been champions of England 11 times – winning the title again had become an obsession at Old Trafford.

By late April 1993, Norwich had dropped out of the race to be the first champions of the new Premier League; then Manchester United strode ahead of second-placed Aston Villa with a win at Crystal Palace on the same night as Villa were beaten at Blackburn. For almost two weeks, with United on the brink, there were no Premier League fixtures because of World Cup qualifying matches.

When the wait for the title finally ended, it wasn't in front of a packed Old Trafford with the eyes of the world watching their joyous celebrations – instead it was huddled around a TV screen or listening to a radio. On Sunday 2 May, United's title was confirmed as Oldham began their unlikely escape from relegation with a 1–0 win at Aston Villa – Liverpudlian Nick Henry scored the goal that sent the gleaming new trophy to Manchester.

Also on this day

1994 A goal from Coventry City defender Julian Darby sealed their 2–1 win over Blackburn at Highfield Road, and in the process Manchester United's ninth title.

1996 Glenn Hoddle accepted an offer to take over from Terry Venables as England manager after the finals of Euro 96.

1998 After one season in the Premier League, Barnsley were relegated following a 1–0 defeat at Leicester.

2004 Three years to the day after drawing with Valencia in the first leg of their Champions League semi-final,

Leeds were relegated out of the Premier League with a 4–1 defeat at Bolton.

2007 Manchester United lost their Champions League semi-final to AC Milan with a 3–0 defeat in the San Siro.

2012 Goal of the Season – Papiss Cissé scored it for Newcastle against Chelsea at Stamford Bridge.

2015 Manchester United lost 1–0 at home to West Bromwich Albion, the first time in 14 years they had lost three league games in succession.

3 MAY
2005 – The 'ghost goal'

The first leg of the Champions League semi-final had been dull, a cagey 0–0 draw at Stamford Bridge that seemed to favour Liverpool. '99.99 per cent of the Liverpool fans think they are in the final,' said José Mourinho. 'They are not.'

At Anfield the Chelsea players walked into their dressing room to see the number 33 written in large red digits on a whiteboard. It was a reminder from Mourinho of their points advantage over Liverpool in the Premier League table – a reminder of the newly crowned league champions' superiority.

Outside that dressing room Anfield was as noisy as in its heyday, and perhaps as hostile as it's ever been, Mourinho later admitting, 'I felt the power of Anfield – it was magnificent.' With every touch of the ball Liverpool players were cheered and Chelsea's whistled, jeered and booed; not just for the first few minutes, but for the whole match.

Liverpool needed only three minutes to take the lead. Steven Gerrard flicked a pass over the Chelsea defence for Milan Baroš to run on to. Immediately sensing the danger, Petr Čech raced from his goal, but Baroš got there first and the Chelsea goalkeeper hammered his countryman to the floor with the impact of his challenge. With Liverpool fans screaming for a penalty, Luis García – the quick-witted Spanish forward – flicked the ball towards the Kop goal, only for Chelsea's William Gallas to stretch every sinew to hook it clear.

Had it crossed the line? Without technology, the referee and his assistants could only decide on the basis of a glance, but after a pause that could have stopped a thousand heartbeats gave the goal – a 'ghost goal', said Mourinho. 'The linesman scored the goal,' he said. 'No-one knows if that shot went over the line. It was a goal that came from the moon – from the Anfield stands.'

Now with a lead to defend, Liverpool set about standing firm under a Chelsea barrage that was extended by six minutes of added time. One goal would put Chelsea through – and in the 96th minute Eidur Gudjohnsen should have scored it, but flashed his shot wide of a gaping net.

Ghosts or greats, Liverpool were in the Champions League Final.

Also on this day

1997 Sunderland played their last game at Roker Park, winning 3–0 against Everton. Eight days later they were relegated.

1998 Arsène Wenger became the first non-British manager to win the league title as Arsenal beat Everton 4–0 at Highbury.

2008 Cristiano Ronaldo scored his 40th goal of the season in Manchester United's 4–1 win over West Ham.

2014 After 13 seasons in the top flight, Fulham were relegated after a 4–1 defeat at Stoke. Cardiff, who lost 3–0 at Newcastle, also went down.

2015 Chelsea clinched the Premier League title with a 1–0 win over Crystal Palace at Stamford Bridge.

4 MAY
1994 – Wonderful, wonderful Copenhagen

Under manager George Graham, Arsenal had won the league title twice, the League Cup twice and the FA Cup. It was a team built on an outstanding goalkeeper in David Seaman, a rock-solid defence of Lee Dixon, Tony Adams, Steve Bould and Nigel Winterburn, the flair of Paul Merson and the deadly opportunism of Ian Wright. They were accused of being dull, but their fans revelled in success and the often-repeated score, which became a song: 'One-nil to the Arsenal.'

In 1994 Graham guided his team to Copenhagen for the club's first European final since 1980 – the Cup Winners' Cup. The odds seemed stacked against them; there was no Ian Wright, their 22-goal top scorer being suspended after a booking in the semi-final against Paris Saint-German. Their opponents were the brilliant Italian side Parma, holders of the trophy from 1993 and blessed with a fearsome forward line of Tomas Brolin, Gianfranco Zola and Faustino Asprilla.

Arsenal were almost behind after less than 30 seconds; Brolin sent Asprilla free, but Steve Bould rescued Arsenal with the first of many saving tackles. Three minutes later Brolin might have scored with a header, and soon the Swede hit the inside of Arsenal's post after a counter-attack had been led by the lightning-fast Asprilla. Arsenal were clinging on.

After dominating for 20 minutes, Parma let their guard slip as Lee Dixon's chipped pass was met by a lazy attempt at a clearance from Lorenzo Minotti that fell to Alan Smith. The Arsenal forward, who so often played second-fiddle to the extravagant Ian Wright, chested the ball down and fired a left-footed half-volley that went in off the inside of the post for only his sixth goal of the season.

With a display of huge determination and organization Arsenal repelled everything that Brolin, Zola and Asprilla could conjure and Parma ran out of energy, hope and inspiration. For the 11th time that season it finished 1–0 to the Arsenal.

Also on this day

2002 **Tony Adams played his 669th and last game for Arsenal as they won the FA Cup for the eighth time with a 2–0 win over Chelsea in Cardiff. Freddie Ljungberg and Ray Parlour scored Arsenal's goals.**

2003 **Sir Alex Ferguson came off the golf course to discover that Manchester United had won their eighth title in 11 years, as Arsenal had been beaten 3–2 by Leeds at Highbury.**

2006 **The FA announced that Steve McLaren would be England's new manager after the World Cup Finals.**

2006 **Sunderland beat Fulham 2–1 at the Stadium of Light to ensure that they would avoid becoming the first Premier League team ever to fail to a win a home game all season.**

2011 **Manchester United completed a 4–1 win over German side Schalke 04 to** **reach the Champions League Final for the third time in four seasons.**

5 MAY
2001 – Coventry down after 34 years

That Coventry survived for so long in the top flight was a remarkable achievement. When they finally went down it was the 20th time they had finished in the bottom seven of the table, and they'd avoided relegation on the final day of a season 10 times. Despite that, at the time of their relegation, only Arsenal, Liverpool and Everton had been in the top division for longer.

Their finest moment had been winning the FA Cup in 1987, beating favourites Spurs 3–2 in a memorable final. In the 1996/97 season another win over Spurs was just as thrilling. With six games to play Coventry were bottom of the league, but beat Liverpool and Chelsea and drew with Arsenal, before saving themselves on the last day of the season with a 2–1 win at White Hart Lane. But it was a controversial escape: traffic problems had delayed the kick-off so with 14 minutes to play Coventry knew that the other results had gone in their favour, and that they could simply defend that crucial lead.

In contrast Coventry threw a lifeline away in 2001. Needing to win their penultimate game at Aston Villa to keep in with a chance of staying up, Coventry led 2–0 at half-time with both goals from Mustapha Hadji. The jubilation among the away fans didn't last. Villa's Darius Vassell pulled a goal back early in the second half, and Juan Pablo Ángel equalized with nine minutes to go. Needing to score, Coventry took risks and conceded a winner to Paul Merson five minutes from the end.

Also on this day

1994 Spurs avoided relegation with a 2–0 win at Oldham.

1996 Manchester United won the title with a 3–0 win at Middlesbrough.

1996 In their final game of the season Manchester City drew 2–2 with Liverpool. In the closing minutes City's manager Alan Ball was incorrectly told that a draw would keep them up, and instructed his players to waste time. In fact they needed to win and were relegated.

2004 Chelsea threw away a two-goal lead at home to Monaco, and lost their Champions League semi-final.

2009 Manchester United won the second leg of their Champions League semi-final at Arsenal 3–1 to reach the final for the second year in succession.

2010 Spurs won 1–0 at Manchester City, pipping them to fourth place

in the league, and a place in the Champions League.

2012 Ashley Cole won a seventh FA Cup winner's medal as Chelsea beat Liverpool 2–1 in the final.

2014 Liverpool lost a three-goal lead to draw 3–3 at Crystal Palace and leave Manchester City as odds-on favourites to win the league.

6 MAY
2009 – Hiddink's Chelsea heartbreak

When Guus Hiddink had replaced Felipe Scolari as Chelsea manager in February 2009 it was to salvage a desperately poor season. Three months later they were on the verge of a glorious cup double.

Chelsea had already reached the FA Cup Final, and looked set to beat Barcelona to set up a Champions League Final against Manchester United in Rome – a repeat of the final that Chelsea had lost in Moscow the previous season.

Chelsea, who had knocked out both Juventus and Liverpool, had drawn 0–0 in the Nou Camp in the first leg of their semi-final against Barcelona. It was the first time that Pep Guardiola's side had failed to score at home all season.

Back at Stamford Bridge Michael Essien took just nine minutes to fire Chelsea in front, striking a left-footed volley that screamed into the roof of the Barcelona net from 25 yards.

Had referee Tom Øvrebø awarded any of four possible penalties in Chelsea's favour, they would surely have put the tie out of Barcelona's reach. However, the Norwegian decided first that Dani Alves's foul on Florent Malouda had been outside the area, then that Éric Abidal had not pulled back Didier Drogba. After half-time Ovrebo waved away appeals against Yaya Touré for another challenge on Drogba, and missed Gerard Piqué's clear handball.

But Chelsea, especially Drogba, had been guilty of missing chances and not every decision had gone Barcelona's way – they were unlucky to see Éric Abidal sent off for an innocuous tangle with Nicolas Anelka.

With the 90 minutes and 2 added minutes of stoppage time played, Chelsea were seconds from the final. Then Xavi fed Dani Alves on the right wing, his deep cross was levered from goal by John Terry, but Essien sliced his clearance straight to Lionel Messi on the edge of the penalty area. With blue shirts hurling themselves in his direction, Messi played a pass to Andrés Iniesta standing 20 yards from goal. Iniesta's rising shot was struck so accurately and with such venom that Petr Čech got nowhere near it.

Yet again, the Champions League Final was a tattered dream for Chelsea.

Also on this day

1997 Manchester United were crowned champions without playing as Newcastle drew 0–0 at West Ham and Liverpool were beaten 2–1 at Wimbledon. Liverpool's goal was scored by Michael Owen on his debut.

2004 Newcastle lost their UEFA Cup semi-final after a 2–0 defeat in Marseille, both goals scored by Didier Drogba.

2007 Chelsea's 1–1 draw at Arsenal confirmed Manchester United as champions for the ninth time under Sir Alex Ferguson.

2014 Caretaker manager Ryan Giggs made his 963rd – and last – appearance for Manchester United as he brought himself on for the last 20 minutes of their 3–1 win over Hull City. Two of United's goals were scored by James Wilson on his debut.

7 MAY
1994 – The scrap to stay up

When the final day of the 1993/94 season kicked off, only Swindon had already been relegated. Two of six other teams would join them, with Oldham and Everton in the relegation places. Ipswich, Sheffield United, Southampton and Manchester City were all in danger too.

The afternoon began appallingly for Everton, who needed to win but were 2–0 down at home to Wimbledon after only 20 minutes. A penalty from Graham Stuart reduced the arrears, but at half-time Everton were still behind.

Elsewhere Oldham, also needing a victory, were losing 1–0 at Norwich. Ipswich and Southampton were drawing at Blackburn and West Ham respectively and Manchester City looked safe despite being a goal down at Sheffield Wednesday. Sheffield United were surely saving themselves, as they were winning 1–0 at Chelsea.

Then Everton equalized against Wimbledon with a fantastic shot from Barry Horne. Oldham scored at Norwich too; but with Sheffield United now 2–1 up at Chelsea, both were still heading down. Manchester City and Southampton were both drawing, and both were safe. Ipswich, still held 0–0 at Blackburn, could be caught only if Everton won.

With 15 minutes to go Mark Stein made it 2–2 between Chelsea and Sheffield United. Oldham, still drawing 1–1 at Norwich, needed to win by three goals to escape but that was far too big a task with so little time.

At Goodison Park, Everton knew they would be relegated unless they scored. In front of tortured Everton fans behind the Gwladys Street goal, Graham Stuart played a one-two with Tony Cottee and

hit a low shot that Wimbledon goalkeeper Hans Segers seemed to misjudge – Everton had saved themselves on the very brink. Stuart's goal took them above both Sheffield United and Ipswich, but it was Ipswich, with inferior goal difference, who were now heading down.

In the last minute of the last game came the last twist of the season. Ipswich didn't save themselves, but were saved by Mark Stein. The Chelsea striker's second goal of the game at Stamford Bridge put Sheffield United 3–2 behind – and out of the Premier League.

Also on this day

2006 On the last day of the 2005/06 season Spurs and Arsenal were battling to finish fourth and qualify for the Champions League. A win for Spurs at West Ham would secure that place, while Arsenal had to beat Wigan to have any chance. On the morning of the match several Spurs players reported feeling ill – they had all eaten lasagne at the team hotel the previous evening. Sluggish and struggling, Spurs lost 2–1 at West Ham while Arsenal took fourth place with a 4–2 win over Wigan in their last ever match at Highbury.

2007 After seven consecutive Premier League seasons Charlton were relegated following a 2–0 defeat at home to Spurs.

2012 Blackburn Rovers were relegated after losing 1–0 at home to Wigan.

2015 Manchester United agreed to pay £25m for PSV Eindhoven striker Memphis Depay.

8 MAY
2013 – Ferguson to retire

He'd said it before, but this time there was no chance of him changing his mind. Aged 71, Sir Alex Ferguson announced his retirement 17 days after having added a 13th Premier League title to his personal haul of honours, which included 5 FA Cups, 4 League Cups and 2 Champions League trophies.

Still the news was a shock; the thought of Manchester United without that familiar figure dominating the dugout was almost unthinkable. 'The decision to retire is one that I have thought a great deal about. It is the right time,' he said. 'It was important to me to leave an organization in the strongest possible shape, and I believe I have done so.'

United still had two more games to play; the first was Ferguson's farewell to Old Trafford against Swansea. After that game the Premier League trophy was presented to United and Ferguson spoke at length to the Old Trafford crowd, taking particular time to stress that: 'When we had bad times here, the club stood by me, all my staff stood by me, the players stood by me. Your job now is to stand by our new manager. That is important.'

Ferguson's last game, his 1500th in charge of the club, was a testament to the attacking principles for which he had stood for over 26 years, though with some untypical defending – it finished in a 5–5 draw at West Brom.

From Prime Minister David Cameron to old rivals José Mourinho and Arsène Wenger, a legion of tributes were paid to the most successful manager that British football has ever seen, or is ever likely to see.

Also on this day

1993 Oldham saved themselves from relegation on the last day of the season with a third consecutive victory. Having won 1–0 at Aston Villa and 3–2 at home to Liverpool, they beat Southampton 4–3 in their last game despite a hat-trick from Matt Le Tissier. Oldham's escape meant that Crystal Palace were relegated on goal difference after a 3–0 loss at Arsenal, for whom former Palace favourite Ian Wright opened the scoring.

2001 Leeds missed the chance to reach the Champions League Final after losing 3–0 in Valencia in the second leg of their semi-final.

2002 Arsenal, who had already won the FA Cup, lifted the Premier League title with a 1–0 win against Manchester United at Old Trafford. Sylvain Wiltord's goal sealed Arsenal's third league and cup double.

2006 Theo Walcott's inclusion in Sven-Göran Eriksson's squad for the World Cup Finals was greeted with astonishment; the 17-year-old had not yet made his Arsenal debut.

2011 Javier Hernández scored after 36 seconds for Manchester United as they won 2–1 against Chelsea at Old Trafford to virtually confirm their 19th league title.

9 MAY
2010 – Chelsea's champagne championship

When Chelsea owner Roman Abramovich had sacked manager José Mourinho in 2007, it was widely believed that it was because Chelsea were not winning with enough style and flair. After the brief reigns of Avram Grant and Felipe Scolari at Stamford Bridge, Guus Hiddink had gone some way to restoring Chelsea's swagger in his months as caretaker manager. But it was under Carlo Ancelotti that Chelsea really took off again.

With Didier Drogba and Nicolas Anelka terrorizing defences and Frank Lampard scoring regularly from midfield, Chelsea recorded some huge wins in the 2009/10 season, the Italian's first as manager. They beat Bolton and Wolves 4–0, Blackburn and Portsmouth 5–0, Sunderland 7–2, Aston Villa 7–1 and Stoke 7–0. Manchester United had done well to keep pace, but on the last day of the season Chelsea needed only a win at home to Wigan to win the title while United had to beat Stoke and hope for news of a miracle in London.

Chelsea took only six minutes to take the lead through Anelka, and doubled it with a Lampard penalty before half-time. In the second half they ran riot. The third goal, from Salomon Kalou, set a new record of 98 goals scored in a

Premier League season, but they took that tally to 103 with 5 more as Anelka got another, Drogba scored a hat-trick and Ashley Cole rounded things off in the last minute. Manchester United had won their game 4–0 against Stoke, but that was immaterial as Chelsea revelled in the 8–0 scoreline, their biggest ever win in 105 seasons of league football.

High in the West Stand of Stamford Bridge, Abramovich beamed his approval.

Also on this day

1993 Liverpool took the unusual step of calling a press conference to announce that their manager Graeme Souness had not been sacked. Souness had been absent from Anfield the previous day as Liverpool beat Spurs 6–2.

2000 Sheffield Wednesday were relegated from the Premier League after losing a 3–1 lead in the last 12 minutes to draw 3–3 at Arsenal.

2001 Harry Redknapp was surprised to be sacked as manager of West Ham after a dispute with chairman Terry Brown over transfer funds. 'When I went into the club I had no intention of leaving,' Redknapp revealed. 'But the chat I had with the chairman got out of hand and now I'm out of a job.'

2015 Burnley were relegated despite a 1–0 win at Hull City.

10 MAY
1995 – Nayim from the halfway line

In the 34-year history of the European Cup Winners' Cup no team had ever retained the trophy. It was almost a curse: Fiorentina in 1962, Atlético Madrid in 1963, AC Milan in 1974, Anderlecht in 1977, Ajax in 1988 and Parma in 1993 had all suffered defeat in the final 12 months after winning the trophy.

Parma's defeat as holders had been at the hands of Arsenal, who reached the final again the following year thanks to goalkeeper David Seaman's heroics in an epic semi-final win over Sampdoria, which had gone to penalties. Arsenal's opponents in the final were Real Zaragoza, conquerors of Chelsea over two legs in their semi-final. Zaragoza's key men were their two South Americans, Uruguayan Gus Poyet as attacking midfielder and the Argentine striker Juan Esnáider. Zaragoza also had a familiar face in midfield in Nayim, who had left north London after five seasons with Spurs two years earlier.

Arsenal, managed by Stewart Houston after the sacking of George Graham, fell behind midway through the second half when Esnáider kept up his record of having scored in every round of the competition. They were only behind for ten minutes as John Hartson, the 20-year-old they had signed in January for £2.5m from Luton, swept home a low cross for his seventh goal for the club.

It was still 1–1 after 90 minutes, and there was little sign of a winning goal in extra-time. In the last minute of the added half-hour, and with both managers inevitably thinking about penalties, a defensive header from Andy Linighan fell to Nayim standing five yards inside the Arsenal half on the right-hand touchline. He controlled the ball on his chest and sent a half-volley rocketing skywards and towards the Arsenal goal. It was such an outrageous effort on goal that it can only have been struck in a flash of either desperation or supreme optimism, but the ball dropped over a despairing, back-pedalling Seaman, who could only push it into the roof of his net. Nayim and Zaragoza had won the trophy, and the curse of the Cup Winners' Cup had struck again.

Also on this day

1996 Chelsea appointed Ruud Gullit as their player-manager to replace Glenn Hoddle, who was to take over as England boss.

1998 Everton escaped relegation on the final day of the season for the second time in four seasons. Needing to better Bolton's result at Chelsea, Howard Kendall's side drew 1–1 at home to Coventry despite missing a

penalty; but it was enough as Bolton were relegated with a 2–0 defeat.

2006 Middlesbrough were beaten 4–0 by Sevilla in the final of the UEFA Cup in Eindhoven.

2015 Requiring an unlikely win to have any chance of avoiding relegation, Queens Park Rangers lost 6–0 at Manchester City.

11 MAY
2013 – The magic of the cup, and the reality of the league

Roberto Mancini had ended Manchester City's 35-year wait for a trophy in 2011 when they won the FA Cup. The Premier League title followed in 2012, and although Manchester United had regained the title in 2013, City at least had the chance to win another trophy having reached the FA Cup Final again. Even so, cup-final day began with newspaper reports that Málaga coach Manuel Pellegrini had already been offered Mancini's job.

City's opponents were Wigan, whom City had beaten without conceding a goal in their previous seven meetings. Under Roberto Martínez, Wigan had become experts in avoiding relegation; but as they headed to Wembley for the FA Cup Final they were three points from safety with only two league games to play.

Watched by their owner Dave Whelan, who had broken his leg playing in the 1960 FA Cup Final for Blackburn, Wigan were rank outsiders for the cup, but they played with style and an intensity that City found hard to match.

With winger Callum McManaman outstanding, Wigan created the better chances in a goalless first half. Although City improved after half-time, Wigan still looked dangerous, and had a numerical advantage when Pablo Zabaleta was sent off with six minutes to go for a foul on the irrepressible McManaman.

Extra-time seemed a certainty when Wigan won a last-minute corner, it was delivered into the box by Shaun Maloney and headed past a helpless Joe Hart by Ben Watson for a magical victory.

Two days later Mancini was sacked by Manchester City; three days later Wigan were relegated after a 4–1 defeat to Arsenal.

Also on this day

1995 Jürgen Klinsmann announced that he would leave Spurs at the end of the season to join Bayern Munich.

1996 Manchester United completed the double with a 1–0 win over Liverpool in the FA Cup Final. Éric Cantona scored the only goal.

1997 FA Cup finalists Middlesbrough were relegated from the Premier League after a 1–1 draw at Leeds.

2003 Jesper Grønkjær's goal gave Chelsea a 2–1 win over Liverpool to edge out the Merseyside club for the last Champions League qualifying spot, attracting the attention of a new would-be purchaser – Roman Abramovich.

2008 Manchester United clinched the Premier League title with a 2–0 win at Wigan while Chelsea could only draw with Bolton at Stamford Bridge.

2008 Manchester City lost 8–1 at Middlesbrough on the last day of the season; manager Sven-Göran Eriksson was sacked three weeks later.

2010 Gianfranco Zola was sacked as manager by West Ham.

2013 Frank Lampard became Chelsea's all-time record goalscorer as he scored his 202nd and 203rd for the club in a 2–1 win at Aston Villa.

2014 Manchester City were crowned champions after a 2–0 win over West Ham at the Etihad Stadium. Norwich were relegated after losing 2–0 to Arsenal.

12 MAY
2001 – The Owen final

In 2001 Liverpool were going for a cup treble. The League Cup had already been won, Gérard Houllier's side had overcome Roma, FC Porto and Barcelona on their way to the final of the UEFA Cup, and they were facing Arsène Wenger's Arsenal in the final of the FA Cup – the first to be held at Cardiff's Millennium Stadium.

Arsenal were denied what seemed a clear penalty in the first half when Thierry Henry raced clear of the Liverpool defence and rounded their goalkeeper Sander Westerveld. Henry's goal-bound shot was deflected wide from off the line by the elbow of Liverpool's Stéphane Henchoz: somehow neither the referee nor the linesman saw it.

Arsenal dominated even more in the second half, and should have scored when Westerveld saved from Henry only for the rebound to fall to Ashley Cole. His shot from six yards out was blocked on the line by Liverpool captain Sami Hyypiä, who rescued Liverpool again when he cleared a Freddie Ljungberg lob off the line.

With 19 minutes to go Arsenal finally claimed the lead they had long deserved. Westerveld's poor clearance was returned to Ljungerg by Pirès, who rounded the goalkeeper to score. Liverpool had to attack, but survived a glorious opportunity for Henry make it 2–0 almost immediately. With eight minutes to go Liverpool won a free-kick that Gary McAllister curled threateningly towards the Arsenal goal; Martin Keown's defensive header rebounded to Michael Owen, who launched an acrobatic right-footed shot into the net.

Unexpectedly back in a game that had been dominated by their opponents, Liverpool sensed Arsenal were vulnerable. With just three minutes left, and with Arsenal on the attack, Patrik Berger sent a long pass ahead of Owen for the Liverpool striker to chase. Neither Lee Dixon nor Tony Adams could stay with the pace of Owen, and his shot crept into precisely the corner of the net that goalkeeper David Seaman couldn't reach.

Arsenal had enjoyed most of the possession and most of the chances, but Liverpool had Michael Owen – and the FA Cup.

Also on this day

1993 A Wembley crowd of only 37,393 watched Parma beat Royal Antwerp 3–1 in the final of the European Cup Winners' Cup.

1999 Four seasons after winning the Premier League, Blackburn Rovers were relegated following a 0–0 draw at home to the team they had beaten to the 1995 title – Manchester United.

2010 Fulham lost the Europa League Final to Atlético Madrid in Hamburg after a 2–1 defeat in extra-time. Simon Davies scored Fulham's goal, but Diego Forlán hit two for Atlético.

2013 Rio Ferdinand scored on his last Manchester United appearance at Old Trafford in a 2–1 win over Swansea, after which Paul Scholes and Sir Alex Ferguson bade farewell.

2014 **After narrowly avoiding relegation, Pepe Mel was sacked as manager of West Bromwich Albion.**

13 MAY
2012 – That Agüero goal

As a climax to a football match it's improbable, as a climax to a season it's unlikely ever to be repeated.

Manchester City and Manchester United were level on points when the last games of the season kicked off, but City's goal difference was superior. They seemingly had the easier game, at home to Queens Park Rangers, while United were away to Sunderland. All City had to do was win.

In Sunderland, Manchester United fans watched their team, but listened to radios and checked their phones even more intently, expecting news of a City goal at any moment. No news was good news; it was still 0–0 at City when Wayne Rooney opened the scoring for United, putting them top of the table.

But not for long; that City goal came six minutes before half-time, Pablo Zabaleta breaking QPR's resistance. At the break it seemed that both Manchester clubs would win, and that City would be champions.

Djibril Cissé's equalizer for QPR changed the mood inside both grounds – advantage United again. Then Rangers made light of the red card to their midfielder Joey Barton to score again, through Jamie Mackie. City were losing and United were winning: United's title, City's despair.

The moments creaked slowly by; United were comfortable against Sunderland, City desperate against Rangers. Ninety minutes came and went, when suddenly tormented City scored. Edin Džeko's header brought tearful, departing City fans rushing back into the stadium.

In Sunderland the final whistle went and United's players waited on the pitch for their cue to celebrate. In Manchester, City's Sergio Agüero dragged himself forward for one last attack. Suddenly the Rangers defence was exposed, goalkeeper Paddy Kenny advanced, and a flying QPR defender lunged. Undaunted, Agüero struck.

As the Argentine peeled away in delirious celebration, the colour drained from United's faces as they sought sanctuary in their dressing room, crushed by the reality that the title was gone.

Also on this day

1997 Stan Collymore joined Aston Villa from Liverpool.

1998 Gianfranco Zola scored 22 seconds after coming on, and won the European Cup Winners' Cup for Chelsea against Stuttgart.

2006 Goal of the Season – Steven Gerrard scored it for Liverpool against West Ham in the FA Cup Final. Gerrard's goal, his second of the game, came in the 90th minute and levelled the match at 3–3. Liverpool won 3–1 on penalties.

2007 Carlos Tévez kept West Ham up, scoring the winner at Manchester United. Sheffield United were relegated after they lost 2–1 at home to Wigan, who stayed up thanks to David Unsworth's penalty.

2007 Fulham's Matthew Briggs, aged 16 years and 65 days, became the Premier League's youngest ever player.

2014 Tim Sherwood was sacked by Spurs.

2014 Yaya Touré's 31st birthday. His agent Dimitri Seluk revealed that Touré was 'very upset' that Manchester City hadn't bought him a present. 'He got a cake,' said Seluk. 'When it was Roberto Carlos's birthday, the president of Anzhi gave him a Bugatti.'

14 MAY
1995 – Blackburn's Anfield joy

After going 26 years without the title, Alex Ferguson's United had become the team to beat having been champions in 1993 and 1994. Blackburn's last championship had been in 1914; but financed by Jack Walker and inspired by the goals of Chris Sutton and Alan Shearer, they had been top since November.

Nevertheless, Blackburn were stumbling. They had dropped eight points in five games, allowing Manchester United to reduce their lead to just two points. On the final day of the season United had to win at West Ham, but their fear was that Blackburn's nerves would be untested in their last match, which was at Liverpool. At Anfield they would much prefer the title to go to their old favourite (and now Blackburn manager) Kenny Dalglish, rather than their old foe Alex Ferguson. Would Liverpool let Blackburn win, and enjoy United's frustration?

After 20 minutes Alan Shearer slammed Blackburn ahead, and their route to the title looked clear when Michael Hughes scored for West Ham. But in the second half Blackburn's stroll in the Anfield sunshine became an agonizing brush with the possibility of failure.

First Brian McClair equalized for Manchester United with a free header – ten minutes later John Barnes scored for Liverpool. With both games tied at 1–1, Blackburn knew that one Manchester United goal would be enough to take the title to Manchester.

In London, United attacked furiously, the unlucky Andy Cole having chance after chance, but West Ham goalkeeper Luděk Mikloško was having the game of his life. Somehow United failed to score.

Deep into injury-time, Jamie Redknapp curled home a brilliant free-kick to put Liverpool 2–1 in the lead. For a desperate instant Blackburn's fans and players alike tried to establish if that goal had cost them the title. Then came news from West Ham that Manchester United had drawn. In a heartbeat Blackburn had lost the game and won the title.

First to reach Kenny Dalglish, and hug him in celebration, was a red-shirted Liverpool fan.

Also on this day

1994 Manchester United completed the league and cup double for the first time, beating Chelsea 4–0 in the FA Cup Final.

1995 With the Premier League to reduce in size from 22 to 20 clubs, Crystal Palace were the unlucky team to be relegated in 19th place after losing at Newcastle.

1995 Manchester City's John Burridge became the oldest player in Premier League history, aged 43 years and 162 days.

2000 Bradford City beat Liverpool 1–0 to stay up. Bradford's win meant that, 12 years to the day since they had won the FA Cup, Wimbledon were relegated.

2007 Managerial changes: Manchester City sacked Stuart Pearce and Paul Jewell resigned from Wigan.

2008 The Eithad Stadium hosted the UEFA Cup Final, which was won by Zenit St Petersburg with a 2–0 win over Glasgow Rangers.

2011 Manchester United won their 19th title with a 1–1 draw at Blackburn.

2012 **Aston Villa sacked manager Alex McLeish.**

15 MAY
2004 – The Invincibles

In the 1888/89 season Preston North End had been unbeaten for the whole season. That season had involved 22 league games; 115 years later Arsenal were edging towards completing a 38-game season without losing.

Having won the league title in their 34th game, a 2–2 draw at Spurs in April, it was perhaps understandable that Arsenal's intensity might drop. An uninspiring 0–0 stalemate at home to Birmingham was followed by a fortunate 1–1 draw at Portsmouth, whose striker Yakubu had missed an inviting chance to put his side in front with less than 15 minutes left.

In the 37th game of the season, Arsenal beat Fulham 1–0. All roads led to Highbury for the final match of the campaign against Leicester City, who had already had their relegation confirmed.

Highbury was full to the brim, and full of expectation that history would be achieved. They hadn't reckoned on Paul Dickov, a former Arsenal striker who had not quite the made the grade at Highbury, but who had enjoyed a productive career at Manchester City and Leicester. Frank Sinclair provided

the cross for Dickov to head past Arsenal goalkeeper Jens Lehmann.

Just after half-time Arsenal's unease evaporated when Ashley Cole was fouled by Sinclair, and Thierry Henry struck home the penalty to become the first Arsenal player to score 30 league goals in a season since 1948. Highbury was relieved more than jubilant, but the real celebrations began after Dennis Bergkamp rolled an inviting pass to Patrick Vieira, who showed great composure to put Arsenal ahead in front of the North Bank stand.

From their 38 league games, Arsenal had 26 wins, 12 draws and no defeats. Arsène Wenger described them as 'immortal'; the newspapers dubbed them 'The Invincibles'.

Also on this day

1993 **Arsenal and Sheffield Wednesday drew 1–1 in the last FA Cup Final to go to a replay.**

2005 **West Bromwich Albion became the first side to avoid relegation from the Premier League having been bottom at Christmas. Bryan Robson's side beat Portsmouth 2–0 on the final day of the season. Southampton went down after losing to Manchester United, Norwich lost 6–0 at Fulham to be relegated and Crystal Palace joined them after a 2–2 draw at Charlton.**

2007 Newcastle appointed Sam Allardyce as manager.

2010 Chelsea completed the league and cup double after beating Portsmouth 1–0 in the FA Cup Final. Both Portsmouth's Kevin-Prince Boateng and Chelsea's Frank Lampard missed penalties as Didier Drogba scored the only goal. The win meant that Ashley Cole received a record sixth FA Cup winner's medal.

2011 West Ham were relegated, and manager Avram Grant sacked, after they let slip a 2–0 lead to lose 3–2 at Wigan.

2013 An injury-time goal from Branislav Ivanović against Benfica won the Europa League for Chelsea and manager Rafa Benítez.

16 MAY
2015 – The greatest escape?

In early February 2015 Nigel Pearson's sacking as Leicester manager was trending on social media. The news wasn't surprising; Leicester had been bottom of the table since November and had just been beaten at home by Crystal Palace. But the news was wrong; Pearson had not been sacked, and took his team to Arsenal two days later, where they lost 2–1.

By late March, when Leicester lost 4–3 at Spurs, Pearson's side were seven points from safety with only nine games to play. The first match was at home to West Ham. Leicester seemed to have thrown away a chance of victory when West Ham equalized after David Nugent had missed a penalty that would have made it 2–0 to Leicester. Crucially Leicester recovered and Andy King scored a late winner: so began an extraordinary sequence of results that seemed to defy all logic.

Leicester won their next match 3–2 at West Bromwich Albion. A 2–0 win over Swansea lifted them off the bottom of the table for the first time in five months. Then there was a 1–0 win at relegation rivals Burnley. A 3–1 defeat at home to Chelsea was shrugged off quickly and Newcastle were swept aside 3–0. When Leicester won 2–0 at home to Southampton, it was their sixth win in seven games.

The incredible escape was confirmed on 16 May with a 0–0 draw at Sunderland. Leicester, who had taken 19 points from 29 games when their run began, had taken another 19 from only 8 matches and were safe with a game to spare. Nevertheless, Pearson was surprisingly sacked only six weeks later.

Also on this day

1998 Arsenal secured the league and cup double with a 2–0 win over Newcastle in the FA Cup Final.

1999 Manchester United's 2–1 win over Spurs at Old Trafford sealed the Premier League title by a single point from Arsenal and kept their dream of a treble alive.

2000 Spurs signed Sergei Rebrov from Dynamo Kiev for a club record £11m, after the Ukrainian striker turned down the chance to join Arsenal.

2001 Liverpool completed a treble of cup wins as they won the UEFA Cup in a thrilling final against Alavés in Dortmund. Liverpool, who led 3–1 at half-time, conceded an 88th-minute equalizer to make the score 4–4. In extra-time Alavés had two men sent off and Liverpool won on the golden-goal rule. Their winner was an own-goal by Alavés defender Delfí Geli.

2007 Following their relegation from the Premier League, Neil Warnock resigned as manager of Sheffield United.

2009 A 0–0 draw at home to Arsenal was enough for Manchester United to clinch the Premier League title for the third season in a row.

2012 Kenny Dalglish was sacked as manager of Liverpool.

2015 Southampton's Sadio Mané scored a hat-trick in 2 minutes and 56 seconds in their 6–1 win over Aston Villa, the quickest hat-trick in Premier League history.

17 MAY
2006 – Wenger's trio

Arsenal had worked hard to reach their first Champions League Final. Having beaten both Real Madrid and Juventus, they had squeezed past Villarreal on penalties to seal their place.

Arsène Wenger's record in European finals was not good. In 1992 as manager of Monaco he had lost to Werder Bremen in the final of the Cup Winners' Cup, and at Arsenal he had lost the UEFA Cup Final to Galatasaray in 2000.

Arsenal's opponents in Paris were Barcelona. They had navigated an equally treacherous route, having beaten Chelsea, Benfica and AC Milan. On paper, it was a final to savour; Barcelona had the deadly Samuel Eto'o and the magical Ronaldinho. But Arsenal had conceded only two goals in 12 games to get to the final, and they had Thierry Henry.

Arsenal's pre-match tactics were thrown into disarray after 18 minutes, when goalkeeper Jens Lehmann was sent off. Ronaldinho played in Eto'o who was fouled by Lehmann outside the penalty area. Barcelona's Ludovic Giuly rolled the ball into the net, but his goal didn't stand, as referee Terje Hauge had already blown his whistle.

Later the referee agreed that he had made a mistake: 'I would like to have taken a few more seconds before I made a decision. If I'd done that, I could have given a goal and given a yellow card (instead of the red).'

That decision seemed to have worked for Arsenal when Sol Campbell rose magnificently to head in a free-kick from Henry before half-time. With ten men, and substitute keeper Manuel Almunia in goal, could Arsenal hold on?

They couldn't. After 75 minutes Henrik Larsson's pass set up Eto'o for an equalizer, and only four minutes later Larsson was provider again, feeding Juliano Belletti, whose shot beat Almunia at his near post.

For the third time, and now once in each of the European competitions, Wenger was on the losing side.

Also on this day

1997 Chelsea won their first major trophy for 26 years, beating Middlesbrough 2–0 in the FA Cup Final. Roberto Di Matteo scored after only 42 seconds, with the second goal coming from Eddie Newton. Mark Hughes became the first player in the twentieth century to win the FA Cup four times, and Ruud Gullit the first foreign manager to win the cup.

2000 Arsenal were beaten by Galatasaray in the final of the UEFA Cup 4–1 on penalties. The match finished 0–0 despite Galatasaray having Gheorghe Hagi sent off in extra-time.

2003 Arsenal beat Southampton 1–0 in the first FA Cup Final to be played under a closed roof. Robert Pirès scored the only goal in Cardiff's Millennium Stadium.

2006 Spurs signed Dimitar Berbatov from Bayer Leverkusen for £10.9m.

2008 Portsmouth's Kanu scored the only goal as they beat Cardiff to win the FA Cup for the first time since 1939.

2014 Arsenal recovered from 2–0 down against Hull City to win the FA Cup Final 3–2, their first trophy since 2005.

18 MAY
1997 – Cantona quits

Éric Cantona's career in England started in February 1992 and ended in May 1997: less than five-and-a-half seasons, and yet he remains one of the most talked-about players of the Premier League era.

Bare statistics tell only half the story, but are impressive nonetheless. He won the title five times, once with Leeds and four times with Manchester United. He scored three goals in two FA Cup Finals, finishing on the winning side both times. In total, he played 220 games and scored 96 goals.

Cantona's most famous kick may have been planted into the chest of a fan rather than onto the leather of a ball; but over the years, even that act of violence has only added to his mystique. His statement about sardines and trawlers might have been knowingly nonsensical, but it sounded like the words of a philosopher and, as he surely knew it would, had the media scrambling for a thread of meaning.

In 1997 Cantona had captained Manchester United to successfully defend their title under pressure from Newcastle, Arsenal and Liverpool, but suffered the disappointment of losing in the Champions League semi-final to Borussia Dortmund. It was after the second leg of that match that Alex Ferguson later revealed that Cantona had told him he intended to retire.

Ferguson had good reason to hope Cantona might change his mind; the player had announced his retirement at the age of 25 when he was playing for Nimes, after being given a two-month ban by the French Federation.

But there was no change of heart this time, and Cantona's teammates were left trying to express the extent of his impact. Ryan Giggs said, 'Gary and Phil Neville, Nicky Butt, Paul Scholes, David Beckham and myself – we all followed his lead.' Gary Neville remembered, 'The young lads had always been in awe of him; there was a vast, unspoken respect for him. We were desperate to impress him.'

Cantona later compared his relationship with Manchester United's fans to a love affair. It's been a lasting one

– almost 20 years after he said goodbye, those fans still sing, 'Ooh, aah, Cantona!'

Also on this day

1993 Arsenal announced that Highbury would become the first ground in England to have video screens installed.

1995 Manchester United winger Andrei Kanchelskis said he was no longer willing to play for manager Alex Ferguson. Kanchelskis was placed on the transfer list, and Ferguson considered whether to buy a new winger or use youngster David Beckham the following season.

1996 Darren Anderton, who had missed most of the season with injury, proved his fitness for Euro 96 by scoring twice in England's 3–0 win over Hungary in a pre-tournament friendly.

2004 Emile Heskey signed for Birmingham City from Liverpool for a club record £6m.

19 MAY
2012 – Chelsea, champions of Europe

Having been beaten finalists once and beaten semi-finalists four times, Chelsea were entitled to wonder if they would ever win the Champions League.

In March 2012 Chelsea sacked André Villas-Boas when another European exit looked likely. Under Villas-Boas they'd been beaten 3–1 at Napoli in the first leg of their knockout tie. Under caretaker manager Roberto Di Matteo, Chelsea had thrillingly overturned that deficit with a 4–1 home win after extra-time. Benfica were beaten in the quarter-final, then came the dramatic two-legged victory over Barcelona.

But in the final Chelsea would face a huge disadvantage – facing Bayern Munich in the Germans' own Allianz Arena.

From the first moment Chelsea's defence, missing both John Terry and Branislav Ivanović, was being tested from every angle. They were grateful for Bayern striker Mario Gómez being wasteful, for the offside flag that ruled out Franck Ribéry's effort and for the post that denied Arjen Robben.

Finally, Bayern's Thomas Müller scored with a bouncing header that fooled an exposed Petr Čech. With only seven minutes to play how could Chelsea, who had hardly managed a shot on target, muster an equalizer?

In the 88th minute Chelsea won their first corner, a first test of Bayern's defence to their aerial threat – Bayern failed it. Mata's cross was met by the flashing head of Didier Drogba, and even the reactions of Bayern's exceptional Manuel Neuer were too slow.

Drogba's header had saved Chelsea, but his foul on Ribéry three minutes into extra-time seemed likely to condemn them to defeat. Bayern's penalty was taken by the former Chelsea forward Robben, whose unconvincing shot was saved by Čech to his left.

Chelsea threw every last drop of effort into defending ever more desperate Bayern attacks. The referee's final whistle confirmed that Di Matteo's team had already beaten overwhelming odds by surviving; now could they beat Bayern from 12 yards?

Mata missed Chelsea's first spot-kick in the penalty shoot-out; but when Čech saved from Olić and Ashley Cole scored, it was 3–3. Bastian Schweinsteiger dithered in his run-up and saw Čech's fingertips push the ball onto the post; the German was in tears long before Drogba strode forward.

Unflinching, Drogba approached the ball – and won the Champions League.

Also on this day

1999 Villa Park hosted the last ever European Cup Winners' Cup Final, Lazio beating Real Mallorca 2–1.

2001 Matt Le Tissier scored as Southampton beat Arsenal 3–2 in the last game played at the Dell.

2007 Didier Drogba's extra-time goal won the FA Cup for Chelsea against

Manchester United, in the first FA Cup Final to be played at the new Wembley.

2013 A day of farewells: Sir Alex Ferguson to Manchester United, David Moyes to Everton and Jamie Carragher, after 737 games, to Liverpool.

2014 Manchester United appointed Louis van Gaal as their new manager.

20 MAY
1995 – Everton's sweet FA

In the 1980s Everton had rivalled Liverpool for football's top honours. Under Howard Kendall they were becoming one of Europe's best sides, a progress that was halted when the ban on English clubs was implemented after Heysel.

In that golden spell Everton had been crowned champions in both 1985 and 1987, won the FA Cup in 1984 and the European Cup Winners' Cup in 1985.

Over the next seven seasons, Everton slipped so far that they only avoided relegation on the last day of the 1993/94 season. The appointment of former player Joe Royle was designed to lift the spirits and restore the team to former glories – both happened sooner than even Royle could have expected.

Everton were the FA Cup's surprise package, making light of both Newcastle and Spurs on the way to Wembley. Still,

Manchester United were expected to win comfortably, spurred on by the disappointment of losing the title race to Blackburn a week earlier.

A dour start was forgotten when Everton's Dave Watson dispossessed Paul Ince and Anders Limpar raced forward from deep inside his own half. Limpar fed Matt Jackson, whose pass found Graham Stuart standing seven yards from an unguarded goal – somehow Stuart hit his shot against the underside of the crossbar rather than into the net. While Stuart flinched at the enormity of his miss, Paul Rideout reacted like a striker should, comprehensively out-jumping Denis Irwin to head in the rebound.

With Éric Cantona serving his lengthy ban and Andy Cole cup-tied, United looked to youth for inspiration. First Ryan Giggs and then Paul Scholes came on to test Everton's experience. Giggs set up first Butt and then McClair, who were both denied by Everton's 36-year-old goalkeeper Neville Southall.

With Dave Watson blocking, marshalling and blocking again, Everton stood firm. Southall's double-save from Scholes drained United of belief, and the game ended with their goalkeeper Peter Schmeichel standing disorientated on the halfway line, having been sent forward for one last corner. Everton's clearance had fallen to Daniel Amokachi, who might have added a second goal had he not run out of energy, and time, before the final whistle went.

Manchester United, who a week earlier had cherished hopes of winning the double, had ended the season with nothing. Everton danced around Wembley with the cup.

Also on this day

1993 Arsenal's Andy Linighan scored in the last minute of extra-time to win the FA Cup Final replay against Sheffield Wednesday. David O'Leary came on for his 722nd and final Arsenal appearance.

2000 Chelsea won the last FA Cup Final to be played at the old Wembley, beating Aston Villa 1–0.

2001 William Gallas joined Chelsea from Marseille for £6.2m.

2003 Aston Villa appointed David O'Leary as their manager.

2010 Avram Grant resigned as manager of relegated Portsmouth five days after losing the FA Cup Final to Chelsea.

21 MAY
2008 – Manchester in Moscow

In 1972 Spurs beat Wolves 3–2 on aggregate in the first ever UEFA Cup Final. As English clubs began to proliferate in the latter stages of the Champions League, it was likely that there would eventually be an all-English final in that competition too.

In 2008, three of the semi-finalists came from the Premier League; Chelsea beat Liverpool and Manchester United defeated Barcelona – so Moscow's Luzhniki Stadium laid out the welcome mat for the English.

In a dramatic final Manchester United struck first, a marvellous header from Cristiano Ronaldo whipping past Petr Čech after 26 minutes. Ten minutes later Čech made a stunning double-save from Carlos Tévez and Michael Carrick, but another United miss, by Tévez from a Wayne Rooney cross, was to prove costly. Seconds before half-time Frank Lampard equalized as Michael Essien's shot deflected kindly into his path. It had been United's half by a distance, but the scores were level.

The second half belonged to Chelsea, but the woodwork denied them when Didier Drogba's shot smacked the post. In Moscow it was long-past midnight, and it was extra-time.

Lampard hit the bar for Chelsea, John Terry headed off the line from Ryan Giggs – who was making a record 759th appearance for United. With tension and tempers rising, referee Ľuboš Micheľ sent off Didier Drogba for a petulant slap at the face of Nemanja Vidić. Four minutes later the referee's whistle blew, and penalties would decide the final.

Tévez, Ballack, Carrick and Juliano Belletti scored. Cristiano Ronaldo became the first to miss and Chelsea's advantage was rammed home by Lampard. Owen Hargreaves and Ashley Cole both converted so, at 4–3 to Chelsea, Nani had to score for United – and did.

John Terry, Chelsea's inspiration for years, strode through the rain with the chance to make history. Terry's foot slipped horribly on the sodden turf just as he struck the ball. The captain, who might have been lifting the cup, instead lifted himself off the ground in disbelief. His shot had hit the post – his slip had thrown United a lifeline.

Into sudden-death penalties, Anderson, Salomon Kalou and Giggs held their nerve as everyone else held their breath. Then came Anelka. The Chelsea striker's kick was not bad, but once Edwin van der Sar had guessed correctly, it was not quite accurate or powerful enough.

For the third time Manchester United were champions of Europe. Not even the Moscow rain could mask Terry's tears.

Also on this day

2001 Manchester City sacked manager Joe Royle.

2002 In a warm-up game for the World Cup Finals, England drew 1–1 in South Korea.

2005 Arsenal won the first FA Cup Final to be decided on penalties, beating Manchester United. José Antonio Reyes was sent off as the game finished goalless, but Patrick Vieira scored the winning penalty after Paul Scholes had missed.

2013 After a seven-year second spell as manager of Stoke, Tony Pulis left the club 'by mutual consent'.

22 MAY
2011 – The dogfight to stay up

When the final day of the 2010/11 season kicked off, there were two relegation places to be filled and five teams that might fill them.

Wigan, Blackpool and Birmingham had 39 points; Blackburn and Wolves – who were playing each other at Molineux – had 40. The winners at Wolves would be safe; the other three could win and still go down – or lose and stay up. They were all away from home, Wigan at Stoke, Blackpool at champions Manchester United and Birmingham at Spurs.

At half-time, the matches involving Wigan and Birmingham were goalless, and Blackpool were drawing 1–1 at Manchester United. Wolves were collapsing: 3–0 down to Blackburn, who looked safe. Wigan and Wolves were in the relegation places, but Birmingham and Blackpool were above them by the slenderest of goal-difference margins.

In the next extraordinary 45 minutes goals flew in as teams moved in and out of the relegation places. First Spurs scored against Birmingham – enough to drop them into the bottom three and lift Wolves out.

Then Blackpool strode nearer to safety when Gary Taylor-Fletcher put them 2–1 ahead at Old Trafford, but only five minutes later Anderson equalized:

although, as things stood, Blackpool were still safe.

At Molineux, a Wolves recovery started, Jamie O'Hara reducing Blackburn's lead to 3–1. Even though Wolves were still behind, the improvement in goal difference could be decisive.

With Manchester United dominant at Old Trafford, Blackpool cracked. When the unfortunate Ian Evatt sliced a cross into his own net it dropped Blackpool back into the bottom three, lifting Birmingham and Wigan nearer to safety.

Grateful to United, Wigan then helped themselves as Hugo Rodallega scored at Stoke. Within seconds Craig Gardner's goal for Birmingham made it 1–1 at Spurs, pushing Wolves back into the bottom three with Blackpool. But Birmingham's advantage was gossamer-thin and would be wiped out by one Wolves goal.

Blackpool now knew they had to draw level at Manchester United, but Michael Owen's 81st-minute goal made it 4–2 to United. Now who would go down with Blackpool – Birmingham or Wolves?

In the 87th minute Stephen Hunt curled in brilliantly for Wolves; their points tally and goal difference were now identical to Birmingham's, but Wolves had scored more goals. Birmingham had to score. Instead they conceded; Roman Pavlyuchenko's injury-time strike for Spurs was the last extraordinary twist.

Birmingham and Blackpool went down, while Wigan and Wolves survived perhaps the greatest relegation battle in Premier League history.

Also on this day

1999 Newcastle lost the FA Cup Final for the second year running as Manchester United completed the league and cup double with a 2–0 win.

2003 Gareth Southgate scored after 36 seconds and England won a friendly 2–1 in South Africa.

2004 Manchester United won the FA Cup with a 3–0 win over Millwall, for whom Curtis Weston, aged 17 years and 119 days, became the youngest ever player in an FA Cup Final.

2011 Carlo Ancelotti was sacked by Chelsea.

23 MAY
2002 – Saipan

Saipan is a tiny island in the western Pacific; in 2002 it became the centre of a story that dominated the build-up to the World Cup Finals.

The FA of Ireland had chosen Saipan as the perfect place to begin their preparations, a relaxing venue for some gentle training before moving to Japan to start the serious work for their opening game against Nigeria.

Ireland's captain and best player was Roy Keane, a world-class midfielder in a squad largely made up of good but not great players. Keane could be brilliant, inspirational, confrontational and unpredictable.

Keane had frequently argued that the FAI's arrangements for their players were inferior to those he was used to at Manchester United; he was unimpressed by the facilities in Saipan. After a row in training, Keane decided to go home. The FAI even went as far as calling up Colin Healy as a replacement – before the captain changed his mind and decided to stay.

It might have ended there, but Keane did an interview with the *Irish Times* in which he outlined exactly what he perceived to be amateurish about the FAI. He told the newspaper, 'I'm not being a prima donna. I came over here to do well, and I want people around me to want to do well. I'm banging my head against a brick wall regarding certain issues about this trip. The training pitch, travel arrangements, getting through the airport when we were leaving, it's the combination of things.'

Ireland's manager, Mick McCarthy, decided to confront Keane with the article in a team meeting. The effect was incendiary as Keane was reported to have exploded at his manager saying: 'I didn't rate you as a player, I don't rate you as a manager and I don't rate you as a person. The only reason I have any dealings with you is that somehow you are the manager of my country.' He threw in several expletives for good measure.

This time there was no coming back; McCarthy told the media, 'I cannot and will not tolerate that level of abuse being thrown at me so I sent him home.' He continued, 'I am happy to go to the World Cup one man down, rather than with a man who shows utter disregard and disrespect for me.'

Later Ireland's Jason McAteer revealed that in the seconds after Keane's rant – when the atmosphere was at its most poisonous – substitute goalkeeper Dean Kiely reduced the room to fits of laughter by joking, 'Mick, if you want I can do a job in midfield.'

Also on this day

1996 England played their first ever match in China, winning 3–0 in a friendly in Beijing as part of their preparations for Euro 96.

2006 Tomáš Rosický joined Arsenal from Borussia Dortmund for £7m.

2007 Filippo Inzaghi scored twice as Liverpool were beaten in the final of the Champions League 2–1 by AC Milan in Athens. Dirk Kuyt scored a late consolation for Liverpool.

24 MAY
1996 – Vialli checks in

In the mid-1990s the Premier League was beginning to establish itself as an attractive destination for some of Europe's top players. Éric Cantona, Jürgen Klinsmann, Dennis Bergkamp, David Ginola and Juninho were at the forefront of the first wave to choose England.

But when one of Italy's top players decided to leave Serie A and move to England, it was a watershed moment for the growing credibility of the Premier League.

Gianluca Vialli was among the greatest Italian strikers of his generation. When he'd moved from Sampdoria to Juventus in 1992, it had been for a world record fee. He'd played at the World Cup and European Championship, and only two days before arriving in England had completed his set of winner's medals from all three UEFA competitions, helping Juventus beat Ajax in the Champions League Final. Vialli was a superstar.

The striker had his pick of clubs, but chose to become Ruud Gullit's first signing at Chelsea. There's no doubt that working with Gullit, a former European Footballer of the Year and AC Milan star, was a major factor in Vialli's decision. If Gullit thought the Premier League and Chelsea were good enough, then few players would argue.

Within weeks Vialli was joined at Stamford Bridge by Roberto Di Matteo from Lazio and Gianfranco Zola from Parma. Ironically, it was Zola's arrival that made life at Chelsea difficult for Vialli. A hamstring injury sidelined Vialli, and Zola's performances in the striking role were so good that Vialli couldn't get back in the team.

Despite being used mainly as a substitute, choosing to stay not only endeared Vialli to the Chelsea fans, but allowed him to take over as Chelsea's player-manager in February 1998 after Gullit's shock departure.

When he retired from playing, Vialli had scored 40 goals for Chelsea in 87 games and won the FA Cup. As Chelsea manager he won the League Cup, the European Cup Winners' Cup and took them into the Champions League for the first time.

Also on this day

2000 Steve McManaman became the first English player to score for a non-English team in the Champions League Final, as Real Madrid beat Valencia 3–0 in Paris.

2001 Seven months after resigning as England manager, Kevin Keegan returned to manage Manchester City.

2004 Despite earning qualification for the Champions League, Liverpool sacked manager Gérard Houllier.

2008 Three days after losing the Champions League Final to Manchester United on penalties, Chelsea sacked manager Avram Grant.

2009 After helping to keep Sunderland in the Premier League, Ricky Sbragia resigned as manager of the club to return to his job as chief scout.

2009 Newcastle were relegated from the Premier League after a 1–0 defeat at Aston Villa.

2015 Hull City were relegated after they drew 0–0 with Manchester United and Newcastle beat West Ham 2–0. After their match, West Ham announced that Sam Allardyce would not have his contract as manager renewed.

2015 Goal of the Season – Jack Wilshere scored it for Arsenal against West Bromwich Albion at the Emirates Stadium.

25 MAY
2005 – Liverpool and the miracle of Istanbul

'I've never seen a game like that. There has never been a better European Cup final.' Jamie Carragher was probably right; the 2005 Champions League Final will take some beating.

It was to be Liverpool's first European Cup Final since the appalling night of

Heysel in 1985, proof of their return to the elite, after years in the shadow cast by Manchester United.

There seemed good reason to think that Liverpool's success was somehow predestined. The late Gerrard thunderbolt against Olympiakos, the brilliant Luis García strike against Juventus, the legend of the 'ghost goal' against Chelsea. Liverpool fans believed their name was on the cup.

By half-time you could have forgiven UEFA's engraver for spelling out the name of AC Milan and leaving early. Liverpool had been utterly outplayed; Milan scored in the first minute through Paolo Maldini and Hernán Crespo added two more.

There are stories that Liverpool heard the Milan players celebrating at half-time or that the defiant singing of the Liverpool fans inspired their team. Jamie Carragher later revealed in his autobiography what actually happened in the dressing room. 'The thought of going home a laughing stock disturbed me,' he wrote. 'It would have felt like the whole city, the whole country, even the whole world was taking the mickey out of us.'

Carragher described how the cool tactical analysis of manager Rafa Benítez encouraged the team. 'Privately, he must have felt the same as us, but the speed with which he made a series of tactical switches showed how sharp he still was.'

Steve Finnan was taken off and Dietmar Hamann sent on. 'Score a goal for those fans,' was the final instruction.

Liverpool did more than that – they scored three in seven dizzying minutes. Gerrard's header had the Liverpool captain flailing his arms to exhort even more backing from the supporters. Vladimír Šmicer's shot two minutes later got Milan panicking, and then Gennaro Gattuso hauled down Gerrard for a penalty. Xabi Alonso's spot-kick was saved by Dida, but Alonso pounced on the rebound; it was 3–3.

The last half-hour of the match, and the extra-time that followed, saw both sides run themselves to exhaustion; but Liverpool goalkeeper Jerzy Dudek's remarkable double-save from Andriy Shevchenko prevented certain defeat with just three minutes left.

In the shoot-out Shevchenko and Dudek faced each other again. Liverpool led 3–2 and the Ukranian had to score. Dudek saved and Liverpool's fifth European Cup was won.

Also on this day

1995 **UEFA threatened to ban all English teams from Europe unless three clubs entered the expanded Intertoto Cup. Sheffield Wednesday, Tottenham Hotspur and Wimbledon were persuaded to do so.**

2001 **Coverage of England's easy 4–0 win over Mexico at Pride Park was**

dominated by discussions of captain David Beckham's new Mohican haircut.

2007 Tottenham Hotspur completed the £5m signing of 17-year-old Gareth Bale from Southampton.

2013 Wembley hosted the Champions League Final, which was won 2–1 by Bayern Munich against Borussia Dortmund.

26 MAY
1999 – Barcelona, Sheringham and Solkskjaer

Reaching the final of the Champions League in 1999 was a triumph for both Manchester United and English football. It was the first time an English club had reached the final of Europe's premier competition since the ban on their participation had been lifted in 1990. For United it was a first chance to be crowned champions of Europe since their only triumph in 1968.

With the league title and FA Cup already won, it was also an opportunity for Manchester United to seal an unprecedented treble.

But United were caught cold after only six minutes. Ronny Johnsen fouled Bayern's Carsten Jancker and Mario Basler scored past Peter Schmeichel. With both Paul Scholes and Roy Keane

suspended, United were struggling to make any impact on Bayern's midfield of Stefan Effenberg and Jens Jeremies, protected by Lothar Matthäus. Their threat was being smothered and Bayern were comfortable. Midway through the second half, Alex Ferguson replaced Blomqvist with Sheringham.

Any hope for Manchester United was almost snuffed out within ten minutes, Mehmet Scholl's chip bouncing off their post. Ferguson responded by sending on Ole Gunnar Solskjaer.

Time favoured Bayern but, crucially, luck favoured United when Jancker's overhead kick hit the bar – there were three minutes to play.

United threw everything at Bayern's goal. As the fourth official held up his board indicating three minutes of injury-time, United won a throw-in deep in Bayern territory – half-cleared, it led to a corner. United's goalkeeper Schmeichel came up in order to unsettle the Bayern defence – it worked. The ball fell to Giggs, whose mis-hit shot was diverted into the net by Sheringham. Bayern's lead, which had lasted for 85 minutes, had gone.

Suddenly Bayern's discipline and belief failed them. Desperately needing the final whistle, they conceded another corner. Beckham delivered, Sheringham flicked at it with his head, and Solskjaer applied the finish.

The body of Bayern defender Sammy Kuffour heaved with uncontrollable tears; United had pulled off surely the greatest injury-time comeback in football history.

Until they had come off the substitutes' bench in Barcelona, Sheringham and Solskjaer had scored just one Champions League goal between them that season; in the space of two minutes they had scored one each. As Alex Ferguson said immediately after the game, 'Football, eh? Bloody hell!'

Also on this day

2001 **Teddy Sheringham rejoined Tottenham Hotspur after four seasons with Manchester United.**

2004 **Despite having said that he would never play for them, Alan Smith left Leeds for Manchester United in a £7m deal.**

2007 **Nine months after dropping David Beckham from his plans, England manager Steve McLaren named him in his squad for England's match against Brazil, their first at the new Wembley.**

27 MAY
2011 – The Celtic Nations Cup

When it ceased to exist in 1984, the Home Championship between England, Scotland, Wales and Northern Ireland had been a staple of British football for a century. Its demise came due to falling attendances, a reluctance to participate on the part of the English FA, increasing hooliganism and the political situation in Northern Ireland, which had caused the cancellation of the 1981 tournament.

After years of playing only occasional fixtures against each other, the Scottish, Welsh and Northern Irish FAs were keen to revive a formal tournament; the English were not. In 2006 the Northern Ireland manager Lawrie Sanchez suggested replacing England with the Republic of Ireland, saying, 'There's a lot in it for us, for Wales and Scotland, but not a lot in it for England.' Two years later, with the Republic of Ireland on board, an agreement was reached for a Celtic Cup.

After postponing plans to play in 2009 because of World Cup qualifying commitments, it was decided to play every two years from 2011. The Republic of Ireland were to be the first hosts, then Wales.

Dublin's new Aviva Stadium, with a capacity of 52,000, was the venue and the first game was between the Irish hosts and Wales in February 2011. Ireland won 3–0 in front of a disappointing crowd of under 20,000, around 5000 fewer than had attended Ireland's previous match – a home friendly against Norway.

The following day fewer than 19,000 saw Scotland's 3–0 win over Northern Ireland. The tournament was under way – though not exactly with a bang. The remaining four matches were to be played in May, when the organizers hoped that better weather would swell the crowds.

But on 24 May just over 12,000 watched the Republic beat Northern Ireland 5–0, while the following day only 6000 saw Scotland beat Wales 3–1.

Crowds had dwindled with each game as the tournament failed to capture the public's imagination. When, on 27 May, the Aviva Stadium welcomed just 529 people for Wales's 2–0 win over Northern Ireland, there was no hiding that the tournament was failing.

Two days later 17,000 watched the Republic of Ireland beat Scotland 1–0 – but everyone knew there would be no Celtic Nations Cup in 2013.

Also on this day

1998 Aged 18 years and 165 days, Michael Owen scored in a win over Morocco to break Tommy Lawton's record and become the youngest player ever to score for England.

2004 Roy Keane made his return to international football two years after walking out of the Republic of Ireland's World Cup squad, playing in a 1–0 win over Romania.

2006 Gareth Bale became the youngest player ever to represent Wales, playing against Trinidad and Tobago in a friendly at the age of 16 years and 315 days.

2009 Samuel Eto'o and Lionel Messi scored the goals as Barcelona beat Manchester United 2–0 in the Champions League Final in Rome.

28 MAY
2011 – United's Wembley final

The 2011 Champions League Final between Manchester United and Barcelona was the sixth to be staged at Wembley and the first since it was rebuilt. It came 43 years after United had won their first European Cup at the same venue with a famous victory over Benfica. But Barcelona also had fond memories of London; Wembley had been the venue for their first European Cup win in 1992.

Hopes were high that, on English soil, United might prevail and take the chance to avenge their defeat at the hands of Barcelona in the final of 2009.

United started well, pressing Barcelona and disrupting their much-admired passing game. Goalkeeper Víctor Valdés had to be alert to foil Wayne Rooney, while Lionel Messi had Park Ji-Sung snapping at his heels every time he got possession.

After ten minutes the tide started to turn. Barcelona began to enjoy having the ball at their feet, their 'tiki-taka' football expending United's energy and putting them under constant pressure; Messi and David Villa both went close.

After 27 minutes Barcelona's goal came, Xavi's pass finding Pedro, who had back-pedalled into space away from Nemanja Vidić and lashed a low shot past Edwin van der Sar.

United's response was quick and brilliant. Rooney exchanged passes with Michael Carrick on the right touchline and drifted infield to the Barcelona penalty area. Another quick exchange, this time with Ryan Giggs, opened the Spanish defence and Rooney's finish curled beyond Valdes.

In the second half United were getting only scraps of possession as their defence worked overtime against Barcelona's relentless attack. One loss of concentration allowed Messi to advance and shoot from just outside the box; it wasn't a great attempt but van der Sar, playing his final game for United, was beaten low to his left.

Now Barcelona turned the screw, denying United any hope of getting back in the game when David Villa curled a brilliant third goal. The last 20 minutes were painful for United as Barcelona left them starved of the ball to seal a comprehensive victory.

'In my time as manager, it's the best team we've faced,' said Sir Alex Ferguson. 'Nobody's given us a hiding like that, but they deserve it. They mesmerize you with their passing and we never controlled Messi. But many people have said that.'

Also on this day

1994 John Stones was born.

1996 England's players, in the Far East as part of their preparation for Euro 96, were accused of vandalism and drunkenness on board their plane bringing them back from Hong Kong.

2003 The Champions League Final was played at Old Trafford, and won by AC Milan against Juventus on penalties.

2014 Mauricio Pochettino was appointed manager of Tottenham Hotspur.

29 MAY
1997 – Al-Fayed buys Fulham

Fulham had just ended the most miserable three years in their history. The club that was associated with Johnny Haynes, Alan Mullery, Bobby Moore, Rodney Marsh and George Best had fallen into the fourth tier of

English football for the first time, with attendances dropping below 5000.

Their Craven Cottage stadium was a crumbling edifice on the north bank of the River Thames, known as a landmark on the course of the University Boat Race as much as for the football that was played there.

Under the chairmanship of Jimmy Hill and the management of Micky Adams, Fulham were promoted into the third tier in the spring of 1997 – but the ambitions of the club were about to change.

Mohamed Al-Fayed, the high-profile Egyptian owner of the west London department store Harrods, bought the club for £30m. He pledged to turn it into the 'Manchester United of the south', and to take Fulham into the Premier League in five seasons. They did it in four.

Within weeks of the Al-Fayed takeover, Kevin Keegan and Ray Wilkins replaced the unlucky Adams. In 1999 they won promotion to the second tier; then under Jean Tigana they made the Premier League in 2001 with 101 points – a record-breaking tally for the second tier.

As the Premier League became richer, the prospect of Fulham ever actually rivalling Manchester United became more remote. However, Craven Cottage was vastly improved and a new training ground built.

Under Roy Hodgson, Fulham married Premier League success – a highest ever seventh-place finish in 2009 – with European glory, as they reached the Europa League Final in 2010.

Al-Fayed was often eccentric and was occasionally ridiculed. His insistence on placing a gaudy statue of Michael Jackson outside the stadium was a particular bugbear for Fulham fans. Nevertheless, for 16 years – 12 of them in the Premier League – Fulham flourished under his ownership.

In July 2013 he sold the club to the American businessman Shahid Khan. Within a year Fulham had been relegated.

Also on this day

1993 Teddy Sheringham made his debut and Ian Wright scored his first England goal as Graham Taylor's side drew their World Cup qualifier in Poland 1–1. Afterwards Taylor said that some of his team had played 'like headless chickens'.

1994 Germany suffered their first home defeat for six years as they lost 2–0 in Hanover to the Republic of Ireland in a friendly. Tony Cascarino and Gary Kelly were Ireland's goalscorers.

2009 With an average age of 21, the youngest Welsh side in history won 1–0 against Estonia in the first international played at Llanelli's Parc y Scarlets.

2013 England drew 1–1 with the Republic of Ireland in a friendly at Wembley in the first meeting of the nations since 1995, when crowd trouble forced the abandonment of a game in Dublin.

30 MAY
2012 – Rodgers or Martínez for Anfield?

From the moment Liverpool announced that they were looking to replace Kenny Dalglish, there were four managers in contention.

Liverpool's former boss Rafa Benítez enjoyed support among many fans, and was still out of work having been sacked by Inter Milan. The highly regarded André Villas-Boas had recently been dismissed by Chelsea. Not far from Anfield, Roberto Martínez had been impressing on limited resources at Wigan. Swansea boss Brendan Rodgers had got the club promoted into the Premier League in his first season in charge, and had then established his team as one to watch in their first top-flight campaign.

Liverpool's owner John W. Henry and chairman Tom Werner quietly distanced themselves from reappointing Benítez. His undoubted success had been built on investing in players at their peak; Henry and Werner preferred a manager with a track record of improving young talent. There was contact with Villas-Boas, but Liverpool didn't pursue their interest.

Instead, they sought permission from both Swansea and Wigan to speak to their managers. Wigan's owner Dave Whelan was quick to recommend Martínez: 'I think he's wonderful, the best manager I have ever worked with,' he said. 'I'd love to keep him but if he wants to move to Liverpool I will have to say good luck.'

In contrast Swansea said little, and Rodgers insisted that he'd be happy to stay in Wales.

When Dave Whelan revealed that Martínez had cut short a holiday to meet Henry and Werner, it seemed the way was clear for him to be appointed. Whelan said, 'He's doing what I gave him permission to do. He has to listen to what they are offering. I've asked Roberto if he will make his mind up as quickly as possible. I'd expect to hear back from him in the next 48 hours or so.'

Privately, Liverpool were incensed at the daily updates on their appointment process coming from Whelan. Their managing director Ian Ayre later said, 'We conducted ourselves properly at all times. It is disappointing, then, that Dave Whelan felt the need to run the kind of sideshow he conducted via various media outlets.'

Martínez left his meeting in Miami with no agreement, and within a week Brendan Rodgers was the new Liverpool manager. 'We make no secret of the fact we spoke with Roberto Martínez, but that is all we did,' said Ayre. 'The only person who was made any offer is Brendan Rodgers.'

Twelve months later Roberto Martínez was the new manager of Everton.

Also on this day

1997 Shay Given joined Newcastle from Blackburn for £1.5m.

2006 Theo Walcott, aged 17 years and 75 days, became England's youngest ever player, making his debut in a 3–1 win over Hungary.

2009 Chelsea, managed by Guus Hiddink, won the FA Cup with a 2–1 win over Everton despite conceding a goal to Louis Saha after 25 seconds – the fastest ever scored in an FA Cup Final.

2013 Mark Hughes was appointed manager of Stoke City.

2015 Arsenal won the FA Cup for a record 12th time with a 4–0 win over Aston Villa; it was Arsène Wenger's sixth FA Cup win as manager, equalling a record set in 1920 by Villa's secretary-manager George Ramsay.

31 MAY
1998 – Hoddle omits Gascoigne

In May 1998 England manager Glenn Hoddle took 30 players to the La Manga resort in Spain as part of their preparations for the World Cup Finals. From there they would fly in and out of Casablanca to play friendlies against Morocco and Belgium; and then Hoddle would tell each player in turn whether or not they had made the final squad of 22 for the finals in France.

In the weeks building up to the trip to La Manga, Paul Gascoigne had been photographed falling drunkenly out of a restaurant and, a few days later, eating a kebab in Soho at 2 a.m.

David Davies, then the FA's director of communications, later recalled how, in La Manga, Gascoigne had been upset and preoccupied by his disintegrating relationship with his wife Sheryl, had been drunk, and had been late for the team bus taking them to the airport for the trip to Morocco.

Hoddle decided that he couldn't pick Gascoigne for the World Cup, writing in his autobiography: 'Physically he wasn't 100 per cent, mentally he was all over the place.'

When Gascoigne was called to Hoddle's room to be told the news of his omission, he exploded. Davies later wrote that Gascoigne 'kicked a chair over and punched a lamp, showering the carpet with glass'.

Hoddle recalled: 'He had snapped. He was ranting, swearing and slurring his words. He was acting like a man possessed. I stood there and he turned as if to go, then he came back with a barrage of abuse.'

Once back in England, Gascoigne spoke to the *Sun* newspaper. 'I wanted Regan [Gascoigne's son] to see me play for England in the World Cup – now I don't know if he'll ever see me in an England shirt again. That breaks my heart.'

Gascoigne was correct; his England career – with all its tears, pranks, laughs and goals – was over.

Also on this day

1995 Chelsea pulled off a major transfer coup by signing Ruud Gullit from Sampdoria. Gullit later revealed that one of the attractions of Chelsea was that they wore white socks, which he considered lucky.

2000 Steven Gerrard won his first England cap in a 2–0 win over Ukraine at Wembley.

2000 Fabien Barthez joined Manchester United from Monaco for £7.8m.

2004 Claudio Ranieri was sacked as manager of Chelsea.

2006 Andriy Shevchenko joined Chelsea from AC Milan for a British record £30.8m.

2011 Paul Scholes announced his retirement after 675 games and 150 goals. He reversed his decision in January 2012 and played a further 42 games for Manchester United, scoring five more goals.

June

1 JUNE
2007 – England and Beckham are back at Wembley

Almost the first thing that Steve McLaren did on taking over as England manager after the 2006 World Cup was to tell David Beckham that he would not be considering him for selection. Beckham was 31 and McLaren said he wanted to move in 'a different direction', prompting the headline 'Mac the Knife'.

Beckham refused to retire from international football, but for 11 months, during which time he announced an impending move from Real Madrid to LA Galaxy, Beckham was an international has-been, marooned on 94 caps.

But with McLaren's team beginning to struggle in their qualifying campaign for Euro 2008 and castigated for a dreadful showing in their last match in Andorra, the England manager performed a U-turn and selected Beckham for a match against Brazil, a friendly to mark the opening of the new Wembley Stadium after a six-year rebuild.

In the build-up to the game Beckham described himself as relaxed and then rolled back the years with a man-of-the-match performance, setting up a goal for new captain John Terry before being substituted to a standing ovation.

Brazil equalized in the last minute but Beckham had done enough. After the game McLaren, who seemed to have changed his tune, told the press that 'when he's playing well there's no better right-sided player in the world'.

Beckham went on to make another 20 appearances for England, captaining the side for a final time in a Trinidad and Tobago friendly exactly 12 months after this recall, before winning his 115th and last cap in 2010.

Steve McLaren was not so fortunate. He lasted just eight more matches as manager before being sacked following England's failure to qualify for the European Championship Finals in Austria and Switzerland. He had lasted just 16 months and 18 games in charge, the shortest reign of any full-time England manager.

Also on this day

1993 England manager Graham Taylor made headlines by expressing concern at how Paul Gascoigne 'refuels' between matches.

2000 Martin O'Neill left Leicester to take over as manager of Celtic.

2009 Carlo Ancelotti was named as Chelsea manager to succeed Guus Hiddink.

2011 Sam Allardyce was appointed as manager of West Ham.

2 JUNE
2004 – Chelsea appoint the Special One

'The Special One'. It's not the only José Mourinho expression to have entered the English football lexicon, but it was the first and it's the most enduring.

Six days after winning the Champions League with FC Porto, Mourinho was introduced to English football at Chelsea. 'I have top players and I'm sorry, we have a top manager. Please do not call me arrogant because what I say is true. I'm European champion, I'm not one out of the bottle; I think I'm a special one.'

At 41, Mourinho's pedigree was obvious; not only for that Champions League win over Monaco, beating Manchester United in the second round, but for having won the UEFA Cup with Porto too, defeating Celtic in 2003. There were also two championships and a cup win in Portugal, making five trophies in two seasons.

Then there was the back story that endeared him to the English media, particularly that Mourinho had worked as an interpreter for Bobby Robson at Sporting Lisbon, Porto and Barcelona and that Robson had offered him the assistant manager's job at Newcastle in 2000, even tempting Mourinho with the promise of allowing him to take over the top job after two seasons.

Chelsea had been the property of Roman Abramovich for almost 12 months but the manager Abramovich had inherited, Claudio Ranieri, had failed to deliver a trophy.

Yes, Chelsea had been Premier League runners-up in 2003/04, their highest league finish since 1955, but there was an 11-point gap between them and Arsenal, and Ranieri's infamous tinkering had probably been the last straw when some strange substitutions allowed Monaco's ten men to score two late goals for a decisive 3–1 first-leg lead in the Champions League semi-final.

Perhaps if Monaco had beaten Mourinho's Porto in that final in Gelsenkirchen then their manager, the 35-year-old former Chelsea player Didier Deschamps, might have been the obvious candidate to be approached to replace Ranieri at Stamford Bridge; but Chelsea and Mourinho seemed made for each other.

Also on this day

1993 England lost 2–0 to Norway in Oslo, leaving qualification for the 1994 World Cup in the balance.

1999 Mark Bosnich joined Manchester United from Aston Villa.

2000 Jimmy Floyd Hasselbaink signed for Chelsea from Atlético Madrid for £15m.

2007 Ryan Giggs played his last international for Wales, a 0–0 draw with the Czech Republic.

2008 Sven-Göran Eriksson was sacked by Manchester City.

2011 Mark Hughes resigned as manager of Fulham.

2012 Paul Lambert left Norwich to take over at Aston Villa.

2015 FIFA president Sepp Blatter unexpectedly announced his intention to resign after 17 years in the job. His announcement came only four days after her had been re-elected as president for a fifth term. Blatter's success in the election had come despite senior FIFA officials having been arrested as part of investigations by Swiss police and the FBI into allegations of corruption and bribery.

3 JUNE
2013 – Chelsea appoint the Happy One

The timing turned out to be perfect. In November 2012 when Chelsea sacked Roberto Di Matteo they had made it clear that the appointment of Rafa Benítez was as an 'interim manager' – to the end of the season and no longer.

If that was designed to tempt Pep Guardiola to Stamford Bridge at the end of his season-long sabbatical, it didn't work; in January Guardiola committed to taking over Bayern Munich.

In April, Real Madrid's José Mourinho was dropping obvious hints about his desire to work in England again. After losing a Champions League semi-final to Borussia Dortmund, Mourinho had told a critical Spanish press that 'I know in England I am loved. I know I am loved by some clubs, especially one.'

In May, Real had seen enough of Mourinho and announced his departure at the end of that season. 'Nobody's been sacked, it's a mutual agreement,' said Madrid president Florentino Pérez.

Perhaps Manchester United might have moved for Mourinho, but Sir Alex Ferguson had recommended David Moyes as his successor and no-one at Old Trafford was about to argue.

Manchester City had sacked Roberto Mancini a week before that Madrid announcement, but Manuel Pellegrini was their choice. There seemed little doubt that Mourinho and Chelsea were inexorably coming together again.

Little doubt, that is, so long as the bitterness of Mourinho's sacking by Abramovich in 2007 could be forgotten when they met. Chelsea supporters needn't have worried: 'I met the boss and in five minutes we decided straight away. I asked the boss, "Do you want me back?" and the boss asked me, "Do you want to come back?" The decision was made.'

When Mourinho met the press a week after his appointment he was inevitably asked if he was still the Special One. 'I am the Happy One,' was his reply.

Also on this day

1995 Gary Neville made his England debut in a 2–1 win over Japan at Wembley.

2003 Sven-Göran Eriksson was criticized for his multiple substitutions that resulted in four different England players (Michael Owen, Gary Neville, Emile Heskey and Jamie Carragher) wearing the captain's armband in a 2–1 friendly win over Serbia and Montenegro.

2004 Jacques Santini was appointed manager of Spurs.

2009 Steve Bruce left Wigan to take the manager's job at Sunderland.

2010 Rafa Benítez left his job at Liverpool.

4 JUNE
1993 – Glenn Hoddle arrives at Chelsea

The 1992/93 season had been a fairly typical one for Chelsea. After a poor run they had sacked manager Ian Porterfield in February, appointed former player Dave Webb until the end of the season and rallied to finish 11th of the 22 teams in the new Premier League.

There had even been a run to the quarter-final of the League Cup before defeat to Crystal Palace.

With chairman Ken Bates having succeeded in a long legal battle to win back the ownership of the stadium and attendances slightly up to an average of almost 19,000, there were plans to build a new North Stand. Promising youngsters Craig Burley, Graham Stuart, Eddie Newton and Frank Sinclair were becoming established alongside favourite Dennis Wise. They even had a Russian goalkeeper in Dmitri Kharine replacing a fading Dave Beasant.

What Chelsea craved was European football and a major trophy, neither of which had come their way in over 20 years.

Glenn Hoddle had been arguably the most gifted English footballer of his generation and at 35 was still a useful player, but it was as a manager that Ken Bates wanted him. In two-and-a-half years at Swindon, Hoddle had guided the club to promotion into the Premier League in a dramatic 4–3 win over Leicester in the play-off final.

Just three days after leading his promoted team on an open-top bus tour of Swindon, Hoddle was installed as player-manager at Chelsea. It was the appointment that set Chelsea's ball rolling.

Helped by more than £25m of investment from millionaire supporter and director Matthew Harding, Hoddle took Chelsea to the FA Cup Final in his first season and back into Europe.

Chelsea soon found that with Hoddle in charge and with European football on offer they could attract an entirely different calibre of player. Ruud Gullit was the first; and if you have Gullit you can get Vialli, and if you have Vialli you can get Zola, and if you have Zola you can get into the Champions League, and if you're in the Champions League you just might get bought by a Russian billionaire.

Also on this day

1997 Arsenal signed Emmanuel Petit from Monaco.

2008 Mark Hughes resigned from Blackburn Rovers and took over at Manchester City.

2011 Kevin Kilbane played his 66th consecutive competitive international for the Republic of Ireland, and his last. A back injury later ruled him out of Euro 2012.

2012 Chelsea completed the signing of Eden Hazard from Lille for £32m.

2012 Dick Advocaat announced that he had reversed an earlier decision to retire from club management and agreed to continue as manager of Sunderland.

5 JUNE
2008 – Luka Modrić signs for Spurs

Spurs were ahead of the game when they signed Luka Modrić just before the European Championships of 2008.

Already a title winner with Dinamo Zagreb, the will-o'-the-wisp playmaker had first come to the attention of a wider audience as the youngest member of Croatia's 2006 World Cup squad. Soon afterwards a key role and a first international goal in a victory over Italy in Livorno confirmed him as one to watch.

A second championship followed and by the time he was helping to knock Steve McLaren's England out of the European Championship in a qualifier at Wembley in November 2007, Modrić was on the list of Europe's most wanted.

Spurs and their manager Juande Ramos acted first with an irresistible bid of £16.5m in April 2008, with the deal to be finalized at the end of the season before the European Championship in Austria and Switzerland. There, the 22-year-old Modrić was his country's outstanding performer as they came within a penalty shoot-out of reaching the semi-final.

A change of manager from Ramos to Harry Redknapp helped Modrić after a difficult start at Spurs, and soon he was delighting fans with his vision and touch and by scoring a rare Tottenham winner against Chelsea.

In 2010/11 Modrić and Gareth Bale were Tottenham's inspiration in a thrilling Champions League campaign that featured victories over both Inter and AC Milan, before a quarter-final defeat to Real Madrid.

Chelsea did all they could to persuade Spurs to sell in 2011, with Tottenham chairman Daniel Levy, stubborn as ever, reported to have rejected a £40m bid. Modrić stayed, but without Champions League football in 2011/12 it seemed certain that his spell at Spurs was nearing its end.

When Real Madrid came calling in August 2012 Levy relented and Modrić left White Hart Lane with a record of 17 goals and many more assists in 160 Tottenham games.

Also on this day

1999 Matt Elliott was sent off as Scotland were held to a draw in the Faroe Islands.

2001 Bryan Robson quit as Middlesbrough manager after seven years.

2002 Steve Staunton became the first Irish player to reach 100 caps as Robbie Keane scored in a 1–1 draw with eventual World Cup winners Germany in Ibaraki.

2005 A record crowd of 29,092 watched England's women beat Finland at the City of Manchester Stadium.

2012 Michael Laudrup was appointed manager at Swansea City.

2013 Roberto Martínez took over at Everton.

6 JUNE
2005 – Manchester United sign Edwin van der Sar

Replacing Peter Schmeichel at Old Trafford was never likely to be straightforward, but nobody could have anticipated that it would take six years to find a really adequate alternative. Alex Ferguson used nine different goalkeepers in that period, none of whom were convincing. Bosnich, van der Gouw, Taibi, Barthez, Carroll, Ricardo, Howard, Goram and Rachubka all pulled on the gloves; of those nine, Fabien Barthez was arguably the best, Massimo Taibi surely the worst.

As Schmeichel was preparing to leave Manchester in 1999, so Edwin van der Sar was packing his bags in Amsterdam where he had won both the Champions League and UEFA Cup with Ajax. United made enquiries, but decided to pursue Aston Villa's Mark Bosnich instead. The Australian Bosnich, who had started his career at Old Trafford, was available on a free transfer, while Juventus paid £5m for the Dutchman.

In his autobiography Sir Alex Ferguson conceded that not signing van der Sar in 1999 was one of his biggest regrets. No doubt Ferguson was as surprised as anybody when in 2001 van der Sar, his place in Turin under pressure from Gianluigi Buffon, left Juventus for newly promoted Fulham.

Four outstanding seasons at Craven Cottage convinced Ferguson that this time he had to act and, approaching his 35th birthday, van der Sar finally became a Manchester United player.

At United van der Sar seemed ageless. In six seasons at the club he played 264 games and won the Premier League title four times, setting a new record of 14 games and 1311 minutes without conceding; there were also two League Cup winner's medals and the Club World Cup. But van der Sar's finest hour came in the Luzhniki Stadium against Chelsea when, in the late-night Moscow rain, he pointed to the left but dived to the right to save Nicolas Anelka's penalty in the shoot-out and won the Champions League for Manchester United.

Also on this day

1995 Bobby Robson accepted that he couldn't break his contract with FC Porto and declined Arsenal's offer to succeed the sacked George Graham as manager.

2006 Gareth Southgate took the manager's job at Middlesbrough, replacing Steve McLaren.

2007 Michael Owen broke the England scoring record for competitive internationals with his 23rd in a 3–0 win over Estonia.

2012 Following Paul Lambert's resignation, Chris Hughton was appointed manager of Norwich City.

7 JUNE
2002 – England 1 Argentina 0: redemption for Beckham

In 1998 David Beckham, after a right-footed flick at Diego Simeone, had been sent off against Argentina in an epic World Cup second-round match that England eventually lost on penalties.

Castigated for his petulance and blamed for the defeat, the following season Beckham was repeatedly booed at games away from Old Trafford.

Bit by bit over three years Beckham won the public round, finally cementing his place as a footballing national hero with the dramatic late goal against Greece that secured England's place at the 2002 World Cup Finals in Japan and South Korea.

It seemed appropriate that when the draw was made for those finals, England and Beckham would be paired with

Argentina, their conquerors not only in 1998 but also, unforgettably, in 1986.

England's campaign didn't start well; a barely deserved draw against Sweden left Sven-Göran Eriksson's team fearful that defeat to Argentina would leave them on the brink of elimination in the group stage.

In Sapporo Beckham faced Simeone again. Michael Owen, as he had four years earlier, flew at the Argentine defence, seeing an early effort hit the inside of the post; Gabriel Batistuta responded with a header well saved by David Seaman.

Seconds before half-time a darting, jink of a run from Owen drew out the leg of Mauricio Pochettino; Owen fell and England were awarded a penalty by referee Pierluigi Collina.

This was the captain's moment and he didn't hesitate. With flashbulbs popping from behind Pablo Cavallero's goal Beckham placed the ball on the spot, took a few deep breaths and attacked the penalty with a low, driven shot just past the goalkeeper's left foot, almost exactly down the centre of the goal.

Elation, relief, redemption or all three? Beckham raced to the corner flag, tugging at his shirt in celebration.

Both England and Argentina drew their final group games, and the South Americans suffered their earliest exit since 1970. England beat Denmark to reach the last eight – where Ronaldinho struck for Brazil.

Also on this day

1993 Relegated Nottingham Forest sold Nigel Clough to Liverpool.

1995 Les Ferdinand joined Newcastle from QPR.

1998 Chelsea signed Brian Laudrup.

2011 Fulham appointed Martin Jol as manager.

2013 Robbie Keane broke Shay Given's national record by winning a 126th cap for the Republic of Ireland

and scored all the goals in a 3–0 win over the Faroe Islands in Dublin.

8 JUNE
1996 – Football's coming home

'Thirty years of hurt, never stopped me dreaming.' The Lightning Seeds, David Baddiel and Frank Skinner provided the soundtrack, and Switzerland provided the opposition for the opening game of Euro 96. It was the start of the first major tournament held on English soil since 1966.

In November 1995 Terry Venables's England side had come from behind to beat Switzerland in a friendly at Wembley in front of fewer than 30,000 people. After that game the Swiss manager Roy Hodgson, who had led them to qualification for the finals, stood down to concentrate on his job at Inter Milan where he had already taken charge.

This game against the Swiss was different: sunshine, a full house, an opening ceremony, a mixture of expectation and some scepticism from a public still digesting details of a Hong Kong drinking session for which England's squad accepted 'collective responsibility'.

It seems unlikely now, but Alan Shearer's place in the side was in doubt. He had not scored an England goal in 12 games and Les Ferdinand and Robbie Fowler were waiting in the wings.

Venables kept faith with Shearer and the Blackburn striker took his opportunity, receiving a pass from Paul Ince to smash a right-footed shot into the roof of the net midway through the first half: 1043 goalless minutes for England ended.

Switzerland were sharp though, and Marco Grassi hit the underside of the crossbar from no more than four yards just before half-time.

After the break England began to struggle with the pace of Johann Vogel and the presence of Kubilay Türkyilmaz: 'We were dead on our feet,' said Terry Venables afterwards.

The introduction of Nick Barmby, Steve Stone and David Platt (for an exhausted-looking Gascoigne) made no difference and with eight minutes left Grassi's flick was handled at close range by Stuart Pearce. Türkyilmaz equalized from the penalty spot.

Just as they had 30 years before, England had started a home tournament with a draw. But soon the team and the nation would be roaring as one.

Also on this day

1995 Arsenal appointed Bruce Rioch as their new manager.

1998 Sepp Blatter won the vote to become FIFA president for the first time.

2007 Manager Stuart Pearce was furious as David Bentley said he was too tired to play at the European Under-21 Championship in Holland.

2012 Steve Clarke became manager at West Bromwich Albion.

9 JUNE
1993 – Yanks 2 Planks 0

The US Cup of 1993 was supposed to be a useful taste for Brazil, Germany and England of what soccer Stateside would be like when the World Cup kicked off in America in 12 months' time.

For Germany and Brazil it probably was.

Graham Taylor had been in trouble as England manager ever since their poor showing in Sweden at the 1992 European Championship. By the time England touched down in Boston in June 1993, the World Cup qualifying campaign was going badly too.

England travelled to America immediately after failing to win either of two qualifiers away from home. First there had been a fortunate draw in Poland, then a numbing defeat in Norway.

Arguably the biggest embarrassment in England's history had come against the USA in Belo Horizonte in Brazil in the 1950 World Cup Finals. Then the US team was a collection of unknown amateurs; in 1993 they were not given credit for having improved much.

In fact, many of the Americans played in strong European leagues and Roy Wegerle was well known in England as a player with Luton, Queens Park Rangers and Coventry. Many others would make their names the following summer.

However, the States had won just one of their previous 15 internationals, and that against Saudi Arabia. Surely even an England team critically low on confidence could gain revenge for the defeat of Belo Horizonte?

Just before half-time England fell behind. Tab Ramos (Real Betis) showed good control to provide a cross that Thomas Dooley (Kaiserslautern) headed past Chris Woods into the England net.

Ian Wright missed a golden opportunity to equalize and with 18 minutes to go the ginger-haired, goatee-bearded, guitar-playing substitute Alexi Lalas rose to head in a corner and settle the game.

The watching press didn't hold back. The *Daily Express* described it as 'abject failure against a third-rate soccer nation', adding that 'English football died of shame in a coffin draped in the Stars and Stripes'. The *Daily Mirror* declared that Taylor was 'Wanted! Dead or alive – the outlaw of English football.'

For the *Sun* it was simple: 'Yanks 2 Planks 0.'

Also on this day

1998 Marcel Desailly signed for Chelsea from AC Milan for a fee of £4.6m.

2011 Liverpool spent £20m on Sunderland midfielder Jordan Henderson.

2014 Jack Colback became the first player to move from Sunderland to Newcastle since goalkeeper Lionel Pérez in 1998.

2015 West Ham appointed Slaven Bilić as their new manager.

10 JUNE
1998 – Scotland's World Cup opener

Not all fans watch every game of the World Cup, but anyone who can surely watches the World Cup's opening game.

Brazil had won the World Cup in 1994, so under FIFA rules at the time, Match One at the finals would see Brazil play in the new Stade de France. The draw in Marseille gave them Scotland.

On the morning of the match one Scottish paper covered its front page with a picture of a blue Parisian sky crossed by two white vapour trails, the Saltire looking down on Saint-Denis.

Brazil's squad included Cafu, Aldair, Dunga and Bebeto, all World Cup winners. First-timers included Rivaldo and Roberto Carlos; then there was Ronaldo, still only 21 but already twice voted World Player of the Year.

Under Craig Brown Scotland included Paul Lambert, a Champions League winner with Dortmund, there was the cultured Monaco-based John Collins, Craig Burley, who was at the peak of his powers with Celtic, and Blackburn stalwarts Colin Hendry and Kevin Gallacher.

Not all the estimated 60,000 Scots in Paris got into the stadium, but those who did saw Brazil take the lead with a fourth-minute header from César Sampaio. Scotland could have crumbled, but instead rallied, matching the Brazilians stride for stride and tackle for tackle. When Sampaio fouled Kevin Gallacher with half-time approaching, John Collins stepped up to face Taffarel from the penalty spot and held his nerve to equalize.

After half-time Jim Leighton saved from Ronaldo and Roberto Carlos and Scotland edged towards a deserved draw until the rampaging Cafu met Dunga's pass and flicked the ball on to Leighton's chest, from where it rebounded onto Tom Boyd and into the Scotland net.

Scotland had been beaten by a fluke. Brazil went on to the final where they lost to France. Unlucky Scotland went home after the group stage – again.

Also on this day

1994 Bobby Charlton was knighted.

1997 Glenn Hoddle's England won the four-team Tournoi de France despite a 2–1 defeat to Brazil.

2001 Gus Poyet moved from Chelsea to Tottenham.

2006 An own-goal helped England beat Paraguay 1–0 in Frankfurt in their opening game of the World Cup Finals.

2012 The Republic of Ireland were beaten 3–1 by Croatia in Poznań in their first match of the European Championship Finals.

2015 Newcastle appointed Steve McLaren as manager.

11 JUNE
2009 – Ronaldo: the Real deal

Real Madrid's pursuit of Cristiano Ronaldo began in earnest in the spring of 2007 when Manchester United were negotiating a new contract with his agent Jorge Mendes. Real, it was reported, were willing to top any contract offer made by United and their president Ramón Calderón said that if United were ready to sell his club would be 'first in the queue'.

Within a few weeks Ronaldo had rejected Real and a new Old Trafford contract was signed; Madrid did a £56m deal for Kaká instead and resigned themselves to not getting Ronaldo – for now.

By the time Ronaldo was preparing for Euro 2008 with Portugal, Real were circling again and United had repeatedly insisted that they would not sell him. Their confidence must have been shaken when Ronaldo gave an interview to a Brazilian journalist stating, 'I want to play for Real Madrid, but only if it's true that they are willing to pay me and Manchester United what they have been promising.'

If United were annoyed with Ronaldo, it was nothing compared to their fury with Sepp Blatter after the FIFA president's observation that Ronaldo was a victim of 'modern slavery', going on to reflect that, 'If the player wants to play somewhere else, then a solution should be found because … it's not good for the player and for the club.'

In December 2008 Sir Alex Ferguson was asked if there was an agreement between United and Real to do business: 'You don't think we'd get into a contract with that mob, do you? I wouldn't sell them a virus.'

With both the European and World Footballer of the Year awards on his shelf, Ronaldo asked to leave Manchester United at the beginning of June 2009. This time there was no persuading him to stay and the club conceded that Real Madrid would have their man, but only in return for a fee eclipsing the previous world record paid for Kaká: Ronaldo would cost them £80m.

Also on this day

1993 The Premier League gave the go-ahead for players to wear shirts with their names and squad numbers on the back.

2003 Michael Owen captained England to a 2–1 win over Slovakia, becoming England's youngest captain in a competitive game.

2005 England's women went out of Euro 2005 after a 1–0 defeat to Sweden in Blackburn.

2005 Liverpool signed Pepe Reina from Villarreal.

2008 The Portuguese FA confirmed that their manager Felipe Scolari would join Chelsea after the European Championship Finals.

2012 England drew 1–1 with France in Donetsk at Euro 2012.

12 JUNE
2000 – England 2 Portugal 3

Kevin Keegan's England had needed a fortunate play-off victory over Scotland to qualify for the European Championship Finals in Holland and Belgium. But they got no luck in the draw for the finals, pitched against Portugal, Germany and Romania. Keegan was one of the few tipping England as possible tournament winners.

There were sighs of relief when Alan Shearer's knee injury responded well to treatment and he was passed fit to partner Michael Owen in the opening game in Eindhoven against the Portuguese. With Beckham lining up for England and Luís Figo for Portugal, Keegan spoke of a battle between 'the two finest number sevens in world football'.

The early battles were conclusively won by Beckham, whose third-minute cross was headed home at close range by Paul Scholes for a goal made in Manchester. Pre-match pessimism was melting away when barely 15 minutes later another Beckham cross found Steve McManaman unmarked. England led by two.

Had England been able to hold that lead until half-time perhaps the belief would have ebbed from Portugal; instead Nuno Gomes put the ball in England's net only to be ruled offside, but Portugal took heart. Later the watching Eusébio said, 'Portugal controlled the game even when they were losing.'

Enter Eusébio's modern equivalent, Luís Figo. Allowed to drive forward from inside his own half, he unleashed a shot that deflected off Tony Adams and flew into the top corner; 2–1 and only 22 minutes played.

Under extreme pressure England were now beginning to unravel and an equalizer came before half-time, a brilliant header from João Pinto from a Rui Costa cross.

With first Michael Owen and then Steve McManaman forced off injured, England's attacking threat had dissolved and Portugal controlled the second half with Rui Costa providing the pass for Nuno Gomes to score the winning goal.

David Beckham's gesture to booing England fans as he left the pitch only deepened the gloom, as did the news that Steve McManaman would miss the last two group games. 'We'll probably have to win them both,' said Keegan.

Also on this day

1997 Jimmy Floyd Hasselbaink joined Leeds for £2m.

2001 Steve McLaren left Manchester United to become manager of Middlesbrough.

2010 In their first match at the World Cup Finals England drew 1–1 USA after a mistake by Robert Green in Rustenburg.

2011 Alex McLeish resigned as manager of Birmingham.

2014 Chelsea signed Cesc Fàbregas from Barcelona.

2015 Gareth Bale scored on his 50th appearance for his country as Wales beat Belgium 1–0 in a European Championship qualifier. The victory left Wales on the brink of a place in their first major tournament finals since 1958.

13 JUNE
2005 – The Glazers in at Old Trafford

After Sir Alex Ferguson's dispute with Manchester United's largest shareholders, Irish race-horse owners J.P. McManus and John Magnier, over part-ownership of the horse Rock of Gibraltar, the club began seeking new investment.

In 2003, Malcolm Glazer and his sons Avram, Joel and Bryan were tempted to extend their sporting interests from the Tampa Bay Buccaneers NFL franchise into English football.

From March to November that year the family increased its stake from nothing to 15 per cent, fuelling speculation of a full-blown takeover bid.

By May 2005 it was unstoppable; the Glazer family were owners of slightly under 30 per cent of the club, the threshold beyond which they would have to launch a formal takeover bid. On 12 May the 28.7 per cent stake of McManus and Magnier was bought and a day later a further 15 per cent.

At the end of the month the Old Trafford board wrote to the remaining shareholders recommending that they sell to the Glazers, who by mid-June owned

97.5 per cent of the club, which was now de-listed from the London Stock Exchange.

The takeover had cost £790m and opponents claimed that the way the takeover had been managed had effectively transformed the richest club in the world into the most indebted.

Breakaway fans formed their own club – FC United of Manchester – while others wore green and gold, the colours of United's very first strip, rather than red and white. The anger was such that on one occasion the Glazer sons had to be smuggled out of Old Trafford in the back of a van.

The takeover, though, was never criticized by Sir Alex Ferguson, before or after his retirement. In October 2013 Ferguson said, 'It created hostility but in my time with them they were nothing but supportive – very strong, single-minded people but always supportive of the manager and the things that happen in the club.'

Malcolm Glazer died on 28 May 2014. He had never set foot in Old Trafford.

Also on this day

2001 **The Premier League announced that a select group of referees were to go full-time.**

2004 **Zinedine Zidane scored twice in injury-time as England were beaten 2–1 in Lisbon in their opening match of the European Championship Finals.**

2011 **Phil Jones ignored late interest from Liverpool to join Manchester United from Blackburn.**

2012 **Harry Redknapp left Spurs.**

2012 **Three weeks after winning the Champions League, Roberto Di Matteo was finally confirmed as Chelsea's permanent manager.**

2015 **The Republic of Ireland and Scotland drew their European Championship qualifier in Dublin 1–1.**

14 JUNE
2001 – Chelsea sign Frank Lampard

Frank Lampard was once known as Frank Lampard junior: soon his dad was to be known as Frank Lampard senior.

Lampard had played 187 games for West Ham and 2 for England when his uncle (Harry Redknapp) and father were sacked as the management team at Upton Park with one game of the 2000/01 season to play. Their sacking made Lampard's departure inevitable.

Chelsea took him to Stamford Bridge for £11m, partnering Lampard in midfield with new signing Emmanuel Petit, having sold both Gus Poyet and Dennis Wise.

He would go on to make 648 appearances for Chelsea, fewer than only Ron Harris, Peter Bonetti and John

Terry. He broke the goalscoring record set in 1970 by Bobby Tambling, finishing with 211 goals and winning another 104 England caps.

Lampard's first headline act for Chelsea was to be sent off for an altercation with Tottenham's Chris Perry in a 3–2 win at White Hart Lane. His first goal came against Levski Sofia in the UEFA Cup his first final was a 2–0 defeat to Arsenal in the FA Cup of 2001.

It was almost four more years before Lampard got his first trophy, the League Cup of 2005. Over the next decade Lampard won four Premier League titles, four FA Cup winner's medals (scoring the winner in 2009 against Everton), another League Cup, the Europa League and in 2012 the Champions League when he scored his penalty in the shoot-out against Bayern Munich.

Lampard's last Chelsea goal was against Stoke in April 2014 and his last game against Norwich at Stamford Bridge the following month.

José Mourinho described his departure from Chelsea as 'a little break' but surprisingly Lampard ended up at Manchester City for the 2014/15 season via an agreement with the new MLS franchise New York City, and returned to Stamford Bridge to play against Chelsea in a 1–1 draw in January 2015.

Also on this day

1994 Spurs were found guilty of financial irregularities. They were fined £600,000, deducted 12 points and banned from the 1994/95 FA Cup. Almost all these sanctions were later overturned.

1998 Wimbledon's Robbie Earle scored for Jamaica in their first ever World Cup Finals match, a 3–1 defeat to Croatia.

2001 Arsenal signed the 'fox in the box', Francis Jeffers, from Everton for £10m.

2005 FC United of Manchester advertised for players to attend a trial day.

2012 The Republic of Ireland were eliminated from Euro 2012 after a 4–0 defeat to Spain.

2013 Manuel Pellegrini was appointed as manager of Manchester City.

2015 Wayne Rooney scored his 48th goal for England in their 3 – 2 win over Slovenia in a European Championship qualifying match in Ljubljana. The goal put Rooney in joint second place with Gary Lineker in the list of England's top-scorers, just one goal behind Sir Bobby Charlton.

15 JUNE

1996 – England 2 Scotland 0

Paul Gascoigne's crowning moments came at Wembley. The first was his free-kick for Spurs against Arsenal in the 1991 FA Cup semi-final, the second came against Scotland in the European Championship of 1996.

England and Scotland had not met since 1989. Fearing crowd trouble, UEFA did initially consider ensuring that they couldn't meet at the group stage of the European Championships either. Only two days before the draw in Birmingham in December 1995 did UEFA decree that there would no 'protection', only four seeds and an otherwise open draw.

Sure enough, England drew Scotland.

Both had drawn their first games in the tournament, and on the Thursday evening Holland had beaten Switzerland 2–0 to go top of the group. The loser on Saturday at Wembley would be in trouble.

Scotland edged the first half with England struggling to find any rhythm. A concerned Terry Venables brought on Jamie Redknapp for Stuart Pearce at half-time.

Soon Redknapp combined with McManaman, who fed Gary Neville, and his perfect cross was met by Alan Shearer. The striker headed in without having to break his stride.

With less than 15 minutes to go Stuart McCall crossed to Gordon Durie in the English penalty area, Tony Adams lunged and missed; penalty to Scotland.

Gary McAllister shot to David Seaman's right, but it was too close and the England goalkeeper made a comfortable save. With the resulting corner cleared to Teddy Sheringham, England broke. Sheringham fed Anderton, who spotted Gascoigne's run. His first touch, with his left foot, lifted the ball over Colin Hendry. His second touch, with his right, was a volley into the corner of Andy Goram's net. It was a flash of extraordinary genius.

Gascoigne's celebration recreated the infamous 'dentist's chair' drinking session in Hong Kong for which England's players, and Gascoigne in particular, had been savaged by the press. Monday morning's *Daily Mirror* read, 'Mr Gascoigne: An Apology'.

Also on this day

1995 Spurs chairman Alan Sugar expressed his disappointment following Jürgen Klinsmann's decision to join Bayern Munich by bemoaning the money being demanded by foreign 'Carlos Kick-a-balls' in the Premier League.

1998 England beat Tunisia 2–0 in their opening game at France 98.

2006 Wayne Rooney made his first appearance at the World Cup, as a substitute in a 2–0 win over Trinidad and Tobago after being rushed back from a metatarsal injury.

2009 Wigan named Roberto Martínez as their new manager.

2014 England lost their opening game at the World Cup Finals 2–1 to Italy in Manaus.

16 JUNE
2004 – Rafa Benítez joins Liverpool

Liverpool had seen what Rafa Benítez could do at first hand when they were outclassed and lucky to lose only 2–0 to Valencia in the Mestalla Stadium in a Champions League game in September 2002. Valencia won the return at Anfield too.

Benítez had made Valencia Spanish champions in his first season after replacing Héctor Cúper, ending a 31-year wait for the title. He'd followed that with a league and UEFA Cup double in 2004.

The disagreement between Benítez and Valencia's director of football Jesús García Pitarch over what type of player they then needed to sign left Benítez saying, 'I was hoping for a sofa and they've bought me a lamp.'

This came at a good time for Liverpool, who were looking to replace Gérard Houllier as manager. Benítez was their man.

First Benítez persuaded Steven Gerrard to stay at Anfield, though not Michael Owen; and then he set about signing Spanish players who'd caught his eye. Xabi Alonso and Luis García were spectacular successes, Antonio Núñez and Josemi were not.

Liverpool's progression past Chelsea to a first European Cup Final since 1985 ensured his lasting place in Liverpool fans' affections; his ability to irritate José Mourinho was uncanny and cherished at Anfield. The nature of their victory against AC Milan in Istanbul practically ensured him Kop immortality.

The FA Cup was won in 2006, and in 2007 another Champions League semi-final victory over Chelsea was followed this time by defeat to Milan in Athens.

The signing of Fernando Torres was designed to turn Liverpool into champions, but the Premier League title continued to be elusive; second place in 2009 was the closest they came under Benítez.

With new American owners at Anfield, the money the manager had been accustomed to spending began to dry up; the sale of Alonso left fans bemused and when in 2009/10 Liverpool went out of the Champions League at the group stage and finished seventh in the league the end came 'by mutual consent'.

Also on this day

1998 Scotland's hopes of progression at the World Cup were in the balance after a 1–1 draw with Norway in Bordeaux.

2002 Robbie Keane scored his third goal of the World Cup Finals but the Republic of Ireland lost to Spain in a penalty shoot-out in Suwon.

2014 Southampton appointed Ronald Koeman as their manager to succeed Mauricio Pochettino.

17 JUNE

2003 – Beckham leaves Old Trafford

In his autobiography of 2013 Sir Alex Ferguson wrote: 'The minute a Manchester United player thought he was bigger than the manager, he had to go. David thought he was bigger than Alex Ferguson. That was the death knell for him.'

Ferguson was used to dealing with famous footballers. He was not accustomed to players whom he felt courted fame outside the game and that, wrote Ferguson, made him feel 'uncomfortable'.

The beginning of the end came when Ferguson sent a boot flying in Beckham's direction after an FA Cup loss to Arsenal, and Beckham made a point of letting the photographers camped outside United's Carrington training ground see the cut on his eyebrow.

After winning his sixth Premier League title in 2003, it quickly became apparent that although the eyebrow had healed, the relationship between Ferguson and Beckham had not.

Barcelona were in the midst of a presidential campaign and candidate Joan Laporta had Beckham as part of his manifesto. Talks with United resulted in an agreement to sell Beckham for around £25m should Laporta win the election.

The only problem with this plan was that Beckham had no interest in signing for Barcelona. Beckham wanted to be a *Galáctico*, part of a Real Madrid midfield that already included Zidane and Figo, not a political pawn in Barcelona's power struggle. He was quoted as being 'disappointed and surprised' at United having agreed a deal with Laporta.

It may be that United were merely trying to create an auction for Beckham to increase his price, but rumoured interest from AC Milan didn't materialize and Real's £24.5m bid was accepted.

When United confirmed the deal to the London Stock Exchange it was with a statement from chief executive Peter Kenyon: 'While we are sad to see David go, we believe this is a good deal for the club. We wish David all the best for his new career in Spain and thank him for his fantastic contribution to the team's achievements.'

Ferguson said nothing.

Also on this day

1997 Arsenal signed Marc Overmars for £7m from Ajax.

1999 David James joined Aston Villa from Liverpool.

2000 England secured their first competitive win over Germany since 1966, 1–0 at Euro 2000.

2004 Aged 18 and 236 days, Wayne Rooney became the youngest ever goalscorer at a European Championship Finals with two against Switzerland in a 3–0 win. The record was broken four days later by Switzerland's Johan Vonlanthen, aged 18 and 141 days.

2011 Alex McLeish took over at Aston Villa.

2015 England's women booked their place in the knockout stage of the World Cup with a 2 – 1 win over Colombia in Montreal.

18 JUNE

1996 – The SAS destroy the Dutch

The Netherlands squad at Euro 96 might not have been the best Dutch squad ever assembled, but England's opponents did include van der Sar, Blind, Ronald de Boer, Seedorf, Bergkamp and Kluivert, and they were coached by Guus Hiddink. This was a team to be reckoned with, but a team that England blew away with arguably the finest performance seen under the twin towers of Wembley for many years.

A draw at Wembley would have been enough to send both teams though to the quarter-final, but defeat would leave either vulnerable to elimination by Switzerland or Scotland, who were playing simultaneously at Villa Park.

England led when Alan Shearer converted a penalty, awarded for Blind's trip on the onrushing Ince. David Seaman denied Dennis Bergkamp with a low save after a mistake by Gareth Southgate, and the Dutch finished the half looking strong.

The news from Villa Park was that Scotland led Switzerland with an Ally McCoist goal; if results stayed as they were the Dutch and the Scots would finish level on points, with goal difference or goals scored to decide who progressed.

In the second half that equation began to swing Scotland's way as England unleashed an 11-minute masterclass in finishing.

First Sheringham climbed to head home a Gascoigne corner on 51 minutes. Six minutes later, Gascoigne found Sheringham, who might have shot but instead rolled a disguised pass delightfully to the unmarked Shearer, who blasted into the roof of the net.

Within another five minutes it was 4–0, Sheringham helping himself to a rebound after van der Sar's save.

Suddenly Scotland, still 1–0 up in Birmingham, were in second place in the group on goal difference above the Dutch, who were heading out unless they scored.

Patrick Kluivert had been on the pitch only a few moments when Bergkamp found him at a narrow angle, but his finish under Seaman was exquisite. It was enough to lift the Netherlands above Scotland in the group.

Try as they might in the last ten minutes, Scotland couldn't find the second goal against Switzerland that would have put them through. Kluivert's strike had eliminated them. For some England fans it was the icing on the cake.

Also on this day

2002 Jay-Jay Okocha joined Bolton from Paris Saint-Germain.

2010 As he left the pitch Wayne Rooney criticized England fans in Cape Town who had booed a dismal team display in the 0–0 draw with Algeria.

2012 Damien Duff signed off from international football with his 100th and last cap in a 2–0 defeat to Italy at Euro 2012. Ireland flew home having lost all three matches.

19 JUNE

1994 – 'You'll Never Beat the Irish!': Ireland 1 Italy 0

If New York is a melting pot of people, many of whom are descended from Irish or Italian families, then the Big Apple was surely split down the middle when the World Cup came to town in 1994.

That's if anyone about town actually understood what it was all about. Before the tournament kicked off one American TV network questioned passers-by about their thoughts on Maradona: a beaming New Yorker replied, 'Oh, she's awesome! I just love her music.'

The Irish got it though: the Giants Stadium was awash with green, Italians vastly outnumbered.

Italy had beaten Ireland in Rome at the quarter-final stage of the World Cup in 1990; they still included Roberto Baggio – The Divine Ponytail – one of the stars of Italia 90, and the might of Baresi and Maldini still marshalled their defence.

Ray Houghton was one of five Irish players who had started in Rome; alongside him were Bonner, McGrath, Townsend and Staunton, joined now by Roy Keane, Denis Irwin and the skilful John Sheridan.

Barely ten minutes into the game, Sheridan's ball was unconvincingly cleared first by Costacurta then by Baresi. It fell to Houghton, who with his weaker left foot sent the ball sailing over Pagliuca in the Italian goal. Houghton, whose header had beaten England in the 1988 European Championship, had done it again.

Italy rarely threatened, Baggio was kept quiet, and the Italian defence was never allowed to rest by the tireless Tommy Coyne, who ran so much he fainted on the team bus after the game.

Ireland won, leaving the Italians to grumble about the ligament trouble that had restricted Baggio.

In the end both teams qualified from the only World Cup group ever to finish with all four teams level on points, Norway being the unlucky losers.

Also on this day

1993 Ossie Ardiles was given the manager's job at Spurs.

2001 John Arne Riise joined Liverpool from Monaco.

2004 Chelsea were reported to have made an approach to sign Steven Gerrard from Liverpool.

2005 Over 21,000 at Ewood Park watched Germany's women win Euro 2005.

2012 England qualified for the last eight of Euro 2012 with a 1–0 win over Ukraine in Donetsk. With no goal-line technology, match officials failed to spot that Marko Dević's shot for the hosts had clearly crossed the England line.

2014 Uruguay 2 England 1. Luis Suárez returned from knee surgery to score twice and leave England on the brink of elimination from the World Cup Finals.

20 JUNE
1995 – Bergkamp arrives at Arsenal

At Highbury, the marble halls felt like a shrine to former manager Herbert Chapman, whose bust greeted those who entered its art-deco surroundings. The Emirates Stadium is almost a monument to Arsène Wenger, who was one of the driving forces behind the project and even had a hand in the design of the dressing rooms.

There's nothing by which to remember Bruce Rioch's time in charge of Arsenal. The club was reeling from the 'bungs' scandal that had cost George Graham his job and, having been unable to persuade Bobby Robson to leave Porto, Arsenal turned to Rioch.

The Scot had been hugely successful at Bolton, taking them to a League Cup Final and winning promotion to the Premier League for the first time. He had also famously beaten Arsenal in an FA Cup fourth-round replay in 1994.

Rioch lasted just one season at Highbury, but his only legacy was a big one: signing Dennis Bergkamp. The Dutchman cost £7.5m after an unhappy spell in Italy with Inter Milan and became one of Arsenal's greatest ever players.

The start of Bergkamp's Arsenal career offered few hints of the glory to come. Inter president Massimo Moratti had sent Bergkamp to London with the words, 'They'll be lucky if he scores ten goals this season.' It looked as though he might be right as Bergkamp failed to find the net in his first seven games, until a brace against Southampton got him started.

Bergkamp stayed at Arsenal for the rest of his career, winning three league titles and four FA Cups, scoring 120 goals in 423 games in 11 seasons.

It could have been more, but Bergkamp was a non-flying Dutchman whose fear of travelling by air ruled him out of many European away games.

Also on this day

1997 Southampton appointed Dave Jones as their new manager.

2000 England were knocked out of Euro 2000 despite Alan Shearer's 30th, and last, international goal. Romania, with an 89th-minute penalty conceded by Phil Neville, won 3–2.

2006 England drew 2–2 with Sweden at the World Cup Finals, Joe Cole scoring brilliantly. Newcastle's Michael Owen, out for the last four months of the previous season, ruptured his knee ligament in the first minute, ruling him out until April 2007.

2014 England's exit from the World Cup was confirmed as Italy lost to Costa Rica in Recife. England's final game, against the Central Americans in Belo Horizonte, would be meaningless.

21 JUNE
1999 – Manchester United's FA Cup withdrawal

By winning the Champions League in 1999, Manchester United had qualified for FIFA's new baby – the Club World Championship.

After one postponement FIFA were now determined to get the event on the football calendar and it was scheduled for 5–14 January 2000, when Brazil would be the host.

The other seven qualifiers were Real Madrid, Corinthians, Vasco da Gama, South Melbourne, Necaxa, Raja Casablanca and the Saudi club Al-Nassr. Some of the eight were keener than others.

Manchester United were concerned about the toll the travel and playing up to four matches in the heat of the southern hemisphere summer would take on their players. A trip to Brazil immediately after the busy Christmas fixtures at home could be damaging to their season, and when would they play the third round of the FA Cup?

United expressed their concerns about taking part to the FA, where their indifference to FIFA's pet project was greeted with horror.

The FA was almost three years into an expensive and bitter campaign to host the 2006 World Cup Finals. The decision on the host nation was to be taken the following July. The FA simply could not countenance an English club irritating FIFA by refusing to play ball in Brazil.

Tense negotiations between the FA and Manchester United began. Could United be given a bye through the third round of the FA Cup? Could they field a reserve team? Neither option was palatable to the FA, but United not going to Brazil was unthinkable.

Finally it was announced that Manchester United, the FA Cup holders, would not defend the cup in the interests of the World Cup bid.

At the announcement of United's withdrawal, the FA's interim executive director David Davies said, 'We can't say we are favourites, but we've had reason in the past 12 months to believe that England's is the bid to beat now.' At the vote in July, Germany did exactly that.

Manchester United went to Brazil but didn't fare much better than the bid, beating only South Melbourne in their three games.

Also on this day

1999 **Didier Deschamps joined Chelsea for £3m from Juventus.**

2002 **Ronaldinho lobbed Seaman and England were out of the World Cup Finals, beaten 2–1 by Brazil.**

2004 **Wayne Rooney scored twice as England beat Croatia 4–2 in Lisbon to set up a European Championship quarter-final meeting with Portugal.**

2011 **Chelsea appointed André Villas-Boas as manager.**

22 JUNE
2006 – Poll's three-card calamity

Graham Poll was undoubtedly a good referee, being selected for his first senior international tournament at Euro 2000.

His first World Cup two years later didn't go too well. Taking charge of Italy's match against Croatia, Poll disallowed two Italian goals on the advice of his Danish assistant as they were beaten 2–1. Afterwards Christian Vieri, one of the disappointed scorers, said, 'Those weren't

division one or even division two officials, they were village officials.'

Mike Riley was appointed as England's representative at Euro 2004.

Poll was back on World Cup duty in 2006. Togo against South Korea and Saudi Arabia vs Ukraine passed without major controversy. Poll's third match took him to Stuttgart for the group game between Australia and Croatia.

It was a game Croatia had to win to stay in the World Cup, while a draw would be good enough for Australia.

It wasn't an easy game to referee. Darijo Srna put Croatia in front, but soon before half-time Craig Moore equalized with a penalty for a handball that some referees might have missed.

Further goals in the second half from Niko Kovač and Harry Kewell left Croatia needing a winner to progress. By this time Poll had booked both Dario Šimić and Josip Šimunić of Croatia as well as Brett Emerton of Australia.

In the closing ten minutes both Emerton and Šimić were shown second yellow cards and dismissed. In the 90th minute Šimunić pulled down Mark Viduka and was booked again, but this time no red card followed. Šimunić did well not to show any surprise, Australia didn't protest and the game moved into stoppage time with Šimunić still on the pitch.

The confusion grew in the final seconds as Cahill thought he'd scored a winner for Australia, only for the whistle to blow with Poll indicating the match was over. Australia celebrated anyway as they were through; Šimunić protested to Poll, who showed him a third yellow card, followed this time by a red.

Poll was not on the list of referees retained for the knockout stages and soon announced his retirement from tournament football.

Also on this day

1995 Paul Ince left Old Trafford to join Inter Milan for £7m.

1996 Stuart Pearce erased memories of the 1990 World Cup by scoring his penalty in the shoot-out against Spain that secured England a semi-final place at Euro 96.

1998 Romania 2 England 1 at the World Cup Finals. Michael Owen staked a claim for a place in the starting 11 by coming on to score.

2005 Rugby World Cup-winning coach Sir Clive Woodward was appointed technical director at Southampton.

2015 Goals from Steph Houghton and Lucy Bronze earned England's women a 2 – 1 win over Norway in Ottawa, and a place in the quarter-finals of the World Cup.

23 JUNE
2011 – Arsenal and Barcelona battle over Fàbregas

Raised a Barcelona fan and a product of their youth academy, it must have been quite a decision for Cesc Fàbregas to sign for Arsenal at the age of 16, but it paid off almost immediately. Fàbregas made his debut just a few weeks after his move to London and became Arsenal's youngest ever first-team player in a League Cup game against Rotherham at Highbury in October 2003.

Five weeks later he made his second appearance, again in the League Cup, and became Arsenal's youngest ever goalscorer in a 5–1 win against Premier League Wolves, who included Paul Ince in their side; it was men against boys, the boys strolled it.

By the summer of 2010, Fàbregas, now 23 and on an 8-year contract, was Arsenal captain but with only one trophy – the 2005 FA Cup – to his name. Recognized as one of the finest midfielders in the world, Barcelona wanted him back.

They were reported to be offering in excess of £30m, and Fàbregas was understood to be tempted, but Arsène Wenger was not. The Arsenal manager spoke to Fàbregas and worked his magic. The midfielder said, 'It was probably the greatest conversation I have had with someone in my life. I respect him so much. He told me to concentrate on my football and the World Cup and he will deal with whatever happens in my future.'

Fàbregas stayed at Arsenal, but the following season brought more disappointment with Barcelona getting the better of them in the Champions League when a Fàbregas mistake had allowed Messi to level the aggregate scores in the Nou Camp.

In late June 2011 Barcelona bid for Fàbregas again, and once more it was rejected; but crucially this time Fàbregas could not be persuaded to stay and Arsenal were forced to negotiate a fee.

Finally Fàbregas left with Arsenal receiving £35m and having reportedly agreed a clause giving them first option to buy him back should he ever leave the Nou Camp. If that clause existed, then three years later Arsenal chose not to use it and Fàbregas signed for Chelsea.

Also on this day

1995 **Mark Hughes joined Chelsea.**

1997 **Andy Gray decided against accepting the job of Everton manager in order to continue his role with Sky Sports.**

1998 **Scotland were eliminated from the World Cup after a 3–0 defeat to Morocco that saw Craig Burley sent off.**

2010 **Jermain Defoe scored the only goal as England beat Slovenia 1–0 to progress to the second round of the World Cup.**

24 JUNE
2004 – The gloves are off and England are out

At Euro 2004 Wayne Rooney emerged onto the international stage as a superstar in the making. Still only 18, the Everton striker had scored two goals against Switzerland and two more against Croatia, helping England to reach the last eight of the tournament, where they faced hosts Portugal.

Rooney was England's new wunderkind, catapulted to fame just as Michael Owen had been at the 1998 World Cup.

Owen was still very much around, however, and put England in front after only three minutes in Lisbon against the Portuguese. England spent much of the next 25 minutes under pressure, then Rooney was challenged by Jorge Andrade and fell to the ground holding his right foot. The broken metatarsal would keep him out until September, by which time he was a Manchester United player.

Without their new hero England held out until the 83rd minute when Hélder Postiga, scorer of just two goals that season for Spurs, converted a Simão cross. With full-time approaching Sol Campbell thought he had won the game for England, only for the referee to disallow the goal. For Campbell it was an agonizing repeat of his disallowed goal in the 1998 World Cup clash with Argentina.

In extra-time Rui Costa scored with a brilliant right-footed strike, only for Frank Lampard to equalize from a corner with five minutes to play.

Just as in 1990, 1996 and 1998, the nation steeled itself for England's latest penalty shoot-out.

Beckham first; and Beckham missed, the turf seeming to give way under his foot. Deco, Owen, Simão and Lampard all scored before Rui Costa's shot flew over the bar, leaving him too cursing the crumbling turf.

Hargreaves, Maniche, Ashley Cole and Postiga (with an outrageous chip) scored to take the shoot-out to sudden death.

As Darius Vassell walked forward for England the Portuguese goalkeeper Ricardo took off his gloves; the message to Vassell was clear – gloves weren't needed to save one of his spot-kicks. The psychology worked, Vassell's kick was saved.

Ricardo had scored a penalty for Boavista in a shoot-out against Málaga in the 2003 UEFA Cup quarter-final, and the goalkeeper stepped forward again to win the match past David James's right hand.

Also on this day

1994 Jack Charlton and John Aldridge lost their cool as Ireland were beaten 2–1 by Mexico in the heat of Orlando. Both were fined for rowing with officials as Aldridge tried to come on as a substitute.

2012 Italy knocked England out of Euro 2012 in a shoot-out after Ashley Young and Ashley Cole missed from the spot.

2014 Already-eliminated England drew 0–0 with Costa Rica at the World Cup Finals. At the same time Luis Suárez was biting Giorgio Chiellini in Uruguay's 1–0 win over Italy.

2015 Liverpool agreed a fee of £29m with Hoffenheim to sign Brazilian international Roberto Firmino.

25 JUNE
2007 – Henry leaves Arsenal

There are very few fans of Premier League football who would not put Thierry Henry in their best ever 11; some would say he was the Premier League's finest ever. Certainly, unlike Cristiano Ronaldo, Henry's best years were in England.

When he left the Emirates in 2007 Henry had scored 226 goals in 370 games, an Arsenal record. He was their top scorer in every season from 1999 to 2006. His lowest goal tally in those seven years was 22 and his highest 39.

Henry scored nine hat-tricks including one in the last ever game at Highbury, won two league titles and three FA Cups and was Arsenal's most capped player, winning the World Cup with France in 1998.

Barcelona signed Henry in 2007 at the fourth attempt. Johan Cruyff had tried to take him from Wenger's Monaco early in Henry's career, club president Joan Laporta tried once more in 2003 and came closest in 2006.

Then Barcelona had just beaten Arsenal in the Champions League Final, the one honour that was missing from Henry's collection. David Dein, vice-chairman at Arsenal, rejected £50m bids from both Barcelona and Real Madrid that would have made Henry the world's most expensive player.

Behind the scenes in spring 2007 Dein left Arsenal in a power struggle that cast doubt on Wenger's future; on the pitch Robin van Persie, six years younger than Henry, was ready to take on the job of being Arsenal's main striker.

When Barcelona came calling again with a £16.1m bid Arsenal accepted, with Arsène Wenger saying that Henry went with his blessing and thanks 'for the huge contribution he has made to the club's success over the past eight years. To his great credit, he has mixed skill and style together with an appetite for winning.'

At Barcelona Henry got his Champions League medal, beating Manchester United in Rome. And in 2012 Arsenal fans were delighted that there would be a postscript to the Frenchman's career in north London.

Also on this day

1995 Kenny Dalglish switched from manager to director of football at Premier League champions Blackburn Rovers, with Ray Harford taking over in the dugout.

2001 Dennis Wise left Chelsea after 11 years at Stamford Bridge.

2003 Carlos Queiroz left his job as assistant manager at Manchester United to take over as manager at Real Madrid.

2006 England progressed to the World Cup quarter-final as David

Beckham scored the only goal against Ecuador in Stuttgart.

26 JUNE
1996 – England, Germany and penalties again

The semi-final of Euro 96 was a glorious occasion, an incredible match, but for England a devastating outcome.

Wembley had seen some of the finest football played by an England team in years, but the wave of euphoria would have to wash away mighty Germany if England were to reach the final.

Germany had won their group and in their quarter-final had seen off Croatia and Davor Šuker at Old Trafford, so headed to Wembley for their first competitive game there since 1972.

England, wearing a grey away strip, struck first, inevitably through Alan Shearer. Gascoigne's third-minute corner was flicked on at the near post by Adams for a stooping Shearer to score his fifth goal at the tournament.

The lead lasted little more than ten minutes, with Stefan Kuntz equalizing from close range. With the tension rising as the clock ticked the game stayed at 1–1 and went to extra-time, during which, under UEFA's 'golden goal' rule, the first goal would win the match.

From now on there would be agony and relief in equal measure.

First McManaman crossed for Anderton, whose shot from six yards smacked against the left-hand post and rebounded into goalkeeper Andreas Köpke's grateful arms. Next Stefan Kuntz headed into the English net only for the referee to disallow the goal for a push no-one could see. Finally Sheringham floated a cross-field ball to Shearer, whose volleyed cross flashed to the back post where Gascoigne was sliding in – he failed to make contact by a hair's breadth in front of an open goal.

Just as in 1990, England and Germany went to penalties in a semi-final. Shearer, Hässler, Platt, Strunz, Pearce, Reuter, Gascoigne, Ziege, Sheringham and Kuntz all scored to take it to sudden death.

Aston Villa's Gareth Southgate rushed at the ball and shot low to Köpke's right, but too close to the goalkeeper, who guessed correctly to give Andreas Müller the chance to win the semi-final. Müller's rising penalty bit into the roof of the net and once again England were out.

In Germany they still sing 'Football's coming home'.

Also on this day

1995 Savo Milošević joined Aston Villa from Partizan Belgrade for a club record £3.5m.

1998 Glenn Hoddle dropped Teddy Sheringham in favour of Michael Owen as England beat Colombia 2–0 to qualify for the knockout stages of the World Cup Finals, where they played Argentina.

2001 Emmanuel Petit signed for Chelsea from Barcelona for £7.5m.

2003 Marc-Vivien Foé, former player with West Ham and Manchester City, collapsed and died during Cameroon's Confederations Cup match against Colombia.

27 JUNE
2010 – England blown away in Bloemfontein

There is an element of Groundhog Day about England's defeats to Germany in major tournaments but while their failure was not without some glory in 1990 and 1996, their exit from the 2010 World Cup was thoroughly merited, though not without controversy.

England had been poor against the USA, worse against Algeria and wasteful against Slovenia. Germany had not been perfect either, 4–0 winners against Australia but then losing to Serbia in Port Elizabeth, where Lukas Podolski missed a penalty and Miroslav Klose was sent off; they'd done enough against Ghana in Johannesburg, but only just. But then Ghana had played much better than England.

Germany were in front after a long clearance from goalkeeper Manuel Neuer caught out both John Terry and Matthew Upson; it bounced twice and was steered in by Klose.

If Germany's first goal was straightforward, the second was woven intricately with half-a-dozen slick passes between static England defenders and finished by Podolski. Two goals in the first 30 minutes and Germany were completely in charge.

England gave themselves a toehold in the game five minutes later when Matt Upson headed home a Gerrard cross. Then came the moment for which the match will be remembered, the moment Capello used in the case for his defence against the charge of having his team comprehensively outmanoeuvred by Germany.

Frank Lampard's improvised chip caught Neuer off his line; the ball hit the bar, dropped a foot or more behind the line and span back up to hit the bar again before being caught by Neuer. By the time the German goalkeeper had the ball in his gloves the England bench and thousands of fans were celebrating an equalizer. Too soon. Somehow neither referee Jorge Larrionda, nor his assistant Mauricio Espinosa, spotted what everyone else had clearly seen.

England left the pitch at half-time in frustration.

At full-time England left in tatters. First Schweinsteiger then Özil provided the opportunities for Thomas Müller to score two more.

Maybe losing on penalties wasn't so bad after all?

Also on this day

1997 Teddy Sheringham joined Manchester United from Spurs for £3.5m.

1997 Howard Kendall was appointed Everton manager for the third time.

2002 David O'Leary was sacked by Leeds.

2005 Arsenal signed Alexander Hleb for £10m from Stuttgart.

28 JUNE
2012 – Beckham's Olympic omission

When the International Olympic Committee announced in 2005 that London was their choice of host city for the 2012 Olympics, Sir Steve Redgrave turned and bear-hugged David Beckham. Football might not be that big in the Olympics but this particular footballer was and he'd worked tirelessly to charm the IOC.

It would be going too far to say that Beckham won the Olympics for London, but having him on board certainly didn't do any harm; bid chairman Lord Coe described him as 'an extraordinary supporter'.

David Beckham's last England game had been in October 2009 – a 115th cap. An Achilles injury meant he was unavailable for the 2010 World Cup, after which manager Fabio Capello suggested the idea of arranging a friendly international in Beckham's honour in order that 'the fans could say goodbye'.

Beckham pointedly rejected the idea, saying that he would never willingly retire from international football so didn't need to say, or hear, any goodbyes.

Nevertheless, Beckham's England career had never resumed. Once the Home Nations had agreed that a combined men's team could compete for Great Britain in 2012, it seemed only natural that Beckham would be there as one of the three overage players allowed. At 37, Beckham was well over that 23-year limit but so was Ryan Giggs, and he too looked a certainty for the 18-man squad to be chosen by manager Stuart Pearce.

Almost a week before the squad was due to be announced, Beckham let it be known that Pearce had contacted him to say that he had not made the cut. Ryan Giggs, Craig Bellamy and Micah Richards would be the overage trio.

There was a huge disappointment among the many thousands who had already bought tickets for the team's group matches in Manchester, London and Cardiff.

At his press conference Pearce, never known for his sense of romance or sentiment, said he had made his decision for 'footballing reasons', adding, 'I'm not picking on personality, I'm not picking on ticket sales and I'm certainly not picking on nationality.'

The tournament was a great success; the Great Britain team was not, losing (on penalties, naturally) to South Korea.

Also on this day

1996 UEFA were criticized for allowing Germany to call Jens Todt into their squad for the final of Euro 96 against the Czech Republic. Germany were without seven outfield players either suspended or injured for the match.

2000 Davor Šuker left Arsenal to join West Ham.

2006 After his error in the Croatia vs Australia match, referee Graham Poll was told he was no longer needed at the World Cup.

2015 England's women reached the World Cup semi-finals for the first time with a 2 – 1 quarter-final win over hosts Canada. Jodie Taylor and Lucy Bronze scored England's goals.

29 JUNE

2008 – Spain 1 Germany 0: *viva España*

Fernando Torres scored 33 Liverpool goals in his first season in English football, and at international level formed a formidable partnership with Valencia's David Villa.

The pair had shared six goals between them in only four games at the 2006 World Cup. But this was another tournament in which the Spanish had looked so promising only to wilt at the crucial time. Spain had won nothing since the European Championship of 1964.

Under manager Luis Aragonés they travelled to the 2008 European Championships unbeaten in 16 games. Spain had perhaps the world's best goalkeeper in Casillas; Puyol, Ramos, Marchena and Capdevila in defence; Xavi, Iniesta, David Silva and Marcos Senna in midfield; and the two razor-sharp strikers up front.

They swept past Russia, Sweden and Greece in their group and then settled in Vienna for the rest of the tournament.

Spain had been eliminated at the quarter-final stage of two World Cups and a European Championship each time on penalties and each time on 22 June, so when they beat Italy on penalties on that date in the Austrian capital, it seemed that their time must be coming at last.

After destroying Russia for the second time in the semi-final, Spain knew that Germany stood between them and the title.

The margin of victory should have been more than 1–0; the Spanish were dominant throughout despite being without the injured Villa.

Torres scored the only goal, firing sweetly past Jen Lehmann after beating Lahm to Xavi's pass. Afterwards the jubilant Torres gushed, 'It's just a dream come true. This is my first title and I hope it's the first of many. We are used to watching finals on television, but today we were here and we won.'

Torres returned to England with a reputation as one of the world's greatest strikers.

Spain's unbeaten run was extended by another 12 months to 35 games, and they broke new ground by winning the World Cup in 2010 and the Euros again in 2012, making them arguably the greatest international team in the history of the game.

Also on this day

1999 Arsenal signed Brazilian Silvinho from Corinthians for £4m.

2007 Spurs signed Darren Bent for £16.5m from Charlton.

2011 Manchester United made David de Gea the most expensive goalkeeper in Britain after a £17.8m move from Atlético Madrid.

2015 Arsenal signed goalkeeper Petr Cech from Chelsea for £10m.

30 JUNE
1998 – Saint-Étienne: England vs Argentina

Of all the agonizing defeats England fans have suffered over the last 25 years this might be the worst. It was defeat with glory, defeat with courage. Perhaps it was a self-inflicted defeat, and – it almost goes without saying – it was a defeat on penalties.

If it were not for Dan Petrescu's last-minute winner for Romania in their group meeting, England wouldn't have been playing Argentina at all. They would have faced Croatia in Bordeaux; not a walk in the park, but not a repeat of the 'Hand of God' match of 1986 either.

There were three goals in the first 16 minutes, two of them penalties. The third was a career-defining run and shot of startling brilliance from a young Michael Owen, who manager Glenn Hoddle had declared was 'not a natural-born goalscorer'.

Owen's goal was stunning; the faces of England substitutes Paul Merson and Teddy Sheringham as they celebrated were a mixture of joy and downright shock. In the seven seconds it took the 18-year-old Owen to control Beckham's pass, run almost half the length of the pitch, beat two defenders and score, he had announced himself as a world superstar.

Paul Scholes missed a glorious chance to make it 3–1, but Javier Zanetti's ingenious equalizer in the closing seconds of the first half should have cleared England heads for what lay ahead.

Only David Beckham can know what was going through his head as he lay on the ground after a challenge from Diego Simeone. Beckham flicked out his right leg in Simeone's direction; referee Kim Milton Nielsen sent him off, with Gabriel Batistuta nodding in pantomime approval.

Sol Campbell had a headed goal harshly disallowed as England's ten men played heroically; inevitably there were more boos for Nielsen.

The outcome of the penalty shoot-out was all too familiar. Crespo missed but so did Ince and it was three penalties each when David Batty stepped forward to take the last.

If Beckham had not been sent off then Batty would surely not have been taking a penalty. David Batty – scorer of just nine career goals, none of which were penalties – but who was brave enough to step forward.

Carlos Roa saved it.

Also on this day

1994 FIFA announced that Diego Maradona had failed a drugs test at the World Cup.

1996 Oliver Bierhoff's golden goal, the first in major tournament history, won Euro 96 for Germany.

1999 Manchester United confirmed their withdrawal from the following season's FA Cup.

2002 Ronaldo scored both goals as Brazil won the World Cup with a 2–0 win over Germany.

2003 Released by Spurs, Teddy Sheringham joined Portsmouth.

2008 Felipe Scolari made Deco his first signing for Chelsea.

2010 Manchester City signed David Silva from Valencia.

2015 UEFA announced that Cardiff's Millennium Stadium would host the 2017 Champions League Final.

2015 Leicester City sacked manager Nigel Pearson, despite him leading them to Premier League safety. In a statement the club cited 'fundamental differences in perspective'.

July

1 JULY
2003 – Roman Abramovich buys Chelsea

It was the atmosphere at Old Trafford that convinced Roman Abramovich he should buy an English football club. The Russian billionaire had seen Manchester United lose their Champions League quarter-final to Real Madrid in April 2003 and found himself beguiled by the English game.

Almost immediately Abramovich started looking for a club to buy. United and Spurs were considered before Abramovich settled on Chelsea.

It wasn't just Chelsea's west London location that appealed and it wasn't just the fact that they already had some great players. What attracted Abramovich might have put off anyone but the very richest investor: Chelsea were on the brink of a financial meltdown.

The club had borrowed against future TV revenues and were struggling to keep up with repayments. The prospect of selling at least one of their star players to pay the bills was looming large. On 11 May Chelsea beat Liverpool 2–1 in the last game of the season, effectively a play-off for the final Champions League place. The money that would generate was a godsend, but soon money would be no object.

Chelsea's chief executive Trevor Birch met Abramovich and said a deal was done 'in ten minutes'.

'Abramovich didn't speak English. There was an interpreter. I wasn't totally convinced he was the real thing. I had googled him but he just didn't appear anywhere. Nobody knew anything about him. So I wasn't sure whether it was a scene from *Candid Camera* and that suddenly Jeremy Beadle was going to jump out at me.'

To buy the club and cover its debts cost Abramovich £140m. Birch advised him that the team needed £20m more spending on it. In the next eight weeks the Russian bought Glen Johnson, Joe Cole, Geremi, Damien Duff, Juan Sebastián Verón, Adrian Mutu, Wayne Bridge, Alexei Smertin, Hernán Crespo and Claude Makélélé. They cost £110m in transfer fees.

The Premier League would never be the same again.

Also on this day

1996 Patrik Berger joined Liverpool from Borussia Dortmund.

1998 Everton appointed Walter Smith as manager.

2006 Portugal knocked England out of the World Cup with Wayne Rooney being sent off. Portugal won 3–1 in the shoot-out.

2007 Owen Hargreaves joined Manchester United from Bayern Munich for £17m.

2012 Spain won the European Championships with a 4–0 win over Italy in the final.

2013 David Moyes started work as manager at Manchester United.

2014 Adam Lallana joined Liverpool from Southampton.

2 JULY
2015 – The broken hearted Lionesses

England began the Women's World Cup in Canada with something of a whimper and they finished it in despair. In between they roared like lionesses, having broken new ground for British women's football.

It started in Moncton, New Brunswick with a tame defeat to France. Neverthless England's manager, Mark Sampson, sounded confident despite the 1 – 0 loss; "I would suggest fans stick with us," he said. Not only did fans stick with England, they began to watch on TV back home in record numbers.

England's second and third group matches were both won. First Mexico and then Colombia were beaten by the same 2 – 1 score line. England finished second in their group and headed for a round of 16 match against Norway in Ottawa.

For the first time in their history England's women won a knock-out game in the World Cup; Steph Houghton and Lucy Bronze scoring as they came from a goal down to win 2 – 1 for the third game running.

Next came hosts Canada in the quarter-final. The Canadians had beaten England in a friendly just prior to the start of the tournament, but this time England raced into a two goal lead through Jodie Taylor and Lucy Bronze. It was enough despite a late Canadian rally: 2 - 1 to England again. Now England were in unchartered territory having reached the last four for the first time. World Champions and

Olympic runners-up Japan waited in the semi-final in Edmonton.

Almost two and half million viewers stayed up until past midnight in the UK to watch the match. They saw Japan take the lead when Claire Rafferty fouled Saori Ariyoshi after 32 minutes and the penalty was converted by captain Aya Miyama.

Only eight minutes later England level having been awarded a penalty of their own. The challenge on Steph Houghton looked inconsequential, but Fara Williams made no mistake from the spot.

In the second half England created the bulk of the chances as Toni Duggan hit the bar and Jill Scott's header flashed just wide. With two minutes of injury time having been played an extra half an hour seemed a certainty when the Japanese broke and Laura Bassett, facing her own goal, stretched to cut out a dangerous cross from Nahomi Kawasumi. The ball looped cruelly over goalkeeper Karen Bardsley and hit the underside of the crossbar, only to bounce over the line and into the English net: 2 – 1 again, only this time to Japan. It was as a cruel an exit as can be.

Also on this day

1995 Manchester City appointed Alan Ball as manager.

1999 Steve Bould left Arsenal for Sunderland, ending 11 years at Highbury.

2000 France were crowned champions of Europe after David Trezeguet scored a golden goal against Italy.

2006 Following England's defeat to Portugal at the World Cup finals, David Beckham announced that he was resigning as team captain.

2009 Michael Owen joined Manchester United on a free transfer from Newcastle.

2010 Manchester City signed Yaya Touré from Barcelona for £30m.

3 JULY
2001 – Tottenham's Campbell becomes a Gunner

Sol Campbell's move from Spurs to Arsenal is perhaps the most controversial transfer ever made in the Premier League.

Campbell spent a short period in West Ham's youth programme, but had joined Spurs in his mid-teens and by the end of the 2000/01 season was the club captain, having played more than 300 games. He had been capped 40 times by England and won the League Cup in 1999.

With Campbell's contract at White Hart Lane due to expire at the end of that season the club had offered to make him the highest-paid player in their history if he stayed.

To their fans' dismay Campbell refused and, under the Bosman ruling, Tottenham accepted that he would leave, with both Inter Milan and Barcelona battling to sign him on a free transfer. It felt like losing one of their own.

Across north London, Arsenal had just bought goalkeeper Richard Wright from Ipswich. A good signing, but not one likely to make that many column inches in the next day's newspapers.

Arsenal called a press conference at their training ground and reporters gathered, preparing their questions for the new young goalkeeper. Richard Wright barely got a mention in the papers the next day, because in walked Arsenal's manager Arsène Wenger with Sol Campbell.

Campbell had just become the first high-profile player to move from Tottenham to Arsenal since Pat Jennings in 1977 and he knew exactly how the Spurs fans were likely to react: 'It is something I am prepared to face and hopefully it won't be a major problem for me.'

That proved to be a false hope. Every time he returned to play at White Hart Lane, Campbell was singled out for some of the bitterest, most vicious abuse any player has ever had to suffer.

Campbell won the double with Arsenal in his first season and went on to win the Premier League again as part of the unbeaten team of 2004; he also won the

FA Cup twice more before moving to Portsmouth and, briefly, Notts County.

He returned to Arsenal in 2010 for a short spell, and is regarded as one of the club's finest defenders. At Tottenham they have still never forgiven him.

Also on this day

1996 **Graeme Souness took over at Southampton.**

2000 **Robert Pirès turned down Real Madrid to join Arsenal from Marseille for £6m.**

2002 **Middlesbrough signed Juninho for the second time.**

2006 **Niall Quinn headed a consortium that agreed to buy Sunderland.**

2012 **André Villas-Boas was appointed manager of Spurs.**

4 JULY
2007 – Fernando Torres to Anfield

When he was captain of Atlético Madrid, Fernando Torres wore an armband with the words 'We'll never walk alone' embroidered on the inside. Later Liverpool fans, mistakenly, took this to be an indication that Torres was hoping for an Anfield move before 2007. In fact, it was more of a statement of belonging to his circle of friends in Madrid. Those friends had got the phrase tattooed, but Torres was aware of the Liverpool connection and instead had it put on the inside of his armband.

Nevertheless, a photographer spotted it during a match against Real Sociedad and Torres later said, 'Maybe that was the day I took my first step towards Anfield.'

Liverpool had come close to winning the European Cup for a sixth time in 2007, losing 2–1 to AC Milan in the final. Liverpool had controlled much of the game but failed to score until it was too late, Dirk Kuyt's header coming with just a minute to play.

What Liverpool needed was a world-class finisher and Torres was that man, with 140 goals in 256 starts for Atlético Madrid, the club he had played for from the age of 17.

Chelsea, Manchester United and Newcastle had all shown an interest in Torres but Liverpool offered more than money; their proposal was in excess of £25m plus the exciting attacking midfielder Luis García.

Atlético couldn't resist and Torres signed a six-year contract, becoming Liverpool's record signing. At Anfield he was an instant hit, scoring against Chelsea on his home debut. He scored 23 Premier League goals in 2007/08, a record for a foreign striker in his debut season, and 34 goals in total.

The goals kept coming for Torres, but so did injuries; he underwent two knee operations in the first four months of 2010. When in July he returned to Anfield as a Spanish World Cup winner, it was to a club now managed by Roy Hodgson and with American owners Tom Hicks and George Gillett in conflict with each other and looking to balance the books.

At the end of August 2010, Chelsea offered the Americans a means to do just that.

Also on this day

1995 Liverpool beat Everton to the signature of Stan Collymore for £8.5m.

1996 Fabrizio Ravanelli signed for Middlebrough from Juventus for £7m.

1998 Arsenal's Dennis Bergkamp scored one of the goals of the World Cup as the Netherlands beat Argentina.

2004 Greece beat Portugal to win the European Championship.

2005 Chelsea made Liverpool a £32m offer for Steven Gerrard.

5 JULY
1996 – Manchester United sign the baby-faced assassin

Manchester United had edged Newcastle to the Premier League title in May 1996, and once the European Championship was out of the way the two clubs began another battle – to sign England hero Alan Shearer from Blackburn Rovers.

Newcastle were about to win that race for a world-record £15m when Manchester United spent one-tenth of that amount on a Norwegian striker who had been offered to, and rejected by, both Everton and Manchester City.

Ole Gunnar Solskjaer looked younger than his 23 years and had scored 31 goals the previous season, his first with Molde in the Norwegian top flight. Alex Ferguson decided he was worth the risk.

Solskjaer's Manchester United career began as a substitute at Blackburn in August 1996 and he scored six minutes after coming on. Over the next 11 seasons he would become English football's most famous substitute since Liverpool's David Fairclough in the 1970s. Of his 369 appearances for United, 150 were as a substitute; once he came off the bench to score four against Nottingham Forest.

Solskjaer's finest moment came on 20 May 1999, when he scored Manchester United's winning goal in the Champions League Final against Bayern Munich in Barcelona. Teddy Sheringham, also a substitute that night, had scored the equalizer in the first minute of added time. Solskjaer provided the winner seconds later.

Injuries meant that he played hardly any football for two-and-a-half years from autumn 2003, but Solskjaer returned to the first team at the beginning of the 2006/07 season and added another ten goals to his tally – four of them after having come on as a substitute.

He won a sixth Premier League title that season, but couldn't quite reprise his late act one last time when, in his final game, he came on with eight minutes of extra-time remaining in the 2007 FA Cup Final only for Didier Drogba to score a winner for Chelsea.

Also on this day

1996 Roberto Di Matteo signed for Chelsea from Lazio for £4.6m.

1999 Chelsea spent £10m on Chris Sutton from Blackburn.

2000 Simon Jordan completed his takeover of Crystal Palace.

2004 Patrick Kluivert joined Newcastle.

2005 Steven Gerrard told Liverpool he would join Chelsea.

2009 Daniel Sturridge left Manchester City for Chelsea.

6 JULY
2005 – Steven Gerrard stays at Liverpool

Steven Gerrard came very close to leaving Liverpool for Chelsea in 2004, but came even closer in 2005.

In the aftermath of a performance that inspired Liverpool to win the Champions League Final against Milan in May 2005, Gerrard had said, 'How can I think of leaving Liverpool after a night like this?'

With two years left on his contract, Gerrard wanted a new deal and expected it to be delivered quickly. But by the time the squad reassembled in late June for pre-season training there had still been no agreement, and there appeared to be little urgency on the part of the club.

At the beginning of July talks finally began but the mood had changed; a report in the Spanish press claimed that Gerrard was tempted by the prospect of a move to Real Madrid.

On 4 July Gerrard's agent, Struan Marshall, broke the stunning news that negotiations between Liverpool and Gerrard had broken down and were 'unlikely to be reopened'.

Liverpool fans were devastated; some were angry with the club, some with the player. But any hope they had of Liverpool keeping Gerrard seemed to evaporate the following day when he confirmed that was leaving, calling it 'the hardest decision I have ever had to make'.

Liverpool received, and rejected, a bid of £32m from Chelsea, who were so confident that he would move to Stamford Bridge that their assistant manager at the time, Steve Clarke, later said that Chelsea considered it a 'done deal'.

Then came the incredible last-minute change of heart. It must have been a long night of soul-searching in the Gerrard house, but the morning papers reporting his impending move to London were already out of date: Rick Parry announced that Gerrard was staying at Liverpool.

Mourinho, who would later call it the biggest regret of his career, growled, 'I can say to him in the next ten years we will compare trophies at Chelsea and trophies at Liverpool, and he will lose.'

Mourinho was right; and even as he signed his new Anfield contract Gerrard probably knew that Mourinho would be right.

Also on this day

1995 David Ginola signed for Newcastle from PSG for £2.5m.

2000 Germany won the right to host the World Cup Finals in 2006 by one vote from South Africa. The FA's £10m campaign yielded just two votes.

2007 Former Thai Prime Minister Thaksin Shinawatra completed his takeover of Manchester City.

2011 Manchester City signed Gaël Clichy from Arsenal.

7 JULY
2007 – Sven arrives at City

Thaksin Shinawatra had a manager in mind when he completed his takeover of Manchester City; it was the former Chelsea boss Claudio Ranieri.

City had sacked Stuart Pearce after a season in which they finished with a whimper, failing to win any of their last six games and finishing 14th. Shinawatra had once been the prime minister of Thailand, ousted by a military coup in 2006, and was living in exile having to deny corruption charges having been filed him against him in Bangkok.

He had previously failed to buy Liverpool, but was courting Manchester City with an £81m takeover, promising his would-be manager £50m more to spend on players.

But Ranieri was unimpressed and took an offer to manage Juventus instead. Sven-Göran Eriksson, who'd been out of work since leaving the England job a year earlier, jumped at the chance to sign a three-year contract with the new City owner.

With over £30m spent on seven new players in less than a month, City started brilliantly. They won their first three games, including the derby against Manchester United, and at Christmas they were in the top four of the Premier League.

In February City beat Manchester United again, winning at Old Trafford for the first time since 1974, but already Shinawatra was unhappy. An FA Cup loss at Sheffield United and defeats to Reading and Birmingham were described by the owner as an 'avalanche of very poor results which is unacceptable at this level'.

In the spring it was announced that Eriksson would not get a second season at the club.

'In the beginning,' said Eriksson, 'it was good with Shinawatra, but he didn't understand football – he hadn't a clue. He thought beating Manchester United twice in one year was normal.'

City's demotivated players lost their last three games of the season, the last of which was an 8–1 defeat by Middlesbrough.

City replaced Eriksson with Mark Hughes, while in 2008 Shinawatra sold Manchester City to the Abu Dhabi United Group for £200m.

Also on this day

1997 Despite being relegated out of the Premier League, Middlesbrough spent £5m on Paul Merson, ending his 13 years at Arsenal.

1998 Arsenal's David Platt retired from the game.

2010 Arsenal signed Laurent Koscielny from Lorient for £8.5m.

2014 Ashley Cole signed for AS Roma, leaving Chelsea.

8 JULY
2014 – Germany 7 Brazil 1

The pressure on Brazil to win the World Cup on home soil had been there since 1950. Then, as hosts, Brazil had failed at the final hurdle, losing 2–1 to Uruguay.

In 2013 the Brazilians had won the Confederations Cup at a canter, hammering World and European champions Spain 3–0 in the final. Maybe that team had peaked a year too soon, because in 2014 they were finding the World Cup much tougher.

They'd been a little lucky to beat Croatia in the opening game in São Paulo, benefitting from a poor decision to award them a penalty when the score was 1–1.

A draw with Mexico followed, then a win over Cameroon that set up a second-round match against Chile. Brazil were taken to the limit physically and emotionally in Belo Horizonte, only winning in a penalty shoot-out.

In the quarter-final the hosts had hung on desperately to a 2–1 lead under enormous pressure from a talented Colombian side led by the superb James Rodríguez. But a second yellow card for captain Thiago Silva and an injury to the wonderful Neymar meant that neither would play in the semi-final against Germany.

The loss of Neymar was incalculable. The 22-year-old forward had scored 35 international goals in just 54 appearances. Pictures of the challenge by Colombia's Juan Zúñiga and a tearful Neymar being stretchered away with a bone broken in his back were perpetually replayed on Brazilian TV.

The Brazilian team arrived in Belo Horizonte wearing hats displaying the message '*Força Neymar*'; they seemed to sing the anthem just for him. The focus of the nation and the team seemed to be on what they were missing rather than what they had, and Germany took full advantage.

Brazil were unbeaten in competitive matches on home soil since 1975, but any hope of extending that 39-year record quickly disappeared. Any hope of even a dignified exit from their own World Cup was obliterated within half an hour, by which time Brazil were 5–0 down and in a state of total disarray.

André Schürrle added two more after half-time as the Germans free-wheeled to the final, Schürrle's Chelsea teammate Oscar scoring a late goal for Brazil that could not even be called a consolation.

A reputation for footballing excellence had been rewritten in 90 truly unforgettable minutes.

Also on this day

2002 Leeds appointed Terry Venables as manager.

2004 Spurs signed Pedro Mendes from FC Porto with Hélder Postiga moving the other way.

9 JULY
2006 – The Zidane final

Zinedine Zidane was voted the best footballer in the world three times. He had won both the World Cup and European Championship with France, and the 2002 Champions League Final, which he sealed for Real Madrid with an extraordinary volley against Bayer Leverkusen.

Zidane had come out of international retirement to help a struggling French team qualify for the 2006 World Cup. Before the tournament began he made it clear that it was his last season with either club or country.

Once at the finals he had excelled, scoring a crucial goal against Spain in the second round and the winner against Portugal in the semi-final.

By the time the final was played in Berlin, he had already been voted the player of the tournament. It seemed as if all that remained was for Zidane to win the game and lift the cup before the curtain fell on his brilliant career.

It took just six minutes for Zidane to become only the fourth player to score in two World Cup Finals, outrageously chipping home a penalty after a challenge by Marco Materazzi on Florent Malouda – what nerve.

Materazzi, the former Everton defender, equalized soon after and an engrossing game went beyond 90 minutes into extra-time with the scores still level.

Twelve minutes from the end came the moment for which Zidane will forever be remembered, overshadowing all the fabulous achievements of the previous 17 years.

As Italy cleared a Malouda cross and launched an attack of their own, Zidane and Materazzi exchanged words. At first Zidane walked past the Italian, but then turned and powerfully butted his head into the defender's chest.

Referee Horacio Elizondo couldn't have seen it, but the cameras had and TV viewers saw a replay within seconds.

In Elizondo's version of events, given to the *Blizzard* football magazine, he was told by the fourth official Luis Medina Cantalejo what had happened. The French suspected that Cantalejo had seen it only on a TV monitor, not with his own eyes – a claim the official rejected.

But Zidane was sent off, leaving the pitch for the last time and walking in disgrace past the trophy itself, standing on its pedestal by the pitch.

Twenty minutes later Fabio Grosso scored the winning penalty for Italy.

Also on this day

2003 Harry Kewell rejected the chance to join Manchester United from Leeds in favour of a move to Liverpool.

2004 Everton were considering making Wayne Rooney their captain as Manchester United denied they were preparing a bid to take him to Old Trafford.

2008 Steve Sidwell joined Aston Villa from Chelsea for £5.5m.

2011 England's women were knocked out of the World Cup by France on penalties at the quarter-final stage.

10 JULY
2014 – Alexis to Arsenal

Liverpool had done everything they could to include Alexis Sanchez as part of the £75m deal that would take Luis Suárez from Anfield to Barcelona. Sanchez was keener on a move to London and Arsenal were looking for a player just like him.

The Gunners had tried to sign Suárez from Liverpool the previous summer, infamously offering £40m plus one pound; 'not the most subtle thing we have done', admitted Arsène Wenger, who believed Suárez had a £40m release clause.

Sanchez, Wenger said, was similar to Suárez: 'Both can play on the flank or down the middle, both are very quick to close you down, both go at you always, and always want to go forward; there are many similarities.'

In three years at Barcelona Sanchez had scored 47 goals in 141 games, but like every forward player at the Nou Camp had to accept that Messi was first and Neymar was second.

Much to Liverpool's disappointment, Arsenal's £35m bid was accepted and Sanchez made his Arsenal debut in a

3–0 win over Manchester City in the FA Community Shield.

In his first season at Arsenal Sanchez scored 25 goals, prompting Thierry Henry to describe him as their best signing of the last six years.

If Henry was peerless at Arsenal, Wenger was soon describing Sanchez as 'one of the best players I have ever worked with – a fighter. The combination of talent and a fighting spirit is very difficult to find and he has both.'

Watching from Barcelona was their new sporting director and former AC Milan transfer chief Ariedo Braida. Sanchez, he said, would never have been allowed to leave under his watch: 'I'd like Sanchez at any club I'm at; he's a great player, one of the world's best in his position. I know him a lot, he has an exquisite technique.'

Arsenal fans would happily agree.

Also on this day

1995 **Paul Gascoigne signed for Glasgow Rangers from Lazio for £4.3m.**

1995 **Arsenal spent £4.75m on David Platt from Sampdoria.**

1998 **James Beattie moved from Blackburn to Southampton.**

2003 **Glen Johnson became Chelsea's first signing under the ownership of Roman Abramovich, signing from West Ham for £6m.**

11 JULY
2014 – Liverpool sell Suárez

The offer from Arsenal in the summer of 2013 was intended to trigger a release clause in Luis Suárez's Anfield contract; in fact it triggered a withering tweet from Liverpool owner John W. Henry: 'What do you think they're smoking over there at the Emirates?'

In fact, the clause in the contract between Liverpool and Suárez only meant that they had to inform him of the bid, not that they had to accept it. Despite Suárez asking to be allowed to move on, Liverpool simply dug in their heels and Suárez had no option but to stay.

If he was unhappy you'd never have known it; having returned from his ten-match ban for biting Branislav Ivanović, Suárez scored 19 goals in his first 13 games of the season before signing a new four-and-a-half-year contract in December 2013.

All seemed well as the goals kept coming, another 12 in 23 games, the last of which was in the agonizing 3–3 draw at Crystal Palace that all but handed the Premier League title to Manchester City. Suárez left the pitch at Selhurst Park in tears.

A knee injury put his World Cup place in doubt, but he recovered in time to score twice against England and line up in Uruguay's final group game against

Italy. Unbelievably and inexplicably, Suárez bit Italian defender Giorgio Chiellini.

FIFA threw Suárez out of the World Cup and banned him from football for four months. Liverpool found themselves at the centre of a storm around their star for the third time. The club had stood by Suárez through the Patrice Evra race row and supported him through the Ivanovic biting ban; now they were ready to sell so long as Suárez moved abroad.

The £75m from Barcelona made Suárez the third most expensive player in the world. When the deal was done the statement on Liverpool's website was brief, the feeling perhaps a mixture of regret and relief that one of the most talented and controversial players the Premier League had ever seen was gone.

Also on this day

2000 Celtic broke the Scottish transfer record with a £6m move for Chris Sutton from Chelsea.

2008 Samir Nasri signed for Arsenal from Marseille.

2008 Peter Crouch joined Portsmouth for a club record £11m.

2010 Howard Webb took charge of the World Cup Final, Spain's bad-tempered 1–0 win over the Netherlands in Johannesburg.

12 JULY
1998 – France 3 Brazil 0

'Arsenal win the World Cup' was emblazoned on the back page of the *Daily Mirror* – a headline that, enlarged to many times its normal size, is still displayed in the media room at the Emirates Stadium.

The headline is a nod in the direction of Arsenal's London rivals West Ham, who claim credit for England's World Cup win of 1966: after all, Geoff Hurst and Martin Peters scored the goals and captain Bobby Moore lifted the Jules Rimet trophy.

There was more than a little journalistic licence in the *Mirror*'s claim; only one Arsenal player, Emmanuel Petit, actually started the final for France, though Patrick Vieira was on the bench. But it was Zinedine Zidane who did most to win the match.

The Brazilian team included the great phenomenon Ronaldo. At first the striker had been left off the official team sheet and then – half an hour later – included on a new one. It caused chaos and confusion in the Stade de France.

Ronaldo, it was later revealed, had suffered a convulsion and had been having cardiac and neurological tests. His roommate, Roberto Carlos, said that Ronaldo had been crying in the night and then been sick with the pressure of what lay ahead. Initially left out of the team, Ronaldo was said to have arrived on his own and late, insisting that he should play.

The drama was stirred in the stadium by dark rumours of a dispute with coach Zagallo; there was even talk of Ronaldo having been the victim of poisoning.

Ronaldo certainly didn't play like the best player in the world and was eclipsed by Zidane, who headed two almost identical goals in the first half to leave Brazil reeling.

With Marcel Desailly sent off midway through the second half, Brazil sensed a route back into the game. But then the Arsenal men sensed glory. In the last minute substitute Patrick Vieira's one-touch pass released the onrushing Petit and his side-footed finish made it three.

Also on this day

1995 Luke Shaw was born.

2001 Juan Sebastián Verón joined Manchester United for £28.1m, a new British transfer record.

2001 Peter Schmeichel moved from Sporting Lisbon to Aston Villa.

2010 Liverpool manager Roy Hodgson denied that Fernando Torres was to be sold to Chelsea.

2013 Shahid Khan completed his takeover of Fulham from Mohamed Al-Fayed.

13 JULY
2009 – Welcome to Manchester

Sir Alex Ferguson had dubbed Manchester City his 'noisy neighbours', and the billboard on Manchester's Deansgate proved it. The picture was of Carlos Tévez with arms outstretched in City's sky-blue; Tévez had swapped Old Trafford for Eastlands.

The route taken by Tévez from Buenos Aires to Manchester was a complex one. Tévez was effectively owned by his advisor Kia Joorabchian's MSI group, an arrangement not uncommon in South America but highly controversial in Britain.

From Boca Juniors to Corinthians and then West Ham, Joorabchian had brought Tévez and countryman Javier Mascherano to Europe.

Tévez was a major factor in West Ham avoiding relegation in 2007, despite the club being fined £5.5m for breaching Premier League rules by engaging in a deal with a third-party owner.

By this time Liverpool had signed Mascherano in a loan deal that, despite the complications, met with Premier League approval. In the summer Manchester United trod the same route to sign Carlos Tévez on a two-year loan, with MSI paying £2m to West Ham to release his registration and United agreeing to a £25.5m option to buy at the end of the loan spell.

After a slow start Tévez soon became an Old Trafford idol; playing with Ronaldo and Rooney the three shared 16 of the 20 Champions League goals United scored as they reached the final and beat Chelsea on penalties in Moscow.

In his second season at Old Trafford, Tévez added a further 15 goals and won a second Premier League title, but in the second half of the campaign increasingly found himself on the bench.

In early May, with the two-year deal close to expiring, United seemed ambivalent about turning his loan into a permanent move. Tévez said he might not stay; fans pleaded with the club to act.

The last game of United's season was again the Champions League Final, this time in Rome. Tévez was again named as a substitute, and although he came on at half-time for Anderson, United were well beaten by Barcelona.

By the time United called Joorabchian to agree to the £25.5m fee it was too late; on 13 July Carlos Tévez picked his next club and it was just down the road.

Also on this day

1995 George Graham was banned from football for one year after being found guilty of taking illegal payments.

1998 After scoring a record 185 goals for Arsenal, Ian Wright left to join West Ham.

14 JULY
2005 – Vieira leaves Arsenal

If there is one player who embodies Arsenal's most successful years under Arsène Wenger it is, surely, Patrick Vieira.

Vieira actually signed for Arsenal before Arsène Wenger joined the club, but it was a move instigated by Wenger, who was waiting for his contract with Nagoya Grampus Eight in Japan to expire before moving to London.

Vieira had spent a short time at AC Milan, playing only twice in their first team, but the midfielder had first caught Wenger's attention at Cannes.

In nine seasons at Arsenal, three as captain, he won the Premier League title three times and the FA Cup on four occasions, scoring the winning penalty in the 2005 shoot-out against Manchester United with his last kick in an Arsenal shirt.

Arsenal fans loved him for his strength and style, and for his epic battles with Roy Keane of perennial rivals Manchester United. Vieira was always combative, ready for any opponent, and his disciplinary record was always an issue; there were a massive 108 yellow cards and 10 reds on his charge sheet.

The relationship between Arsenal and Vieira wasn't always trouble-free: in 2001 he threatened to leave Arsenal, with both Juventus and Manchester United offering a change of scene. Three years later Real Madrid tried their luck, and a deal seemed to have been agreed, with Arsène Wenger even discussing signing Michael Carrick as a replacement, only for Vieira to change his mind.

The following summer Juventus enquired about Robert Pirès; the Italians couldn't get him, but discovered that they could get Vieira. A fee of £13.75m was agreed and Arsenal's captain left for Turin.

Arsène Wenger paid tribute as he left: 'Patrick was a great player for us, one of the greatest in the club's history, and I feel I had a special relationship with him because I made him come here. I think his impact, not only at Arsenal but in English football overall, was just tremendous.'

Vieira was 28, and many Arsenal fans felt he was being allowed to leave too soon. But Arsène Wenger had a replacement raring to go and he wouldn't cost a penny; aged only 18, Cesc Fàbregas was ready.

Also on this day

1993 David Platt signed for Sampdoria from Juventus for £5.2m and on the same day Sampdoria agreed to sell Des Walker to Sheffield Wednesday for £2.7m.

1995 Manchester City agreed a £2m transfer with Dinamo Tbilisi for Georgi Kinkladze.

1997 David Ginola joined Spurs from Newcastle for £2.5m.

2015 Raheem Sterling completed a record breaking £49m move from Liverpool to Manchester City.

15 JULY
1994 – The SAS are born

In the 1992/93 season Alan Shearer had scored 22 goals for Blackburn and his partner Mike Newell had scored 21. The following campaign Shearer scored an explosive 34 goals, with Newell, and now also Kevin Gallacher, chipping in but getting nowhere near Shearer's tally.

Meanwhile at Carrow Road, Norwich City manager Dave Stringer had seen something in a young centre half who was breaking into the first team. Stringer decided it was worth experimenting with Chris Sutton as a centre forward alongside the experienced Mark Robins. In 1992 Norwich replaced Stringer with Mike Walker and, now alternating between defence and attack, Sutton scored ten goals in the 1992/93 season, enough to persuade both manager and player that his future lay in attack.

That decision paid handsome dividends as Sutton, now partnered by Efan Ekoku and supported by Ruel Fox, finished the 1993/94 season as Norwich's top scorer with 28, despite another change of manager as Walker went to Everton to be replaced by John Deehan.

Having only just turned 21, Sutton was the big clubs' must-have striker of the summer and had the choice of moving to Arsenal or Blackburn, both of whom had agreed a British record £5m fee with Norwich.

Sutton spent 14 July meeting representatives of both clubs and overnight decided on Blackburn. The Shearer and Sutton partnership, the SAS, would wreak havoc with defences over the following season.

With Stuart Ripley and Jason Wilcox providing the ammunition, Shearer and Sutton shared 57 goals in the 48 league and cup games they played together in 1994/95, winning the Premier League title. They were unstoppable, either Sutton or Shearer, or both, scoring in all except three of their league games before Christmas. Shearer ended the season with 37 goals in league and cup and Sutton with 21.

It seemed that Blackburn's strike partnership would lift them to even greater heights, but it wasn't to be. Kenny Dalglish made the shock decision to leave the day-to-day management to Ray Harford, Sutton picked up an injury early in the following season, and even Shearer's 31 league goals weren't enough to sustain a title challenge.

Shearer left Blackburn for Newcastle in the summer of 1996, and the SAS partnership was finished. For one magical season it had been truly glorious.

Also on this day

1997 Danny Murphy, the latest star graduate of Crewe's successful youth system, signed for Liverpool.

2014 Diego Costa signed for Chelsea from Atlético Madrid for £32m.

16 JULY
1997 – Ferguson picks captain Keane

Éric Cantona's sudden retirement from football at the age of 30 came as a shock to Manchester United. Alex Ferguson said, 'Eric basically believes that he must go out at the top. Now he's gone, I don't feel let down. There can't be any recriminations in my heart.'

In appointing a new captain Ferguson chose the most forceful voice in his dressing room, the unpredictable, incendiary, brilliant Roy Keane. The Irishman would turn out to be one of United's finest captains.

It didn't start that way. No sooner had Keane got used to the grip of the armband on his biceps than he was injured, out of action for ten months.

Keane and Leeds's Alf-Inge Haaland clashed in a game at Elland Road, leaving the Manchester United captain with a cruciate knee injury. As Keane lay on the ground in agony Haaland accused him of feigning injury to cover for an attempted foul – not something Keane would forget.

As captain, Keane would add four Premier League titles to the three he had already won as well as doubling his haul of FA Cup winner's medals from two to four.

Keane was not a company man, sometimes willing to criticize teammates and famously ready to point the finger at the fans for a lack of atmosphere. After United's win over Dynamo Kiev at Old Trafford in November 2000 Keane said, 'Away from home our fans are fantastic, I'd call them the hardcore fans. But at home they have a few drinks and probably the prawn sandwiches, and they don't realize what's going on out on the pitch. I don't think some of the people who come to Old Trafford can spell football, never mind understand it.'

Keane's finest hour came in Turin, when he scored the first goal for United as they launched the unlikely comeback at Juventus that took them to the Champions League Final of 1999. Keane would not play in that final, having been booked in the first half in Turin, but despite that personal disappointment his sheer determination to prevail seemed to drag United through.

Without Roy Keane the Champions League and the great treble of 1999 may very well never have been won.

Also on this day

1993 Peter Beardsley rejoined Newcastle from Everton.

2001 Christian Ziege signed for Spurs from Liverpool for £4m.

2005 Shaun Wright-Phillips completed a £21m move from Chelsea to Manchester City.

17 JULY
1998 – Liverpool's job-share

When Liverpool appointed Roy Evans as manager in 1994 to take over from Graeme Souness, it was a move that continued a tradition stretching back to 1959 and the arrival of Bill Shankly.

Liverpool's famed boot-room – the meeting place for the coaching staff to have post-match discussions and drinks – had produced a succession of managers as Liverpool appointed from within. Shankly's successor Bob Paisley had been followed by Joe Fagan, then Kenny Dalglish as player-manager, former player Souness, and finally Roy Evans, who had joined the club in 1965 as a player only to be advised by Shankly to take up coaching.

Evans's four years in charge at Liverpool had been frustrating; pleasing on the eye, Liverpool had been League Cup winners in 1995, beaten finalists in the 1996 FA Cup and semi-finalists in the European Cup-Winners' Cup the following season when they had also faded badly after mounting a serious challenge to win the league.

There was a feeling that off the pitch discipline was not what it should be; Liverpool's young team were dubbed the Spice Boys.

Perhaps that's why the club turned to a former school teacher to help Evans out.

Gérard Houllier, who had even spent a year teaching in Liverpool in the early 1970s, seemed perfect. After a spell as an amateur player he had forged a career as a coach that took him all the way to the top as manager of France's national team. Houllier had stood down after their failure to qualify for the 1994 World Cup, but was still employed by the French Federation as part of their much-admired Clairefontaine academy.

With Arsène Wenger blazing a trail at Arsenal and France having just won the World Cup, French coaches and players were in vogue. Houllier fitted the bill.

The decision to have joint managers seemed a fudge – it would hardly have been at Evans's suggestion – but the club were reluctant to sack such a loyal and popular man.

The arrangement lasted just 18 matches, of which only 7 were won. With the team playing badly it was clear that job-sharing didn't work and equally clear that the new man wasn't likely to get the blame.

After a home defeat to Spurs, Evans resigned.

Also on this day

1994 Italy's Roberto Baggio missed the decisive kick in the penalty shoot-out as Brazil won the World Cup.

2000 Paul Gascoigne was reunited with manager Walter Smith when he signed for Everton from Middlesbrough.

2014 Following his release by Manchester United, Rio Ferdinand signed for QPR.

18 JULY

2005 – Ashley Cole to stay at Arsenal

When Ashley Cole signed a new contract with Arsenal in July 2005, it seemed to be bringing down the curtain on one of the most protracted and ugliest transfer sagas in the Premier League's history, and one that contributed greatly to the antipathy between Arsène Wenger and José Mourinho.

In January 2005 contract negotiations between Cole and Arsenal were not going well. On 27 January Cole and his agent Jonathan Barnett met Chelsea manager José Mourinho, chief executive Peter Kenyon and agent Pini Zahavi in London's Royal Park Hotel.

The meeting, instigated by Cole's agent, was one about which Arsenal knew nothing: they believed that, in football parlance, Cole was being 'tapped-up'.

When Arsenal complained to the Premier League, Chelsea argued that they had no intention of discussing any potential transfer, but were simply interested in hearing about the inner workings of a rival club from a disgruntled employee. Mourinho stated that he would have no interest in signing Cole anyway, because at five feet eight inches he was too short.

Arsenal viewed it differently and so did the Premier League. The fines were huge: Chelsea were ordered to pay £300,000, Mourinho £200,000, Barnett and Cole £100,000 each.

Mourinho and Cole had their fines reduced to £75,000 on appeal but the atmosphere between the clubs was poisonous. Chelsea chairman Bruce Buck said, 'None of the scenarios I'm thinking about are positive when it comes to Chelsea and Arsenal, but we can try.'

Cole returned to Arsenal and signed a new contract, but injury meant that he would play only 16 more games for the club. A year later, without having grown at all, Cole moved to Chelsea in a deal that saw William Gallas and £5m go the other way.

Cole's parting shot to Arsenal was that they had 'fed him to the sharks' over the tapping-up affair. Arsenal fans never forgave Cole and the relationship between Wenger and Mourinho remains as frosty as ever.

Also on this day

1997 Liverpool signed former Manchester United midfielder Paul Ince from Inter Milan for £4.2m.

2000 Nick Barmby became the first player to join Liverpool from Everton since Dave Hickson in 1959. The fee was £6m.

2009 Emmanuel Adebayor moved from Arsenal to Manchester City for £25m.

2013 England's women lost their final match at the European Championship 3–0 to France, going home with just one point from three games.

19 JULY
1993 – Keane to Old Trafford

Roy Keane would never have signed for Manchester United if his handshake with Kenny Dalglish at Blackburn Rovers hadn't come late on a Friday afternoon.

Keane, 'the hottest property in football right now' according to Brian Clough, had a clause in his contract saying he could leave Nottingham Forest if they were relegated. Clough's impending retirement made his departure a certainty. 'He virtually is Nottingham Forest in my eyes,' said Keane. Relegation came and Keane left, knowing he was far too good to play outside the top division.

Arsenal and Blackburn were leading the race, with both willing to break the British transfer record to get their man, but Rovers manager Kenny Dalglish had

the edge after spending several months making it clear that he wanted the midfielder at Ewood Park.

On 16 July a deal was agreed. Blackburn would pay Forest £4m for Keane, whose contract was settled, and all that remained was for the paperwork to be signed. Unfortunately for Blackburn the offices at Ewood Park were empty and there was nobody to complete that paperwork – it would have to wait until Monday morning.

Alex Ferguson, fresh from leading Manchester United to their first Premier League title and looking for a replacement for Bryan Robson, saw a window of opportunity.

Having been told on Saturday that Keane's move to Blackburn had not been signed off, Ferguson invited him to his house, where they played snooker.

Keane later wrote, 'I liked him straight away, for a man managing Manchester United he was unaffected, funny and reassuringly human. He was also clearly hungry for more trophies. There were a few obstacles to overcome before a deal could be done. We agreed that I would tell Dalglish our deal was off.'

How Ferguson must have enjoyed putting one over Dalglish, one of his oldest adversaries. Blackburn, who signed David Batty instead, complained bitterly that a handshake should be binding; but on the Monday morning Keane signed for

Manchester United, where he would stay for 12 seasons, winning seven league titles and four FA Cups.

Also on this day

1995 Arsenal striker Alan Smith was forced to retire from football with a knee injury.

2005 Liverpool signed Peter Crouch for £7m from Southampton.

2006 David O'Leary left the manager's job at Aston Villa by mutual consent.

20 JULY
2004 – Chelsea sign Didier Drogba

Didier Drogba had scored 32 goals for Marseille in the 2003/04 season including 2 against Liverpool and 2 against Newcastle in their march to the UEFA Cup Final. He was the reigning French Footballer of the Year and had been nominated for the World Player of the Year award.

Drogba had been a late developer, already 21 when he signed as a professional at Le Mans in the French second division. Arsenal manager Arsène Wenger had noticed him there, but it was top-flight Guingamp who were willing to take a chance on Drogba. Once there he developed quickly, scoring 20 league goals over two seasons and earning a move, for that one stellar season, to Marseille.

Already 26, it was not unreasonable that many coaches wondered if Drogba's season at Marseille might not be a flash in the pan. And the French club were not short of money; they would demand a big fee for a player they'd had for only a short time.

At Chelsea José Mourinho had been manager for barely six weeks. His FC Porto side had been drawn against Marseille in their Champions League group the previous season and Drogba had impressed in both games, scoring in Marseille's 3–2 defeat in France.

Roman Abramovich was said to be encouraging Mourinho to make a bid for Ronaldinho, but the new manager preferred the hungrier Drogba.

A bid of £24m was enough for Marseille's resistance to yield. Drogba started slowly at Stamford Bridge, only scoring once in his first five games and coming under pressure for his place from Mateja Kežman. Any doubts were eradicated by a fabulous display and two goals against Paris Saint-Germain in France, and Drogba's place as Chelsea's senior striker was assured.

Drogba signed for Chelsea on the same day as Portuguese midfielder Thiago; one is barely remembered, the other will never be forgotten for 157 goals in 342 games. And that was only in his first spell: in 2014 Chelsea fans were delighted to discover that Drogba was coming back.

Also on this day

1998 UEFA gave the go-ahead for Arsenal to play their Champions League fixtures at Wembley.

2003 Ronaldinho disappointed Manchester United by rejecting a move to Old Trafford and joined Barcelona instead.

2004 Liverpool broke their transfer record to sign Djibril Cissé from Auxerre for £14m.

2012 Swansea signed Michu from Rayo Vallecano for £2m.

21 JULY
2002 – Elland Road to Old Trafford, Ferdinand on the move

Rio Ferdinand was the best English ball-playing central defender of his generation. Others might head, tackle, clear, block and battle; Ferdinand would always try to play.

Singled out early in his career at West Ham as a possible successor to Bobby Moore, Ferdinand played his last game for the Hammers at Elland Road against Leeds in November 2000. Elland Road is where

he stayed, now the world's most expensive defender at £18m, aged only 22.

At Leeds Ferdinand flourished immediately, helping them reach the semi-finals of the Champions League. Their fourth-place finish in the Premier League left them in the less lucrative UEFA Cup the following season.

The Leeds team of 2001/02 was one of the most expensive ever assembled: playing alongside captain Ferdinand were Robbie Keane, Mark Viduka, Robbie Fowler, Olivier Dacourt and Lee Bowyer. Chairman Peter Ridsdale paid for the best and rewarded them accordingly, but Leeds once more failed to qualify for the Champions League and manager David O'Leary was replaced by Terry Venables.

By now Leeds United's accounts showed debts of around £100m.

Ferdinand went to the 2002 World Cup, where he played every minute of every game and scored in the 3–0 win over Denmark.

Manchester United had sold Jaap Stam the previous autumn; Laurent Blanc was an able but ageing replacement. What Alex Ferguson needed was a Rio Ferdinand.

Relations between Leeds and Manchester United have never been cordial. In 2002 they were rivals at the top end of the Premier League, with Leeds fans still haunted by the sale of Éric Cantona for a meagre £1.2m to their bitter Lancastrian foes.

When Manchester United first enquired about signing Ferdinand, it seemed a deal to which Leeds could never agree. A look at their accounts soon made it obvious that they had no choice but to agree.

At first Ridsdale insisted on £35m and a quick deal, but dropped both demands as a contract at Old Trafford was hammered out.

Ferdinand signed for £30m, restoring his status as the world's most expensive defender. Ridsdale countered the inevitable dismay by saying, 'People need to look at how much we've invested in the last three or four years – we're hardly a selling club.'

Within months Keane, Bowyer, Fowler and Woodgate had also been sold; two seasons later Leeds were relegated.

Also on this day

2000 Mark Viduka joined Leeds United from Celtic.

2003 Chelsea beat Liverpool to the £17m signature of Damien Duff.

2014 Steven Gerrard announced his international retirement after 114 caps for England.

22 JULY
1995 – Cologne 8 Spurs 0

The Intertoto Cup was a summer tournament designed to give meaningful matches that European football pools companies could include on a betting coupon, and to offer some summer football to teams who failed to qualify for any of the major European competitions. It had been run – outside UEFA's jurisdiction – since 1961 without anyone in Britain taking any notice.

In 1995, UEFA adopted the tournament as one of its own, offering two winning clubs entry to the UEFA Cup. The FA accepted the offer of three places, assuming that there would be interest from the Premier League. Unanimously all 20 top-flight clubs rejected the chance to take a spot in the competition, understandably put off by a start date of 24 June.

Initially UEFA threatened to fine the FA £150,000 for their clubs' non-participation. This didn't ruffle many feathers in England so UEFA upped the penalty for ignoring the Intertoto Cup to elimination of all English clubs from all European competition. Now they were listening at the FA and the Premier League.

Blackburn, Manchester United, Nottingham Forest, Liverpool, Leeds and Everton were off the hook. They'd all already qualified for Europe, but unless they could persuade three volunteers to step forward for the Intertoto Cup, all six might be barred from taking part.

Eventually, and only after a deadline was extended, Sheffield Wednesday,

Wimbledon and Tottenham Hotspur agreed to play, though none at their usual home ground. Wimbledon and Spurs both played at the Goldstone Ground in Brighton, Sheffield Wednesday at Rotherham's Millmoor.

None of the three English clubs progressed beyond the group phase, though Sheffield Wednesday did best, winning two of their four games and using many of their senior players including Chris Waddle, Des Walker and Mark Bright.

Wimbledon, fielding a team of youth players, scored only one goal in four games and didn't register a win.

The most eye-catching result of all came at Cologne's Müngersdorferstadion. There Spurs picked a team including a youthful Stephen Carr, the on-loan and ageing Barnet defender Mark Newson and a 33-year-old Alan Pardew who had recently been released by Charlton and was about to sign for Barnet.

The Germans took the game uncharitably seriously and won 8–0, still Tottenham's heaviest ever defeat.

Also on this day

1999 Dietmar Hamann joined Liverpool from Newcastle.

2006 The Emirates Stadium hosted its first match, a testimonial for Dennis Bergkamp.

2014 Stoke City signed Bojan Krkić from Barcelona.

23 JULY

2004 – Everton capture Cahill

Either Tim Cahill was so good, or the Samoan Under-20 team was so bad, that Cahill played for them when he was just 14. Born in Sydney, Cahill had family in Samoa and viewed his call-up as a chance to visit relatives at someone else's expense. It was a decision that cost him the chance to represent the Republic of Ireland (he had an Irish grandfather) at the 2002 World Cup.

Under FIFA rules at the time, a player couldn't switch allegiance once he had played any representative game at any age group. Mick McCarthy was the disappointed Irish manager who had offered Cahill a place in his squad. Once FIFA changed their rules on national affiliation in 2004, Cahill became a full Australian international, playing and scoring in three World Cups.

By the time he was 24, Cahill had six seasons at Millwall under his belt and had played in the FA Cup Final, losing to Manchester United in 2004.

Millwall's south London neighbours Crystal Palace agreed a £2m fee to take Cahill to Selhurst Park, only for the deal to fall through. Within two weeks David

Moyes had swooped and Cahill was an Everton player.

The 2004 Olympic football tournament delayed his arrival at Goodison, but once he got there his impact was immediate, scoring the winning goal against Manchester City – and being sent off – in only his second game. His second goal, against Portsmouth two weeks later, was another classic header and soon Premier League defences were wary of this five-foot-ten midfielder whose timing was so immaculate that he could out-jump much taller defenders.

Cahill was Everton's top scorer in his first season and soon his trademark goal celebration of shadow-boxing the corner flag became a familiar sight.

Over eight seasons at the club he scored 68 goals, 5 of them in Merseyside derbies. He also lost a second FA Cup Final, this time to Chelsea in 2009.

Sent off in his second game for Everton, Cahill was also dismissed in his last – or more accurately, *after* his last game. He was shown a red card after the final whistle for violent conduct after grabbing Newcastle's Yohan Cabaye by the neck. It didn't deter the New York Red Bulls from taking him to the MLS.

Also on this day

2001 Junichi Inamoto became the first Japanese player to move to the Premier League, signing for Arsenal from Gamba Osaka.

2002 Gary Lineker opened Leicester City's new Walkers Stadium.

24 JULY
1995 – Grobbelaar, Fashanu and Segers bailed over match-fixing allegations

English football was shaken by the allegations of match-fixing made against three high-profile players. Bruce Grobbelaar was the former Liverpool goalkeeper who was now playing at Southampton, John Fashanu was a former England international and Wimbledon striker recently signed by Aston Villa, and Hans Segers was a Dutch goalkeeper who had played in England for ten years representing both Nottingham Forest and Wimbledon. Malaysian businessman Heng Suan Lim was also accused of involvement.

The *Sun* newspaper had secretly filmed Grobbelaar discussing fixing matches in the past. In his defence Grobbelaar said that he had been going along with the discussion in order to gather evidence, which he intended to pass to the authorities.

In the video Grobbelaar discussed accidentally making a brilliant save against Manchester United for Liverpool, and thus losing the chance of a £125,000 payment. The newspaper alleged that Fashanu and Lim were middle-men for a betting syndicate, with Grobbelaar and Segers paid to deliver the correct results.

When the case came to trial, the jury were unable to come to a verdict. A second trial also failed to reach a verdict and all four of the accused were acquitted in November 1997.

An FA inquiry found that Grobbelaar and Segers had breached betting rules and both were given suspended bans.

The fall-out didn't end there for Grobbelaar: he sued the *Sun* and won £85,000 in damages, only for an appeal to result in a House of Lords judgement cutting the award to Grobbelaar to just £1, the minimum allowed. Eight years after the allegations were made, Grobbelaar was also ordered to pay legal costs of £500,000, which resulted in him being declared bankrupt.

Also on this day

1998 David Unsworth, wanting to move nearer his Merseyside home, joined Aston Villa from West Ham for £3m. A month later he joined Everton for the same fee without ever playing for Villa.

2007 Manchester United manager Sir Alex Ferguson refused to allow defender Gabriel Heinze to sign for Liverpool.

25 JULY
2003 – Raúl says no to Roman

Money, it turned out, cannot get you everything.

Roman Abramovich had bought Chelsea and set about the biggest spending spree that English football had ever seen. The Blues had already snapped up Damien Duff, Geremi, Joe Cole and Juan Verón.

It had not all been good news for Chelsea fans that summer: even the promise of a new super-charged Chelsea couldn't persuade the adored Gianfranco Zola to go back on his promise to finish his career at his home-town club Cagliari. No replacement had been bought and it was clear that a big-name goalscorer would be recruited to go alongside Eidur Gudjohnsen and Jimmy Floyd Hasselbaink, who were already at the club.

In 2003 there were few bigger names than Raúl.

In nine years in the first team at the Bernabéu , Raúl had won the Spanish league four times and the Champions League on three occasions, becoming the first player to score in two finals.

Real planned to make him their club captain following the departure of Fernando Hierro, but then Chelsea called his agent Ginés Carvajal offering to double his salary of around £4m a year.

Carvajal later told Spanish journalists, 'I called and told him that Chelsea had made a very good proposal. He would not let me continue. He flatly refused. I insisted, but it was impossible. He told me not to tell anything. It was the only time Raúl came close to leaving Madrid.'

Seven years later Raúl did eventually move on, to Schalke 04 in Germany, but not before he had scored a staggering 323 goals for the club, breaking Alfredo Di Stéfano's record.

Chelsea looked elsewhere for their superstar striker and bought Adrian Mutu and Hernán Crespo instead.

Also on this day

1997 Newcastle signed Inter Milan's Alessandro Pistone for £4.5m.

2003 Arsenal signed goalkeeper Jens Lehmann from Borussia Dortmund for £1.25m.

2009 Manchester City failed in their bid to sign John Terry from Chelsea.

2014 Two years after leaving Stamford Bridge, Didier Drogba returned to Chelsea on a free transfer from Galatasaray.

26 JULY
1992 – Alan Shearer joins Blackburn Rovers

In 1992 English transfer fees were lagging way behind the deals being done by the wealthiest Serie A clubs in Italy. The world transfer record was broken three times that year: first by AC Milan, who spent £10m on Jean-Pierre Papin from Marseille, then by Juventus paying £12m to Sampdoria for Gianluca Vialli, and finally by AC Milan again when they signed Gianluigi Lentini from Torino for £13m. Glasgow Rangers held the British record with the £5.5m they had paid Marseille for Trevor Steven. The English record stood at £2.9m, Liverpool signing Dean Saunders from Derby County.

Blackburn, with Jack Walker funding them and Kenny Dalglish managing, had finished only sixth in the second division in 1991/92, but had beaten Derby and Leicester in the play-offs to be promoted into the top flight for the first time since 1966; now they were ambitious to make an immediate impact.

David White of Manchester City, David Hirst of Sheffield Wednesday and Kevin Campbell at Arsenal were other young English strikers making a name for themselves, but Alan Shearer was the youngest and the most highly rated. After scoring 13 goals in 11 games for England Under-21s he had made a very promising start with the senior England team, scoring on his debut against France.

Shearer had spent four years in Southampton's first team, becoming the youngest player to score a top-flight hat-trick, and hit 21 goals in his last season at the Dell. Manchester United, Leeds and Liverpool had all been impressed and were linked with a move for the 21-year-old striker.

With Shearer a part of the England squad at Euro 92, Southampton's then manager Ian Branfoot accepted that a sale was inevitable; and when Blackburn offered £3.6m plus David Speedie Southampton had the deal they wanted.

Shearer's first game for Blackburn came on the first weekend of the brand-new Premier League; it was at Selhurst Park against Crystal Palace – and it was a thriller.

Mark Bright headed Palace in front, only for another new signing, Stuart Ripley, to equalize for Blackburn. Gareth Southgate scored his first league goal for Palace and then Shearer exploded. His first was a dipping right-footed half-volley from around 25 yards, his second a bending shot, again off the right foot, this time from even further out. Simon Osborn equalized for Palace with almost the last touch of the game, but Shearer and Blackburn had announced their arrival.

27 JULY
1997 – Les Ferdinand leaves Newcastle

Les Ferdinand spent only two seasons at St James' Park, but what great seasons they were.

Signed from Queens Park Rangers for £6m in June 1995, Ferdinand set a post-war record by scoring in eight consecutive matches for the club in his first season, scoring 29 goals in all and becoming the first Newcastle player to be named the PFA Players' Player of the Year – receiving the award from Pelé.

Premier League runners-up that season, Newcastle added Alan Shearer to their squad for the 1996/97 campaign, with Ferdinand letting the new man take the famous number nine shirt and switching to number ten.

In his second season in the northeast, Ferdinand scored 21 goals, despite a fractured cheekbone and a hamstring injury costing him ten games, and despite the shock resignation in January of Kevin Keegan, who was replaced by Kenny Dalglish. Ferdinand's willingness to act as an unselfish foil for 28-goal Shearer made him hugely popular and kept Faustino Asprilla out of the starting 11 for much of the campaign, but again Newcastle came just short of winning the Premier League.

In the summer of 1997 there were rumours that Newcastle's finances had become precarious and that Dalglish would have to sell to get in the new faces he wanted at the club. At first Ferdinand was reluctant to leave, but when Spurs signed his Newcastle teammate David Ginola and then had an offer of £6m accepted, Ferdinand moved back to London.

Ferdinand scored 50 goals for Newcastle in 84 games, and when he returned to St James' Park with Tottenham the following October he was overcome by the reception he got from the home fans.

Dalglish replaced Ferdinand with Jon Dahl Tomasson and ageing ex-Liverpool stars Ian Rush and John Barnes, and the team slumped from runners-up in 1997 to finishing 13th in 1998.

Ferdinand spent five-and-a-half seasons at Spurs, but scored fewer goals with them than he had in just two seasons at Newcastle.

It was short, but very sweet.

Also on this day

2001 Rangers boss Alex McLeish and his Celtic counterpart Martin O'Neill jointly urged the Premier League to consider allowing their clubs entry to the English top flight.

2004 Ricardo Carvalho signed for Chelsea from FC Porto for £19.8m.

2006 Real Madrid completed the £10.3m signing of Ruud van Nistelrooy from Manchester United.

28 JULY
2011
– 'AgüeroOOOOOOO!'

The man who scored 'that' goal to win the Premier League title for Manchester City in 2012 was already a world star before he ever came to Eastlands.

Agüero had won the Under-20 World Cup twice with Argentina (as top scorer and having been voted best player in the 2007 tournament), in 2008 he'd won Olympic gold and beaten Lionel Messi to the title of the Spanish league's best player, and in 2010 he'd won the Europa League and the European Super Cup with Atlético Madrid and played in his first World Cup.

It's a lot to achieve by the age of 22, but then Agüero started early. He was only 15 years and 13 days old when he made his debut for the Buenos Aires-based club Independiente, breaking a record set by his future father-in-law Diego Maradona.

Inevitably, as with that other Atlético hero Fernando Torres, a move away from Madrid's second club was certain to happen sooner or later. The usual suspects – Inter Milan, Real Madrid and Chelsea – were all linked with Agüero after the 2010 World Cup.

Agüero stayed for another season, scoring 27 goals in a struggling side, but before leaving for the 2011 Copa America in Argentina, he told Atlético he wanted to leave.

There must have been conflicting influences in that Argentina dressing room; just prior to the tournament kicking off City striker Carlos Tévez had told an Argentine TV chat show, 'There's nothing to do in Manchester, there are two restaurants and everything is small. It rains all the time and you can't go anywhere. I will not return to Manchester, not for a vacation, not anything.'

Luckily for Manchester City, right-back Pablo Zabaleta was also in that Argentine squad and he had a different tale to tell.

After completing his £35m move in July 2011, Agüero said, 'I spoke to Zabaleta and he spoke really positively about the club. There will be friends and family coming to see me and I'm sure I'm going to enjoy myself here; life will be fine.'

Also on this day

1993 Harry Kane was born.

2000 Coventry sold Robbie Keane to Inter Milan for £13m.

2000 Marc Overmars and Emmanuel Petit left Arsenal for Barcelona for a joint fee of £30m.

2002 World Cup winner Gilberto Silva joined Arsenal for £4.5m from Atlético Mineiro.

2010 Mark Hughes was named as the new manager of Fulham.

29 JULY
1996 – Alan Shearer, the world's most expensive player

It took Alan Shearer ten years to sign for his home-town team. Shearer was discovered by Jack Hixon, a full-time British Rail clerk but hugely respected football scout. The young Shearer was playing for Wallsend Boys Club, whose former players include Peter Beardsley, Steve Bruce, Michael Carrick, Michael Bridges and Fraser Forster.

Hixon might have been watching the playing fields of Newcastle and the northeast, but he was working for Southampton; and that's where Shearer headed at the age of 16.

Seven years at Southampton and four at Blackburn had seen Shearer become the mainstay of England's attack, finish as top scorer at Euro 96, win a Premier League title with Blackburn and come third in the FIFA vote for World Player of the Year.

Blackburn hoped to keep Shearer in the summer of 1996, but Manchester United and Newcastle were ready to break not only the British transfer record, but the world record; both were offering £15m.

Blackburn's strong preference was for Shearer not to join Manchester United, the club they had battled for the 1995 Premier League title. United's chairman Martin Edwards was later quoted as saying, 'There was no way that Rovers would let him come here.'

In fact Shearer nearly did sign at Old Trafford; talks with Alex Ferguson were productive and a deal seemed possible. But Newcastle had Shearer's childhood hero Kevin Keegan as their manager, and Keegan's enthusiasm and determination swung the decision their way: 'What a player. What a man. What a signing!' he said.

At his unveiling at St James' Park 20,000 Newcastle fans came to make sure that he knew he'd made the right decision. Shearer said, 'I drove past the old house and the old piece of grass where I used to play. Why? Just to say officially, "Look, I am back in Newcastle, and this is where it all started." There is a special feeling of being a Geordie. If you go away you always want to come back.'

In ten seasons Shearer scored 206 Newcastle goals in 405 matches, scoring 20 goals or more in six of those campaigns. Loyal to Newcastle, he never won a major trophy with the club, but nobody has come close to matching his record of 260 Premier League goals.

Also on this day

1994 Tottenham signed Jürgen Klinsmann from Monaco for £2m.

1999 The FA confirmed that the twin towers of Wembley would not be preserved in the rebuilt stadium's design.

2008 Liverpool paid Spurs £19m for Robbie Keane.

2009 Kolo Touré swapped Arsenal for Manchester City in a £16m deal.

30 JULY
2008 – Spurs buy Bentley

David Bentley was to be the 'new David Beckham'. Like Beckham, his crossing ability was uncanny despite not being blessed with fantastic pace.

Starting at Arsenal, he was quickly earmarked as a star in the making for club and country.

His first Arsenal senior goal was a wonderfully executed chip against Middlesbrough in an FA Cup tie in 2004, scoring an equally brilliant goal against the Netherlands on his debut for the England Under-21 side a few days later.

A season on loan at Norwich gave him a taste for regular first-team football and in the summer of 2005, despite being only 20, he told Arsène Wenger he wasn't willing to wait his time at Arsenal. Perhaps to Bentley's surprise, Arsenal didn't argue.

Later Bentley would admit that gambling was becoming a problem for him at this time; maybe Arsenal could see there was something wrong, or maybe his self-confidence, bordering on arrogance, was just too much?

A loan spell to Blackburn was arranged, and quickly made permanent by boss Mark Hughes. Arsenal's loss seemed to be Blackburn's gain when, in his first game after that deal was agreed, he scored a hat-trick against Manchester United.

Bentley, who had now overcome his gambling habit, spent three seasons at Blackburn where everything went right. He played for England and was linked with both Manchester clubs and Liverpool; but it was Spurs who got in first for £15m.

There was soon a new manager at White Hart Lane, as Harry Redknapp took over from Juande Ramos. In his second game in charge Redknapp watched as Bentley converted one of the best goals ever seen in a north London derby, a dipping volley from 40 yards in a 4–4 draw.

That was as good as it got at Tottenham. Bentley missed a penalty in the League Cup Final shoot-out defeat to Manchester United and over the last four years of his contract played only 27 more games for Spurs. Unsuccessful loans to Birmingham, West Ham, FC Rostov and Blackburn followed.

He played his last game of football at the age of 28 and after 12 months without a club retired in 2014.

In an interview with the *Sunday People* Bentley said, 'I had the tools but I don't think I had [tapping his head] that.'

Also on this day

1998 Newcastle signed Dietmar Hamann from Bayern Munich and Nolberto Solano from Boca Juniors.

1999 Middlesbrough bought Paul Ince from Liverpool.

2000 Aston Villa spent £3m on David Ginola from Spurs.

2014 Everton broke their transfer record, signing Romelu Lukaku from Chelsea for £28m.

2012 – Houghton the Wembley wonder

Many of the most memorable moments of the London 2012 Olympic Games belonged to triumphant women: Katherine Grainger, Victoria Pendleton, Laura Trott, Jessica Ennis, Charlotte Dujardin, Nicola Adams and Jade Jones were all fêted as gold-medallists.

There were no medals for Hope Powell's Great Britain football team, but there were plenty of plaudits as the women's football tournament proved to be every bit as exciting and popular as the men's.

Despite having four international goals for England, Steph Houghton was something of an unlikely goalscoring sensation at the Olympics; she was the left back in a team containing renowned finishers Kelly Smith, Karen Carney and Eni Aluko.

It was Kelly Smith who looked favourite to take a 64th-minute free-kick in Britain's first match against New Zealand in Cardiff; but Smith was a decoy, and Houghton swept home for an edgy 1–0 win.

The second match saw Cameroon beaten 3–0 in the Millennium Stadium, Houghton scoring an excellent third after goals for Jill Scott and Casey Stoney. Great Britain knew they were through to the quarter-finals no matter what happened in the last group game, against the mighty Brazil at Wembley.

From 1921 to 1969 the FA had banned women from playing football on league grounds. Now they were playing at the home of the FA.

A crowd of 70,584, a new record for a women's game in Britain, watched as Houghton scored in the second minute from a narrow angle after some great work by Carney, her third goal in as many games.

Brazil, ranked fourth in the world, came back strongly, hitting the post, but even though Kelly Smith missed a penalty, Britain deservedly won. They had played three games, won them all without conceding, and for Steph Houghton there were three goals scored.

Tickets for the quarter-final against Canada in Coventry were suddenly among the hottest at the games.

This time Houghton's hot streak ended and Canada won 2–0 but, in not much more than a week, women's football in Britain had probably made more progress than it had in decades.

Also on this day

2001 Edwin van der Sar joined Fulham from Juventus.

2006 Michael Carrick moved from West Ham to Manchester United.

2012 Steven Pienaar rejoined Everton from Spurs.

2014 Hull City played their first ever game in Europe, a 0–0 draw at AS Trenčín in Slovakia.

August

1 AUGUST
2006 – McLaren starts work for England

The idea that you had to have been a top-class player to be a top-class coach had long since been disproved by 2006; Wenger, Mourinho and Benítez barely had playing careers at all.

Steve McLaren's modest talents as player had taken him to five clubs in the lower leagues, but his credentials as a coach were impeccable and he had learned from the very best.

Denis Smith at Oxford and Jim Smith at Derby had first spotted McLaren's coaching potential; both had been impressed by his attention to detail, use of technology and psychology, and his ambition. It was still a surprise, though, when Alex Ferguson asked McLaren to take over as his assistant manager following the departure of Brain Kidd. The Manchester United boss said, 'We needed someone with the right credentials and we kept coming back to Steve. When I checked him out I knew he was the right man and he has deeply impressed me. I expect him to go on to great things.'

Within a few months Manchester United had won the treble and McLaren was a well-liked and highly respected part of the Old Trafford machine.

When, in October 2000, Peter Taylor was in temporary charge of the England team following the resignation of Kevin Keegan, he looked for a Manchester United influence on his squad by naming David Beckham as captain and McLaren as one of his coaches. It was an opportunity neither would let slip.

New England boss Sven-Göran Eriksson asked McLaren to continue in his part-time role and in the summer of 2001, when McLaren made it clear he wanted to be a club manager in his own right, he had the pick of Southampton, West Ham and Middlesbrough. McLaren chose Middlesbrough and in six seasons took them to two FA Cup semi-finals, the UEFA Cup Final, and won the League Cup – their first major trophy.

McLaren left his coaching role with Eriksson's England in late 2002, only to return in 2004 – again replacing Brian Kidd – and helped them to qualify for the World Cup in 2006, after which Eriksson stuck to his promise and stood down.

The FA had tried, and failed, to entice Portugal manager Felipe Scolari. Even so, the FA's chief executive Brian Barwick said, 'My first choice was always Steve. He was my first choice and the FA board's unanimous choice.'

The media weren't convinced and dubbed the new manager 'Second Choice Steve'.

Also on this day

2001 Fulham signed Edwin van der Sar from Juventus.

2004 FA chief executive Mark Palios resigned over his affair with Faria Alam.

2006 William Gallas refused to return to Chelsea after the World Cup.

2 AUGUST
1999 – Henry and Šuker to Highbury

The 1998/99 season could have been a second successive double season for Arsenal; instead it was Manchester United's treble year. Arsenal had finished one point behind United in the Premier League and been beaten by them in an epic FA Cup semi-final that might have gone either way.

Perhaps the difference between the two teams had been the sheer weight of goals provided by the Manchester United front pair of Andy Cole and Dwight Yorke. The United duo had scored 53 times between them that season, compared to Bergkamp and Anelka's combined 34 for Arsenal. On his substitutes' bench Alex Ferguson had the options of Ole Gunnar Solkskjaer and Teddy Sheringham while Arsène Wenger had Christopher Wreh and Luís Boa Morte.

With Anelka looking set for a move to Real Madrid, Wenger decided to act

and did so decisively, bringing in two new strikers. The first was Davor Šuker from Madrid. It was unlike Wenger to sign a 31-year-old, but the Croatian Šuker had been one of the best players at Euro 96 and had been top scorer at the World Cup in 1998, where he was voted the tournament's second best player after Ronaldo. He was a proven goalscorer and available for just £1m having lost his place at Real since the emergence of the Morientes/Raúl partnership.

Also unveiled by Wenger was the intriguing Thierry Henry. Wenger had given the Frenchman his first professional contract at Monaco, where he had blossomed into a goalscoring winger for club and country.

In a formation that employed only one striker, coach Aimé Jacquet preferred Stéphane Guivarc'h for the final. Henry had been used in midfield during the tournament but lost his place in the starting line-up after the second-round match against Paraguay.

If Henry was intent on convincing the new France manager Roger Lemerre that he should be the main striker for Les Bleus after the World Cup, the 1998/99 season didn't help his cause. Henry scored just one goal in 20 games for Monaco, eclipsed by David Trezeguet, before moving to Juventus where he found himself back on the left wing, scoring only 3 times in 16 appearances.

It seemed that Henry might be destined to be a nearly man; clearly a great talent, but on the fringes of the action. Juventus didn't take much persuading to accept Arsène Wenger's £10m offer – probably the best money Arsenal have ever spent.

Also on this day

2000 **Playing their matches at West Bromwich Albion's Hawthorns ground, Aston Villa were knocked out of the Intertoto Cup by Celta Vigo.**

2001 **Boudewijn Zenden joined Chelsea from Barcelona for £7.5m.**

3 AUGUST
2004 – Paul Scholes's England retirement

'The truly great English midfield player of the generation. He didn't just play the game, he thought about the game. You could see every pass, every decision, was based on his intelligence and understanding.'

Those were the words of the Italian master Andrea Pirlo about Paul Scholes.

Glenn Hoddle gave a 22-year-old Scholes his England debut in May 1997 against South Africa at Old Trafford, and by the time that summer's four-team Tournoi de France tournament had finished he had his first goal, against Italy in Nantes.

At his first World Cup Scholes started every game, scoring against Tunisia, but was left to rue a missed chance in the second phase against Argentina that would have made the score 3–1. Scholes had been replaced by Paul Merson by the time England lost the game in a shoot-out.

Like most England players, Scholes's international career was characterized by a few highs and too many lows. In 1999, in a win over Poland, Scholes became the first England player for six years to score a hat-trick, only to become the first England player ever to be sent off at Wembley in his next game against Sweden.

Two goals at Hampden Park against Scotland ensured that England qualified for Euro 2000; but despite a goal against Portugal, Scholes and England slumped out of the tournament. In the 2002 World Cup he shrugged off an injury scare to start every game, but again England went home early.

In 2004, Sven-Göran Eriksson began playing Scholes on the left of midfield to accommodate Lampard and Gerrard in the centre. He ended 29 England games without a goal, finding the net in a 4–2 win over Croatia at Euro 2004, but Scholes's last England game was in the quarter-final against Portugal – another penalty shoot-out and another defeat watched from the bench after being replaced by Phil Neville.

Six years later Fabio Capello asked Scholes to come back for the 2010 World Cup Finals, giving him just two hours to make a decision. Scholes said no.

Later, though, he admitted regretting turning down the opportunity, despite England's poor showing in South Africa: 'I am not saying I would have made a difference. I am saying I might have made the wrong decision.'

Also on this day

2009 Liverpool agreed to sell Xabi Alonso to Real Madrid for £30m.

2012 Great Britain's women were knocked out of the Olympic football tournament, losing 2–0 to Canada.

2014 Manchester City announced that they had agreed a shock deal to sign Frank Lampard.

4 AUGUST
2012 – The Olympic shoot-out

At first the football associations of the four home nations were sceptical about entering a team at the London Olympics at all, fearful that it might jeopardize their separate status within FIFA. Then there had been worries that a Great Britain men's Olympic squad might be booed if they played outside England, from where the bulk of players were expected to be selected. No-one need have worried on either count; but soon the sense of anticlimax was all too familiar.

Manager Stuart Pearce risked being booed himself after leaving David Beckham out of his 18-man squad, selecting 5 Welshmen alongside the English, but no Scots or Northern Irish. Ryan Giggs, aged 38, was captain in his first senior international tournament. The draw placed Britain in a group against Senegal, the UAE and Uruguay, with matches at Old Trafford, Wembley and the Millennium Stadium.

A 1–1 draw with Senegal in Manchester was an underwhelming way to start Britain's first Olympic football tournament since 1960. Craig Bellamy scored the goal, but Britain conceded a late equalizer.

At Wembley a crowd of more than 85,000 watched as the UAE were dispatched 3–1 in the second match, with Ryan Giggs scoring the first. But the result was flattering – Scott Sinclair's and Daniel Sturridge's goals came late in the game.

Uruguay, with both Luis Suárez and Edinson Cavani in their squad, were one of the favourites for gold but had lost to Senegal. Cardiff played host to the final group game, which turned out to be the high point for the British team; Sturridge was again on target in a 1–0 win in front of an enthusiastic full house.

In the quarter-final, Britain faced South Korea, who'd had two 0–0 draws and a narrow win over Switzerland in their group games; Stuart Pearce's side were expected to progress.

Sunderland's Ji Dong-Won hardly ever featured for his club in the Premier League, but gave his South Korean Olympic side a deserved lead in Cardiff before Aaron Ramsey equalized from the penalty spot. Five minutes later Ramsey had another penalty saved by Jung Sung-Ryong.

The South Koreans created the better chances, but a penalty shoot-out seemed an inevitable outcome. The first eight kicks were all scored, before Daniel Sturridge had his effort saved and Ki Sung-Yeung, about to sign for Swansea, knocked Great Britain out.

Also on this day

1993 Saido Berahino was born in Burundi.

1994 Wimbledon sold John Fashanu to Aston Villa for £1.35m.

2005 Phil Neville joined Everton from Manchester United for £3.5m.

2006 Aston Villa appointed Martin O'Neill as their new manager.

5 AUGUST
2009 – Aquilani to Anfield

The sale of Xabi Alonso to Real Madrid didn't just upset Liverpool's fans – it upset Steven Gerrard too. 'He's easy to play with,' said Gerrard. 'I love it when he's in the team because I know I'm going to see lots of the ball.'

Liverpool's very public pursuit of Gareth Barry from Aston Villa had left Alonso feeling undervalued, aware that it was his place in the centre of midfield that manager Rafa Benítez was trying to fill. 'I prefer not to think too much about how I was treated. It was a new situation for me, something I had never experienced before,' said the Spaniard, who had become hugely popular at Anfield.

The fact that Liverpool failed to sign Barry didn't quell Alonso's unease and the following summer Real Madrid were encouraged by his lingering sense of having been undermined. By now Barry had signed for Manchester City, and Liverpool needed a replacement for Alonso, who was set on a move to Madrid.

Alberto Aquilani had a couple of nicknames; the more flattering one was 'Il Principino' – the Little Prince – for his elegant playing style with AS Roma. The other nickname was 'Swarowski', a reference to his ankle, which was inclined, like crystal, to be damaged on impact. A succession of injuries had limited him to just 48 Serie A games in three seasons when Liverpool decided he was to be their replacement for Alonso.

By 2009 Liverpool were under the ownership of Americans George Gillett and Tom Hicks, whose willingness to support Rafa Benítez's penchant for spending was wearing thin. Alonso had cost Real £30m; Aquilani, who was injured when Liverpool signed him, was therefore priced accordingly – 'a bit cheaper', said Benítez – at £20m.

It took Aquilani more than four months to get fit enough to start a Premier League match and in his entire Liverpool career he played just 28 games, only 3 times for 90 minutes. Season-long loans to Juventus and AC Milan followed with neither wanting to take up their option to buy.

Three years after joining Liverpool, Aquilani moved to Fiorentina on a free transfer.

Also on this day

1995 **Middlesbrough manager Bryan Robson spent £5.2m on Nick Barmby from Spurs.**

1997 **Sheffield Wednesday bought Paolo Di Canio from Celtic for £4.5m.**

1999 **Arsenal sold Nicolas Anelka to Real Madrid for £22.3m.**

6 AUGUST
2003 – Sporting Lisbon 3 Manchester United 1

It was the weekend before they were due to play Arsenal in the FA Charity Shield, and Manchester United were warming up in Lisbon, invited as special guests to play the first ever game at Sporting's new stadium, the Estadio José Alvalade.

Wearing Sporting's number 28 shirt and ready to dance his way through a full repertoire of tricks was Cristiano Ronaldo.

Ronaldo had broken into Sporting's first team the previous season, playing 28 games as they finished third. His performances that year, and his proactive agent Jorge Mendes, had alerted Europe's top clubs to the precocious winger from Madeira making a name for himself in Lisbon.

Mendes had already held talks with Arsenal vice-chairman David Dein. In his autobiography Mendes would later write, 'There was a moment in which I really thought he was going to Arsenal. David Dein is a spectacular person but, with the construction of their stadium, they were left with very little money and it wasn't possible.'

Ronaldo himself had been talking up the possibility of moving to England, briefly touting himself to Liverpool: 'one of the best clubs in England. It would be a dream for any player to represent a club of such traditions. I will have to hope they make an offer that is good for both Sporting and myself.'

Alex Ferguson knew all about Ronaldo from his Portuguese assistant manager Carlos Queiroz, who had joined United the previous summer after resigning from his job as national coach of South Africa. Ferguson also knew that it was likely Ronaldo would leave Sporting in the next 12 months; what Ferguson had not done was see Ronaldo play in the flesh.

By half-time Ferguson had seen enough of Ronaldo; so had John O'Shea, who had been teased and turned almost to distraction. Ferguson later wrote that at half-time he asked the United kit man to find chief executive Peter Kenyon and tell him to start negotiations with Sporting as soon as possible: 'John O'Shea's ended up with a migraine! Get him signed.'

United had just received £25m from Real Madrid for David Beckham, almost exactly half of which was spent on Ronaldo. United had a new number seven, and soon it was obvious they had a new superstar.

Also on this day

1996 20,000 Newcastle fans greeted the unveiling of new signing Alan Shearer at St James' Park.

1999 Middlesbrough signed Christian Ziege from AC Milan for £4m.

2007 Newcastle signed José Enrique from Villarreal for £6.3m.

7 AUGUST
1999 – Bradford City join the big guns

Bradford City's finest hour came in 1911 when the club, managed by 37-year-old former player Peter O'Rourke, won the FA Cup and finished fifth in the Football League's Division One.

Bradford had remained in Division One until 1922, when they were relegated and began a 77-year wait to get back into the top flight. The trials of seven decades of relegation and promotion between Divisions Two, Three and Four were nothing compared to the ordeal the club and the city suffered when 56 fans were lost in the fire that broke out at their Valley Parade stadium on 11 May 1985.

In May 1998, Bradford had asked assistant boss Paul Jewell to take over from the sacked manager Chris Kamara and the results had been immediate. Driven on by the goals of Lee Mills and Robbie Blake, Bradford went into the final game of the 1998/99 season in second place, needing to win at play-off-chasing Wolves to be sure of promotion.

They fell behind, but a goal from Peter Beagrie and one each from Mills and

Blake secured a 3–2 win, and Bradford's long wait was over.

Football in Yorkshire had seldom been stronger, with Bradford joining Leeds United and Sheffield Wednesday in the top flight; and when the fixtures for the new season were announced, the Premier League computer sent Bradford to Middlesbrough's Riverside Stadium on the opening day, 7 August.

Jewell was busy in the summer, signing David Weatherall, Gunnar Halle and Lee Sharpe from neighbours Leeds and, two days before the start of the season, veteran striker Dean Saunders from Benfica. Bradford had been trying to get international clearance through to play Saunders, but red tape delayed confirmation of the move to the last minute. The paperwork was completed just in time for him to be named as a substitute.

Middlesbrough dominated the first half completely – 'We took a battering,' admitted Jewell after the game – but they didn't score. David Weatherall cleared their best chance from Brian Deane off the line. But in the second half Saunders replaced Dean Windass for Bradford, and with two minutes to go he was picked out by a Lee Mills pass. Saunders, once English football's most expensive player, didn't hesitate to control the ball and shot low past Mark Schwarzer.

It was a win that had been 77 years in the making.

Also on this day

1992 Dion Dublin joined Manchester United from Cambridge for £1m.

2003 Juan Sebastián Verón moved from Manchester United to Chelsea for £12.7m.

2012 Santi Cazorla signed for Arsenal from Málaga for £15m.

8 AUGUST
1992 – Eric, the King of Elland Road and Wembley

Éric Cantona had retired from football at the age of 25 in protest at a two-month ban from the French Federation. It was a long way from being a first offence.

The ban came at the end of four eventful years in which he had played for five different clubs. Auxerre had fined Cantona for punching his own goalkeeper; the French Federation had disciplined him for a tackle so bad that they banned him for two months; he'd been banned for one month by Marseille for ripping off his shirt and kicking the ball into the crowd when he was substituted in a friendly match; he was banned from international football for a year for insulting national coach Henri Michel in an interview; Montpellier had banned him for ten days for throwing his boots at a teammate; and, finally, the Federation banned him again, for a month, for throwing the ball at a referee. This final ban had later been extended to two months when Cantona insulted the members of the disciplinary panel.

Changing his mind about retirement, Cantona was invited for a two-week trial at Sheffield Wednesday by manager Trevor Francis in January 1992. 'Trev swoops for Mad Eric!' said the newspaper headline.

Cantona appeared only once for Wednesday, in a six-a-side exhibition game against Baltimore Blast indoors at the Sheffield Arena; not quite what Cantona had in mind.

Two weeks later he was making his debut for championship-chasing Leeds. Three months after that Cantona was on an open-topped bus celebrating United's title win and telling fans in stumbling English, 'I don't know why, but I love you.'

The 1992/93 season was the first of the new Premier League. Some things hadn't changed though; champions Leeds played cup winners Liverpool at Wembley in the FA Charity Shield.

Loving the stage, Cantona shone and scored his first career hat-trick as Leeds won 4–3. Afterwards manager Howard Wilkinson stressed that Cantona had been working hard on both his fitness and language skills in pre-season: 'When I say nice things to him, he understands

me very well. When I suggest he works harder, he finds it more difficult.'

Also on this day

1995 Éric Cantona, serving a nine-month ban for kicking a Crystal Palace fan, had a transfer request turned down by Manchester United.

1997 Graeme Le Saux rejoined Chelsea after four years away in a £4m deal from Blackburn.

2010 Manchester United won the FA Community Shield with a 3–1 win over Chelsea.

9 AUGUST
2010 – O'Neill resigns from Aston Villa

Sixth in the Premier League is as high as Aston Villa have finished since 1997; and it's where they finished for three consecutive seasons under the management of Martin O'Neill. Villa, it seemed, were getting somewhere under the Irishman.

After an apprenticeship at Grantham and Wycombe, O'Neill was briefly the manager at Norwich before enjoying four-and-a-half hugely successful years at Leicester in which they were promoted to the Premier League and won the League Cup twice.

Five seasons at Celtic followed, winning seven domestic trophies and reaching the 2003 UEFA Cup Final, beating Blackburn, Celta Vigo, Stuttgart and Liverpool on the way to an extra-time defeat in Seville by Mourinho's FC Porto.

O'Neill was appointed Aston Villa's manager in August 2006 and immediately made his mark with some eye-catching transfers: Stiliyan Petrov from Celtic and Ashley Young from Watford were joined by Nigel Reo-Coker and John Carew.

Under O'Neill, Villa improved their points tally in four consecutive seasons; finishing 11th and then in 6th place three times. They qualified for the UEFA Cup in 2008/09 and beat Ajax only for O'Neill to then prioritize their league position and pick a weakened team at CSKA Moscow, where they were knocked out. Villa fans' disappointment was compounded when they failed to win any of their next eight league games and slipped out of contention for the top four.

Defeat in the final of the League Cup and the semi-final of the FA Cup followed in 2010, with the team again failing to sustain the top-four place that had been theirs at Christmas.

Villa were beginning to look like nearly men; good enough to embark on promising league campaigns and lengthy cup runs, but without the quality and depth of squad needed to sustain them. Villa had sold Gareth Barry to Manchester City in 2009 and were now on the point of selling James Milner to the same club. Maintaining a position in the top six looked like it would be getting harder; improving on it looked as though it might be impossible within the financial constraints being set by owner Randy Lerner.

In an echo of his sudden resignation from Norwich over transfer policy, O'Neill decided to leave Aston Villa just five days before the start of the new season. When Villa lost 6–0 at Newcastle two weeks later, he probably felt he'd made the right decision.

Also on this day

2009 **Chelsea won their first ever competitive penalty shoot-out, beating Manchester United 4–1 on spot-kicks in the FA Community Shield after a 2–2 draw.**

2012 A new record crowd for an Olympic women's match and a record for a women's match in Britain – 80,203 – watch USA beat Japan 2–1 at Wembley to win gold at the London Olympics.

10 AUGUST
1994 – Bonds out, Redknapp in

In their 92-year history, West Ham had only had seven managers and one of them, Lou Macari, had lasted only seven months in the job. It was a remarkable statistic and a testimony to the stability behind the scenes at Upton Park.

Billy Bonds had been at the club since 1967, making a record 663 league appearances, playing until he was nearly 42 and spending ten years captaining the team. He stayed as a coach at West Ham and applied for the manager's job in the summer of 1989, only for Lou Macari to be appointed; another unsuccessful candidate for the job had been Bonds's former West Ham teammate Harry Redknapp, who was managing Bournemouth with considerable success.

When Macari resigned in February 1991, West Ham appointed Bonds; in the summer of 1992 Bonds made Redknapp his assistant manager.

In his first three seasons in charge, Bonds saw West Ham promoted into the top flight, relegated out of it, and then promoted again. In 1993/94 Bonds's team finished 13th in the Premier League, their best position in eight years.

That summer of 1994, Redknapp was linked with a move to manage Southampton and had been asked to return to his old job at Bournemouth where Tony Pulis had just been sacked.

Redknapp was keen to be a manager again rather than an assistant, and West Ham were deeply reluctant to risk losing him. The board had clearly not forgotten their relegation under Bonds in 1992, and recognized Redknapp's part in stabilizing the squad and earning promotion again in 1993.

The two men have differing versions of whether Redknapp engineered the change, or whether the West Ham board members decided to act of their own accord, but the outcome was the same. With the start of the season ten days away, Billy Bonds was sacked and Harry Redknapp was installed as West Ham's new manager.

Also on this day

1994 Newcastle signed Philippe Albert from Anderlecht.

1997 Teddy Sheringham missed a penalty against former club Spurs on his Manchester United debut. Despite the miss, United won 2–0.

2006 Steve McLaren dropped David Beckham from his first squad as England manager and chose John Terry over Steven Gerrard as his new captain.

2007 Carlos Tévez joined Manchester United from West Ham.

11 AUGUST
2010 – Robbie Keane 100 not out

It was a historic day for the Republic of Ireland and for Robbie Keane, who had been singled out for great things from a very early age.

Keane had scored twice on his debut for Wolves when he was just a month past his 17th birthday and scored nine more in 37 further games in that 1997/98 season. By the end of the campaign, Keane had also become the Republic of Ireland's second youngest international ever, making his debut against the Czech Republic, and played his first 90 minutes for his country against an Argentina side preparing for the 1998 World Cup Finals.

In 2010, 12 years and 43 international goals later, Keane was lining up against Argentina again in an impressive new home for Irish football. He was only the fourth Irish player to reach 100 caps, following Steve Staunton, Shay Given and Kevin Kilbane into the record books.

The team had led a nomadic existence since 1996 when Lansdowne Road, their home since 1971, had been demolished. Matches had been played at Croke Park, the imposing home of Gaelic football and hurling; at Thomond Park, which is Munster's rugby union ground in Limerick; and at another primarily rugby union stadium, the RDS Arena, home of Leinster.

Finally, after a €400m rebuild, Ireland were in their new home – the 51,000-capacity Aviva Stadium. The new ground was packed as Keane, with his son Robbie junior in his arms as mascot for the night, took to the field.

With Lionel Messi outstanding, Argentina ensured that Ireland couldn't quite provide the fairy-tale end to the evening. Ángel Di María scored the only goal of the game with Martín Demichelis denying Ireland an equalizer with a superb 90th-minute tackle as Keane seemed poised to score. Argentine defenders don't sacrifice results in the interests of sentiment.

Also on this day

1994 Southampton signed Bruce Grobbelaar from Liverpool.

1996 Alan Shearer's debut for Newcastle ended in a 4–0 defeat in the FA Charity Shield against Manchester United.

2006 David James joined Portsmouth from Manchester City.

2012 Mexico won gold at the London 2012 Olympic men's football tournament, beating Brazil 2–1 in the final at Wembley.

12 AUGUST
1996 – Bruce Rioch sacked by Arsenal

Bruce Rioch was given just 61 weeks in charge of Arsenal, the shortest tenure of any of the club's 19 managers; appointed in June 1995, he took charge of just 46 matches.

An English-born Scot, Rioch had coped admirably with managing in the midst of financial meltdown at Middlesbrough, had been briefly in charge of Millwall and then guided Bolton through two promotions into the Premier League, reaching the League Cup Final and winning an FA Cup replay at Highbury against Arsenal for good measure.

After the turmoil of George Graham's fall from grace, the straight-talking, no-nonsense Rioch seemed the perfect man for the job.

It started well enough. With new signing Dennis Bergkamp settling in, Arsenal were unbeaten in their first eight games of the season and were third at the start of December.

The optimism was short-lived. A run of one win in eight games left them falling short of the title pace and in early January there were eyebrows raised when Division One Sheffield United drew at Highbury in the FA Cup third round and might easily have won.

In the replay at Bramall Lane, Arsenal lost 1–0 and an emotional Ian Wright was reported to have had a furious row with the manager after the game.

One point from home games against Everton and Coventry left Arsenal fans disheartened. At the top of the table Manchester United, Newcastle and Liverpool were playing thrilling, attacking football, and the comparison left them gloomy.

In February the last chance of a trophy went with a League Cup semi-final defeat to Aston Villa, and although they salvaged fifth place and a UEFA Cup spot on the last day of the season there was a feeling of despondency at Highbury.

Vice-chairman David Dein was busy in the summer, and when Rioch's sacking was confirmed, Arsenal announced that a new manager had been identified and would soon be in place.

The newspapers went into overdrive and speculation had it that Johan Cruyff was the man. When the *Evening Standard* later discovered the identity of the actual replacement for Rioch they asked in a back-page headline, 'Arsène Who?'

Also on this day

2001 The first domestic match to be played indoors was the FA Charity Shield between Liverpool and Manchester United under the closed roof of Cardiff's Millennium Stadium. Liverpool won 2–1.

2003 Cristiano Ronaldo completed his move from Sporting Lisbon to Manchester United for £12.24m and inherited David Beckham's number seven shirt.

2006 Chelsea made a £23m bid for Ashley Cole of Arsenal.

13 AUGUST
2004 – Owen's Anfield exit

In a little over seven seasons in Liverpool's first team Michael Owen played 297 games for the club, scoring 158 goals. He won the FA Cup, UEFA Cup, League Cup twice and was voted European Footballer of the Year in 2001. All this despite being only 24 and having been dogged by muscle injuries from an early age.

Owen's father, Terry, was a striker who had played twice for Everton before having a career in the lower leagues taking in Bradford, Chester, Rochdale and Port Vale.

By the time his son was five, Terry Owen knew he had a special talent: 'His

co-ordination and eye for a ball were quite exceptional. Most lads of that age are just toe-punting the ball but Michael was tucking shots into the corner of the net with the side of his foot. You would have thought he was three or four years older than he was. It was remarkable.'

At ten, Owen scored a record 97 goals in a season for Deeside School's under-11 team, a record that had been set by Ian Rush 20 years earlier.

Despite the Goodison connection – and the young Owen was an Everton fan – Terry Owen encouraged his son to sign for Liverpool after receiving a letter from the Anfield head of youth development Steve Heighway.

Playing for England's under-15 and under-16 teams, Owen scored 28 goals in 20 games and scored 11 in 5 matches as Liverpool won the FA Youth Cup in 1996. Heighway told manager Roy Evans, 'He is ready for whatever you throw at him; nothing fazes Michael Owen. He's ready.'

A first-team debut came as a substitute in May 1996 at Selhurst Park against Wimbledon – Owen scored in a 2–1 defeat.

Real Madrid had first tried to sign Owen in 2002, manager Gérard Houllier saying, 'They might be able to afford Ronaldo but they can't afford Michael Owen.'

In 2004, mindful that five years earlier they had lost Steve McManaman to Real Madrid on a free transfer under the Bosman ruling, Liverpool had been hoping to extend Owen's contract, but little progress had been made. When Real Madrid called again Liverpool accepted their £8m offer, with makeweight midfielder Antonio Núñez included as part of the deal.

Owen later remembered, 'It was never my intention to leave Liverpool. I had always thought I'd be a one-club man and when Real Madrid called I didn't know whether to laugh or cry.'

Also on this day

1997 The first game at Derby's new Pride Park stadium was abandoned after 56 minutes due to a floodlight failure. Derby were leading Wimbledon 2–1 when the lights went out.

1997 John Barnes joined Newcastle on a free transfer from Liverpool.

2010 Manchester City spent £22.5m on Mario Balotelli from Inter Milan.

14 AUGUST
2010 – Blackpool rock Wigan

Blackpool hadn't played in the top flight of English football since 1971; 39 years later, under manager Ian Holloway, they won promotion to the Premier League with a thrilling 3–2 win over Cardiff in the play-off final.

Having spent much of the previous two seasons battling relegation, promotion surprised Blackpool almost as much as anyone else and there was a huge amount to do before the historic new season could begin.

First there was their Bloomfield Road stadium. A brand new south stand, named after their former England captain Jimmy Armfield, had been open only a few months, taking capacity to a little over 12,000. The East Stand, a small temporary structure, didn't meet with Premier League standards and the race was on to replace it in time for the start of the season; in July the club had to admit defeat and asked Wigan to switch the first game of the season from Blackpool to their DW Stadium.

Then there was the team. Promotion through the play-offs delayed the process of improving a squad and weeks went by with only one new player, the almost-unknown Israeli Dekel Keinan, having been signed.

Holloway and Blackpool's chairman Karl Oyston spoke of being inundated by calls from agents, Oyston saying, 'I'm not sure that I've got the right approach for this division. We are the employers. We are the ones offering the terms, the contracts. It's up to us what we do and the way we go about things. There are people who we should have given short shrift to earlier on.'

In the last week before the opening game at Wigan, six new players were signed. Five of them made their Blackpool debuts at Wigan and one of them, Marlon Harewood, scored twice in a remarkable 4–0 win. For a couple of hours, until Chelsea beat West Bromwich Albion 6–0, Blackpool were top of the table.

Ian Holloway said, 'It's the maddest world I've ever known but I've had another good day today. Our fans deserve them and hopefully there will be an even better day at Arsenal next week, but I doubt it, to be perfectly honest.'

He was right, Arsenal won 6–0.

Also on this day

1993 **Arsenal were stunned by a Mick Quinn hat-trick that gave Coventry a 3–0 win at Highbury on the opening day of the season.**

1996 **With Arsène Wenger waiting to join them, Arsenal signed Patrick Vieira and Rémi Garde.**

2014 **Tony Pulis resigned as manager of Crystal Palace.**

15 AUGUST
1992 – The Premier League's opening day

There were nine matches played on the opening day of the new Premier League, with 27 goals scored.

If the Football League was looking on with envious eyes, fearing an exodus of fans to the new FA-run league, then they would have been encouraged that none of those nine games could attract a crowd bigger than the 28,545 that watched Newcastle beat Southend. That was in Division One, which now, counter-intuitively, was England's second tier.

The biggest attendance in the new Premier League was at Bramall Lane where Sheffield United beat Manchester United 2–1 in front of 28,070; the 12,681 who watched Coventry beat newly promoted Middlesbrough by the same score at Highfield Road was the smallest crowd.

Sheffield United also had the first goal of the opening day, Brian Deane scoring after five minutes to put them in front and later adding a second against Manchester United from the penalty spot.

At Elland Road, champions Leeds began with a win over Wimbledon, Lee Chapman scoring twice. At Selhurst Park, promoted Blackburn – with new English record signing Alan Shearer hitting two – drew 3–3 at Crystal Palace. After six years out of the top league, Ipswich returned with a 1–1 draw at home to Aston Villa.

There were draws between Everton and Sheffield Wednesday (1–1) and Southampton and Spurs (0–0).

The biggest surprises came in London. At Stamford Bridge, Chelsea were held to a draw by Oldham, Mick Harford scoring for Chelsea with Nick Henry equalizing. Meanwhile at Highbury, Arsenal conceded four times in the last 21 minutes as Norwich turned a two-goal deficit into a 4–2 win, Mark Robins coming off the bench to score twice and spark the comeback.

But perhaps, with the benefit of hindsight, the most surprising fact about the first day of the new Premier League was that of the 198 players who started the nine inaugural matches, only nine were not British or Irish.

Also on this day

1993 Alex Oxlade-Chamberlain was born.

2004 José Mourinho's Chelsea beat Manchester United 1–0 in his first game as manager.

2010 Joe Cole and Laurent Koscielny were both sent off on their debuts as Liverpool and Arsenal drew 1–1 in Roy Hodgson's first game in charge at Anfield.

2011 Cesc Fàbregas completed his move from Arsenal to Barcelona.

16 AUGUST
2008 – Ring the bells for Hull

Kingston upon Hull was famously the largest city in England never to have hosted top-flight football. Hull boasted two fine rugby league clubs; but since its formation in 1904, the closest the football club had come to achieving promotion to the top division was in 1910, when Oldham went up instead thanks to a superior goal average.

In 2001, owned by former British tennis player David Lloyd, the club came within an ace of going bust. Their Boothferry Park ground was padlocked, a winding-up order was issued at the High Court on behalf of the Inland Revenue and the club was placed into administration. A consortium led by former Leeds United commercial director Adam Pearson saved the Tigers.

Local business executives paid the bills to keep the club afloat through its the darkest hours, and they presented Hull City with a bell, asking that should the club ever reach the top division it should be rung to herald the new era.

The move in 2002 to a new home, the KC Stadium, started a dramatic upturn in Hull's fortunes and in just five seasons they rose from the bottom division to the Premier League.

Nobody could have envisaged that the bell would be rung just seven years after their 2001 crisis. Live on BBC TV's *Football Focus*, chairman Paul Duffen said, 'I dedicate the ringing of this bell to the generations of the Tiger-nation who never got to see this day.'

Fulham provided the first opposition for Hull, and they took the lead though an early goal by Seol Ki-Hyeon. Hull fought back and, on his debut, their Brazilian former Barcelona, Benfica and Manchester City striker Geovanni scored a suitably brilliant equalizer; substitute Caleb Folan swept home a winner to seal Hull City's first ever top-flight win.

Also on this day

1992 Teddy Sheringham scored the first goal in the Premier League to be televised live. He scored the only goal of the game for Nottingham Forest against Liverpool on Sky TV.

2003 Cristiano Ronaldo made his first appearance for Manchester United, as a substitute for Nicky Butt against Bolton at Old Trafford.

2008 Samir Nasri scored after only 3 minutes and 42 seconds on his debut for Arsenal against West Bromwich Albion.

17 AUGUST
1996 – Beckham from the halfway line

On 11 August 1996 David Beckham had set up two goals and scored one in Manchester United's demolition of Newcastle in the Charity Shield. His goal had been a lob over the advancing Pavel Srníček as he scurried on to a Cantona pass. It was a small taste of what was to come six days later.

That Wembley lob had been Beckham's 10th United goal in his 51st appearance for the club. He had already won the double with United in 1996 and had been capped nine times at England Under-21 level. Beckham was being strongly tipped for inclusion in the new England manager Glenn Hoddle's squad for a World Cup qualifier in Moldova in September.

What happened at Selhurst Park made his immediate inclusion in the England team, let alone the England squad, a near-certainty.

United were cruising at 2–0 up when, with time almost up, Efan Ekoku was dispossessed and the ball was played into Beckham's path; from a foot inside his own half he smashed a right-footed shot so cleanly that it never deviated in its path over the top of Wimbledon goalkeeper Neil Sullivan's head and underneath the crossbar.

On *Match of the Day* John Motson called out, 'Oh, that is absolutely phenomenal, what an astonishing goal by David Beckham! A goal that will be talked about and replayed for years.'

In 2002, Beckham's lob was named Goal of the Decade in a vote to mark the first ten years of the Premier League; though it didn't win the BBC's vote for Goal of the Season for 1996/97, that award going to Trevor Sinclair of Queens Park Rangers.

Beckham would score another 75 goals for Manchester United but it was the goal at Wimbledon that is most remembered; the goal that started the process of turning an outstanding 21-year-old into perhaps the most famous footballer in the world.

Also on this day

1996 Fabrizio Ravanelli scored a hat-trick on his debut for Middlesbrough in a 3–3 draw with Liverpool.

2000 Everton bought back fans' favourite Duncan Ferguson from Newcastle for £3.75m.

2002 Wayne Rooney made his Everton debut in a 2–2 draw with Tottenham at Goodison Park.

2004 Xabi Alonso moved from Real Sociedad to Liverpool.

2005 England suffered their worst defeat for 25 years, a 4–1 loss to Denmark in Copenhagen.

2012 Robin van Persie completed his move from Arsenal to Manchester United for £22.5m.

18 AUGUST
2002 – Arsenal beat Birmingham for 14 in a row

Arsenal's remarkable run of victories began on 10 February with a 1–0 win at Goodison Park and it ended on 24 August with a draw at West Ham; in between Arsène Wenger's side won a record 14 consecutive top-flight league matches.

Sylvain Wiltord was the scorer of the first winning goal. Arsenal's victory at Everton kept them in touch with leaders Manchester United, who won at Charlton on the same night. Arsenal were fourth in the table behind United, Liverpool and Newcastle – but the Gunners had a game in hand.

Fulham were dispatched next, 4–1 at Highbury, before a crucial 2–0 win at Newcastle. Arsenal were above Newcastle and second behind Manchester United only on goal difference.

A narrow home win over Derby, who had held Manchester United to a draw two days earlier, sent Arsenal top with nine games to play.

Arsenal then recovered from a home defeat to Deportivo La Coruña in the Champions League to win at Aston Villa, and showed their powers of recovery again when, after suffering European elimination at Juventus, they beat Sunderland, Charlton and Spurs in a week.

An FA Cup semi-final win over Middlesbrough was followed by three successive 2–0 Premier League wins against Ipswich, West Ham and Bolton – the last of which sent Arsenal five points clear at the top of the table with just two games to play.

The FA Cup was won against Chelsea in Cardiff followed by the Premier League title, and the double, which was sealed at Old Trafford with a 1–0 win.

In celebratory mood, Arsenal trailed 2–1 to Everton on the last day of the season before recovering to win 4–3; it was the only time in the winning run that Arsenal had fallen behind.

The top-flight record of 13 consecutive victories jointly held by Tottenham, Preston and Sunderland was beaten in the first league game of the following season, Henry and Wiltord scoring in a 2–0 win over Birmingham. West Ham ended the sequence six days later when Arsenal came from 2–0 down but had to settle for a draw.

Also on this day

1992 Alan Shearer made it three goals in two games at the start of his Blackburn career, with the winner against Arsenal on his home debut.

2010 James Milner completed his move from Aston Villa to Manchester City in a deal worth around £26m, including Stephen Ireland moving in the opposite direction.

19 AUGUST
1995 – The kids are alright

It is possibly the most famous piece of football punditry in the English game. Alan Hansen, winner of 17 major honours with Liverpool, was analysing a youthful Manchester United team's defeat at Aston Villa for *Match of the Day*.

It was the opening day of the 1995/96 season and United had sold two of their most senior players, Mark Hughes and Paul Ince, in the summer; Andrei Kanchelskis was putting the finishing touches to a move to Everton. Playing for United that day at Aston Villa were Phil Neville (18), Gary Neville (20), Nicky Butt (20), Paul Scholes (20) and David Beckham (20). Villa beat them 3–1.

Hansen said, 'I think they've got problems. I wouldn't say they have got major problems. Obviously three players have departed and the trick is always buy when you are strong. So he needs to buy players. You can't win anything with kids.'

'He almost ruined my night that night,' said Phil Neville some 20 years later. 'I came home to watch *Match of the Day* with my mum and dad and when he speaks, the country listens.'

That United generation turned out to be the most successful in the club's history, winning the double nine months later and proving Hansen wrong time and time again.

Hansen would never be allowed to forget his assessment of the United 'kids', but when he retired from the BBC in 2014 he reflected that, 'It was the line that made me. I'd be at Euston station or Heathrow airport and they'd be shouting it at me. To this day, I stand by that line. How many times have you seen a manager pick experience over youth – it happens all the time.'

Also on this day

1995 A brilliant hat-trick from Matthew Le Tissier was not enough to prevent Southampton losing to Nottingham Forest 4–3.

1999 Robbie Keane became British football's most expensive teenager when he moved from Wolves to Coventry for £6m.

2005 Michael Essien signed for Chelsea from Lyon for £24m.

2009 Burnley beat champions Manchester United 1–0 in their first home game in the Premier League.

20 AUGUST
1994 – Klinsmann's diving debut

Jürgen Klinsmann was not very popular in England. The man who had scored goals for Stuttgart, Bayern Munich, Inter Milan and Monaco was a key part of the German team that had knocked England out of the 1990 World Cup at the semi-final stage. Klinsmann also had a reputation for diving that followed him to White Hart Lane when he signed for Spurs from Monaco for £2m.

As the most high-profile German by far ever to play in England, opposition fans, and some media, were ready to give Klinsmann a hard time in the Premier League.

Before his first press conference at Spurs, Klinsmann knew the barbs that would be coming his way and decided to disarm the press before they had the chance to unleash them. 'Is there a diving school in London?' he asked.

Klinsmann later told *FourFourTwo* magazine that he had a snorkel and face-mask with him in his bag, but the joke went down so well that he didn't need the props.

Klinsmann's plan to get the English on his side could not have worked better had it been orchestrated by a PR guru. By smiling a lot, speaking excellent English, being self-deprecating and driving a VW Beetle rather than a typical footballer's sports car, Klinsmann was soon an object of affection rather than derision.

All those little touches were genuine and important, but nothing won the public round like his first goal celebration on English turf.

Tottenham were at Hillsborough on the opening day of the 1994/95 season playing Sheffield Wednesday. Spurs manager Ossie Ardiles started the season playing five attackers: Darren Anderton, Nick Barmby, Ilie Dumitrescu, Teddy Sheringham and Klinsmann. The result was that Tottenham were involved in some thrilling games in which they scored plenty of goals, but conceded plenty too. The Hillsborough game was a classic example.

Teddy Sheringham and Darren Anderton put Spurs 2–0 up, Dan Petrescu and a Colin Calderwood own-goal made it 2–2, Barmby scored for Tottenham and then Anderton set up Klinsmann, who headed his first goal in England.

Klinsmann sprinted in celebration towards the touchline before remembering a suggestion of Teddy Sheringham's and launching himself into the air in a spectacular swallow dive; it was one of the images of the season.

David Hirst's goal for Wednesday made it 4–3, but it was Klinsmann who stole the headlines – and a few hearts.

Also on this day

1998 Manchester United broke their transfer record by paying £12.6m for Dwight Yorke from Aston Villa.

2004 Jonathan Woodgate joined Real Madrid from Newcastle for £15.7m.

2013 Hope Powell was sacked as manager of the England women's team after 15 years in the job.

21 AUGUST
2014 – Balotelli back in England

Mario Balotelli had been described as 'unmanageable' by José Mourinho at Inter Milan and as a 'another one of my children' by Roberto Mancini at Manchester City; carrot or stick, the result was the same – in the end Balotelli was discarded.

By January 2013 it seemed Balotelli and Manchester City had had enough of each other; a miserable last five months brought him only three goals in 20 games and he was sold to AC Milan for £16m. Inspired and energized by the move back to Italy, Balotelli then scored 12 goals in 13 games for Milan between February and May.

His record the following season, 2013/14, was 16 goals in 38 games; but increasingly it was the old, disengaged Balotelli. His performances at the 2014 World Cup were similarly frustrating.

Having sold Luis Suárez to Barcelona, Liverpool had tried and failed to land a big-name striker as a replacement; Sanchez, Cavani, Falcao, Higuaín and Lavezzi had all been considered, some had been pursued, but only Rickie Lambert had been signed.

On Liverpool's pre-season tour of America, manager Brendan Rodgers had been asked whether he might consider bringing Balotelli to Anfield – the reply was unequivocal: 'I can categorically tell you that he will not be at Liverpool.'

With the season having started and the close of the transfer window looming, Rodgers's options were diminishing by the day. Could he risk going into a Premier League and Champions League campaign with only Sturridge, Lambert and Fabio Borini, a player he'd been trying to sell all summer, as recognized strikers?

Rodgers's choice boiled down to Samuel Eto'o, 33 and released by Chelsea, or the 24-year-old Balotelli, who was now unwanted at Milan.

Rodgers chose Balotelli, calling the move 'a risk worth taking'. Back in Milan

the former Inter and Italy striker Christian Vieri described selling Balotelli as 'the biggest coup in AC Milan's history'. Italian journalist Mario Sconcerti told Sky Italia that when it comes to Balotelli, 'champagne corks are popped when he arrives – but also when he leaves'.

It took the Italian six months to score his first Premier League goal for Liverpool.

Also on this day

2005 Arsène Wenger's 500th game for Arsenal ended in a 1–0 defeat at Chelsea.

2014 Malky Mackay, who had been expected to join Crystal Palace as manager, was alleged to have exchanged offensive texts with Palace's sporting director Iain Moody when the pair were together at Cardiff City. Moody resigned from his post at Palace and Mackay was no longer under consideration for the manager's job.

22 AUGUST
2008 – Kompany for Manchester City

In 2006 Vincent Kompany was 20, had already played three full seasons for Anderlecht, and as one of the brightest young defensive prospects around was on the radar of some of Europe's top clubs.

His agent had talks with Real Madrid and Arsenal, but wanted his client to go a club where he would be guaranteed first-team football straight away rather than waiting his turn. Germany's Hamburg offered that opportunity, and Kompany headed for the Bundesliga.

In 2008, Kompany was selected for Belgium's Olympic squad at the Beijing games, only to be sent off in their first match in China, a 1–0 defeat to Brazil.

With Kompany facing a one-match suspension in China, Hamburg demanded that he be released from the squad to return to his club. Kompany refused until the Belgian FA intervened and advised him to do so. Reluctantly back in Germany, he came on in Hamburg's first league game of the season, a 2–2 draw at Bayern Munich.

Manchester City's new manager, Mark Hughes, heard that Kompany might be so upset at not being allowed to stay at the Olympics that he'd consider a move away from Hamburg.

Hughes needed new players, City's weakness exposed by an embarrassing home defeat to Midtjylland in the UEFA Cup second qualifying round. City's finances were complicated by the charges of corruption being contested by owner Thaksin Shinawatra in the courts in Thailand, where he had been ousted as prime minister.

But the sale of the club was imminent and the promise of what might lie ahead was enticing to Kompany, who joined City for £6m. He was the club's last signing before the Dubai takeover ten days later, when the spending really began.

Also on this day

1992 Coventry City were setting the pace at the top of the first Premier League table after a 1–0 win at Wimbledon maintained their 100 per cent start to the season.

1998 Charlton played their first top-flight game at the Valley since 1947. Between 1985 and 1992 the club had ground-shared with first Crystal Palace and then West Ham.

2004 Arsenal recovered from 3–1 down to beat Middlesbrough 5–3 at Highbury. The result took Arsenal's unbeaten league run to 42 games, equalling the record of Nottingham Forest.

23 AUGUST
2000 – Ferguson's second coming

With full-time approaching it seemed as though Everton's home game against Charlton would be remembered, if at all, for an energetic performance from Paul Gascoigne, who had moved to Goodison

Park from Middlesbrough on a free transfer in the summer.

Carl Tiler's red card for Charlton had given Everton a numerical advantage that they made use of early in the second half, taking the lead with a goal created by Gascoigne, scored by Francis Jeffers.

A run-of–the-mill game so far, but then Duncan Ferguson came off the bench to replace Mark Hughes. With his Everton tattoo on his shoulder, Ferguson had been a hero in his first spell at the club in which he'd scored 42 goals in 133 games. But it wasn't just his goals that made Ferguson such a favourite; it was the aggressive determination, the surprisingly elegant footwork for a man rightly feared for his aerial strength, and above all the emotion with which he played the game.

When Ferguson had been sold to Newcastle for £7m in 1998, it was without manager Walter Smith's knowledge. The deal was conducted between Everton chairman Peter Johnson and his Newcastle counterpart Freddie Shepherd during a game between the two clubs at Goodison Park. Such was the level of anger among Everton fans that Johnson was forced to resign a week later.

Now, after just over 18 injury-hit months at Newcastle, Ferguson was back for a cut-price £3.75m. In the 84th minute he slotted home a pass from Thomas Gravesen, and in the last minute added

a second with a powerful, deflected shot. Goodison Park shook with approval.

It was typical of Ferguson that there was still time for him to injure himself with an ill-timed attempt at a tackle that put him out of action for four months.

Also on this day

1992 At the third attempt, Arsenal won their first Premier League points with a 2–0 victory over Liverpool.

2003 Ruud van Nistelrooy scored in his tenth successive Manchester United Premier League match, finding the net against Newcastle in a 2–1 win.

2004 Newcastle had a £20m bid for Everton's Wayne Rooney rejected.

2006 Portsmouth's Pedro Mendes was knocked unconscious and taken to hospital after receiving an elbow from Manchester City's Ben Thatcher. The FA later banned Thatcher for eight games.

2007 Chelsea sold Arjen Robben to Real Madrid for £25m.

2008 Stoke City won their first top-flight game for 23 years in a 3–2 success over Aston Villa.

2011 Manchester City signed Samir Nasri from Arsenal for £23m.

24 AUGUST
2005 – Everton's Champions League woe

Everton had twice been denied a place in the European Cup when, with English clubs banned from Europe following the Heysel Stadium disaster, they were champions in 1985 and 1987.

For a brief time in 2005 it seemed as though they might be denied again. Under David Moyes, Everton had finished fourth in the Premier League, one place above Liverpool. That would normally be enough to qualify for the Champions League, but when Liverpool then won the Champions League Final in Istanbul it gave UEFA a problem.

Nobody at Europe's governing body had anticipated a team winning the trophy having not already qualified for the following season's competition through its league position.

Either UEFA accepted a fifth English team, or they denied Liverpool the chance to defend their title, or they gave the fourth qualifying place to Liverpool at the expense of Everton.

UEFA went for the least unpalatable option – allowing Liverpool entry to the tournament at the first qualifying stage and allowing Everton to enter at the third qualifying round as normal.

So Everton went into the draw for Europe's top prize for the first time since 1971 – and that draw could not have been less kind.

Villarreal had finished third in Spain the previous season, and reached the last eight of the UEFA Cup. They had Diego Forlán, Juan Riquelme, Juan Pablo Sorín, Marcos Senna, Antonio Valencia and Santi Cazorla in a squad managed by Manuel Pellegrini.

Everton's worst fears were confirmed when Villarreal won 2–1 at Goodison in the first leg. Everton would have to win in Spain if they were to reach the sought-after group stages of the competition.

In the second leg, Villarreal took the lead when Sorín scored, only for Mikel Arteta to equalize with a glorious free-kick. Needing another goal to take the tie to extra-time, Everton hit the bar through Tim Cahill and had a Duncan Ferguson header brilliantly saved.

Ferguson then headed in, only for referee Pierluigi Collina to disallow the goal for a foul by Marcus Bent; replays showed there had been no foul. In the last minute Forlán added a second goal for a relieved Villarreal.

Everton dropped into the UEFA Cup, where they were immediately knocked out by Dinamo Bucharest. Villarreal progressed to the Champions League semi-final, where they were beaten by Arsenal.

Also on this day

1992 **After two defeats and a draw, Manchester United celebrated their first ever win in the new Premier League – Dion Dublin scored the only goal of the game at Southampton.**

1998 **Manchester United pulled the plug on Ole Gunnar Solskjaer's proposed £5.5m move to Tottenham.**

2011 **Juan Mata left Valencia to join Chelsea for £23.5m.**

25 AUGUST
1999 – Newcastle 1 Sunderland 2

The Labour politician Gerald Kaufman famously described his party's 1983 general election manifesto as the longest suicide note in history. Ruud Gullit's team sheet for the 1999 Tyne–Wear derby might have been the shortest: Gullit dropped Alan Shearer and Newcastle lost.

Gullit had been in charge for a season and failed to improve on the 13th-place finish of his predecessor Kenny Dalglish. Gullit, just as Dalglish had the season before, steered the club to the FA Cup Final only to lose; Dalglish's team had been beaten 2–0 by Arsenal, Gullit's lost by the same score to Manchester United.

Newcastle's start to the following season had been awful. With only one point taken from their first four games, they had lost the lead in their last three matches and were 18th in the table. The rumour mill had it that Gullit could not survive another defeat, least of all against their closest and bitterest rivals, Sunderland.

It was a filthy, wet Wednesday night at St James' Park. With so much at stake there was incredulity when it was announced that Alan Shearer was a substitute and 20-year-old Sunderland-born Paul Robinson partnered by Croatian Silvio Marić were preferred up front. Neither had scored a goal for the club.

Kieron Dyer's first goal for Newcastle gave them the lead, but with the weather worsening Sunderland equalized through a Niall Quinn header.

As the rain poured onto the roof of the dugout and the fans implored the manager to bring him on, Shearer stood just over Gullit's shoulder and watched – not so much the Angel of the North as the Angel of Death.

Eventually Gullit took heed of the pleading fans and Shearer went on, only for Kevin Phillips to score the winning goal for Sunderland.

Three days later Gullit resigned, saying he could no longer tolerate the intrusion on his private life. When Bobby Robson took over a week later he said, 'Under Gullit the best players were on the bench, we have to face the fact he did nothing for this club.'

Also on this day

1992 Tottenham's Gordon Durie became the first player ever to be charged with feigning injury by the FA.

1997 Blackburn beat Sheffield Wednesday, who had Benito Carbone sent off, 7–2 at Ewood Park.

2004 Arsenal extended their unbeaten league record to 43 games with a 3–0 win over Blackburn. Cesc Fàbregas, at 17 years and 113 days, became their youngest ever league scorer.

2004 Manchester United bid £25m for Everton's Wayne Rooney.

2010 Spurs qualified for the group stages of the Champions League for the first time when Peter Crouch scored a hat-trick in a 4–0 win over Young Boys Bern.

26 AUGUST
2014 – Manchester United win Di Maria but lose to MK Dons

When David Moyes took over from Sir Alex Ferguson at Manchester United in the summer of 2013, Cesc Fàbregas had been at the top of a long list of transfer targets. Like most of the names on that list, Fàbregas didn't move to Old Trafford. Moyes's only significant signing that summer was Marouane Fellaini from Everton.

When Louis van Gaal became manager in 2014 it was a different story: Ander Herrera and Luke Shaw were first into Old Trafford, deals for Marcos Rojo and Daley Blind were well advanced, with Radamel Falcao's expensive loan from Monaco to follow.

The biggest deal United did, though, was to sign Argentine Ángel Di María from Real Madrid for a British record £59.7m.

Di Maria, having won both league and cup with Real, had been voted man of the match in the 2014 Champions League Final win over city rivals Atlético. A thigh injury in the World Cup quarter-final win over Belgium had ruled out him out of the World Cup Final in which Argentina had lost to Germany.

United fans licked their lips at the prospect of watching another tricky, lightning-quick winger in their finest traditions.

United, who had failed to win either of their first two matches under van Gaal, had a match on the night Di Maria signed. If the new signing was too busy unpacking his suitcase to watch the League Cup second-round tie at MK Dons from League One, it was probably just as well. United lost 4–0 to a team that had cost a total of less than £500,000 to assemble. They didn't even manage a shot on target until they were losing 3–0.

If Di Maria did tune in to familiarize himself with some of the faces he'd soon meet at training, he was wasting his time. Van Gaal, nothing if not ruthless, moved on Javier Hernández, Shinji Kagawa, Anderson, Michael Keane, Marnick Vermijl and Danny Welbeck within a few weeks.

Also on this day

1993 Peter Reid was sacked as player-manager of Manchester City.

1995 Middlesbrough beat Chelsea in the first match at their new Riverside Stadium.

2001 Jaap Stam was sold to Lazio by Manchester United, whose manager

Alex Ferguson had taken exception to Stam's autobiography.

2009 Arsenal beat Celtic 3–1 at the Emirates Stadium to qualify for the group stages of the Champions League. Celtic, 5–1 losers on aggregate, complained about an Eduardo dive that won a penalty for the first Arsenal goal.

2014 After winning 106 caps with England and scoring 29 goals, Frank Lampard retired from international football.

27 AUGUST
1997 – Bergkamp's brilliant treble

Filbert Street was the venue for a Wednesday evening that had one of the most dramatic endings and most memorable hat-tricks of any Premier League year.

Dennis Bergkamp scored his first goal after less than ten minutes. Leicester allowed Marc Overmars to find Bergkamp from a corner, and a magnificent right-footed curling shot hit the inside of the far post and bounced past a startled Kasey Keller.

Bergkamp, who had scored twice at Southampton four days earlier, got his second goal soon after half-time. Patrick Vieira won possession deep inside his own half, exchanged passes with Ray Parlour, and picked out Bergkamp's run, which had pierced the Leicester defence. Keller advanced but couldn't stop the chip from going in.

Leicester boss Martin O'Neill sent on substitutes Tony Cottee and Garry Parker and the change worried Arsenal. Parker's long ball caused confusion between Lee Dixon and David Seaman, and Emile Heskey scored a tap-in: 2–1 to Arsenal with six minutes to play.

Filbert Street was energized, responding to Martin O'Neill's trademark nervous prancing on the touchline. In the 90th minute, having battered the Arsenal defence with a string of corners, Leicester equalized. Central defender Matt Elliott scored with a low drive that deflected through a crowd of bodies into the bottom corner.

The ground was now shaking with excitement, and in the third minute of injury-time, David Platt chipped a pass towards Bergkamp, who, as ever, was already on the move. With the ball dropping over his shoulder, Bergkamp controlled it with his right foot, then flicked it with his left past Elliott. Knowing what was coming, Eliott tried to grab Bergkamp as he glided past but his right-footed shot curled beyond Keller into the far corner. It was a sublime, almost astonishing, way to complete a hat-trick. Bergkamp would later rate it his best ever Arsenal goal.

However, Arsenal didn't win the game. One last Leicester corner was headed back across goal by Steve Walsh, then back again by Spencer Prior for Walsh to slam a gleeful header past Seaman for 3–3. The goal came in the sixth minute of stoppage time. A furious Ian Wright led the Arsenal protests to referee Graham Barber when the final whistle blew – from their point of view a moment too late.

Also on this day

1998 Newcastle sacked Kenny Dalglish and appointed Ruud Gullit as manager.

2010 Javier Mascherano signed for Barcelona from Liverpool.

2014 Neil Warnock was appointed Crystal Palace manager for the second time.

28 AUGUST
2009 – Shevchenko leaves Chelsea

When Chelsea broke the British transfer record to sign Andriy Shevchenko in May 2006, it brought owner Roman Abramovich's personal pursuit of the player to a successful conclusion.

Shevchenko was 29 when he signed for £30m, almost 18 months after Chelsea had first attempted to buy him. He had scored 298 career goals at an average of almost 25 per season for Dynamo Kiev and AC

Milan. Milan had done everything they could to keep a player who seemed to guarantee goals.

From the moment he was unveiled at Chelsea there was debate as to whether Mourinho had wanted the celebrated Ukrainian at Chelsea as much as Abramovich had. Chelsea already had Didier Drogba, and Mourinho – who had seen a Drobga partnership with Hernán Crespo fail to flourish – preferred to play with just one central striker.

Later Mourinho would admit that the Ukrainian was not his top choice: 'We wanted to buy Samuel Eto'o; he was our target. He was the player I wanted. Why? Because Eto'o was the only player I could play with Didier Drogba.'

In his first season Shevchenko scored 14 goals, but only 4 of them in the Premier League. Shevchenko often found himself either being substituted or being used as a substitute and played a full 90 minutes in only five games all season.

When Mourinho was sacked the following September, his reluctance to use Shevchenko was rumoured to be one of the reasons.

Shevchenko's second season was disrupted by injury, and he managed only eight goals. In 2008 he was allowed to go back to AC Milan on loan, but he couldn't reproduce his magic in Italy either. Once the loan had finished Milan chose not to buy him back.

Shevchenko found himself back in London in the summer of 2009 with Carlo Ancelotti, his old manager from those heady days from his first spell at Milan, now in charge of Chelsea. The Italian gave Shevchenko five minutes as a substitute in a 3–1 win at Sunderland, but had seen enough. Chelsea paid up the remaining nine months of his contract and allowed Shevchenko to sign for Dynamo Kiev on a free transfer.

As Mourinho said: 'Even with the top dogs – when you buy for £30m, £40m, £50m or £60m – sometimes it doesn't work. It doesn't mean you or the club made a big mistake. It just doesn't work.'

Also on this day

1992 **Tottenham signed Teddy Sheringham from Nottingham Forest for £2.1m.**

1994 **Robbie Fowler scored a hat-trick against Arsenal in 4 minutes and 33 seconds. It was the Premier League's fastest ever hat-trick until Southampton's Sadio Mané beat the record in May 2015.**

2011 **Manchester thrashed London as two matches produced 16 goals in one day. Manchester United hammered Arsenal 8–2 at Old Trafford and Manchester City trounced Spurs 5–1 at White Hart Lane.**

29 AUGUST
2009 – Wenger sees red

Arsenal had started the 2009/10 season in fantastic style: a 6–1 win at Everton, a comfortable two-legged victory over Celtic in a Champions League qualifier and a thumping home league win over Portsmouth. They went to Manchester United as confident as could be, despite having only one victory at Old Trafford in their last nine visits.

The game started with Arsenal looking powerful and in control – it ended with Arsène Wenger standing helplessly on a ledge above the dugouts, his arms outstretched in hopeless protest, surrounded by laughing, taunting Manchester United fans. It is one of the enduring images of the seemingly constant feud that was Arsenal vs Manchester United.

Wenger's frustration began when Arsenal, who had been beaten in the Champions League semi-final by United the previous May, were denied a penalty when referee Mike Dean saw nothing wrong with Darren Fletcher's challenge on Andrey Arshavin. It seemed not to matter when, within moments, the Russian had lashed a shot past Ben Foster and Arsenal had the lead they deserved.

United had been outplayed, but equalized when Arsenal goalkeeper Manuel Almunia needlessly rushed out to Wayne Rooney and conceded a penalty, which Rooney converted himself. Almunia claimed Rooney had dived and Wenger called the penalty award 'Old Trafford-ish' afterwards.

If Almunia's decision-making had been strange, Abou Diaby's was inexplicable just five minutes later when he headed a Giggs free-kick into his own net.

Arsenal had conceded two needless goals, missed some routine chances, had a clear penalty rejected and had hit the bar. It seemed nothing could get worse when in the fifth minute of injury-time Robin van Persie had an equalizer ruled out for offside. Not seeing the flag, Wenger turned and punched the air, only for the celebration to fizzle out in yet more despair. It was a correct decision but, unable to believe his luck, Wenger took a swipe at a water bottle and chipped it down the touchline.

Fourth official Lee Probert called Mike Dean over, and Wenger was sent off, something for which the official later apologized. Defiant, the Arsenal manager climbed, like a newly crowned Wimbledon tennis champion, over the wall and onto the ledge above the Manchester United dugout, standing there with arms outstretched in supplication until a steward came to lead him away.

Also on this day

2003 Steve McManaman joined Manchester City from Real Madrid.

2008 Newcastle sold James Milner to Aston Villa for £12m, less than two weeks after manager Kevin Keegan said that Milner would not be sold.

30 AUGUST
2005 – Owen to Newcastle

Michael Owen was not a failure at Real Madrid, far from it. His record of 19 goals in 43 games is very decent, but tells only some of the story, because Owen played all 90 minutes in only 11 of those games.

Battling for game-time with the great Brazilian Ronaldo and the untouchable Raúl was always going to be hard, but when Real bought Robinho from Santos and Julio Baptista from Sevilla in July 2005, it was clear that life would only get harder for Owen if he stayed.

Owen had left Liverpool the previous summer for a cut-price £8m due to his contract only having a year to run. His preference on leaving Spain was to return to Anfield, but manager Rafa Benítez had his reservations. Having won the Champions League in his first season in charge, the only blot on the Spanish manager's copybook had been his inability to convince Owen to stay at Liverpool the previous summer.

Fearing his place in the England team might come into doubt, Owen began talks with both Liverpool and Newcastle.

When Newcastle boss Graeme Souness offered £17m, he blew Liverpool out of the market, with the Anfield board of directors unwilling to pay more than double the fee they'd received for Owen only a year before.

Owen had a good relationship with, and huge admiration for, Alan Shearer. Soon, the prospect of playing every week alongside his former England partner was too appealing to turn down, despite a last-minute phone call from Everton manager David Moyes.

More than 20,000 Newcastle fans turned up at St James' Park to welcome Owen. However, a thigh injury meant that Owen missed the start of the season, and it set the tone for the four years ahead.

Also on this day

1998 Michael Owen rubbed his hands in glee after scoring a 16-minute hat-trick as Liverpool won 4–1 at Newcastle.

1999 Andy Cole hit four for Manchester United in a 5–1 win over his former club Newcastle.

2002 Tottenham signed Robbie Keane from Leeds for £7m.

2004 Two days after a 4–2 defeat at Aston Villa, Newcastle sacked manager Bobby Robson, who had been due to stand down at the end of the season.

2011 Arsenal signed Per Mertesacker from Werder Bremen for £8m.

2013 Christian Eriksen signed for Spurs from Ajax for £11m.

31 AUGUST
2004 – United get Rooney

Wayne Rooney had enjoyed a sensational Euro 2004, making his name on the international stage with four goals before suffering a foot injury in the quarter-final defeat to Portugal. Still only 18, he had played 77 games for Everton and scored 17 goals, many of them spectacular. His status as one of the hottest prospects in Europe was indisputable.

In 2002, after scoring in the FA Youth Cup Final against Aston Villa, the 16-year-old Rooney had shown off a shirt on which he'd written 'Once a Blue, always a Blue'; now there were clubs queuing round the block to see if that was still the case.

Manchester United had been happy to monitor Rooney's progress for a further 12 months, but were spurred into action when Newcastle made a £20m bid, a record for a teenager.

Everton rejected the bid and, although they had already made Rooney a millionaire, offered him a new contract reported to be worth £50,000 a week. United had to act now or face the prospect of missing out on a player whom Arsène Wenger had described as the best British prospect he had ever seen.

United's first £25m bid was rejected, and Everton said they wouldn't consider selling for anything less than £40m. Rooney's written transfer request changed that. Now Everton had to accept that keeping the player they'd nurtured since he was nine was impossible.

Sir Alex Ferguson later admitted that his request to the Old Trafford board to improve on their offer meant that 'there were plenty of eyebrows raised', but their second bid of £27.5m was accepted.

'His age is a great thing,' said Ferguson. 'Manchester United couldn't afford to miss him.'

Also on this day

1999 Manchester United signed goalkeeper Massimo Taibi from Valencia.

2001 Liverpool signed two goalkeepers on the same day: Chris Kirkland from Coventry for £5m and Jerzy Dudek from Feyenoord for £4.75.

2002 The first summer transfer window in English football closed.

2006 Ashley Cole signed for Chelsea from Arsenal, with William Gallas going the other way.

2006 West Ham signed Carlos Tévez and Javier Mascherano.

2010 Rafael van der Vaart joined Spurs from Real Madrid for £8m.

2011 Stoke signed Peter Crouch from Tottenham for £10m.

2011 Mikel Arteta moved from Everton to Arsenal for £10m.

September

1 SEPTEMBER
2008 – All change at Eastlands

The takeover of Manchester City was announced on the morning of transfer deadline day. The Abu Dhabi United Group, led by Sheikh Mansour, bought the club from its previous owner Thaksin Shinawatra for a reported £200m.

Following the model set by Roman Abramovich's takeover at Chelsea, that outlay was only the beginning. But Abramovich had bought Chelsea in July, leaving two months to buy new players; at Eastlands they had a day. City's chief executive Gary Cook was suddenly cash-rich but time-poor.

His first move was for Dimitar Berbatov. The Bulgarian had been tracked by Manchester United for over a year, with Spurs complaining bitterly that United had been 'disgraceful'. What better way for Cook and City to make a splash on day one than to gazump their neighbours?

With Tottenham chairman Daniel Levy furious at United, and Berbatov intent on leaving White Hart Lane, the Londoners were only too happy to accept a bid in excess of £30m from Manchester City. The final figure was expected to set a new British transfer record, but possibly only for a matter of minutes, as Robinho's move from Real Madrid to Chelsea was about to be completed too.

With the clock ticking to the close of the transfer window, the truculent Berbatov threw his spanner in the works. He refused to sign for Manchester City, insisting that he go to Old Trafford. This left Spurs with a problem because they hadn't agreed a fee with United, it left City with a problem because they needed a landmark signing, and soon it would leave Chelsea with a problem too because City decided that if they couldn't get Berbatov, they'd have Robinho.

There followed a maelstrom of negotiations involving Real Madrid, Manchester City, Manchester United, Chelsea and Spurs. The five played a furious game of monopoly until the midnight deadline struck. When the last chime faded United had Berbatov for £30.75m, City had Robinho for £32.5m and Chelsea got nothing.

At Eastlands a dazed Robinho told the press, 'On the last day, Chelsea made a great proposal and I accepted.' 'You mean Manchester?' said a reporter. 'Yeah, Manchester, sorry!' came the reply.

Also on this day

1996 David Beckham won his first England cap in Glenn Hoddle's first game as manager, a 3–0 win in Moldova.

1997 Bolton's first game at the new Reebok Stadium ended in a 0–0 draw with Everton.

2001 England won on German soil for the first time since 1965; Michael Owen scored a hat-trick as England won 5–1 in Munich.

2003 Chelsea signed Claude Makélélé from Real Madrid.

2013 Gareth Bale joined Real Madrid for a world record fee of £85.3m.

2 SEPTEMBER
2014 – Welbeck to Arsenal, Falcao to United

For some it was the end of an era for Manchester United. Danny Welbeck had never been in the same class as some of the club's greatest home-grown talents – nor had he claimed to be – but he was United born and bred, having been with them since the age of eight.

When Welbeck completed his transfer deadline day move to Arsenal, United's former assistant manager Mike Phelan said, 'They have probably lost the way of Manchester United a little bit. Someone like a Danny Welbeck has been part of United's identity and that thread has been broken now.'

When Phelan expressed his reservations people would listen, but when David Beckham joined in it was headline news. Beckham said, 'Seeing Danny leave Manchester United is sad. Danny being

such a young kid and having grown up at Manchester United, it's sad to see.'

At Old Trafford, new manager Louis van Gaal had other things on his mind. They'd already spent £13.8m on Daley Blind earlier in the day, and had allowed Javier Hernández to go to Real Madrid on loan. He'd broken the British transfer record for Ángel Di María, but United looked a striker short. Van Gaal's solution was Radamel Falcao.

The Colombian had missed the World Cup Finals with a knee injury sustained in January with Monaco. Two goals in three games with Monaco at the start of the 2014/15 season suggested that his recovery was complete and a move to Real Madrid was reported to be close when United stepped in with one of the most expensive loan agreements ever.

Monaco received £6m in a loan fee, and Falcao would be paid an estimated £265,000 a week by United, who had first option to buy in the summer of 2015 for £43.5m. The move was not a success and Falcao left Old Trafford having scored only four goals in 29 matches in his only season at the club.

Also on this day

1993 After a protracted legal battle with Alan Sugar, Terry Venables sold his shareholding in Spurs and resigned from the board.

1997 Rio Ferdinand, seemingly about to become the youngest England international since Duncan Edwards in 1955, was dropped from the squad by Glenn Hoddle after being banned from driving for failing a breathalyser test.

2007 With Chelsea losing 2–0 at Aston Villa, Roman Abramovich left Villa Park early. The exit was interpreted as being a sign of his displeasure with José Mourinho.

2013 Arsenal broke their transfer record with a £42.4m deal to sign Mesut Özil from Real Madrid.

3 SEPTEMBER
1999 – Bobby Robson comes home

Bobby Robson, one of the great Geordies, had been in football for almost 50 years when he was employed for the first time by the club he loved most of all.

As a boy, Robson had signed for Fulham when their manager, Bill Dodgin, had made the journey to his home at Langley Park in County Durham to persuade him to move to London. Eleven seasons at Craven Cottage were split by six at West Bromwich Albion. Robson won 20 England caps too, before a spell in America at the end of his playing days.

Robson returned to Fulham to start the managerial career that would take him to the very top. The FA Cup and UEFA Cup were won at Ipswich where he stayed for 13 years. With England there was some shocking treatment from the press and some fans, before the wonder and eventual woe of Italia 90.

PSV Eindhoven, Sporting Lisbon, FC Porto, Barcelona and PSV again had all benefited from Robson's management – there were championships in Holland and Portugal, cups in Portugal and Spain and the Cup Winners' Cup with Barcelona.

Robson was 66 when he returned to England to a role with the FA that looked like semi-retirement. But when Ruud Gullit resigned at Newcastle, who were in the bottom three and in disarray, there was only one man the fans wanted to take over.

With bookies having stopped taking bets on Gullit's successor, Robson told the *Mail on Sunday*, 'I would love that job more than anything else in the world. It is impossible to put into words what it would mean to become manager at Newcastle.'

Two days later, Robson was confirmed as manager. Home, at last.

Also on this day

1998 With Arsenal and Manchester United expressing their interest in a proposed European Super League, UEFA hinted at giving England a third qualifying place in the Champions League. They also raised the prospect of merging the UEFA and Cup Winners' Cups.

2004 Scotland's friendly game against Spain at Levante was abandoned with the score at 1–1 after a power failure.

2008 After West Ham sold Anton Ferdinand and George McCartney to Sunderland without his approval, Alan Curbishley resigned as manager at Upton Park.

2013 Marouane Fellaini signed for Manchester United for a fee of £27.5m.

2014 More than two years after his last appearance for his country, Shay Given played for the Republic of Ireland against Oman, his 126th cap.

4 SEPTEMBER
2008 – Keegan resigns, again

When Kevin Keegan returned to manage Newcastle in January 2008 he was welcomed if not as a messiah, certainly as a prodigal son. Newcastle had been through six managers in the 11 years since Keegan had first left the club. The last of these, Sam Allardyce, had stayed just eight months.

Keegan's first spell had been characterized by his commitment to attacking football, goals at any cost. A decade later he had England failure and self-confessed tactical flaws on his CV. If Keegan had changed, so had Newcastle: in 1997 John Hall had been the owner, now it was Mike Ashley in charge with a complicated management structure of Chris Mort as chairman, Derek Llambias as managing director, Dennis Wise as executive director and Tony Jimenez as head of player recruitment.

For all the enthusiasm that greeted Keegan, his second spell started badly. There were nine games without a win in which Newcastle scored only four goals.

A flurry of wins against Fulham, Spurs and Reading ensured there would be no relegation battle, but even a win against Sunderland didn't add much gloss to a season that ended with consecutive defeats and Newcastle in 12th place.

Keegan wanted a major investment in the summer but had already expressed his reservations about the board's willingness to deliver. Argentines Jonás Gutiérrez and Fabricio Coloccini were signed along with Danny Guthrie, but when Aston Villa declared their interest in James Milner, Keegan publicly said he wanted the midfielder to stay. When Villa improved their offer to £12m, Newcastle accepted it and Keegan was left explaining the deal to unhappy fans, and promising new players before the transfer deadline.

The players he was presented with by Newcastle's recruitment team were Xisco and Ignacio González. Before either had pulled on a Newcastle jersey Keegan had resigned, saying, 'It's my opinion that a manager must have the right to manage and that clubs should not impose upon any manager any player that he does not want.'

Three weeks (and three defeats) later, Joe Kinnear was appointed as Keegan's replacement.

Also on this day

1996 **Vinnie Jones was sent off for the 12th, and last, time in his career as Wimbledon won 1–0 at home to Tottenham.**

1999 **Alan Shearer scored his first England hat-trick in a 6–0 win over Luxembourg.**

2004 **A mistake by David James helped Austria hold England to a 2–2 draw in Vienna in their World Cup qualifier.**

2006 **Sir Alex Ferguson joined calls for the Premier League to take a two-week winter break after the Christmas fixtures.**

5 SEPTEMBER
2001 – Scotland's World Cup exit

It was the Belgians who ended Scotland's dream of qualifying for the 2002 World Cup Finals. Scotland, who had proudly featured in all but one of the World Cups played since 1970, were hoping to make it seven World Cups in eight attempts – two more than England.

In their qualifying group, Craig Brown's team were drawn with San Marino, Latvia, Croatia and Belgium – with only one team guaranteed to make it to Japan and South Korea, the second place side to go into a play-off.

Seven points from their first three games, all away, was a great start. Latvia and San Marino were first to be beaten, followed by a draw in Zagreb with Croatia.

Scotland's first home game in the group was against Belgium, who had just fired ten past San Marino. Scotland led 2–0 after only half an hour, and the Belgians were down to ten men after Éric Deflandre had handled the ball on the line – Billy Dodds scoring the penalty.

Marc Wilmots pulled one back for Belgium soon after half-time and Scotland lost their composure; in the 92nd minute Daniel van Buyten headed an equalizer. Years later Craig Brown described it as 'the game that haunts me. That's the worst pain of any game I had from 70 with the team.'

Scotland, Belgium and Croatia each had two games to play by September 2001. Belgium had 14 points, Scotland and Croatia 12 each. With Croatia almost certain to beat San Marino, the Scots knew that they must not lose to Belgium in Brussels.

Scotland were optimistic until Niko van Kerckhoven opened the scoring after 28 minutes. In the last minute, with Scotland seeking an equalizer, Belgium broke for Bart Goor to make it 2–0. Scotland digested defeat along with the news of Croatia's 4–0 win in San Marino.

Only an unlikely sequence of results in the final round of games could see Scotland qualify for the play-offs. 'The World Cup is over for us now,' said Brown. 'I don't fault the guys for effort but the best side won.'

Scotland beat Latvia in their final game, but Croatia topped the group after winning against Belgium, who qualified by beating the Czech Republic in the play-off.

Craig Brown, arguably Scotland's most successful manager, resigned.

Also on this day

1994 Leeds signed Lucas Radebe from Kaizer Chiefs in South Africa.

1998 Paul Ince was sent off for England as they lost their European Championship qualifier in Sweden 2–1.

2009 Northern Ireland kept alive their hopes of qualifying for the World Cup Finals with an excellent 1–1 draw in Poland.

6 SEPTEMBER
1995 – Higuita the scorpion

From Manchester City's Bert Trautmann, who played the last 15 minutes of the 1956 FA Cup Final with a broken neck, to São Paulo's Rogério Ceni, the Brazilian with over 60 goals in his career – goalkeepers have always had a reputation for being a bit different. Colombia's René Higuita was certainly one of those.

Colombia, who came to England having finished third in the Copa America, had Carlos Valderrama and Faustino Asprilla, who were supposed to be the star attractions. At 34, Valderrama was famous for his performances at the 1990 and 1994 World Cups, but also for his crazy mop of frizzy blond hair. Asprilla was nine years younger and had been part of the Parma team that had made three successive European finals, winning the Cup Winners' Cup and UEFA Cup either side of a defeat to Arsenal in the Cup Winners' Cup.

Higuita was just the goalkeeper, albeit one who had three international goals to his credit – like Rogério Ceni he had a penchant for free-kicks and penalties.

If England fans had had any inkling of what Higuita would do, many more than the meagre crowd of 20,038 at Wembley would have turned up to watch.

Jamie Redknapp hit the shot. It was from around 30 yards out, not very hard and straight at the goalkeeper standing in the centre of the goal. A ten-year-old would have been disappointed not to save it in their sleep.

Perhaps deciding that such an elementary save was beneath him, Higuita dived forwards, head first, under the ball and flipped his feet in the air to volley clear with his heels. In a move that might have come from a break-dancing manual he then landed on the palms of his hands and flipped back to his feet. It was the scorpion kick.

The game finished 0–0.

Also on this day

1999 Mikaël Silvestre chose Manchester United over Liverpool and left Inter Milan for £3.2m.

2002 Peter Schmeichel signed for Manchester City.

2003 Aged 17 years and 317 days, Wayne Rooney became England's youngest ever goalscorer in a 2–1 win in Macedonia.

2004 Graeme Souness resigned as manager of Blackburn Rovers.

2006 David Healy scored a hat-trick for Northern Ireland, who beat Spain 3–2 in Belfast in a European Championship qualifier.

2009 England's women beat the Netherlands 2–1 in extra-time to reach the European Championship Final.

2011 England all but sealed a place at Euro 2012 with a 1–0 win over Wales at Wembley.

7 SEPTEMBER
2005 – Irish eyes are smiling

Northern Ireland had improved immeasurably in the 20 months Lawrie Sanchez had been in charge. After two years in which they had failed to even score a goal under Sammy McIlroy, there was a new optimism at Windsor Park.

Flying the flag for this new Northern Irish team was David Healy, who had scored ten goals in the 17 games Northern Ireland had played under Sanchez. A former Manchester United trainee, Healy had been a success at Preston and was now playing as a midfielder for Leeds in the Championship, but for his country he was seen as an out-and-out striker.

There was great excitement in Northern Ireland, Wales and England when the three countries were drawn together in qualifying for the 2006 World Cup.

By the time England travelled to play in Belfast for the first time since 1987, they had already beaten Wales home and away and won against Northern Ireland at Wembley, while Wales and Northern Ireland had drawn in Cardiff.

Northern Ireland hadn't scored against England in the last eight meetings stretching back to 1980, and hadn't beaten them since 1972. Both records were about to end.

Windsor Park was full to the brim. With 14,000 fans crammed inside the ageing stands, they watched an England side containing Gerrard, Lampard, Beckham, Rooney and Owen put in an abject display.

At 0–0 with 17 minutes to go the critics already had the knives out for Sven-Göran Eriksson. Things got worse when Frank Lampard failed to control a clearance from Paul Robinson and

Steven Davis advanced for the home side. Davis spotted Healy's run and delivered a chipped pass over the England defence, which appealed for offside. Correctly the flag stayed down, and Healy controlled the pass before unleashing a half-volley across Robinson into the far corner.

England's inquest lasted almost as long as Northern Ireland's celebrations.

Also on this day

1994 England got some measure of revenge for their 1993 defeat by winning 2–0 against the USA at Wembley.

1996 Struggling Leeds lost 4–0 at home to Manchester United, former Leeds man Cantona netting the fourth.

1998 Under pressure from unhappy fans, the FA asked for the government to get involved in BSkyB's proposed takeover of Manchester United.

2002 Lee Bowyer won his only England cap in a 1–1 draw with Portugal at Villa Park.

8 SEPTEMBER

1998 – Sky's Old Trafford offer accepted

Even in some of their less successful eras there had always been someone interested in buying Manchester United. In 1984 it had been Robert Maxwell, in 1989 it was

Michael Knighton, but neither attempt was as close to success as BSkyB's in 1998.

Sky's head Rupert Murdoch saw his £625m offer accepted by the Old Trafford board in early September 1998. Anger at the proposed deal rose almost as quickly as the club's share price. United fans formed a 'Shareholders against Murdoch' group; in Parliament the cross-party Football Group demanded that the deal be put before the Office of Fair Trading.

The politicians were concerned about a conflict of interest; that when TV rights were being negotiated, United might pass privileged information from rival broadcasters to its parent company Sky. The TV executives countered by saying that they'd be happy for Manchester United to take no part in any such negotiations to ensure a fair process.

With pressure from fans, Parliament and the Independent Television Commission, the deal was referred to the Monopolies and Mergers Commission, whose findings would be put to the Trade and Industry Secretary, Stephen Byers.

In March 1999 it was rumoured that the MMC would advise the Department of Trade and Industry to block the deal as it found it was not in the public interest. The lobbying continued until April when it was confirmed that the proposed Sky takeover was found to be anti-competitive and would have an adverse effect on the wider football industry.

Sky's reaction was reported to be one of 'disbelief' and their chief executive Mark Booth said, 'This is a bad ruling for British football clubs, who will have to compete in Europe against clubs who are backed by successful media companies.'

The Shareholders against Murdoch group said, 'The most remarkable thing is that a politician has at last stood up to Rupert Murdoch.'

Also on this day

1998 Paul Merson signed for Aston Villa for £6.75m from Middlesbrough.

1999 David Batty was sent off as England drew 0–0 in Poland. The result left Kevin Keegan's side relying on a favour from Sweden to qualify for Euro 2000.

2003 Manchester United chief executive Peter Kenyon left Old Trafford to join the Abramovich revolution at Chelsea.

2010 Gérard Houllier was appointed manager by Aston Villa.

9 SEPTEMBER
1996 – Leeds sack Howard Wilkinson

It couldn't have been an easy decision to sack Howard Wilkinson. In his time at Leeds he had taken the club back into the top division after eight years in the second tier and they had been crowned champions of England in 1992, the last year before the formation of the Premier League.

The list of players whom Wilkinson had either bought or developed included Gordon Strachan, Gary McAllister, Lee Chapman, Gary Speed, David Batty and Steve Hodge. He was a Yorkshireman taking arguably Yorkshire's biggest club to the very top.

Unfortunately for Wilkinson they didn't stay there very long. United's defence of the title was catastrophic, finishing 17th the following season, avoiding relegation by only two points and failing to win a single game away from Elland Road. Wilkinson also sanctioned the sale of Éric Cantona to Manchester United, which came back to haunt him and the club.

The following two seasons were much better, Leeds finishing fifth each time and in 1995 unearthing a jewel in Tony Yeboah. It seemed as though the man nicknamed Sergeant Wilko had got his troops in order again.

It didn't last. In the 1995/96 season, while Cantona continued to flourish across the Pennines, Leeds invested in the unfit, seemingly uninterested, Tomas Brolin from Parma. It didn't help that Leeds had sold Cantona for just £1,2m, but signed the Swedish Brolin for a club record £4.5m. Leeds were well beaten by PSV Eindhoven in the UEFA Cup, and

lost 12 of their last 16 league games with Brolin failing to score in any of them. Leeds limped home in 13th place.

The following season started in similar vein. Two days after losing 4–0 at home to Manchester United, Wilkinson was sacked after eight years in charge. He was replaced by George Graham, who returned to management after 19 months on the sidelines.

Also on this day

1992 Vinnie Jones rejoined Wimbledon from Chelsea.

1998 After being 3–0 down after 27 minutes, Wimbledon came back to win 4–3 at West Ham.

2006 Everton beat Liverpool 3–0 at Goodison Park with Andrew Johnson scoring twice, their biggest win in the Merseyside derby since 1964.

2009 England sealed qualification for the 2010 World Cup with a 5–1 win over Croatia at Wembley, maintaining their 100 per cent record from eight qualifying games played.

10 SEPTEMBER
2008 – Walcott the Boy Wonder

There had been widespread astonishment when Sven-Göran Eriksson called up

Theo Walcott for the 2006 World Cup Finals in Germany on the advice of Arsenal manager Arsène Wenger. Walcott, who'd been signed from Southampton, had only just turned 17, hadn't made his Arsenal debut and Eriksson admitted he had only seen him play on TV. The decision seemed all the more surprising when Walcott didn't play a single minute of football in Germany.

Steve McLaren took over from Eriksson immediately after England's elimination from the World Cup, and relegated Walcott to the Under-21 side.

In 2006/07, his first full season with Arsenal, Walcott played regularly and scored his first goal in the League Cup Final defeat to Chelsea, but couldn't break into the senior England squad despite its failure to qualify for Euro 2008.

It was under Fabio Capello that Walcott got his England chance again, playing the last 25 minutes of a friendly win in Trinidad. Capello had seen enough to include the now 19-year-old Walcott in his starting line-up for England's next match. He played all 90 minutes as England began their 2010 World Cup qualifying campaign with a 2–0 win in Andorra.

England's next match was on 10 September in Croatia, the team that had qualified for Euro 2008 at England's expense. Walcott kept his place, keeping David Beckham on the bench, and

England took revenge, with Walcott stealing the show.

Walcott's first goal was smashed into the bottom corner after a mistake by Robert Kovač, his second was lashed in after Rooney's assist. Rooney and Mario Mandžukić traded goals before Walcott was sent clear by another Rooney pass and raced away to finish, becoming the youngest player ever to score a hat-trick for England.

Afterwards Capello said of his new star, 'I decided to put in Theo because I saw the game against Andorra at the weekend and also how he was in training – and at this moment he is fantastic psychologically and physically. At this moment, he is difficult to contain. I hope he doesn't get any injuries because he is so fast and so dangerous.'

When Capello left Walcott out of the squad for the 2010 World Cup Finals, it was almost as big a shock as when Eriksson had included him in 2006. Injury meant that Walcott missed out in 2014 too.

Also on this day

1995 Jack Grealish was born.

2009 England's women lost their first major international final 6–2 to Germany in the European Championship in Helsinki, the Germans scoring three in the last 30 minutes.

2013 Frank Lampard won his 100th England cap in a 0–0 draw in Ukraine.

11 SEPTEMBER
2008 – West Ham hope for Zola power

Gianfranco Zola might have been a Chelsea legend, but so special were his skills – and so infectious his smile – that even Chelsea's rivals could hardly help but admire him.

Zola's skills as a manager were almost untested when West Ham appointed him as their successor to Alan Curbishley. Zola had spent two years as assistant manager for Italy's Under-21 team and had filled the same role with the 2008 Olympic squad, but that was his only experience.

Curbishley's exit had been over transfer policy, not results. West Ham were fifth in the league when he stood down in protest at the sale of first Anton Ferdinand and then George McCartney.

Zola's start at West Ham was a difficult one; they slumped to 17th by Christmas and then sold Craig Bellamy to Manchester City in the January transfer window. Their results and performances rallied from January, and when West Ham finished ninth, higher than in the previous two seasons, it was a job well done by Zola, who had the team playing the kind of football West Ham's tradition demands.

There were question marks about his signings though: Savio had cost £9m from Brescia in January and had failed to score, Radoslav Kováč from Spartak Moscow had been unconvincing.

In the summer Alessandro Diamanti from Livorno, Manuel da Costa from Fiorentina, Hérita Ilunga from Toulouse and Guillermo Franco from Villarreal were all signed relatively cheaply and with varying degrees of success. Soon West Ham were in a relegation battle.

In January it looked as though co-owner David Sullivan might have taken the responsibility of transfer policy away from his manager. First West Ham signed Mido and Benni McCarthy, moves that smacked of desperation, then Sullivan suggested that the entire squad with the exception of Scott Parker was for sale. Soon Zola was claiming that he'd had no say in an unsuccessful move for West Brom's Graham Dorrans.

Despite losing 8 of their last 12 games West Ham stayed up, finishing one place above the relegation zone, but to no-one's surprise Zola was sacked two days after the season finished.

Also on this day

1998 Arsenal signed Freddie Ljungberg from Halmstads for £3m.

2001 A minute's silence was observed before all Champions League matches after the attack on New York's World Trade Center. UEFA announced that all Champions League matches scheduled for the following day would be postponed.

2004 Tim Cahill was sent off in only his second game for Everton, after getting a second yellow card for pulling his shirt over his face after scoring the winner at Manchester City. Referee Steve Bennett said FIFA laws gave him no choice; Sepp Blatter said, 'I don't agree with the referee.'

12 SEPTEMBER
2009 – Adebayor's Arsenal taunt

The route from Arsenal to Manchester City was to become a well-trodden one once City had Sheikh Mansour's money at their disposal. The first player to make that journey was Emmanuel Adebayor.

In his three-and-a-half seasons at Arsenal, Adebayor had normally played second fiddle, initially to Thierry Henry and then to Robin van Persie. Like his Arsenal predecessor Nwankwo Kanu, Adebayor clearly had a huge talent but sometimes seemed to lack the application to make the most of it.

Perhaps it was no coincidence that by far Adebayor's best season for Arsenal had been in 2007/08, when Henry had left

for Barcelona and van Persie was injured for much of the campaign. Adebayor had scored 30 goals that season, which included two hat-tricks, both scored against Derby.

Adebayor and his agent spent much of the summer talking about a transfer away from Arsenal. AC Milan and Barcelona were both said to be keen but, after testing the patience of Arsenal fans and manager Arsène Wenger, he signed a new contract at the club.

The next season saw van Persie restored to fitness and Adebayor restored to his role of support act. Sixteen goals was a decent return from 37 games, but only five of those were scored after Christmas and he didn't play 90 minutes in a league match from the start of February to the end of the season.

When Manchester City offered £25m for Adebayor, Arsenal decided to take the money.

Arsenal fans at City's Etihad Stadium taunted Adebayor throughout the clubs' first meeting since the transfer. Kolo Touré, who had made the same move a few days after Adebayor, got off relatively unscathed. But then Touré was not such a divisive figure.

Adebayor had already aimed a kick at Robin van Persie's head, which referee Mark Clattenburg missed, when he scored his goal. It was a magnificent header that put City 3–1 up with ten minutes to play. He could have celebrated with his new teammates, he could have charged towards the City fans, but instead Adebayor ran the length of the pitch to slide on his knees in front of the Arsenal supporters at the other end of the stadium.

There were two more goals as City won 4–2, but Adebayor had guaranteed himself both the headlines and punishment from the FA. He was banned for three matches for the kick at van Persie and fined £25,000 for his celebration sprint.

Also on this day

2000 To general astonishment Chelsea sacked manager Gianluca Vialli.

2007 James McFadden scored the only goal as Alex McLeish's Scotland won 1–0 in France in their Euro 2008 qualifier.

13 SEPTEMBER
1997 – Ian Wright: 179 Just Done It

Cliff Bastin's goalscoring record for Arsenal had stood for 58 years. Despite the fact his career at Highbury was interrupted by the Second World War and despite playing many of his games on the left wing, Bastin scored 178 goals for Arsenal. Ian Wright broke that record in spectacular fashion, scoring a hat-trick against Bolton at Highbury in 1997.

Wright had joined Arsenal from Crystal Palace in September 1991. He had scored on his debut and went on scoring until he moved to West Ham in the summer of 1998.

In the 1991/92 season Wright scored 26 goals for Arsenal (plus 5 for Palace before his move), thereafter his goal tallies for the next five seasons were 30, 35, 30, 23 and 30; incredibly consistent and remarkably injury-free. The chant of 'Ian Wright, Wright, Wright!' became a Highbury constant.

By the autumn of 1997, Wright was approaching his 34th birthday and even he couldn't continue forever, particularly with Arsène Wenger having invested in the teenage prodigy Nicolas Anelka.

Wright started the season with a goal at Leeds in a 1–1 draw, then scored both in a 2–0 win over Coventry; 177 goals and counting.

Dennis Bergkamp then scored five in two games against Southampton and Leicester while Wright remained one short of equalling the record. No doubt he was hoping to break it against Spurs at Highbury, but the north London derby finished 0–0.

Then came Bolton. Wright's first goal came after 20 minutes; he immediately tore off his jersey to reveal a printed T-shirt declaring, '179 Just Done It'. Except that he hadn't: that was goal number 178 – the record-equalling strike.

The record-breaker was a tap-in five minutes later and a relieved Wright sprinted away with his Arsenal shirt over his head revealing that T-shirt again. The icing on the cake, and the 180th goal, came nine minutes from time.

Also on this day

1993 Andy Roxburgh resigned as Scotland manager having equalled Jock Stein's record of 61 games in charge.

1996 On the same day that caretaker manager Stewart Houston left Arsenal to take over at Queens Park Rangers, Tony Adams admitted to his teammates that he was an alcoholic.

2004 Graeme Souness was appointed manager of Newcastle, replacing Bobby Robson.

2006 In the Champions League Manchester United beat Celtic 3–2 at Old Trafford in the first ever competitive meeting between the clubs.

2008 Robinho scored on his debut for Manchester City but they lost 3–1 at home to Chelsea.

14 SEPTEMBER

1994 – Manchester United 4 Gothenburg 2: the ever-expanding Champions League

UEFA had begun changing the format of the European Cup in 1991. It was a response to the ever-present threat of Europe's top clubs breaking away to form their own European Super League.

For the powerful elite the old, unseeded, knockout competition between all of Europe's champion clubs had all kinds of drawbacks. It didn't provide enough games, there was too great a risk of being knocked out early, and the format allowed entry to the champions of, say, Malta but only one club from each of the major leagues.

UEFA's new idea for 1991/92 was to have two knockout rounds as usual, followed by a group stage with two pools of four teams, the winners of each meeting in the final. So when Barcelona beat Sampdoria 1–0 at Wembley in the final, it was their 11th money-spinning game in the tournament, whereas the 1991 winner Red Star Belgrade had played only 9.

For the 1992/93 season UEFA stuck with the format but introduced a new name, the Champions League. In 1993/94 they introduced a semi-final stage for the top two teams from each group, increasing the number of games for the winner to 13.

There were still problems though – it was too easy for those big clubs to get knocked out. The English champions had failed to reach the group stage in all three seasons, the German champions had missed out in two and even Barcelona hadn't progressed beyond the knockout stage in 1993.

So, for the 1994/95 season UEFA effectively crumpled up their competition and started again. For starters the champions of the so-called 'smaller nations' were shunted into the UEFA Cup. There was a knockout phase, but only for the mid-ranking leagues – the champions of Spain, Germany, England, Italy, Russia, Portugal, Holland and Belgium were all straight into a new expanded 16-team group stage, no questions asked.

So it was that Manchester United beat Gothenburg in the first Champions League group game to be played on English soil.

Also on this day

2002 Manchester United lost 1–0 at Leeds three days after losing by the same score at home to Bolton. Eight points from six games was their worst start to a Premier League season. They still won the league by five points.

2004 Mark Hughes agreed to become manager of Blackburn Rovers, while continuing in his job as manager of Wales for the upcoming World Cup qualifying games against England and Poland.

15 SEPTEMBER
2004 – Van Nistelrooy's European record

Denis Law had scored 28 goals in European competition for Manchester United in just 33 games. It was a club record that stood for 35 years until, also in his 33rd game in Europe, Ruud van Nistelrooy passed it.

The Dutchman, who had scored nine goals in 15 European games for PSV Eindhoven, joined United in 2001 but failed to find the net in his first two Champions League games against Lille and Deportivo La Coruña. Van Nistelrooy's double in the home game against Deportivo were his first, but they couldn't prevent a 3–2 defeat.

Eight more European goals followed that season, including one in the semi-final, which United lost on away goals to Bayer Leverkusen.

In 2002/03 van Nistelrooy scored 14 times in Europe as United went out in the quarter-final to Real Madrid. His goal in Madrid was his 23rd in Europe, putting him ahead of Bobby Charlton and behind only Law on United's list. Van Nistelrooy scored again in the second leg at Old Trafford, but Madrid won 6–5 on aggregate.

FC Porto were the next to knock United out of the Champions League, winning at the second-round phase. In the group matches, van Nistelrooy had scored two goals against Stuttgart and two against Rangers taking his total to 28 – the same as Law – but he had to wait for the chance to break the record.

Injury meant that van Nistelrooy missed the start of the 2004/05 season and a two-legged qualifying win over Dinamo Bucharest, but he returned for the trip to the Stade Gerland in Lyon in September. United were 2–0 down at half-time, but two goals from van Nistelrooy in the space of five minutes earned a draw.

Afterwards Denis Law paid tribute to the man who broke his long-standing record, 'He deserves this. I'm delighted for Ruud. It could not happen to a nicer guy.'

Van Nistelrooy added another eight goals to that record before leaving Manchester. Like Law, who missed the 1968 European Cup Final with a knee injury, he never lifted a European trophy or played in a final.

Also on this day

1999 Chelsea played their first ever Champions League game, a 0–0 draw at home to AC Milan.

2000 Claudio Ranieri was appointed Chelsea manager.

2007 Goal of the Season – Emmanuel Adebayor scored it for Arsenal against Spurs at White Hart Lane.

16 SEPTEMBER
2002 – Enckelman's derby horror

It was the first derby match between Birmingham City and Aston Villa in the Premier League, and the first in any league for 15 years. It will forever be Peter Enckelman's match.

Enckelman, signed from his native Finland, had played only 37 games for Villa in two seasons, but when Peter Schmeichel was sold to Manchester City in 2002, the 25-year-old became Villa's first-choice goalkeeper.

Things were going well; Enckelman conceded only seven goals in his first eight games of the season. Villa weren't scoring many at the other end, but he couldn't be blamed for that.

Nor could he be blamed for Birmingham's first goal at St Andrew's. A cross from Kenny Cunningham bounced off Robbie Savage into the path of Clinton Morrison, who scored.

Enckelman was not guilty for Birmingham's third goal either. Villa's defender Alpay was caught in possession by Geoff Horsfield, who finished into the corner.

But in between those goals, Enckelman had made one of the worst errors by any goalkeeper in the Premier League's history.

Olof Mellberg took a defensive throw-in, aiming the ball back to his own goalkeeper standing on the right corner of the six-yard box. Enckelman was under no pressure and had no need to hurry, but took his eye off the ball for a split second and it bounced under his foot and into the net.

The 'goal' could not stand if Enckelman hadn't touched the ball, the laws stating that, 'A goal cannot be scored directly from a throw-in.'

If Enckelman had looked unconcerned and apologized to all concerned then perhaps the goal would have been disallowed. In fact he chased the ball into the net and stood, horrified, with his head in his hands. Referee David Elleray couldn't possibly be sure that Enckelman had touched the ball, and if he had it must have been the slightest of grazes. Enckelman's reaction might have led him to give the goal.

Enkelman has always denied that he touched the ball, and therefore claims that the goal should not have stood.

Also on this day

1997 Steve McManaman ran from the halfway line to score a brilliant individual goal in Liverpool's 2–2 draw at Celtic in the UEFA Cup.

1998 Southampton agreed to sell the Dell for housing development and to purchase a disused gasworks as the site for a new stadium.

2014 Mario Balotelli scored his first Liverpool goal in their 2–1 win over Ludogorets in the Champions League.

17 SEPTEMBER
1997 – Tino of the Toon

Faustino Asprilla is sometimes seen as the man who derailed Newcastle's 1996 title bid. Kevin Keegan signed the Colombian for Newcastle from Parma when they were nine points clear at the top of the Premier League with Keith Gillespie, David Ginola, Peter Beardsley and Les Ferdinand tearing defences apart. Accommodating Asprilla, usually at the expense of Gillespie, seemed to unbalance the side. Newcastle lost at West Ham on his full debut and won only 5 of their remaining 12 games, allowing Manchester United to win the league.

Nevertheless the unpredictable Asprilla was a fans' favourite for his extravagant skills and famous somersault goal celebration.

By 1997, with Alan Shearer injured, Asprilla was playing up front with Jon Dahl Tomasson and Newcastle were managed by Kenny Dalglish. Their first ever game in the Champions League group stages could not have been much tougher: Barcelona were at St James' Park.

Asprilla was sensational, scoring a 29-minute hat-trick and running the Barcelona defenders into the ground. His first goal was a penalty he won himself, the second and third fantastic powerful headers from Gillespie crosses. Luis Enrique and Luís Figo scored late goals for Barcelona, but Asprilla had done enough to win the game.

Nobody could have anticipated that these would be Asprilla's last goals for Newcastle. An operation on a stomach injury ruled him out for two months and he was sold back to Parma in January 1998.

Also on this day

2002 Liverpool were outplayed and beaten 2–0 in their Champions League match at Rafa Benítez's Valencia.

2005 Sunderland ended their 20-game losing streak in the Premier League with a 1–1 draw at West Brom.

2007 Derby beat Newcastle 1–0 in what turned out to be their only Premier League win of the season.

2007 José Mourinho was asked about the quality of his squad in a press conference the day before a Champions League game against Rosenborg. He replied, 'But it is omelettes and eggs. No eggs – no omelettes. It depends on the quality of the eggs. In the supermarket you have class one, two or class three eggs and some are more expensive than others and some give you better omelettes. So when the class one eggs are in Waitrose and you cannot go there, you have a problem.' Three days later Roman Abramovich cracked and sacked him.

18 SEPTEMBER
2011 – Torres and the open goal

Fernando Torres had scored one goal in his first 23 games in a Chelsea shirt when André Villas-Boas took his side to Old Trafford in 2011.

The only fans enjoying Torres's torturous start to life at Chelsea as much as Liverpool's were Manchester United's. Torres had destroyed their defence in Liverpool's 4–1 win in Manchester in the spring of 2009, and the Stretford End had not forgotten it.

Manchester United were top and Chelsea third after the opening four games of the season and this was bound to be a game between two teams who would be aiming for the title in May.

It was an extraordinary match that could have had many more than four goals. United led 3–0 at half-time: Smalling with a header, a blast from Nani and a tap-in from Rooney. But Chelsea should have scored at least twice, Torres missing after a mistake by Anderson and David de Gea making a remarkable stop from a wasteful Ramires.

Those United fans had reason to be wary when Torres scored in the first minute of the second half, receiving a pass from Anelka and clipping superbly over De Gea – Torres at his best.

Chances continued to flood at both ends; then Nani hit the bar for United and was fouled in going for the rebound. Rooney slipped as he approached the penalty and put it wide. Then, to the delight of mocking United fans, Torres volleyed over after his own skill had created panic in the United defence. Rooney hit the post when it seemed easier to score, but that was a long way from being the miss of the game.

Making a run behind Phil Jones, Torres was released by a perfect Ramires pass. As David de Gea charged out to meet him, a sublime Torres step-over sent him past the goalkeeper, where an empty net at the Stretford End was yawning wide and unguarded. From seven yards out Torres inexplicably shot wide.

The cheering reverberated down the East Lancashire Road all the way to Anfield and back again.

Also on this day

1998 John Gregory left Wycombe Wanderers to take over as manager at Aston Villa.

2005 Michael Owen scored his first goal for new club Newcastle in only his second game, a 3–0 win at Blackburn.

2007 Chelsea were held to a 1–1 draw by Norway's Rosenborg in their Champions League group game at Stamford Bridge. The game attracted a crowd of only 24,793, Chelsea's lowest attendance for four years.

19 SEPTEMBER
1992 – Rocket Ron gets it wrong

Ronny Rosenthal's arrival at Liverpool late in the 1989/90 season had gone a long way to helping them win the First Division title; he'd scored seven times in his first eight games for the club at the very end of that campaign.

Direct, powerful and nicknamed 'Rocket Ron', Rosenthal was not the most elegant striker, but worked prodigiously hard and was a reliable finisher – most of the time. He was usually on the bench for Liverpool the following season, but scored five goals in 16 appearances as they finished runners-up to Arsenal.

In 1991/92, Rosenthal was hardly involved as Liverpool won the FA Cup, and he scored only three goals in the league.

After a poor start to the first ever Premier League season (Liverpool were 15th after the first seven games), they sold Dean Saunders to Aston Villa. Manager Graeme Souness decided that Rosenthal should take Saunders's place and, when his side went to face Villa and Saunders at Villa Park, it was only the Israeli's sixth start of the calendar year.

Saunders had only left Liverpool nine days earlier and this was his home debut. He scored twice as Villa, also with Liverpool cast-offs Staunton and Houghton in their side, won 4–2. Rosenthal did get one goal, a late consolation, but he'll never be allowed to forget his miss when the score was 0–0.

Rosenthal latched on to a mistake by Shaun Teale and darted past goalkeeper Nigel Spink. From barely eight yards he could have rolled the ball gently into the empty net but instead tried to hammer it home. He hit the bar – a miss that must have been on every compilation of footballing calamities ever since.

Also on this day

1998 Dave Watson became only the third Everton player to reach 500 appearances for the club.

1999 Newcastle beat Sheffield Wednesday 8–0 with Alan Shearer scoring five in Bobby Robson's first home game as manager. It was Newcastle's biggest win since Len Shackleton scored six on his debut in a 13–0 thrashing of Newport in 1946.

2000 Leeds beat AC Milan 1–0 in the Champions League.

2004 José Mourinho accused Spurs of 'parking the bus' when Jacques Santini's side held on for a 0–0 draw at Stamford Bridge.

2013 Swansea City won 3–0 at Valencia in the Europa League.

2014 UEFA announced that Wembley Stadium would host the semi-finals and final of the 2020 European Championships.

20 SEPTEMBER
2007 – Mourinho sacked

There had been clues: Roman Abramovich walking out of Villa Park early with Chelsea losing, Mourinho's complaints about the quality of 'eggs' he was able to buy. There had been the appointment by Abramovich of his friend Avram Grant as director of football and Mourinho's apparent suspicion of Abramovich's favourite player, Andriy Shevchenko, whom

Mourinho seemed to regard as a Trojan horse sent from the owner rather than a very expensive gift from the heavens.

There were definitely clues, but when the end came it came quickly and left Chelsea fans in a state of shock.

In a little over three seasons Mourinho had won two Premier League titles, the FA Cup and the League Cup twice. But he'd failed to bring the Champions League to Stamford Bridge.

While Abramovich wanted fantasy football, Mourinho was more prosaic. When Chelsea were labouring to beat Birmingham and Portsmouth at Stamford Bridge at the start of the 2007/08 season it wasn't the kind of football anyone would dream about.

Problems mounted when Chelsea were beaten at Villa, drew 0–0 at home to Blackburn and then drew 1–1 at home to Rosenborg.

If Mourinho was under pressure he'd been doing his best to sound unconcerned: 'If the club decide to sack me because of bad results that's part of the game. If it happens I will be a millionaire and get another club a couple of months later.'

The morning after the Rosenborg draw, Mourinho was summoned to a meeting with Abramovich, chief executive Peter Kenyon and director Eugene Tenenbaum. Whether the intention was to sack Mourinho or not is unclear,

but by the end of the meeting that had become a real possibility.

In the evening Mourinho and the bulk of his squad attended a showing of the film *Blue Revolution* about the club's recent success. Afterwards Mourinho is said to have shaken the hand of every player and returned to Stamford Bridge for the meeting to reconvene.

At 1.45 in the morning Chelsea released a 15-word statement: 'Chelsea Football Club and José Mourinho have agreed to part company today by mutual consent.'

Also on this day

1995 Manchester United lost 3–0 at home to York City in the League Cup.

2004 Rio Ferdinand returned from his eight-month ban for missing a random drugs test as Manchester United beat Liverpool 2–1.

2006 Xabi Alonso scored for Liverpool against Newcastle from inside his own half, measured at 58 metres or 63 yards.

2009 Michael Owen scored in injury-time to seal a dramatic 4–3 home win for Manchester United over Manchester City.

21 SEPTEMBER
2003 – Keown vs van Nistelrooy

Such was the enmity between Manchester United and Arsenal that every meeting, however early in the season it might come, was played as though the title depended on it – which often it did. The meeting at Old Trafford in the early stages of the 2003/04 season goes down as one of the most turbulent. It became known as 'The Battle of Old Trafford'.

The two sides had met in the Community Shield six weeks earlier, a game marred by a red card for Arsenal's Francis Jeffers for aiming a kick at Phil Neville.

In this second match, which Alex Ferguson described afterwards as 'ferocious', Patrick Vieira was sent off for a second yellow card with nine minutes to go. He had jumped with Ruud van Nistelrooy for a high ball and landed on his back as the Dutchman stayed on his feet. Vieira flicked out with his foot as though to kick van Nistelrooy, though his foot actually came nowhere near him. The United striker, maybe needlessly, jumped back out of the way of Vieira's foot and referee Steve Bennett sent off the Arsenal captain. Arsenal were incensed with van Nistelrooy and almost everyone except the two goalkeepers got involved in a pushing match as Vieira was led away.

Still at 0–0, the game went into injury-time when Martin Keown and Diego Forlán dived for a cross and Steve Bennett decided there was a push – penalty to Manchester United. Van Nistelrooy smashed it right-footed as hard as he could, and saw it cannon back off the crossbar.

The man who had conceded it, Martin Keown, dashed to taunt van Nistelrooy, and when the final whistle blew a few seconds later the United man was surrounded by jeering Arsenal players with Keown dancing in front of his face.

The fall-out was wide-ranging; Arsenal were fined £175,000, Keown banned for three games and fined £20,000, Lauren banned for four games and fined £40,000, Ray Parlour banned for one game and fined £10,000, Patrick Vieira banned for one match and fined £20,000 and Ashley Cole fined £10,000. For United Ryan Giggs was fined £7,500 and Cristiano Ronaldo £4000.

A very expensive day out.

Also on this day

2003 Glenn Hoddle was sacked by Spurs and replaced by David Pleat.

2014 Frank Lampard scored for Manchester City against former club Chelsea in a 1–1 draw at the Etihad Stadium.

2014 Manchester United lost 5–3 at newly promoted Leicester, manager Louis van Gaal's third defeat in his first six games.

22 SEPTEMBER
2013 – Sunderland sack Di Canio

Paolo Di Canio was a controversial appointment when he took over at Sunderland in March 2013. The new manager had previously admitted to having some extreme political views, telling an Italian news agency in 2005, 'I am a fascist not a racist.'

Sunderland's vice-chairman (and former candidate for the leadership of the Labour Party) David Miliband resigned when Di Canio was appointed, saying, 'In the light of the new manager's past political statements, I think it right to step down.'

The club were only one point above the relegation zone when Martin O'Neill was sacked and replaced by the Italian, who had got Swindon promoted from League Two the previous season before his unexpected resignation.

Di Canio's finest hour at Sunderland was a 3–0 derby win at Newcastle in his second game; he celebrated it by sliding down the touchline on his knees. But that was one of only two wins in the last seven games of the season in which there was also a 6–1 defeat to Aston Villa. Sunderland did just enough to stay up, finishing 17th.

Fourteen new players were signed in the summer, but Di Canio claimed they weren't his choices, rather those of the director of football Roberto De Fanti and chief scout Valentino Angeloni.

At the training ground, Di Canio banned tomato ketchup and mayonnaise. He claimed the players were unfit and unprofessional.

Sunderland took just one point from the first five games of the following season, a League Cup win over MK Dons being their solitary victory. After a 3–0 defeat at West Bromwich, Di Canio indulged in a bizarre mime act in front of the Sunderland fans, gesturing to them to keep their chins up. Those fans seemed split over whether to applaud or abuse the manager. 'I was absorbing the energy of the fans,' he said.

At beginning of the following week a group of senior players were reported to have approached chief executive Margaret Byrne – 'cowards', said Di Canio later – and on Tuesday he was sacked.

Under his management Sunderland had played 13 games – winning 3, drawing 3 and losing 7.

Also on this day

1992 Liverpool came from 3–1 down and 4–2 down to draw 4–4 with Chesterfield at Anfield, the most goals Liverpool had conceded at home in a cup tie since 1898.

2005 Jonathan Woodgate was sent off on his debut for Real Madrid.

2007 England's women lost 3–0 to the United States in their World Cup quarter-final.

2010 Liverpool were knocked out of the League Cup at Anfield by Northampton Town in a penalty shoot-out.

23 SEPTEMBER
2003 – Ferdinand's missed drugs test

Rio Ferdinand was told twice at Manchester United's training ground that he had to undergo a routine drugs test that day. For whatever reason, he forgot.

Soon after leaving the training ground, Ferdinand realized his mistake, but the testers had gone and reported Ferdinand for having failed to take the test. A day

later a test proved negative, but the damage was done.

In October, with Ferdinand's case waiting consideration by a disciplinary commission, the FA delayed the naming of the England squad to play Turkey in a European Championship qualifier. A day later they decided that playing Ferdinand would be inappropriate. The squad, without Ferdinand, was named.

Once that squad assembled, the players took a vote and agreed that they might boycott the match in protest at Ferdinand's omission. It took hours of diplomacy to persuade them to board the flight to Istanbul.

Football had been under pressure to stick to the guidelines of the World Anti-Doping Agency (WADA), whose policy was that missing a test was as serious as failing a test. The commission recommended that Ferdinand be banned from football for eight months, and in December the FA accepted their findings – ruling Ferdinand out of the rest of the season and Euro 2004.

United called the ban 'savage', comparing it to the nine-month ban for Mark Bosnich, who had actually tested positive for cocaine a year earlier. WADA chief Dick Pound said Ferdinand had been lucky the ban was not longer.

In his autobiography ten years later, Sir Alex Ferguson wrote that 'my indignation endures to this day', blaming the testers for not keeping an eye on Ferdinand at the training ground.

In an interview with the BBC two months into the ban Ferdinand said, 'I love playing for England, I love playing for my club … and to have that taken away from me in such a way was disheartening and something that really did shock me. I'm man enough to admit that I did cry.'

Also on this day

1995 Goal of the Season – Tony Yeboah scored it for Leeds at Wimbledon.

1995 Dennis Bergkamp scored his first Arsenal goals, getting two in a 4–2 win over Southampton, his seventh game for his new club.

2015 In the League Cup, Liverpool beat Middlesbrough in a penalty shoot-out at Anfield. The shoot-out went to 30 kicks before Liverpool won 14–13.

24 SEPTEMBER
2003 – Robinson sees off Swindon

Rarely has a League Cup second-round tie provoked such emotion, especially when the Premier League team progresses at home to a side drawn from two divisions below them, but Leeds United's match against Swindon was no ordinary League Cup tie.

Leeds were 2–0 down with barely 15 minutes to play. Swindon captain Andy Gurney had scored the first just before half-time with a superb free-kick and Sam Parkin got their second from close-range deep into the second half.

Ian Harte pulled a goal back for Leeds almost immediately, volleying home an Aaron Lennon corner. Swindon goalkeeper Bart Griemink was then sent off after bringing down Alan Smith just outside the area. Swindon manager Andy King brought on substitute goalkeeper Rhys Evans, with Sammy Igoe being taken off.

Four days earlier, Sunderland goalkeeper Mart Poom had headed a last-minute equalizer at Derby in Division One. Leeds keeper Paul Robinson would certainly have known about the goal, and maybe he had seen it. With time almost up, Robinson came forward for a corner and, with a wonderful leap, planted a powerful header beyond Evans into the Swindon net. The goalkeeper was submerged under a pile of jubilant teammates.

Robinson wasn't finished there. After three penalties each Swindon led 3–2 in the shoot-out; Ian Harte had missed and Sam Parkin's for Swindon had hit the post and rebounded in off Robinson's back. Then Roque Júnior scored for Leeds and Robinson flung himself to the left to save from Stefani Miglioranzi: 3–3.

Lucas Radebe scored the next Leeds penalty so Andy Gurney had to score. Robinson's save to the right post sent Elland Road into the kind of ecstasy normally reserved for a cup final.

After all that, Leeds were knocked out by Manchester United in the next round; Robinson added another goal to his tally in 2007, this time for Spurs against Watford.

Also on this day

1994 **After winning their first six games as a Premier League club, Newcastle were held to a 1–1 draw by Liverpool.**

2000 **Steve Bould retired from playing after a 20-year career taking in over 600 games.**

2009 **Portsmouth sacked manager Paul Hart.**

25 SEPTEMBER
1999 – Taibi: the Blind Venetian

For every goalkeeper who is a hero, there's another who is a villain. Massimo Taibi was certainly that at Old Trafford. After just four games for the club he was moved on, having lost a reputation for being a reliable shot-stopper and gained a nickname courtesy of the English tabloids: 'The Blind Venetian'.

Taibi was actually from Palermo, but Venezia was the most recent of six clubs he had represented in Italy's top three divisions. He'd spent the two seasons before his move to Manchester in Serie A, with first AC Milan and then Venezia, and at 29 should have been at his peak when United paid £4.5m for him.

With Mark Bosnich injured, Taibi went straight into the side for United's match at Anfield in mid-September. The Italian was named man of the match in a 3–2 United win. Taibi's second game was a disappointing 1–1 draw at home to Wimbledon, and his third was the visit of Southampton to Old Trafford.

There wasn't much Taibi could have done to prevent Southampton's first goal from Marian Pahars. Teddy Sheringham and Dwight Yorke restored normal service to put United 2–1 in front – and then came the moment for which Taibi will always be remembered.

Matt Le Tissier scored many great goals with long-distance shots that sprang from his right foot into opposition nets. This was not one of those. In fact Le Tissier was so disgusted with his shot that he turned away in frustration.

Somehow Taibi allowed the ball to squirm through his arms, under his torso and through his legs into the net. Le Tissier looked embarrassed, Taibi mortified. The game finished 3–3.

Alex Ferguson must have been alarmed, but picked Taibi again for the visit to Chelsea the following weekend. United lost 5–0 with Taibi at fault for the first and fifth.

Taibi never played for Manchester United again; he was quickly loaned to Reggina with the move being made permanent at the end of the season for £2.5m. In Italy Taibi played for another eight seasons and remained highly regarded. In Manchester they prefer to forget him.

Also on this day

1993 Efan Ekoku scored four goals in Norwich's 5–1 win at Everton.

1997 Fabrizio Ravanelli left Middlesbrough for Marseille in a £5.5m deal.

2002 Gilberto Silva scored for Arsenal at PSV Eindhoven after 19.4 seconds, the fastest scored in the Champions League. Arsenal won 4–0.

2013 The statue of Michael Jackson was removed from Craven Cottage.

2014 Luis Suárez returned from his ban for biting Branislav Ivanović as Liverpool lost 1–0 at Manchester United in the League Cup.

26 SEPTEMBER
1998 – Di Canio pushes Alcock

With AC Milan, Juventus and Napoli on his CV, signing Paolo Di Canio was quite a coup for Celtic. The Italian spent only one season there but did so well that there was an outcry from their fans when he was sold to Sheffield Wednesday for £3m.

He was soon every bit as popular in Sheffield as he had been at Celtic, scoring 14 times to become their top scorer in season 1997/98. Di Canio had three goals in the first eight games of the 1998/99 season when Arsenal went to Hillsborough.

A challenge from Wim Jonk started an explosion of anger. Patrick Vieira, the target of the tackle, took exception and threw Jonk to the ground. As Di Canio rushed over to get to Vieira, he was grabbed by Martin Keown. Di Canio kicked Keown and the two then started pushing their hands into each other's faces. When it had calmed down enough for him to get their attention, referee Paul Alcock sent both Di Canio and Keown off.

Then the Italian did it. He looked Alcock in the face, raised his hands and pushed the referee hard in the chest with both palms. Almost comically, Alcock back-pedalled furiously before finally falling over.

After an FA hearing at Bramall Lane the next month Di Canio was banned for 11 games. Immediately after the ban was imposed he seemed to be genuinely remorseful: 'I want to say that I'm very, very sorry for what's happened. I had a fair hearing. I'll see the Sheffield Wednesday fans on Boxing Day, the first game after my suspension.'

In fact Di Canio never played for Sheffield Wednesday again. He went back to Italy during his suspension and failed to return for that game on Boxing Day. He was sold to West Ham in January 1999 for £1.7m.

Also on this day

1995 Peter Schmeichel scored with an 89th-minute header in a 2–2 draw with Rotor Volgograd at Old Trafford. The goal didn't prevent United going out on away goals, but did save them from a first ever home defeat in Europe.

2008 Joe Kinnear was appointed manager of Newcastle.

2009 In his 25th game, Gareth Bale finally played in a Spurs team that won. Bale came on for the last five minutes in their 5–0 win over Burnley.

2009 Avram Grant was appointed manager of Portsmouth.

27 SEPTEMBER
2011 – Bayern Munich v Manchester City / Mancini v Tévez

Manchester City's 2011/12 Champions League campaign had started poorly when they were held to a home draw by Napoli. It got worse in Munich, but their 2–0 defeat to Bayern paled into insignificance when manager Roberto Mancini claimed that Carlos Tévez had refused to come off the substitutes' bench to play.

Mancini, who had seen his expensive side outclassed in Bavaria, said, 'If we want to improve like a team, like a squad, Carlos cannot play with us. With me, no – it is finished. For me, if a player earns a lot of money playing for Manchester City in the Champions League and he behaves like this, he cannot play again. Never.'

At first Tévez said, 'I didn't feel right to play, so I didn't.' The next day, he had changed his tune saying it was a misunderstanding and that, 'I had warmed up and was ready to play … I wish to state that I never refused to play.'

City's owners found themselves having to either back their manager or one of their most important players; Mancini's position was stronger and Sheikh Mansour backed him not his striker.

Tévez found himself in limbo as City fined him and told him to stay away from the club, but they weren't willing to sell him cheaply. Only West Ham made an offer and that was for a loan deal, which City rejected.

Back in Argentina, Tévez at first claimed that he'd been treated 'like a dog' by Mancini. Eventually, and with both sides looking for a solution, Tévez was persuaded to apologize and return to Manchester.

Mancini made him wait for a chance to play again, giving Tévez a personal training programme before he was named as substitute and finally played his first City game in six months, coming on against Chelsea in a 2–1 win.

By the end of the season, Tévez was back in the team and even scored a hat-trick against Norwich. He started the game against Queens Park Rangers in May 2012 that brought City their first Premier League title, but it was still something of a surprise that he stayed at the club for the following season.

In fact Tévez outlasted Mancini at Manchester City by a month, before being sold to Juventus.

Also on this day

1999 Sander Westerveld, Steven Gerrard and Francis Jeffers were all sent off as Everton won 1–0 at Anfield with a goal from Kevin Campbell.

2008 Hull came from behind to win 2–1 at Arsenal and go into the top six in their first ever Premier League season.

28 SEPTEMBER
2004 – Rooney's Manchester debut sensation

Wayne Rooney was a month short of his 19th birthday when he made his Manchester United debut in the Champions League against Turkish side Fenerbahçe at Old Trafford. Having broken a metatarsal playing for England in the quarter-final of Euro 2004, Rooney had to wait for his debut until almost the end of September. Once he was fit he didn't just get into Alex Ferguson's side, he exploded into it.

United were expected to win, and a hungry Rooney was always likely to make an impact, but his hat-trick left the Turkish side reeling and the home fans ecstatic. It was his first senior hat-trick and made him the youngest player to hit three in the Champions League.

His first was hammered into the roof of the net after Ruud van Nistelrooy's pass sent him clear. His second was from further out, right-footed again, this time fizzing past keeper Rüştü in the bottom corner. His third was a brilliant free-kick that

Rüştü stood and watched, knowing he had no chance of saving. Three Rooney goals in the space of 36 minutes. Old Trafford stood to acclaim a new hero as United won 6–2.

Afterwards Sir Alex Ferguson was practically drooling. 'I don't suppose I've seen a debut like it,' he said. 'What you saw tonight is the reason why we signed him and I think he can only get stronger now. We think the boy has great potential and it was a great performance and a great start by him.'

Unencumbered by the need to keep Rooney's feet somewhere near the ground, the Fenerbahçe coach Christoph Daum said, 'Maybe he will become the player of the century.'

The only question was what might Manchester United achieve when Rooney was unleashed alongside the 19-year-old Cristiano Ronaldo, who had watched the drama unfold from the substitutes' bench?

Also on this day

1994 Manchester United drew 0–0 at Galatasaray in the Champions League despite the home fans' best attempts to intimidate them as they had when knocking United out the previous season.

2003 Kevin Lisbie scored a hat-trick for Charlton in a thrilling 3–2 win over Liverpool at the Valley.

2008 Spurs were beaten 2–0 at Portsmouth, increasing the pressure on Juande Ramos, who was overseeing their worst start to a season for 53 years.

29 SEPTEMBER
2007 – Portsmouth 7 Reading 4

There were eight matches in the Premier League on Saturday 29 September 2007, and with Manchester United, Chelsea, Arsenal and Liverpool all in action nobody could have expected a game between 11th-placed Portsmouth and 16th-placed Reading to be the back-page lead in the Sunday papers. But of the 23 goals scored in those games, 11 came in that one match.

The first half was good – without Kanu, who was injured, Portsmouth manager Harry Redknapp gave a start to Benjani. The Zimbabwean put the home side in front after seven minutes and got an excellent second eight minutes before half-time, only for Stephen Hunt to bundle one back for Reading just before the break. It was only their second away goal of the season.

A David James mistake allowed Dave Kitson to equalize for Reading just after half-time, but Hermann Hreidarsson scored his first goal for almost three years to make it 3–2 after 55 minutes. All over the country football followers were beginning to take notice of the game at Fratton Park.

With 20 minutes to go, Reading were awarded a penalty that Nicky Shorey took, and that David James saved. Benjani then completed his hat-trick, and it seemed the game was up for Reading when Niko Kranjčar made it 5–2 with 15 minutes to play.

Reading had other ideas and Shane Long deflected in a James Harper shot to make it 5–3. At the other end, Ívar Ingimarsson was credited with an own-goal after deflecting in Sean Davis's effort: 6–3 with nine minutes to play. There was still time for Sulley Muntari to score a 90th-minute penalty to make it 7–3, before Shorey's shot deflected in off Sol Campbell in injury-time. Portsmouth 7 Reading 4.

Reading's manager Steve Coppell, who had seen his side score four away, miss a penalty and still lose, decided it was best to draw a line under the defeat: 'It's difficult to analyse a match like that, and if you try you'll be there a long time.'

With nine different players contributing 11 goals, it's the highest-scoring game in Premier League history.

Also on this day

1994 **Aston Villa knocked Inter Milan out of the UEFA Cup on penalties.**

2001 **Manchester United came from 3–0 down at Tottenham to win 5–3 in what Alex Ferguson described as the best performance away from home by any of his teams.**

2012 **Tottenham won at Old Trafford for the first time since 1989, Clint Dempsey scoring the winner.**

30 SEPTEMBER
1998 – The Gunners at Wembley

Frustrated by the difficulties of trying to expand Highbury, Arsenal had tried to buy Wembley Stadium for £100m in the spring of 1998.

Although the North Bank and Clock End at Highbury had been redeveloped, the work was to meet with the recommendations of the post-Hillsborough Taylor Report, and the stadium's capacity was still only 38,500. Nestled in densely populated Islington streets, there was no way Arsenal could extend their ground to keep pace with the expansion of rivals Manchester United and the big European clubs.

When Arsène Wenger's side qualified for the Champions League for the first time in 1998 they were confronted with Highbury's capacity being further reduced to around 35,000 in that competition by UEFA's demands for extra space to be given over to more advertising boards and sponsors' logos.

Vice-chairman David Dein and Arsène Wenger embraced the idea of playing the games at Wembley. The FA took a little persuading but eventually agreed, stating, 'Bearing in mind Arsenal's exceptional circumstances, the demands of UEFA and the fact that the matches are in Europe's premier club competition, the FA feels able to consent – on this occasion.'

Some Arsenal fans were not keen on the prospect of the arduous travel problems associated with getting to and from Wembley, and Arsène Wenger described it as a 'risk', aware that the opposition might be given a lift by playing at the famous old stadium.

The first visitors, on 30 September, were Panathinaikos, who had lost the European Cup Final in the same venue in 1971. The Greek side lost again, Tony Adams and Martin Keown scoring in a 2–1 win watched by 73,455 fans.

Attendances were similar for the home win over Dynamo Kiev and the crucial home defeat to Lens, which cost Arsenal

the chance to progress to the next phase.

AIK Solna, Barcelona and Fiorentina attracted equally large crowds the following season but Barcelona and Fiorentina both beat Arsenal. The commercial argument for playing at Wembley had been won, but too many games had been lost. Arsenal clearly needed a bigger stadium, but one that felt like home.

As Wenger said at the time: 'So what other choice is there than to move from Highbury? Sometimes you're in a situation where you either improve or die.'

Also on this day

1992 Leeds beat Stuttgart 4–1 at Elland Road in the Champions League but went out on away goals. Leeds were then reprieved when it was discovered that the Germans had fielded one too many foreign players. UEFA ordered a re-match on a neutral ground, which Leeds won 2 – 1.

2006 Gary Speed marked his 750th club game with a goal in Bolton's 2–0 win over Liverpool.

October

1 OCTOBER
1996 – Wenger's first day

Bruce Rioch had been sacked in August, caretaker manager Stewart Houston had left abruptly for QPR, Tony Adams had announced that he was an alcohOlić and Borussia Mönchengladbach had knocked them out of the UEFA Cup.

Arsenal were in some disarray when Arsène Wenger finally started work at Highbury on the expiry of his contract in Japan with Nagoya Grampus Eight.

Arsenal vice-chairman David Dein had chosen Wenger as the man to sort the club out. They had first met in January 1989 when Wenger, returning to his club Monaco after a scouting trip to Galatasaray, decided to call into London to watch Arsenal play Spurs.

Wenger later told *Arsenal* magazine, 'I immediately thought that football in England was great. There was a fantastic atmosphere at Highbury and I just wondered, "Is everywhere like this?" Even at that time I thought it would be great to be part of that. Obviously on that day I could never imagine that I would come back one day as manager, it was not even in my head.'

Dein and Wenger had been for dinner after that game, and ending up playing charades. A lasting friendship was formed.

Some of the Arsenal squad were less convinced as to whether Wenger would last at the club. Captain Tony Adams recalled, 'At first, I thought, what does this Frenchman know about football? He wears glasses and looks more like a schoolteacher. He's not going to be as good as George Graham. Does he even speak English properly?'

While his contract had been running down in Japan, Wenger had been influential in Arsenal's transfer business. Patrick Vieira and Rémi Garde had been signed as early as mid-August when the club were still refusing to confirm the identity of their proposed new manager.

Comically, Arsenal's cover had been blown when, at his first press conference, Garde had told the media how much he was looking forward to working with Arsène Wenger.

The *Evening Standard* had famously printed 'Arsène Who?' – but soon everybody knew.

Also on this day

1995 Éric Cantona returned to the Manchester United team for the first time after his eight-month ban for kicking a supporter. He scored a penalty in a 2–2 draw with Liverpool.

1998 George Graham took charge at Tottenham having left Leeds.

2002 Wayne Rooney scored his first senior goals, coming on as a substitute to get two of Everton's three in a League Cup win at Wrexham.

2008 Joe Kinnear gave his first press conference as manager of Newcastle, aiming 20 expletives in the first minute at journalists Simon Bird and Niall Hickman.

2012 West Ham collected a record eight yellow cards in one game against QPR.

2 OCTOBER
2005 – Chelsea destroy Liverpool

Rafa Benítez and José Mourinho had been appointed as the new managers of their clubs just two weeks apart in June 2004, and they were cast as rivals from the beginning. From 3 October 2004 to 2 October 2005, the two clubs played each other a remarkable seven times. In those games, all desperately close encounters, Mourinho and Chelsea could boast that they had usually had the upper hand, while Liverpool and Benítez could argue they had the won the match that mattered most.

The first two meetings of season 2004/05 were in the Premier League. Chelsea had won both 1–0, and had then won the 2005 League Cup Final in Cardiff, needing extra-time to squeeze a 3–2 victory. Two months later, in the Champions League semi-final, there had been a 0–0 draw at Stamford Bridge followed by Liverpool's 1–0 win at Anfield that took them to Istanbul.

After a summer in which the clubs and managers had fought over Steven Gerrard's future, they were then drawn together in the group stage of the Champions League in 2005/06. The meeting at Anfield at the end of September had been goalless, and three days later Chelsea headed back to Liverpool for the first Premier League meeting of that campaign.

Liverpool had started the league season poorly, with one win and four draws from their opening five games. In contrast Chelsea had played seven league games and won them all. Even so, the expectation was for another tense, tight and very close game. In reality, it was anything but close.

With Didier Drogba rampant, Chelsea tore Liverpool apart. Drogba scored the first, only for Gerrard to equalize, but Damien Duff's goal just before half-time restored Chelsea's deserved advantage.

In the second half Drogba continued to terrorize Jamie Carragher and Djimi Traoré, allowing Joe Cole and Geremi to add further goals.

The win left Chelsea nine points clear at the top of the league, and 17 points ahead of Liverpool. 'Your season's over!' sang the jubilant away fans; but in April Liverpool got their revenge, beating Chelsea in the FA Cup semi-final.

Also on this day

1997 Bolton signed Dean Holdsworth from Wimbledon for a club record £3.5m.

2002 Chris Coleman was forced to retire from playing because of the injuries he sustained in a car crash in January 2001.

2011 Fulham beat Queens Park Rangers 6–0 in their west London derby, their biggest ever win over their near neighbours.

3 OCTOBER
2002 – Chelsea pillaged by Viking

By 2002 Chelsea had grown into an important club at home and in Europe. Under Gianluca Vialli they won the Cup Winners' Cup, the Super Cup, and experienced their first taste of the Champions League. But there had also been some embarrassments along the way: UEFA Cup defeats against St Gallen and Hapoel Tel Aviv in the two previous seasons had been hard to explain.

As FA Cup winners in 2002, Chelsea were entered into the UEFA Cup again, and fewer than 16,000 fans watched them beat Viking Stavanger of Norway in the first leg of the first-round match at Stamford Bridge. Some of those had already left when Ben Wright, a former

Kettering and Woking striker who had been released by Bristol City, scored a late goal for Viking in Chelsea's 2–1 win.

If the atmosphere in west London had been flat, it was anything but that in west Norway for the return leg. The only stand of the Stavanger Stadium was packed as Chelsea emerged from the dressing room. The team Claudio Ranieri had picked was: Cudicini, Gallas, Terry, Huth, Le Saux, Grønkjær, Lampard, Petit, Stanić, Hasselbaink and Zola – surely far too good for the Norwegians, whose manager, Benny Lennartsson, had won only 6 of 31 games in a spell in charge of Bristol City.

Viking's star man was Erik Nevland, who had played six games for Manchester United, scoring once in 1998. They had Erik Fuglestad, who'd been at Norwich, and Brede Hangeland, who later joined Fulham.

Viking wiped out Chelsea's aggregate lead inside 35 minutes with goals from Morten Berre and Peter Kopteff. Frank Lampard levelled the tie just before half-time but Nevland made it 3–1 on the night and 4–3 on aggregate with a header after an hour. Chelsea were back under intense pressure in an exuberant atmosphere.

Soon John Terry managed to bundle in a corner – 4–4 on aggregate, with Chelsea in front courtesy of the away-goals rule. Finding reserves of energy from somewhere, Viking scored again three minutes from the end, Nevland getting in front of Terry to steer in a cross. Chelsea were out, and as Benny Lennartsson danced on the pitch, his opposite number Claudio Ranieri shook his head in the press conference and said, 'Unbelievable, just unbelievable.'

Also on this day

1992 Goal of the Season – Dalian Atkinson scored it for Aston Villa against Wimbledon at Selhurst Park.

1994 Rangers's Duncan Ferguson, facing assault charges for a head-butt on Raith's John McStay, joined Everton, initially on a three-month loan.

2005 For the first time Manchester United didn't top Deloitte's list of the world's richest clubs. Real Madrid were the new number one and have been there ever since.

4 OCTOBER
2009 – Wenger's Arsenal record

Herbert Chapman was the first great Arsenal manager, winning the championship in 1931, 1933 and 1934 and the FA Cup in 1930. For many years it was Chapman's bust that stood in the marble entrance halls at Highbury.

Arsenal's second great manager was certainly the man who succeeded him,

George Allison. Following greatness is not easy, as many good managers have found; but Allison won the league for Arsenal in 1935 and 1938 and won the FA Cup in 1936.

Allison, first described as Arsenal's 'secretary-manager', was in charge 4 years longer than Chapman, 13 years in total, and until Arsène Wenger broke his record in October 2009, was Arsenal's longest-serving boss.

It seemed appropriate that Wenger should pass Allison's mark with a home game against Blackburn, the team who had provided the Frenchman's first opposition in 1996. That game had been won 2–0 at Ewood Park with a double from Ian Wright; in 2009 Arsenal won 6–2, despite being behind twice.

Steven N'Zonzi and then David Dunn scored for Blackburn either side of a Thomas Vermaelen strike, only for Robin van Persie and Andrey Arshavin to give Arsenal a half-time lead that they built on with goals from Fàbregas, Walcott and Bendtner in the second half.

It was masterful attacking display that was watched by an impressed Thierry Henry, enjoying a day off from scoring goals for Barcelona. The manner of the win left Wenger purring and meant that 15 different Arsenal players had already scored in the first 12 games of the season. 'Our culture is scoring goals and going forward,' he said. 'The whole team goes forward. There is fantastic potential in this team and the presence of Henry certainly inspired our strikers – they wanted to show him how good they are and they did in style today.'

Impressive though Arsenal were, in May it was Chelsea who won the league by a point from Manchester United, with Arsenal in third, a further ten points behind.

Also on this day

1997 **Tottenham started the second half of their 1–0 defeat at Newcastle with only nine men as their former Newcastle players Les Ferdinand and Ruel Fox were in the toilet.**

2003 **Alan Shearer scored his 250th career goal for Newcastle in their 1–0 win over his former club Southampton.**

5 OCTOBER
2014 – Mourinho vs Wenger: Mourinho wins again

The relationship between Arsène Wenger and José Mourinho was chilly from the start and has been getting colder ever since.

Mourinho famously called Wenger a 'voyeur' in 2005, saying, 'he speaks, speaks and speaks about Chelsea'. Wenger replied that Mourinho was 'disconnected with reality and disrespectful. When you give success to stupid people, it makes them more stupid sometimes and not more intelligent.'

Even when he was abroad Mourinho was happy to remind journalists about the Arsenal trophy drought. When he was about to join Inter Milan in 2008, Mourinho said, 'The English like statistics a lot. Do they know that Arsène Wenger has only 50 per cent of wins in the English league?'

In 2010, when he was at Real Madrid, Mourinho tried again: 'Maybe Wenger should explain to Arsenal fans how he cannot win a single little trophy since 2005.'

In 2014 Mourinho stoked the fires again by calling Wenger a 'specialist in failure', and the mutual dislike came to a head in a typically charged meeting at Stamford Bridge the following October.

It was 0–0 when Gary Cahill was booked for a tackle on Alexis Sanchez. While Sanchez was getting treatment Mourinho began to shout at the referee, which irritated Wenger. The Arsenal manager walked across to the Chelsea technical area and was told to go back by fourth official John Moss. A few seconds later, with Mourinho still shouting, Wenger walked across again and pushed the Chelsea manager in the chest, Mourinho flicking out his right hand in a dismissive gesture.

It was rather a feeble confrontation, and seemed to sum up Arsenal's impotence in matches against Chelsea and Wenger's personal frustration when confronted by Mourinho. That's probably understandable – this was the 12th meeting between a team managed by Wenger and one of Mourinho's, with Chelsea's 2–0 victory meaning José had won seven and drawn five with Arsenal yet to win any.

Asked if he regretted pushing Mourinho, Wenger said, 'No, not at all.' A week later the Frenchman did apologise, saying it was 'not the way to behave'.

Also on this day

1993 Robbie Fowler scored all five goals for Liverpool in their League Cup win over Fulham at Anfield. It was only Fowler's fourth game for the club.

2008 Hull City won 1–0 at Spurs a week after winning 2–1 at Arsenal. The win put Phil Brown's side into third place in the Premier League in their first ever season in the top flight.

6 OCTOBER
2001 – Beckham saves Sven

England's World Cup qualifying group started in September 2000 and was decided in the last minute of the last game 13 months later.

The team top of Group 9 would go straight to the World Cup Finals, while the runner-up would face a difficult play-off against Ukraine. Going into the final day, England and Germany both had 16 points but England were top on goal difference thanks to their 5–1 win in Munich.

England's last game was at home to Greece in Manchester, while simultaneously Germany played against Finland in Gelsenkirchen. England were overwhelming favourites to win comfortably and seal that one guaranteed World Cup place.

Soon England began to think again. The first half belonged to the Greeks, with England creating nothing in attack. It was no surprise when Greece took the lead through Angelos Charisteas. In Gelsenkirchen, though Oliver Bierhoff had hit the Finnish post, it was still Germany 0 Finland 0. Now the Germans were topping the group.

Twenty minutes into the second half, Sven-Göran Eriksson made a change, bringing on Teddy Sheringham, who equalized with his first touch just ten seconds after running on. If England thought they had saved themselves they were wrong – Greece scored again only two minutes later through Demis Nikolaidis.

In Gelsenkirchen, Bierhoff hit the underside of the bar for Germany with Oliver Neuville hitting the inside of the post from the rebound. It was still, somehow, 0–0 in Germany.

At Old Trafford, England poured forwards with Heskey, Sheringham, Beckham, Scholes and Gerrard all going close.

In the 93rd minute England were given a free-kick for a foul on Teddy Sheringham. The final whistle blew in Gelsenkirchen – Germany 0 Finland 0, so one England goal would be enough. The free-kick was 25 yards from goal and there were seconds to play.

Beckham hit it so sweetly, so perfectly, that the Greek goalkeeper Antonos Nikopolidis didn't move as the ball ripped into his net.

In his autobiography Beckham revealed that Teddy Sheringham had wanted to take the kick: 'Nothing was going to stop me taking that free-kick. I felt confident, calm, certain. I knew I could make it.'

Also on this day

1998 UEFA countered the ongoing threat of a breakaway European Super League by confirming that the Champions League would be expanded from 24 to 32 teams to accommodate more teams from the major leagues. They also announced that the Cup Winners' Cup would be scrapped.

2004 Spain coach Luis Aragonés was filmed using racist language about Arsenal's Thierry Henry during a training session. Aragonés said he was merely encouraging Henry's club colleague José Antonio Reyes to believe he was as good as the French striker.

7 OCTOBER
2000 – The end of the line for Wembley and Keegan

It was a day of firsts and lasts. It was England's first game of the 2002 World Cup qualifying campaign, the last at the old Wembley Stadium and, unexpectedly, the last as manager for Kevin Keegan.

Wembley was to be demolished and rebuilt into a stadium fit for the twenty-first century. The first England game under the twin towers of what was first called the Empire Stadium was in 1924, and initially the only games England played there were against Scotland. Argentina in 1951 were the first opponents other than the Scots to play there.

The match against Germany was the 223rd played by England at Wembley, and in very few of the previous 222 could England have been so desperately poor. Dietmar Hamann scored the only goal as Germany took revenge for their defeat to England at the finals of Euro 2000 less than four months earlier.

In grim rain, England and Keegan trudged off the pitch for the last time to a chorus of disapproval from the fans, but there was still one more drama to come. Keegan sought out the FA's executive director David Davies and told him he wanted to resign.

In his book *FA Confidential*, Davies recalls looking for somewhere private to talk to Keegan in an attempt to persuade him to think again. Eventually he took the England manager into a toilet cubical. Davies wrote that Keegan said, 'You can't change my mind, I'm out of here. I'm not up to it. I can't motivate the players.'

Keegan, who had bowed to the pressure of being the overwhelming choice of fans to take the job in the first place, had resigned after only 18 months and 18 games – of which he won only 7.

Also on this day

1995 Juninho joined Middlesbrough from São Paulo for £4.75m.

2002 After more than seven years in charge, Peter Reid was sacked by Sunderland.

2006 Aged 17 years and 35 days, Gareth Bale became Wales's youngest ever scorer, but couldn't prevent a 5–1 defeat to Slovakia.

2011 England clinched a place at Euro 2012 with a 2–2 draw in Montenegro despite Wayne Rooney's red card.

2012 Brad Friedel's record of playing 310 consecutive league matches ended when Hugo Lloris played in goal for Spurs against Aston Villa.

8 OCTOBER
2005 – England win their World Cup place

David Beckham knows more than most people about being an England hero and an England villain. Sent off in 1998, Beckham had then been the man who got England to the 2002 World Cup Finals with a late goal against Greece, and once at those finals he had scored the winning penalty against Argentina.

England's 2006 World Cup qualifying campaign had far fewer headlines then four years earlier. There had been the numbing defeat in Belfast but no managerial resignation, no triumph in Munich, no last gasp free-kicks from Beckham.

England had dominated a group containing Austria, Poland, Wales, Northern Ireland and Azerbaijan from the start. By the time Austria came to Wembley, England had 19 points from eight games with six wins, one draw and that one defeat against Northern Ireland.

They knew a win over Austria at Old Trafford would all but seal a place in the finals. The Austrians knew they had no chance of reaching the World Cup and came to England having recently lost in Poland and drawn in Azerbaijan.

England did enough, but only just. They were grateful for a penalty in the first half after Paul Scharner had fouled Michael Owen. Beckham had missed his last three spot-kicks for his country so Lampard stepped up and put England in front.

The game might have been memorable for little else, except that Beckham fouled Austria's Andreas Ibertsberger after 57 minutes and was booked. A little over a minute later he was judged to have fouled the same player again, and the Spanish referee sent him off. David Beckham became the only England captain ever to be shown a red card and the only England player ever to be sent off twice – this one coming seven years after his red against Argentina in Saint-Étienne.

England held on to win 1–0 and results in the evening confirmed that it was enough to qualify for the finals in Germany with a game to spare.

Also on this day

2005 **Wales won their World Cup qualifier against Northern Ireland 3–2 in Belfast.**

2010 **Northern Ireland held Italy to a 0–0 draw in Belfast in their European Championship qualifier.**

2014 **Gus Poyet was appointed manager of Sunderland, only to be sacked within six months.**

9 OCTOBER
1992 – Leeds vs Stuttgart: take three

In 1992 UEFA's rules over foreign players were complex, and forced many clubs to field seriously weakened teams in European competitions.

Those rules stated that a club was allowed to play up to three foreign players and two 'assimilated' players – those who had played for five years in the country of the club. It was an administrative calamity waiting to happen – and it did.

In the first round of the 1992/93 Champions League, Leeds were drawn against VfB Stuttgart. The first leg was played in Germany and Leeds were hammered 3–0. Howard Wilkinson's side were given little chance in the return game at Elland Road – no British team had ever overturned a three-goal deficit.

It turned out to be an epic match, with Éric Cantona playing perhaps his finest game for the club. Leeds were 2–1 in front at half-time, Gary Speed and Gary McAllister scoring either side of an Andreas Buck goal for Stuttgart.

Leeds tore into their opponents after half-time, with Cantona getting a third and Lee Chapman a fourth to make it 4–4 on aggregate. But Stuttgart had an away goal and Leeds couldn't find a fifth to win the tie, leaving the Germans to celebrate the narrowest of victories.

However, Stuttgart had brought on Jovica Simanić with eight minutes to go. Simanić was Serb, as was Slobodan Dubajić. Eyjólfur Sverrisson was from Iceland and Adrian Knup was Swiss – four foreigners was one too many.

Stuttgart admitted their mistake and, after long deliberations, a rematch was ordered at a neutral venue, Barcelona's Nou Camp.

At the third time of asking Leeds won. The massive 120,000-capacity stadium had only 7,000 fans inside as goals from Gordon Strachan and Carl Shutt knocked the Germans out 2–1.

A month later Leeds had no reprieve when Rangers beat them home and away.

Also on this day

1996 Estonia's national team boycotted their World Cup qualifier at home to Scotland. The kick-off time had been changed at 24 hours' notice after Scotland complained about the poor floodlights. In protest, Estonia didn't turn up at the new, earlier, time and Scotland kicked off without any opposition. The game lasted three seconds before it was abandoned.

2004 David Beckham deliberately got himself booked playing for England against Wales. He fouled Ben Thatcher and was cautioned, meaning that he would miss the game in Azerbaijan four days later. Beckham felt that an injury sustained earlier in the game against Wales would rule him out of the Azerbaijan game anyway. He later apologized.

10 OCTOBER
2001 – Leicester appoint Harry

Leicester City had enjoyed unprecedented success under Martin O'Neill's management, winning promotion to the Premier League and reaching three League Cup Finals – winning two of them. When O'Neill left to become Celtic manager in the summer of 2000, Leicester turned to Peter Taylor to continue that line of success.

Taylor was given a big transfer budget and spent over £11m on new players for the start of the season – almost half of that was on Ade Akinbiyi from Wolves. The early games were encouraging, with Leicester unbeaten in the first eight matches of the season, but they faded as the year progressed and finished 13th – Akinbiyi scored only four league goals after Christmas.

The next season was to be the last at their Filbert Street ground. With the new stadium taking shape down the road, Leicester started with a 5–0 defeat at home to Bolton, then a 4–0 loss at Arsenal. By the time Taylor was sacked in late September they had just four points from their first eight games. Harry Redknapp and George Graham were the front-runners to get the job, but instead Leicester turned to Dave Bassett, known to everyone in football as 'Harry'.

On 10 October, the day the appointment was confirmed, Leicester were playing at home to Leeds in a League Cup tie – with Bassett watching on, they lost 6–0.

Wins over Sunderland and Aston Villa were promising, but from December to March Leicester failed to win any of their 16 league games and they were relegated in early April. This made Bassett the only manager to be relegated out of the Premier League three times. He had suffered the same fate at Sheffield United in 1994 and had been Nottingham Forest manager for the last three months of their 1996/97 relegation season.

At least Leicester won their last ever game at Filbert Street, beating Spurs 2–1.

Also on this day

1998 A Craig Bellamy goal gave Wales a superb 2–1 win in Denmark in their European Championship qualifier.

2009 The Republic of Ireland and Italy drew 2–2 in front of more than 70,000 fans at Croke Park in their World Cup qualifier. The result sealed a play-off for Ireland and a place in the finals for Italy.

2010 Robert Green was sent off as England were beaten 1–0 by Ukraine in Dnipropetrovsk. The result ended England's 100 per cent record in the qualifying campaign for the 2010 World Cup.

11 OCTOBER
2006 – Robinson's Zagreb misery

When the draw for the Euro 2008 qualifying groups was made, Sven-Göran Eriksson was the England manager. England were drawn in a group with Croatia, Russia, Israel, Estonia, Macedonia and Andorra – with the top two teams to qualify. Eriksson had already announced that he'd be stepping down after the upcoming World Cup, so could offer an unbiased opinion on how tough, or otherwise, the group would be.

'I think England should be happy with that draw. I'm convinced they will pass through rather easily,' he said.

Eriksson's words would hang round Steve McLaren's neck like the proverbial millstone for the 18 months that he was the England manager.

McLaren started well enough: a friendly win over Greece was followed by two European qualifiers against Andorra and Macedonia, both of which were won.

England had very little luck in their next game, Rio Ferdinand injuring himself in the warm-up and Gary Neville and Steven Gerrard hitting the woodwork as Macedonia held on for a 0–0 draw at Old Trafford.

McLaren tried a new system in Zagreb, introducing a 3-5-2 formation that only played into Croatia's hands as they ripped into England's defence. Goalkeeper Paul Robinson had made several important saves before Eduardo gave Croatia a deserved lead.

England were brutally exposed but, whatever the system, Croatia's second goal was a nightmare for Gary Neville and Robinson. Neville's back pass hit a divot just as Robinson's boot was about to make contact. The ball bobbled in the air, over the keeper's boot and rolled into the England net.

The inquest began. Was it Gary Neville's fault for aiming a back pass on target at the goal, Robinson's fault for not having replaced the divot probably caused by one of his own goal-kicks, or McLaren's fault for the wrong formation?

Of the three only Neville had a long-term England future.

Also on this day

1995 Everton striker Duncan Ferguson was jailed for a head-butt on John McStay when he had been playing for Rangers.

1997 England and Scotland booked their places at the 1998 World Cup Finals: England by drawing in Italy, and Scotland with a win over Latvia.

2002 George Burley was sacked by Ipswich after eight years as manager.

2003 England drew 0–0 in Turkey to qualify for Euro 2004.

2008 Scotland striker Chris Iwelumo was guilty of a memorable miss in their game against Norway.

2014 Robbie Keane hit a hat-trick in 12 minutes as the Republic of Ireland beat Gibraltar 7–0.

12 OCTOBER
1996 – The Bosnich salute

Alex Ferguson, who signed Mark Bosnich from Aston Villa as a replacement for Peter Schmeichel, once claimed that the Australian turned up three hours late for training on one of his first days at Manchester United. In his autobiography Ferguson even went so far as calling Bosnich 'a terrible professional'.

He was a good goalkeeper though. United had released him as a teenager only for Bosnich to earn a contract at Aston Villa, where he thrived and earned a reputation for being one of the best young keepers around.

Aged only 21, Bosnich took the place of Nigel Spink in the Villa goal in October 1993 and made an immediate impact. He saved three Tranmere Rovers penalties in the League Cup semi-final shoot-out and won the trophy at Wembley against Manchester United.

He won the League Cup again with Villa in 1996, but missed the first ten games of the 1996/97 season with injury – his first game back in the side was at White Hart Lane against Spurs. During the match the home fans were chanting the name of their former striker Jürgen Klinsmann every time the Villa keeper got the ball. This was a reminder of an incident in which Bosnich had knocked Klinsmann unconscious with a rough challenge in their game at Villa Park in January 1995.

Bosnich responded by turning to the Spurs fans and doing a Nazi-style salute. There was a furious response – Tottenham have a strong Jewish heritage of which their fans are very proud.

Afterwards Bosnich was interviewed by the police following complaints from Tottenham fans and that night he called BBC Radio's *606* programme to apologize. 'To be honest I'm a bit distraught,' he told presenter David Mellor. 'I'd just like to say that it was something done out of ignorance. For me it was a real joke, but it's been taken so much out of proportion and I'm so, so sorry. I thought the crowd were laughing with me. Obviously I was mistaken. It's been taken out of context and I'm really sorry.'

The FA fined Bosnich £1000 and warned him about his future conduct.

Also on this day

1992 Leeds and Rangers agreed to ban away fans from each leg of their forthcoming Champions League tie.

1994 Tony Adams captained England for the first time in a 1–1 draw with Romania.

2005 Brian Kerr's last match in charge of the Republic of Ireland ended in a 0–0 draw with Switzerland.

2010 Fabio Capello was under pressure as England manager after a 0–0 draw at home to Montenegro.

13 OCTOBER
1993 – Do I not like that!

England's attempt to qualify for the 1994 World Cup Finals lurched from one calamity to another. Graham Taylor's side put in some abject displays, and by the time they went to play the Netherlands in Rotterdam they were in serious trouble. To make matters worse for Taylor, a film crew were following him everywhere making a fly-on-the-wall documentary that was meant to chart England's route to the World Cup in the USA. Instead the documentary captured the manager's increasing desperation as England floundered. "Do I not like that!" was the expression that Taylor repeatedly used as qualification slipped away.

Norway were the surprise package, winning the group. England and the Netherlands were playing for the runners-up spot that would also ensure a place in the World Cup.

With Gascoigne suspended and Stuart Pearce injured, England knew that if they lost in Rotterdam there was almost no chance of qualifying. At half-time it was 0–0 but Frank Rijkaard had seen a goal wrongly disallowed, and the Dutch looked the better side.

Ten minutes into the second half, David Platt outpaced Ronald Koeman and the Dutch defender pulled him back on the edge of the penalty area. Referee Karl-Josef Assenmacher pointed to the spot and Platt already had the ball in his hands for the penalty when the referee changed his mind and gave a free-kick outside the box. England complained that not only should it be a penalty, but that Koeman should be sent off – crucially he was only booked.

Three minutes later, in similar circumstances, the Dutch were given a free-kick on the edge of the England box. The reprieved Koeman, one of the best free-kick takers in the world, blasted a shot that was blocked by Paul Ince – but again the referee incensed England by deciding that the kick should be retaken.

ITV commentator Brian Moore called it brilliantly: 'He's going to flip one now, he's going to flip one, he's going to flip one … and it's in!' Exactly as Moore had predicted, Koeman had delicately 'flipped' the ball over the wall and into the England net.

On the touchline, that documentary crew captured Taylor's agony as he approached the linesman: 'What sort of thing is happening here? You know it. Linesman! You see at the end of the day, I get the sack now … the referee's got me the sack. Thanks ever so much for that.'

Moments later Dennis Bergkamp made it 2–0. England were as good as out, and so was Taylor.

Also on this day

1999 England were drawn to play Scotland in a play-off for a place at Euro 2000.

2001 Liverpool manager Gérard Houllier was rushed to hospital at half-time in their game with Leeds. Houllier underwent a life-saving heart operation.

2013 England qualified for the 2014 World Cup Finals with a 2–0 win over Poland.

14 OCTOBER
2014 – O'Shea's dream century

John O'Shea's first 100 caps for the Republic of Ireland began and ended with late drama. As a 20-year-old in 2001, O'Shea's injury-time handball against Croatia cost Ireland victory in a friendly at Lansdowne Road. The young

Manchester United defender certainly paid for the mistake, having to wait 15 months for his next cap against Greece.

O'Shea then missed only 7 of his country's next 68 competitive internationals over 12 years – add in friendly appearances and he was on 99 caps when they went to Gelsenkirchen to play world champions Germany in a European Championship qualifier.

Even though Ireland had started their group well, with a 2–1 win in Georgia followed by a 7–0 thumping of minnows Gibraltar, they were given no chance against a German side who had beaten them 6–1 in Dublin and 3–0 in Cologne during the 2014 World Cup qualifying campaign.

There were no thrashings this time; Germany were frustrated by the Irish until Toni Kroos scored with only 19 minutes to go. It seemed certain that Ireland would leave defeated until, with the last kick of the game, John O'Shea got to a Jeff Hendrick cross ahead of Mats Hummels and scored to ignite jubilant green celebrations.

It was only O'Shea's third international goal and after the game he said, 'I think we might have to find a frame for my shirt. I'm not one for hanging stuff but I think this one could be heading for the mantelpiece at my mum and dad's house.'

Also on this day

1992 Paul Gascoigne returned to the England team after missing 21 international games, including Euro 92, with a knee injury. England could only draw 1–1 with Norway at Wembley.

1997 Arsenal's Jason Crowe was sent off 33 seconds into his debut after coming on as a substitute in a League Cup game against Birmingham.

1998 Robbie Keane became the Republic of Ireland's youngest ever scorer with two goals in a 5–0 win over Malta.

2006 Chelsea's Petr Čech suffered a depressed fracture of his skull in a collision with Stephen Hunt at Reading. Čech's replacement, Carlo Cudicini, was also injured later in the game, leaving John Terry to play in goal.

2009 David Beckham won his 115th and last England cap in a 3–0 win over Belarus.

2009 Shay Given and Kevin Kilbane both won their 100th caps for the Republic of Ireland in their 0–0 draw with Montenegro.

15 OCTOBER
2011 – The Luis Suárez race row

The fixture between Liverpool and Manchester United is always laced with enmity, but the meeting in the autumn of 2011 may be the most infamous of them all.

Luis Suárez and Patrice Evra had been tussling throughout the match at Anfield, but a particularly animated war of words broke out between them at a Liverpool corner. After the game, which was drawn, Evra reported to the referee Andre Marriner that he had been racially abused by Suárez.

In December the FA found Suárez guilty of using the Spanish word '*negrito*' to Evra, banning him for eight matches and fining him £40,000. Both Suárez and Liverpool argued that in Uruguay *negrito* is not a derogatory term and called the judgement 'extraordinary'.

Liverpool decided to stand by their player and issued a statement saying, 'Nothing we have heard in the course of the hearing has changed our view that Luis Suárez is innocent of the charges brought against him, and we will provide Luis with whatever support he now needs to clear his name.'

With the saga seriously impacting on the image of both Suárez and Liverpool, the club eventually accepted the ban and dropped their appeal.

If Liverpool hoped that might draw a line under the affair, they were wrong. It was unfortunate that the Uruguayan's second game back in the Liverpool team after his ban was at Old Trafford. As the players performed the pre-match handshake, Suárez refused Evra's hand. It set the tone for an ugly game high on emotion and aggression that United won 2–1, with Suárez scoring for Liverpool.

Police had been needed at half-time to prevent a scuffle between players of both sides from turning into a fight. At the full-time whistle Evra danced his way around the pitch and celebrated provocatively in the face of the Uruguayan as he left the pitch; again stewards and police were needed.

When Liverpool manager Kenny Dalglish was told by Sky TV that Suárez had refused to shake Evra's hand, he said, 'I think you're bang out of order to blame Luis Suárez for anything that happened here today.'

Alex Ferguson saw it differently: 'He's a disgrace to Liverpool Football Club and should never be allowed to play for them again.'

Also on this day

1994 Jack Charlton ruled out the possibility of replacing Graham Taylor as England manager.

1997 Ian Rush equalled Geoff Hurst's League Cup scoring record with his 49th goal in the competition playing for Newcastle against Hull City.

2008 Wales were unlucky to lose 1–0 to a late Piotr Trochowski goal for Germany in Mönchengladbach.

2010 John W. Henry took over ownership of Liverpool from Tom Hicks and George Gillett.

16 OCTOBER
1995 – Hodgson into Inter

In demand abroad, but unfancied at home. Until he took over as Fulham manager in 2007, Roy Hodgson had nothing like the acclaim on English shores that he'd enjoyed in Europe. Bob Houghton, then manager of Swedish club Malmö, recommended Hodgson to Halmstads BK of Sweden in 1976 and over the next 20 years he enjoyed great acclaim in both Sweden and Switzerland, but in his home country he only had a brief and unsuccessful spell at Bristol City.

In 1992, after a season as manager of Neuchâtel Xamax, Hodgson was named as the national manager of Switzerland, who had failed to qualify for a major tournament since the 1966 World Cup.

In a group containing Italy, Portugal and Scotland, the Swiss lost only one qualifying game and booked their place at the World Cup Finals of 1994. Once there, Hodgson's team drew with hosts the United States, beat Romania and lost to Colombia before going out in the second phase at the hands of Spain.

Hodgson's standing in Switzerland was further enhanced when they qualified impressively for Euro 96, but the manager's plans to lead to his team to the finals in England changed when Inter Milan offered him the chance to move to Serie A.

The job title at the San Siro was 'technical consultant' – this would get round the Italian FA's ban on foreign coaches – but everyone knew that Hodgson was the manager in all but name. At first Hodgson juggled both his role with the Swiss FA and Inter Milan, but once Switzerland's friendly against England at Wembley had been played, Hodgson moved to Italy full-time.

At the San Siro, Hodgson took Inter to the UEFA Cup Final of 1997, which they lost to Schalke 04 on penalties.

Despite that defeat, Hodgson was offered a new contract at Inter by club president Massimo Moratti, which he declined in favour of trying to make his name at home; Blackburn Rovers were his next stop.

Hodgson's impression on Moratti was so strong that he was twice asked to return to the club. When he became England manager in 2012, Inter issued a statement offering their congratulations, describing Hodgson as 'a person who had always shown honesty and generosity towards Inter, qualities that formed a rapport of true friendship'.

Also on this day

1998 Gerry Francis was appointed Queens Park Rangers manager for the second time.

2002 Craig Bellamy scored the winning goal when Wales beat Italy 2–1 in Cardiff in a European Championship qualifying match.

2004 Ten-man Liverpool recovered from 2–0 down to win 4–2 at Fulham, the first away win for new manager Rafa Benítez.

17 OCTOBER
2009 – Life's a beach for Sunderland

Sunderland had won just one home game against Liverpool in 51 years when Rafa Benítez took his side to the Stadium of Light in 2009 to play Steve Bruce's team.

Bruce, who had joined Sunderland in the summer from Wigan, had signed Darren Bent from Spurs in the summer transfer window. Bent already looked like a bargain, scoring seven goals in his first eight games for the club, and was being tipped for a return to the England side.

Like Bent, Steve Bruce had started well with four wins and a draw at Old Trafford from the first eight matches. After the game against Liverpool, Bruce not only looked like a *good* manager, he looked like a *lucky* manager.

Sunderland's first stroke of luck was that after five minutes a red beach ball was thrown onto the pitch by a Liverpool fan just as a Sunderland attack was building. Their second bit of good fortune was coming soon; a cross was deflected into the path of Bent, whose shot hit the beach ball. The lightweight, red ball deflected crazily to goalkeeper Pepe Reina's right while the actual ball went to his left and into the net. Later Reina told Spanish radio, 'I went for the red ball instinctively as it was the closest to me and the other went past me. It all happened very quickly. I didn't know what to do.'

Neither did referee Mike Jones – after consulting with his assistants he gave the goal. That was Sunderland's third bit of luck, because the laws of the game state that in the case of any outside influence there should be a drop-ball. Former referee Jeff Winter told the *Daily Telegraph*, 'It's a basic law of the game that a referee would learn on his initial refereeing course, it's just absolutely amazing that the goal was allowed to stand.'

Not surprisingly, a smiling Steve Bruce didn't see it that way: 'If anybody knew that rule – that it is supposed to be a drop-ball – then you are a saddo. They have got it pictured on telly, with the guy who threw it on, and it's got Liverpool crests all over it. What a shame!'

Also on this day

2001 Six Chelsea players decided against travelling to Israel to play Hapoel Tel Aviv in the UEFA Cup. Desailly, Gudjohnsen, Le Saux, Ferrer, Gallas and Petit all chose not play amid safety fears in Israel.

2007 Sammy Lee left his job as Bolton manager 'by mutual consent' after winning only one of his 11 league games in charge.

2007 England lost their crucial European Championship qualifier 2–1 against Russia in Moscow, increasing the pressure on manager Steve McLaren.

2010 Goals from Tim Cahill and Mikel Arteta gave Everton a 2–0 win over Liverpool at Goodison Park in Roy Hodgson's first Merseyside derby as Liverpool manager.

18 OCTOBER
2014 – When the Saints go marching in

When Southampton ended the 2013/14 season in eighth place, it was as high as they had finished a season in the top flight since 1990. It also heralded an exodus of staff that seemed to guarantee that it would be a long time before they finished as high again.

First to go was the manager Mauricio Pochettino, who was lured to Tottenham. Following him out of St Mary's were Rickie Lambert, Dejan Lovren and Adam Lallana, all to Liverpool, Luke Shaw to Manchester United, and Callum Chambers to Arsenal. Almost £100m was brought in, but the heart of the team was torn out. The first thing new manager Ronald Koeman did was to insist that midfielder Morgan Schneiderlin would not be allowed to leave as well – Pochettino wanted to take his former player to Spurs.

With Koeman bringing in players he knew from the Dutch league, but who were not well known in England, Southampton were many pundits' pick to be relegated.

After a faltering start, Koeman's first win was in the League Cup at Millwall; it seemed to spark them into life. Suddenly new signing Graziano Pellè was scoring regularly, fed with chances by Dušan Tadić – another Koeman signing from the Dutch league.

Southampton won six consecutive matches from the end of August until a narrow loss at Tottenham – against Pochettino – at the beginning of October.

The manner in which Koeman's side bounced back was sensational. Sunderland came to St Mary's on 18 October fresh from a 3–1 win over Stoke, but they were overrun by a Southampton side that recorded its biggest ever Premier League victory.

Sunderland helped them by scoring a remarkable three own-goals and with an inept performance, but Pellè scored two, Tadić, Jack Cork and Victor Wanyama the others as Southampton ran their visitors ragged. Southampton won 8–0.

'I wasn't happy at the beginning of the game. It was not perfect,' said the demanding Koeman.

Also on this day

1992 Ian Rush surpassed Roger Hunt's Liverpool goalscoring record with both goals in a 2–2 draw against Manchester United. The goals took Rush to 287 for the club.

2001 Chelsea lost 2–0 in Tel Aviv in their UEFA Cup game against Hapoel.

2005 Thierry Henry passed Ian Wright's Arsenal scoring record with two goals against Sparta Prague, his 185th and 186th for the club.

2009 The first Blackburn vs Burnley derby in the top flight since 1966 finished with a 3–2 win for Rovers at Ewood Park.

19 OCTOBER
2010 – No new deal for Rooney

There had been rumours ever since the 2010 World Cup Finals that Wayne Rooney was disillusioned with life at Manchester United, and his form at the start of the following season had been poor.

In September, Rooney was substituted in a 2–2 draw at home to Bolton – and he was left out completely when United played Valencia in the Champions League and Sunderland in the Premier League. Rooney, Sir Alex Ferguson said, had an ankle injury.

But Rooney did play for England in a 0–0 draw with Montenegro, and afterwards denied that he had been injured at all. 'I've had no ankle problem all season,' he stressed.

A week later, with rumours rife of a fall-out between Ferguson and Rooney, the Manchester United boss attended a press conference ahead of a Champions League tie against Bursaspor and dropped a bombshell to United's fans. Ferguson revealed that Rooney's agent had told the club in the summer that the striker wanted to leave.

'I've had no argument with him at any time,' said Ferguson. 'I had a meeting with him, and he intimated to me that he wanted to leave. I feel that we've got to keep the door open for him because he's

such a good player. We're as bemused as anyone because we don't know why he'd want to leave, and we've done nothing but help him since he got here.'

Rooney said that money was not the issue, the strength of the team was, and he was upset that the club had failed to 'give me any of the assurances I was seeking about the future squad'.

United fans protested outside Rooney's house, and for a few days it seemed certain that he would leave. Worse for United, it seemed likely that Manchester City would be his destination. That would have been a deal to stun United even more than the loss of Carlos Tévez to City had a year earlier.

Then, two days later, a change of heart. A new five-year contract to stay at Old Trafford had been agreed, with Rooney saying, 'The manager's a genius and it's his belief and support that convinced me to stay.'

Also on this day

1993 Jeremy Goss and Mark Bowen scored the goals as Norwich won 2–1 against Bayern Munich in Germany in the UEFA Cup, arguably the most famous result in their history.

2002 Wayne Rooney scored his first goal in the Premier League to become its youngest ever scorer at 16 years and 360 days old. The spectacular last-minute shot secured Everton a 2–1 win over Arsenal.

2013 Goal of the Season – Jack Wilshere scored it for Arsenal against Norwich at the Emirates Stadium.

20 OCTOBER
1996 – Howay 5-0!

Of all the many thrilling and unpredictable days for Newcastle United under the management of Kevin Keegan, this must go down as the best.

Briefly, the rivalry between the two Uniteds – Newcastle and Manchester – had English football enthralled. Newcastle had lost a 12-point lead over Manchester United in an emotionally charged climax to the previous season. Keegan had famously lost his cool in a TV rant at Alex Ferguson as the title, which Newcastle had not won since 1927, slipped through their fingers.

The summer had been spent with the two clubs battling over the signature of Alan Shearer, a tussle Newcastle won. Then the season had started, with Manchester United crushing Newcastle 4–0 in the Charity Shield at Wembley.

At St James' Park, Keegan took his revenge, as his side ripped the champions apart playing breathtaking football.

Newcastle's first goal was hotly contested by Manchester United, who felt that Denis Irwin had cleared Darren Peacock's effort before it crossed the line. There was no argument about the second goal – a fantastic, long-distance curling shot from David Ginola.

Many managers would have instructed their team to be cautious with a two-goal lead at half-time and protect the advantage they had – not Keegan and not Newcastle. Later Alan Shearer would say, 'Kevin Keegan went for broke with an attacking team. He loved to see all-out attack, often to his downfall, but when it came off it was spectacular to watch.'

Keegan's men poured forward looking for more goals, and scored three in a sublime 20 minutes. First Shearer provided a stunning cross for Les Ferdinand to head in off the underside of the crossbar, then Shearer converted after Schmeichel's heroics had denied first Beardsley and then Ferdinand.

Newcastle's fifth goal was perhaps the best, and summed up Keegan's philosophy. The tall Belgian central defender Philippe Albert strode forward like an attacking midfielder and perfectly executed an audacious chip over Schmeichel from almost 40 yards.

It was Manchester United's biggest defeat for 12 years, and it was impossible to imagine that within three months Keegan would resign.

Also on this day

2001 Peter Schmeichel became the first goalkeeper to score a Premier League goal. The Dane's shot following a last-minute corner was not enough to prevent Aston Villa's 3–2 defeat at Everton.

2010 Gareth Bale scored a fabulous hat-trick for Spurs in the San Siro against Inter Milan, but still finished on the losing side. Spurs had goalkeeper Heurelho Gomes sent off after ten minutes and were trailing 4–0 at half-time – the game finished 4–3.

21 OCTOBER
1996 – London calling

It had been clear for some time that, despite the addition of a new Olympic gallery for corporate clients, Wembley was unsustainable as the home of English football and as a venue for major events. England needed a new national football stadium and Wembley had strong competition from both Manchester and Birmingham.

Manchester had bid unsuccessfully to host both the 1996 and 2000 Olympic Games but had won the bid to host the Commonwealth Games in 2002. A site for a stadium in east Manchester had long since been identified and plans existed for that stadium to be built to a capacity of 80,000 if need be.

Birmingham had bid for the Olympic Games of 1992 – losing to Barcelona – and argued that its location in the centre of the country made it a natural, convenient base for the new stadium.

On the face of it, Wembley – with its tired infrastructure and notorious transfer links – seemed to have only history on its side.

The London bid was further complicated by Wembley's unwillingness to accommodate a running track, so ruling it out as the centre of proposed bids for the 2005 World Athletics Championship and a 2012 Olympic bid. History suggested that those bids would only be successful if they came from London, and the government wanted a new national stadium, not just a new national football stadium.

The Football Association and Football League's decision to support Wembley over Birmingham and Manchester in autumn 1996 didn't finish the argument – Coventry launched a campaign of their own when the Wembley project ran into financial difficulties – but it was influential in the 1997 decision that the new home of English football had to be the old home, rebuilt.

Also on this day

1992 Rangers won the first Champions League 'Battle of Britain', beating Leeds 2–1 at Ibrox with a winner from Ally McCoist.

1995 Les Ferdinand scored a hat-trick and Vinnie Jones ended up in goal after Paul Heald was sent off in Newcastle's 6–1 win over Wimbledon.

1998 Martin O'Neill rejected the chance to take over as Leeds United manager, preferring to stay at Leicester.

2014 Didier Drogba scored the first goal of his second spell at Chelsea as they recorded their biggest ever Champions League win, 6–0 against Maribor.

22 OCTOBER
2005 – Henry and Pirès pay the penalty

In 1982 Johan Cruyff and Jesper Olsen had pulled off a penalty routine for Ajax that Thierry Henry and Robert Pirès tried to recreate for Arsenal 23 years later.

At Ajax's Olympic Stadium, in a 5–0 win over Helmond Sport, Cruyff had taken a penalty for Ajax. Rather than shooting at goal, Cruyff had passed to his left where an onrushing Jesper Olsen had drawn the goalkeeper and then passed back to Cruyff, who scored into an empty net.

The Ajax duo might have been aware that it had been done before, by Belgian pair Rik Coppens and André Piters, who converted a two-man penalty in Belgium's 8–2 win over Iceland in 1957. It's unlikely that Cruyff had seen Plymouth's Johnny Newman pass a penalty to Mike Trebilcock, who scored against Manchester City in a Division Two game in 1964.

Robert Pirès had already scored one spot-kick against Manchester City in the game at Highbury, beating David James in the conventional manner. When they were awarded a second penalty, Pirès and Henry decided to recreate the Cruyff/Olsen penalty of 1982.

Henry was ready, standing to the left of Pirès on the edge of the box. Pirès approached the ball and tried to touch it to his left, only to miss the ball almost completely, making only the faintest of contact with his studs, not even enough to move the ball from the spot. Because Pirès had touched the ball, however faintly, another player had to make the next contact – and that player was Manchester City's Sylvain Distin, who cleared.

Afterwards, with Arsenal having won 1–0, Arsenal manager Arsène Wenger saw the funny side: 'I think he is vaccinated now against taking a penalty like that again, which is a positive. He's a lucky boy because the team has not been punished.'

A laughing Henry admitted, 'It was my idea, but not for his leg to go numb. I don't know why his leg went numb, but in future I'll be taking the penalties.'

Also on this day

2001 Gordon Strachan was appointed Southampton manager.

2003 A rare goal from Phil Neville gave Manchester United a 1–0 win at Ibrox against Rangers in the Champions League.

2006 Jermain Defoe appeared to bite West Ham's Javier Mascherano in a game at White Hart Lane. Spurs manager Martin Jol described it as a 'comical nibble', Defoe said it was 'mischievous' and the FA decided to take no action.

23 OCTOBER
2011 – The John Terry race row

Queens Park Rangers beat Chelsea 1–0, but the consequences of the meeting between the London rivals were still being felt long after the result had been forgotten. The toxic row contributed to the end of the international careers of two senior players and the resignation of the England manager.

With five minutes to go at Loftus Road, John Terry and Anton Ferdinand argued over a claim for a Chelsea penalty. It seemed routine until, in the hours after the game, a clip of the TV footage of the exchange began to spread on social media. It appeared to show John Terry racially abusing Ferdinand.

The story grew so quickly that by the evening Terry had issued a statement saying, 'I thought Anton was accusing me of using a racist slur against him. I responded aggressively, saying that I never used that term.' Soon both the FA and the Metropolitan Police were investigating.

In early February, Terry's lawyers entered a plea of not guilty to committing a racially aggravated public order offence and a court date was set for July – clearing him to play at Euro 2012. Two days after that plea, the FA stripped Terry of the England captaincy until the proceedings against him were concluded. Speaking on Italian radio, England manager Fabio Capello criticized the FA for their decision, and two days later he resigned.

Meanwhile Rio Ferdinand, Anton's elder brother and England's vice-captain under Terry, was back to fitness and form for Manchester United. Could the elder Ferdinand play alongside Terry for England while the case against Terry's alleged abuse of his brother was ongoing? England's new manager, Roy Hodgson, left Rio Ferdinand out of his squad for Euro 2012 saying that it was for 'footballing reasons'. Rio Ferdinand never played for England again.

After the European Championships, Terry was found not guilty at the criminal proceedings against him. With the police case finished, the FA charged Terry with 'using abusive and/or insulting words and/or behaviour'. The day before his hearing at the FA on that charge, Terry announced his retirement from international football.

The FA found Terry guilty, saying his defence was 'improbable, implausible and contrived', though saying they did not believe that Terry was racist. He was fined £220,000 and banned for four matches.

Also on this day

1999 Kanu scored a hat-trick in the last 15 minutes as Arsenal came from 2–0 down to win 3–2 at Chelsea.

2011 Manchester City won 6–1 at Old Trafford against Manchester United. Mario Balotelli, in the news after a firework set off in his bathroom had started a fire, scored twice and revealed a T-shirt printed with the words 'Why Always Me?' It was Manchester United's worst home defeat since 1955.

2013 Ian Holloway left Crystal Palace 'by mutual consent'.

24 OCTOBER
2004 – Pizzagate: the Battle of the Buffet

Arsenal had won the Premier League title without being beaten in 2003/04, and had extended their record-breaking run without losing a league game to 49 matches when they went to Old Trafford in October 2004.

The match was dramatic enough, but the occasion is remembered far more for what happened in the Old Trafford tunnel afterwards.

Arsenal lost 2–0, but were unhappy with referee Mike Riley, who they thought should have sent off Rio Ferdinand for an early foul on Freddie Ljungberg and then gave Ruud van Nistelrooy the benefit of the doubt for a stamp on Ashley Cole. The FA later reviewed that challenge and banned the Dutchman for three games.

With just under 20 minutes to play, Riley awarded Manchester United a penalty when Sol Campbell was adjudged to have fouled Wayne Rooney. It was the eighth penalty Riley had awarded United in the eight matches he'd officiated at Old Trafford – and van Nistelrooy scored it.

Afterwards Wenger said, 'Riley decided the game, like we know he can do at Old Trafford. There was no contact at all for the penalty. We can only master our own performance, not the referee's performance.'

In the last minute, Rooney added a second goal and Arsenal's long run was over. But that was only the beginning.

In the tunnel there were arguments and scuffles, and with the Arsenal manager criticizing van Nistelrooy for his tackle on Cole, Wenger was confronted by Sir Alex Ferguson.

Suddenly, with bedlam breaking out and soup and coffee being spilt, a pizza was thrown. In his autobiography United's Andy Cole recalled that it hit Ferguson full in the face and rolled down his suit.

Ferguson later wrote, 'I was in control of my emotions and the next thing I knew, I had pizza all over me. They say it was Cesc Fàbregas who threw the pizza at me but, to this day, I have no idea who had the culprit is.'

Although Fàbregas has never admitted it, he's also never denied the various hints

from witnesses that it was him who'd taken aim.

In 2015 Arsène Wenger said, 'It still hurts today – losing the 50th game, I think that hurt us the most.'

Also on this day

1994 The Football League decided not to punish Manchester United for fielding a weakened team in their second-round League Cup tie against Port Vale. They also announced that in future teams playing in European competition would enter the League Cup at the third-round stage.

2006 West Ham's worst run of defeats for 74 years was extended to eight games after losing 2–1 at Chesterfield in the League Cup.

2007 Steve Staunton left his job as Republic of Ireland manager 'by mutual consent'.

25 OCTOBER
2008 – Ramos out, Redknapp in

Juande Ramos was another Tottenham manager who, like Christian Gross and Jacques Santini before him, had arrived with a big reputation and left with not much more than a whimper.

Spurs were in 18th place in the Premier League when Ramos took over from

Martin Jol, and although they finished 11th and won the League Cup – beating Chelsea in the final – they'd finished the 2007/08 season with only one win in their last seven games. Spurs wanted to qualify for the Champions League and, if he was to keep his Tottenham bosses happy, Ramos needed a good start to the following campaign.

In fact, Tottenham had their worst ever start to a Premier League season, failing to win any of their first eight games and losing their opening UEFA Cup match to Udinese. They were bottom of the table and four points adrift when the Spaniard was sacked along with sporting director Damien Comolli.

In his second spell at Portsmouth, Harry Redknapp had led the club to their most successful period in over 50 years. Not only had he staved off near certain relegation in his first season, they had won the FA Cup in 2008, finishing in the top ten of the Premier League for a second consecutive season.

Redknapp was the obvious choice to take over at Tottenham and Portsmouth let him go, negotiating a £5m compensation fee.

Three days after his resignation from Portsmouth, Redknapp had to run the gauntlet of a mixed reception when he returned there to receive the Freedom of the City; if that timing was unfortunate, then everything else was

perfect for Redknapp, who said, 'It's a big opportunity to manage a big club before I retire.'

Portsmouth replaced Redknapp with Tony Adams, who lasted less than four months in the job. At Spurs they recovered to finish eighth and reached the League Cup final again, losing to Manchester United on penalties.

Within two years Portsmouth were in administration and Tottenham were in the Champions League.

Also on this day

1996 Ray Harford resigned as manager of Blackburn Rovers.

1998 After Martin O'Neill turned down the job, David O'Leary was appointed Leeds manager.

2007 Martin Jol was sacked by Spurs after a 2–1 home defeat to Getafe in the UEFA Cup.

2007 Gary Megson was appointed manager of Bolton Wanderers.

26 OCTOBER
1996 – Southampton 6 Manchester United 3

Six days before their trip to Southampton, Manchester United had been beaten 5–0 at Newcastle and Alex Ferguson had called it a blip. It didn't look like a blip when they conceded six at the Dell in their next league game.

Southampton manager Graeme Souness had brought in three new faces at the start of October: Ulrich van Gobbel from Galatasaray for £1.3m, Egil Østenstad from Viking Stavanger for £800,000 and Eyal Berković coming on-loan from Maccabi Haifa.

The three had all played in Southampton's disappointing 2–2 draw at home to Lincoln in the League Cup on the previous Wednesday, and Souness made only one change to that team for the visit of Ferguson's United. For Berkovic and Østenstad it was a day to remember.

Berkovic took only six minutes to get his first goal for his new club, hammering home after Schmeichel's save from an Østenstad shot. Roy Keane, already booked for dissent, was then late into a challenge on Claus Lundekvam and was sent off. Southampton took full advantage with a brilliant chipped goal from Matt Le Tissier, before a Beckham free-kick put United back in the game.

The reprieve didn't last long. Østenstad beat Schmeichel at his near post to make it 3–1 and register his first Southampton goal.

During half-time the previous season, United had changed their kit from grey to blue and white, saying it was hard to see each other in the grey. There wasn't much Ferguson could do this time, although David May did pull a goal back with a header from a Cantona corner.

There were four goals in the last seven minutes. First an outstanding Berkovic volley made it 4–2, then Østenstad added his second goal from a Berkovic pass for 5–2, before Paul Scholes scrambled in another United goal. The Norwegian Østenstad had the last word though, completing his hat-trick in stoppage time.

'My first goals in English football,' recalled Østenstad, 'and they came as a hat-trick against Manchester United. Four weeks earlier, I had been watching them on television back in Norway.'

Things got worse for Manchester United: they lost a 40-year unbeaten home record in Europe to Fenerbahçe in their next match.

Three weeks later Southampton lost 7–1 at Everton.

Also on this day

1993 David Batty signed for Blackburn Rovers from Leeds.

2002 Diego Forlán scored his first Premier League goal for Manchester United, after nine months and 23 games. Forlán's goal came in a 1–1 draw with Aston Villa at Old Trafford.

2004 After winning only one of their first ten games of the season, Gary Megson was sacked by West Bromwich Albion.

2008 Chelsea's 86-game unbeaten league run at Stamford Bridge was ended by Liverpool. Xabi Alonso scored the only goal of the game at Stamford Bridge.

27 OCTOBER
2007 – Manchester United's 4x4

Manchester United's tradition of playing attacking football has arguably never been adhered to more wholeheartedly than in the 2007/08 season when Cristiano Ronaldo, Wayne Rooney and Carlos Tévez were cut loose and wreaked havoc across Europe.

By the end of the season Manchester United had won the Premier League and Champions League titles, with Ronaldo scoring 42 goals, Tévez 19 and Rooney 18. The rest of the squad shared a further 51 goals between them.

The season hadn't started particularly promisingly; United scored only ten times in their first 12 matches of the season, drawing with Reading and Portsmouth and going out of the League Cup at home to Coventry. Nobody could have predicted that within a month they would equal a century-old club-scoring record.

A 1–0 Champions League win at AS Roma seemed to galvanize them, and in their next match United beat Wigan 4–0 at Old Trafford with Ronaldo getting two goals, Tévez and Rooney one each.

Their next match, at Aston Villa, saw Rooney score twice and miss a penalty in a 4–1 win. Rio Ferdinand and Ryan Giggs got the other goals as Ronaldo was rested for the upcoming Champions League game in Kiev.

Suitably refreshed, Ronaldo scored twice in the Ukrainian capital; a Rooney goal and another from Ferdinand secured a 4–2 win.

United's final October match was back at Old Trafford against Middlesbrough, who scored after six minutes to make it 1–1 following an early long-range strike from Nani. Wayne Rooney then took control with United's second goal and a back-heeled assist for Tévez to make it 3–1. The Argentine hit the fourth with five minutes to go.

It meant that United had scored four times in four consecutive games for the first time in 100 years.

Also on this day

1994 FIFA decreed that all leagues must award three points for a win.

1999 Liverpool's Titi Camara scored the only goal as West Ham were beaten at Anfield, despite learning of his father's death just prior to kick-off.

2001 Aston Villa went top of the Premier League for the first time in three years with a win over Bolton.

2002 A James Beattie hat-trick helped Southampton come from 2–0 down to beat Fulham 4–2.

28 OCTOBER
2003 – Fàbregas's Arsenal debut

He was so obscure that the newspapers called him by his full name, FranCesc Fàbregas Soler, soon much better known as Cesc Fàbregas. At 16 years and 177 days, Fàbregas broke a record set by Jermaine Pennant to become the youngest ever player to appear for Arsenal in a first-team game. This was only a few weeks after being signed from a Barcelona youth system that included Lionel Messi.

There were fewer than 28,000 fans at Highbury to watch the League Cup third-round match against Rotherham, who were near the bottom of the second tier – then called Division One. Fàbregas wasn't the only unfamiliar name on the Arsenal team sheet: Graham Stack, Justin Hoyte, Jerome Thomas, Gaël Clichy, and substitutes Ryan Smith, John Spicer and Quincy Owusu-Abeyie all made their debuts while Efstathios Tavlaridis was playing his sixth game and Jérémie Aliadière his eighth. Only Edu, Pascal Cygan and Sylvain Wiltord would normally be anywhere near the first team.

Arsenal went in front through Aliadière early on, but Rotherham equalized in the last minute with a Darren Byfield goal. Despite Rotherham keeper Mike Pollitt being sent off in extra-time, Arsenal couldn't find a winner and the game went to penalties.

As the senior striker, Wiltord took Arsenal's first kick and it was saved by Rotherham's substitute keeper Gary Montgomery. The shoot-out went into sudden death and after everyone, including the goalkeepers, had taken a penalty it was 8–8. Then Chris Swailes missed for Rotherham and, second time around, Wiltord scored to put Arsenal through.

Fàbregas had been taken off five minutes from the end of normal time, but had made his mark and a bit of Arsenal history. He would make more history by becoming Arsenal's youngest ever goalscorer in the next round of the League Cup against Wolves.

Also on this day

2003 Leeds announced a record pre-tax loss of £49.5m, taking their debts to £78m. On the pitch they lost 3–2 to Manchester United in the League Cup, Alan Smith earning a two-match ban for throwing a plastic bottle back into the crowd after it landed on the Elland Road pitch. The bottle hit the sister of one of Smith's best friends.

2007 Juande Ramos was appointed manager of Tottenham Hotspur.

2008 Tony Adams took over from Harry Redknapp as manager of Portsmouth.

29 OCTOBER
2011 – Chelsea 3 Arsenal 5: van's the Man

Chelsea were having a difficult week and Arsenal were having a difficult season.

Chelsea had been embroiled in the accusations of racial abuse by their captain John Terry during the match at Queens Park Rangers six days earlier. The FA investigation and the Metropolitan Police's interest in the affair were just beginning.

Arsenal had already been beaten at home by Liverpool, lost 8–2 at Manchester United, 4–3 at Blackburn and 2–1 at Spurs. The highest they'd been in the Premier League table all season was seventh, but Robin van Persie – whose nine goals already that season were keeping Arsenal afloat – was about to make John Terry's week even more difficult.

Chelsea took the lead, Frank Lampard heading in Juan Mata's textbook cross, but Aaron Ramsey's pass allowed Gervinho

to run clear for Arsenal and provide van Persie with a tap-in to equalize. Arsenal weren't level for long as Terry bundled Chelsea back in front from a Lampard corner and took the acclaim of the supportive home crowd.

Again Arsenal equalized, André Santos latching on to Alex Song's pass and beating Petr Čech with almost the first attack of the second half. Theo Walcott then blasted Arsenal in front with a brilliant individual goal before Juan Mata replied with ten minutes to go: 3–3.

Then the turning point: Terry tried to receive a back pass from Florent Malouda but slipped face-down to the floor, allowing Van Persie to sprint clear and score. Van Persie completed his hat-trick, and Chelsea's misery, when he beat Čech in injury-time for a 5–3 Arsenal win.

Chelsea's shell-shocked manager André Villas-Boas said, 'Luck doesn't want anything to do with us now. Emotions took control and we needed to be cold-blooded.'

Arsène Wenger – who had made an impassioned speech at the club's AGM only the day before – said, 'To come here and score five goals is absolutely amazing. Football is difficult enough if you are united, if you are disjointed you have no chance'.

Also on this day

1996 Everton signed Nick Barmby from Middlesbrough for £5.75m.

2004 Chelsea sacked Adrian Mutu after he tested positive for cocaine.

2005 Manchester United lost 4–1 at Middlesbrough. A few days later Roy Keane gave his opinions on the game in a frank interview with MUTV, which would result in him leaving the club.

2008 Arsenal and Spurs drew 4–4 at the Emirates Stadium in only Harry Redknapp's second game as Tottenham manager. David Bentley scored a brilliant goal for Spurs against his former club.

30 OCTOBER
2000 – England turn to Eriksson

Walter Winterbottom was the first England manager; prior to his debut in 1947, a selection committee had picked the England team and appointed coaches on a match-by-match basis. Over the 53 years that followed Winterbottom's ground-breaking appointment, a total of 11 men had been given the responsibility of picking the national team and all had been English.

When Kevin Keegan suddenly resigned in October 2000, the FA were left with a headache. Howard Wilkinson took charge of the next game, a 0–0 draw in Finland, but was not a contender to take the job on a full-time basis.

Arsène Wenger and Sir Alex Ferguson were both given serious consideration, but it was Wenger's great friend, Arsenal's vice-chairman and influential FA insider David Dein, who was first to suggest Sven-Göran Eriksson.

The Swede's credentials appeared impeccable. He had won the UEFA Cup with Gothenburg, reached two European finals with Benfica and two more with Lazio, winning the Cup Winners' Cup in 1999. Lazio had also just won the Italian league and cup double and, like most Swedes, Eriksson spoke perfect English.

According to the former FA executive director David Davies in his book *FA Confidential*, David Dein and FA chief executive Adam Crozier flew to Rome to meet Eriksson in a flat owned by Dein's daughter, who was studying in Rome. A deal was agreed, and Eriksson was signed to join England the following July.

The appointment was not universally popular. PFA head Gordon Taylor said, 'I think it's a betrayal of our heritage, of our culture and of the structure of the game in this country.'

To the FA's relief – he had once gone back on an agreement to manage Blackburn – Eriksson left Lazio earlier than planned, and his first of 67 games as manager was against Spain at Villa Park in February 2001. By the time he left in 2006, the idea of a foreign manager taking charge of England seemed entirely normal.

Also on this day

1996 Manchester United lost a home match in Europe for the first time, to Turkish side Fenerbahçe 1–0.

2004 Djibril Cissé suffered a double fracture of his leg in Liverpool's match at Blackburn. Cissé suffered the injury when his studs got caught in the turf and he later revealed that but for the prompt action of the medical staff he might have had to undergo an amputation.

2010 After eight games without a win, struggling Wolves shocked Manchester City with a 2–1 victory at Molineux.

2013 Arsenal recovered from 4–0 down to win 7–5 at Reading in the League Cup fourth round. Theo Walcott scored a hat-trick, including a last-minute equalizer to take the game into extra-time.

31 OCTOBER
2010 – No stopping Nolan: Newcastle 5 Sunderland 1

Chris Hughton had been appointed as Newcastle manager in the aftermath of their relegation out of the Premier League in 2009. Promoted back to the top flight as champions, it was quickly evident that it was going to be an interesting season when Newcastle began with a 3–0 defeat against Manchester United followed by a 6–0 win over Aston Villa.

When the first Tyne–Wear derby for 18 months came round, Newcastle were in mid-table, a point behind their neighbours who had conceded only seven goals in their first nine league games of the season. By half-time at St James' Park, Sunderland had conceded three more.

Kevin Nolan got the first with a close-range overhead kick from a corner and he added a second when Andy Carroll's mis-hit shot fell to him in the penalty area. On a hat-trick, Nolan must have been tempted to take the penalty that followed in first-half stoppage-time, but allowed regular taker Shola Ameobi to make it 3–0.

Shortly after the break Newcastle's joy was increased when Sunderland's Titus Bramble, a former Newcastle player, was sent off for a trip on Carroll, who hit the bar from a Danny Simpson cross soon afterwards only for Ameobi to smash in the rebound for 4–0.

Nolan's hat-trick, the first in this fixture since Peter Beardsley scored three goals on New Year's Day in 1985, was completed with an instinctive header after Ameobi had flicked on a corner. Darren Bent pulled one back for Sunderland in the last minute, but by then most of their fans had long since left for home.

It was Newcastle's biggest win over Sunderland since 1956 and the Newcastle fans serenaded their manager with the song, 'Chris Hughton is a Geordie!'

Five weeks later, Hughton was sacked.

Also on this day

2002 Adam Crozier, credited with modernizing the FA beyond recognition despite strong internal resistance, resigned from his job as its chief executive.

2006 After making team changes in 99 consecutive matches, Rafa Benítez picked an unchanged side for their 3–0 win over Bordeaux in the Champions League.

2009 After Robbie Keane had suggested that they were better than Arsenal, Spurs lost the north London derby 3–0 – conceding two goals in 11 seconds of playing time at the end of the first half.

November

1 NOVEMBER
1994 – Spurs sack Ardiles

When Ossie Ardiles, along with Ricky Villa, signed for Spurs just after they'd been part of Argentina's successful 1978 World Cup campaign, Tottenham fans immediately took him to their hearts. A skilful but tough midfielder, Ardiles scored some spectacular goals and delighted fans with his style of play and chirpy personality.

In 1981, Spurs reached the FA Cup Final and the pop charts with 'Ossie's Dream', though it was Ricky Villa, not Ardiles, who won the cup in the replay against Manchester City with a wonderful goal.

Ardiles's management career began at Swindon, where they won the play-off final only to be denied promotion to the top flight as a punishment for the club's financial turmoil. An unsuccessful year at Newcastle was followed by a season at West Brom, where Ardiles achieved promotion out of Division Two.

When Tottenham's chairman Alan Sugar sacked manager Doug Livermore in the summer of 1993, the appeal of the Argentine was too big to resist. With a return to Tottenham on offer, Ardiles resigned from West Brom and took over at White Hart Lane.

Assisted by another Spurs legend, Steve Perryman, there was no shortage of goodwill for the new management team – but the 1993/94 season was not a success. Spurs relied heavily on the goals of Teddy Sheringham, but even so relegation wasn't avoided until a win at Oldham in the penultimate game of the season.

Alan Sugar's response to this poor campaign was to allow Ardiles to go on a summer spending spree. Romanian World Cup stars Ilie Dumitrescu and Gică Popescu were signed, along with German superstar Jürgen Klinsmann.

Tottenham felt re-energized as a club and the team was reinvented. Ardiles's philosophy was simply to be so committed to attack that they stood a chance of outscoring the opposition, however many goals they conceded. Spurs played with five forwards: Klinsmann and Sheringham supported by Anderton, Barmby and Dumitrescu.

Tottenham's season started with a 4–3 win at Sheffield Wednesday and a 2–1 win over Everton, but the brave new world lasted only three months. After that bright beginning Spurs won only two of nine league games culminating in a 5–2 loss at Manchester City. Then they lost 3–0 at Notts County in the League Cup.

A win over West Ham the following weekend was welcome, but not enough to prevent his sacking. Ossie's dream was over.

Also on this day

1994 James Ward-Prowse was born.

1997 Costa Rican Paolo Wanchope made it nine goals in his first 11 games of the season with 2 for Derby as they beat Arsenal 3–0.

2003 Cristiano Ronaldo scored his first goal for Manchester United in their 3–0 win at home to Portsmouth.

2004 Bertie Vogts resigned from his job as Scotland manager.

2 NOVEMBER
2013 – Begović scores

Goalscoring goalkeepers are a rarity, and so are goals scored after only 13 seconds of a game – so the main event at the Stoke City vs Southampton game in 2013 is unlikely to be repeated in a hurry.

Southampton travelled to the Potteries with the best defensive record in the Premier League, having conceded just three goals in nine games from the start of the season, while Stoke had failed to score in four of their last six league games.

It was a typically windy afternoon at the Britannia Stadium, and some fans were still taking their seats when Southampton kicked off. Rickie Lambert gave the ball to James Ward-Prowse, who tried to slip a pass through the Stoke defence. It was easily cut out by Erik Pieters, who passed back to his goalkeeper.

Asmir Begović stepped forward and gave the ball a mighty punt with his right foot. Stoke's pitch is exactly 100 metres (109 yards) long and, with the wind behind it, the ball travelled about 70 metres before it bounced. Southampton goalkeeper Artur Boruc was standing on the penalty spot as the ball veered high in the air. Realizing what was about to happen, Boruc turned and scrambled towards his goal, but the ball was already past him and with one more bounce landed in the back of his net.

The convention is that goalkeepers shouldn't celebrate if they embarrass their opposite numbers, and Begović didn't, saying afterwards, 'I feel a bit sorry for Boruc, it's not a nice thing when that happens to you as a goalkeeper – but it's a cool feeling to score.'

Jay Rodríguez equalized for Southampton and the match finished 1–1.

Also on this day

1994 Manchester United were beaten 4–0 at Barcelona in a Champions League group game, Hristo Stoichkov scoring twice.

2000 Leicester City unveiled plans for a new 32,000-capacity stadium adjacent to Filbert Street.

2006 Tim Krul, aged 18, made an outstanding debut for Newcastle in a 1–0 UEFA Cup win in Palermo.

2010 Tottenham beat Inter Milan 3–1 in the group stage of the Champions League.

2013 Manchester City beat Norwich 7–0 at the Etihad Stadium, with seven different players getting on the score sheet. David Silva, Yaya Touré, Edin Džeko, Álvaro Negredo and Sergio Agüero all scored for City, as did Norwich's Bradley Johnson and Russell Martin with own-goals.

3 NOVEMBER
1993 – 'Welcome to Hell'

Galatasaray's Ali Sami Yen Stadium was arguably the most volatile football arena in Europe. Sir Alex Ferguson described the atmosphere that awaited Manchester United on their visit there in 1993 as the most intimidating he had ever experienced.

The first leg of the Champions League second-round tie at Old Trafford had been a classic, the Turks recovering from 2–0 down to lead 3–2 until Éric Cantona's late equalizer.

When they arrived at Istanbul airport, United's players were greeted by Galatasaray fans bearing banners saying 'RIP Manchester' and 'Welcome to Hell'.

In the hotel, reception staff put phone calls through to the players' rooms in the middle of the night and on the way to the stadium the windows of their team bus were pelted.

The stadium was full eight hours before kick-off and when the United players went out to warm up they needed a police escort.

United were second-best in the match and never looked like getting the win they needed to go through. Galatasaray were happy to time-waste and draw 0–0 to progress on the away-goals rule. On the final whistle Cantona snapped and threw the ball into the crowd before confronting the referee – he was shown a red card.

Bryan Robson recalled in his autobiography that he and Cantona were ushered into the tunnel by a policeman as bedlam broke out all around them. Robson wrote, 'I was just about to thank the policeman when he punched Eric. Eric stumbled down a couple of steps, so I turned to throw a punch at the copper. As I did, a shield smashed into the back of me.'

Robson needed stitches in his elbow, Steve Bruce, who had dodged a flying brick, had a gash on his hand from a riot shield, Paul Parker had been punched and Cantona had to be restrained from going back out to find the policeman who had hit him.

Welcome to hell indeed – though when asked about the trip Alex Ferguson did once quip, 'You've obviously never seen a Glasgow wedding.'

Also on this day

1998 **Liverpool had both Steve McManaman and Paul Ince sent off in their 2–2 draw at Valencia in the UEFA Cup, but progressed on away goals.**

1999 **Brian Kidd was sacked by Blackburn Rovers after 11 months as manager, coach Tony Parkes taking over as caretaker manager for the fifth time. Parkes would go on to fill the caretaker role again in 2004 following the departure of Graeme Souness but was never offered the job on a full-time basis.**

4 NOVEMBER
2000 – Viduka's four-goal blast

Mark Viduka had scored 35 goals for Celtic in only 48 games when Leeds prised him from Glasgow with a £6m offer. That looked like a lot of money to pay when Viduka failed to score in his first five games in English football, and then went back to Sydney for a month to play in the Olympic football tournament for his country. Australia lost all three games and Viduka didn't score.

The striker's first game back at Leeds saw him break his duck in a 6–0

Champions League romp against Beşiktaş, quickly followed by two goals against Spurs and two more against Charlton. Viduka was off and running.

When Liverpool came to Elland Road in early November they were third in the Premier League table, just behind Manchester United and Arsenal, and had won five successive games. Gérard Houllier's side were 2–0 up after 18 minutes through Sami Hyypiä and Christian Ziege; Leeds, fresh from a League Cup defeat to Tranmere, seemed to be in disarray.

A mistake by Ziege allowed Viduka to score his first goal midway through the first half. Soon after half-time it was 2–2, Viduka converting with a powerful header from Gary Kelly's cross. Vladimír Šmicer then put Liverpool 3–2 up, which only seemed to galvanize Leeds United's rampaging centre forward.

Viduka's hat-trick goal came after 73 minutes, as he showed great agility and balance to pirouette through the Liverpool defence and finish from a narrow angle. His fourth, and the winning goal, came less than two minutes later when he controlled a shot from Olivier Dacourt and turned to chip delightfully over Liverpool goalkeeper Sander Westerveld. It was the first time a Leeds player had scored four goals in one game since Allan Clarke in 1971.

In four seasons Viduka scored 72 goals for Leeds before he was sold to

Middlesbrough, one of many players to leave in an attempt to ease the club's financial crisis.

Also on this day

1992 Rangers knocked Leeds out of the Champions League, winning 2–1 at Elland Road and 4–2 on aggregate.

2003 Despite having Glen Johnson sent off, Chelsea won 4–0 at Lazio in the Champions League.

2010 Manchester City came home from Poland with nothing after losing 3–1 at Lech Poznań in the Europa League, but the City fans brought home a new goal celebration – The Poznań.

2014 Brendan Rodgers dropped his captain Steven Gerrard for Liverpool's 1–0 Champions League defeat at Real Madrid.

5 NOVEMBER
2006 – Wenger vs Pardew

José Mourinho, Martin Jol, Sir Alex Ferguson and Alan Pardew will all confirm that Arsène Wenger is not always the calm, sage, unflappable person his image portrays.

One of Wenger's biggest touchline rows came with Alan Pardew at the end of Arsenal's game at West Ham on the afternoon of 5 November 2006. The headlines about fireworks were inevitable after Wenger lost his cool after West Ham scored a late winning goal.

It had been a frustrating week for Arsenal. Held to two home draws by first Everton in the Premier League and then CSKA Moscow in the Champions League, they were off the early pace in the title race, which was being set by Manchester United and Chelsea, each seven points better off than Arsenal.

West Ham were in the bottom three after winning only two of their first ten league games and the pressure was piling on manager Pardew despite their FA Cup Final appearance the previous May.

Arsenal had edged the game, but had seen Robin van Persie hit by a coin thrown from the crowd, and been knocked off their stride by West Ham's unusually physical approach. Wenger already looked angry before Marlon Harewood tucked in a Matthew Etherington cross in the 89th minute.

The goal sparked some wild celebrations in the West Ham dugout and Wenger took exception, pushing Alan Pardew in the chest and having to be restrained by referee Rob Styles from going back to Pardew for another confrontation.

Afterwards the canny Pardew apologized to Wenger: 'He is a top guy and I really respect him. I thought I was entitled to celebrate the goal after a pulsating game. I was celebrating our goal, nothing more, but I apologize to him again and to Arsenal.'

The FA fined Wenger £10,000 and warned him about his future conduct. Six weeks later Alan Pardew was sacked.

Also on this day

2002 **After almost seven successful years in charge of the Republic of Ireland, Mick McCarthy resigned.**

2004 **Jacques Santini resigned as manager of Spurs, leaving his assistant Martin Jol to take over.**

2007 **Chris Hutchings was sacked by Wigan Athletic after only 12 Premier League games in charge.**

2011 **Martin O'Neill was appointed manager of the Republic of Ireland with Roy Keane to be his assistant.**

6 NOVEMBER
2007 – Liverpool's Champions League record

Liverpool, beaten Champions League finalists in 2007, were in danger of an early exit from the competition the following season after a terrible start to the group stage of the tournament. Having drawn in Porto, Rafael Benítez had seen his team lose at home to

Marseille and lose in Istanbul against Beşiktaş. Going into their fourth game Liverpool were bottom of the group with only one point; Beşiktaş had three, Porto were on five and Marseille on seven.

To make matters worse for Liverpool their new striker Fernando Torres, who had played only one half of football in a month for Liverpool because of a thigh strain, was only fit enough to be named as a substitute. Torres wasn't needed as Beşiktaş were overwhelmed.

Peter Crouch and Yossi Benayoun scored in the first half for Liverpool, and before the hour-mark Benayoun had completed his hat-trick to make it 4–0. Urged on by the Kop, Liverpool added four more goals in the last 20 minutes as Steven Gerrard, Ryan Babel twice and Crouch with his second made it 8–0. It was the heaviest ever defeat for any side in a Champions League group stage or knockout match.

Liverpool's last two games saw them win 4–1 against Porto at Anfield and then 4–0 in Marseille. They finished second in the group behind Porto and qualified for the knockout stages. They went on to beat Inter Milan and Arsenal before losing to Chelsea in the semi-final.

Beşiktaş used the memory of their humiliation as fuel when the two clubs met again in the Europa League in 2015, with the Turkish side winning after a penalty shoot-out.

Also on this day

1995 Vinnie Jones was sent off for the tenth time in his career as Wimbledon lost 4–1 to Nottingham Forest.

2008 Mark Hughes's Manchester City beat Steve McLaren's FC Twente 3–2 in the UEFA Cup.

2009 The Court of Arbitration for Sport ruled that a transfer ban on Chelsea should be suspended. Chelsea had been forbidden from buying players until January 2011 after being found guilty of inducing Gaël Kakuta to break his contract at Lens.

7 NOVEMBER
2006 – Manchester United back to their Roots

The day before Manchester United travelled to Southend's Roots Hall ground there had been celebrations marking Sir Alex Ferguson's 20 years at the club. What happened at Southend in the League Cup was one of the biggest surprises in those two decades.

Ferguson usually treated the earlier rounds of the League Cup as an opportunity to rest players; but having needed extra-time to win at Crewe in the previous round, it was a strong Manchester United team that took to the field, with both Wayne Rooney

and Cristiano Ronaldo in the starting line-up.

Southend, who were managed by their former player Steve Tilson, had drawn four and lost eight of their previous twelve league games and were bottom of the Championship.

With Cristiano Ronaldo being booed every time he touched the ball, United might have taken the lead twice early on, only for Southend keeper Darryl Flahavan to save twice from Rooney.

The home side took the lead with an exceptional free-kick from Freddy Eastwood, a striker who had been signed from non-league Grays Athletic. From 30 yards, Eastwood curled a tremendous shot past Tomasz Kuszczak into the United net.

Within moments David Jones almost equalized, but saw his shot hit the post. The rest of the game seemed to become a personal duel between Ronaldo and Flahavan in the Southend goal, with Ronaldo being repeatedly denied by some astonishing goalkeeping.

Afterwards Sir Alex Ferguson said of Eastwood's goal, 'I bet he doesn't score another goal like that in his life. If you are going to lose, it might as well be to something special like that. It is a great reminder to everyone at the club that football can smack you in the face. I have been here 20 years and I am not impervious to it either.'

Southend went on to lose 1–0 at Spurs in the League Cup quarter-final, while Eastwood later played for Wolves and Coventry, and scored four goals in winning 11 caps for Wales. Flahavan stayed at Southend for two more years before moving to Crystal Palace, where he was understudy to Julián Speroni.

Also on this day

1992 Ian Rush scored his 200th league goal in Liverpool's 4–1 win over Middlesbrough.

2003 Lazio's Siniša Mihajlović was banned for eight matches after being sent off for spitting at Chelsea's Adrian Mutu in their Champions League meeting in Rome.

8 NOVEMBER
1996 – Chelsea sign Zola

Gianfranco Zola had a great teacher. Zola's first major club was Napoli and their star was Diego Maradona. 'I learned everything from Diego,' said Zola. 'I used to spy on him every time he trained and learned how to curl a free-kick just like him. After one year I had completely changed.'

Zola moved on to Parma, where he formed a partnership with Faustino Asprilla, Tomas Brolin playing just behind. At Parma he lost to Arsenal in the 1994 Cup Winners' Cup Final, but they beat Juventus to win the UEFA Cup the following season.

When Ruud Gullit took over as Chelsea manager in 1996, replacing Glenn Hoddle, the club were able to target still more high-profile players. Few foreigners had ever been so well regarded in Italy as Gullit, who had starred for AC Milan and Sampdoria. Italy is where Gullit started looking for Chelsea's new stars.

Gianluca Vialli from Juventus was the first to come to London, followed by Roberto Di Matteo from Lazio. When Gullit heard that Zola was becoming disillusioned with life under Carlo Ancelotti at Parma, Chelsea acted quickly and paid £4.5m for him.

At the time it seemed a lot to pay for a striker who was already 30. But Zola had been a relatively late developer and Gullit knew there were plenty of matches in him yet, though nobody could have anticipated that six seasons later Zola would still be able to play every Premier League game of Chelsea's season.

When Zola left Chelsea in 2003 at the age of 37, it was to keep a promise he'd made to finish his career at home in Sardinia playing for Cagliari. Roman Abramovich, who had just bought Chelsea when Zola departed, was rumoured to have offered to buy Cagliari as well if they allowed him to return.

Zola played 312 games and scored 80 goals for Chelsea – he created many more.

He won the FA Cup twice, scored the winning goal in the 1998 Cup Winners' Cup Final, won the League Cup and was voted Footballer of the Year.

He was one of the greatest players the Premier League has ever seen.

Also on this day

2000 **Leeds drew 1–1 in the San Siro with AC Milan, and progressed in the Champions League at the expense of Barcelona despite the Spanish side's 5–0 win over Beşiktaş.**

2005 **After 11 wins and a draw from the start of the season, champions Chelsea were beaten at home by Manchester United, who won 1–0 with a goal from Darren Fletcher.**

9 NOVEMBER
2002 – City vs United: the Maine Road farewell

Maine Road was home to Manchester City from 1923 to 2003. It was also home to Manchester United from 1945 to 1949 – Old Trafford had been requisitioned as a depot during the Second World War and was so badly bombed that the rebuild took four years to finish. In fact Manchester United's record attendance for a home game is the 83,260 who watched them play Arsenal at Maine Road in 1948.

The last Manchester derby at City's old ground would turn out to be a treasured memory for the home fans to carry with them to the new City of Manchester Stadium.

City hadn't won a derby game since 1989 when Alex Ferguson's side had been beaten 5–1, heaping more pressure on the under-fire United boss. More than a decade later Kevin Keegan, who had plenty of history with Ferguson and Manchester United from his time at Newcastle, had got City promoted back into the Premier League, and the 127th Manchester derby was his first.

It was one to forget for Manchester United's Neville brothers. First Philip Neville was dispossessed by Nicolas Anelka. He outpaced Rio Ferdinand and fed Shaun Goater, whose shot was parried by Fabien Barthez only to rebound to Anelka, who scored with ease.

Ole Gunnar Solskjaer equalized almost immediately for United, but soon Gary Neville was caught dawdling in possession by Goater, who beat Barthez from a narrow angle. Early in the second half a stray pass from Philip Neville conceded possession. City gave it to Eyal Berković and his pass released Goater to make it 3–1. The Bermudan striker, who had been released by United as a teenager without getting near their first team, celebrated his 100th goal for City.

It was their first victory over United for 13 years, their first in the Premier League and the last at Maine Road.

Also on this day

1996 Wales suffered their worst ever World Cup qualifying defeat, 7–1 against the Netherlands in Eindhoven.

1997 A late David Platt winner sealed Arsenal's thrilling 3–2 win over leaders Manchester United, who had recovered from 2–0 down.

2004 Bryan Robson was appointed manager of West Bromwich Albion.

10 NOVEMBER
1994 – Royle's return

Until the emergence of James Vaughan in 2005, Joe Royle was the youngest player ever to represent Everton – more than 100 goals in nine seasons with the club made him one of their greats.

Royle's managerial career began at unfashionable Oldham and almost took him to the very top when he was shortlisted for the England manager's job after the departure of Bobby Robson. Pipped to the England job by Graham Taylor, Royle stayed at Oldham for 12 years, taking them into the Premier League and reaching the FA Cup semi-finals twice and the League Cup Final once.

After three years in the top flight Oldham were relegated in 1994, but Royle stayed on until November 1994 when Everton, who had just sacked Mike Walker, offered him the chance to return to Goodison Park and the Premier League.

Everton were bottom when Royle took over, with only one win from 14 games. Their next match was the Merseyside derby, and who better to lead them into it than Royle? It was the stuff of dreams for Everton and their new manager as they won 2–0 at Goodison with goals from Duncan Ferguson and Paul Rideout.

The transformation had been immediate – and it lasted. Royle dubbed his team 'The Dogs of War'; they lost only two of their next dozen games and embarked on a run in the FA Cup in which they would concede only one goal in six games before lifting the trophy against Manchester United at Wembley.

It was Everton's first major honour since the league title in 1987 and, to date, their last.

Also on this day

1994 **Despite being Premier League runners-up in 1993 and League Cup winners in 1994, Aston Villa sacked manager Ron Atkinson.**

2003 **After only six months in charge, Peter Reid was sacked as manager of Leeds United following a 6–1 defeat at Portsmouth.**

2010 **Ian Holloway made ten changes to his Blackpool side for their game at Aston Villa, which they lost 3–2. Afterwards he said he would resign if the FA tried to fine him for fielding a weakened team. Three days later, and with his first team restored, Blackpool earned a valuable point at fellow-strugglers West Ham.**

11 NOVEMBER
2012 – Edin Džeko: the unwilling super-sub

Bosnian Edin Džeko made his name in Germany with 92 goals in four seasons at Wolfsburg before Manchester City spent £27m bringing him to England in 2011.

Džeko's impression on the Premier League had been immediate, scoring seven goals in his first four games, including four in a 5–1 win at Tottenham. Competition for places in City's attack was intense with Sergio Agüero, Mario Balotelli and Carlos Tévez also at the club. No player was safe from an afternoon on the substitutes' bench.

In May 2012, City won the Premier League title with Džeko coming on as a substitute to score the 92nd-minute equalizer that made Agüero's title-winning goal possible. It was the fifth time manager Roberto Mancini had seen Džeko come on as a substitute and score.

The following season began with Džeko on the bench again as City won the FA Community Shield against Chelsea. He then came on and scored in matches against Southampton, Real Madrid, Fulham and West Brom – against whom he scored twice. Five of his six goals had been as a substitute, and City had never lost a league game in which he'd come on and scored.

Džeko pleaded not to be typecast: 'I was never a super-sub before I came to City. I used to play always from the beginning and I scored a lot of goals not as a sub. In the last few games it's a situation like this and I am just happy I am scoring goals. But I will never be a super-sub. I want to play.'

On 11 November Manchester City's unbeaten home record of 34 league games came under serious threat from Spurs. City fell behind to a Steven Caulker goal and Emmanuel Adebayor might have doubled Tottenham's advantage.

With just over 20 minutes to go Sergio Agüero equalized, and almost immediately Džeko began to warm up on the touchline. Having replaced Carlos Tévez, Džeko then won the game with two minutes to play, exchanging passes with David Silva before firing past Brad Friedel.

As commentator Gerald Sinstadt once said about Liverpool's David Fairclough, 'Super-sub strikes again.'

Also on this day

1993 UEFA found that Éric Cantona was not guilty of suggesting that the referee in Manchester United's Champions League game at Galatasaray had taken a bribe.

2000 The Professional Footballers' Association allowed women members for the first time, accepting 14 members of the Fulham Ladies squad to their ranks.

2011 The Republic of Ireland all but sealed their place in the Euro 2012 Finals with a 4–0 win in Estonia in the first leg of their play-off. Keith Andrews, Jonathan Walters and Robbie Keane (with two) got the goals.

12 NOVEMBER
2009 – No entry for Celtic and Rangers

The first British club to win the European Cup was Celtic in 1967. Hibernian reached the semi-finals in 1956. The first to reach a Cup Winners' Cup Final was Rangers in 1961. Dundee reached the European Cup semi-final in 1963 and Dundee United did the same in 1984. Aberdeen won the Cup Winners' Cup in 1983 and reached the semi-final the following season. Even Dunfermline and Kilmarnock had European semi-finals in the 1960s.

There was a time when Scottish clubs could match and beat the achievements of their English rivals in Europe. Top English players were only too happy to move to Celtic and Rangers in the late

1980s and early 1990s when Rangers knocked Leeds out of the Champions League. Later Celtic beat both Liverpool and Blackburn on their way to the 2003 UEFA Cup Final.

But the more the revenue from English TV deals grew and the less competitive the Scottish league became, the wider the gap grew between Scotland and England. Eventually both Celtic and Rangers argued that they had outgrown the Scottish leagues and that a move into the Premier League in England would benefit both them and the English league.

Everton manager David Moyes voiced the case in favour: 'Both Celtic and Rangers have as big a support as any team in England. From that point of view it would help the game in England if we need a boost in revenue.'

In the autumn of 2009 Bolton Wanderers chairman Phil Gartside proposed a second division of the Premier League that would include the Glasgow Auld Firm.

In November of that year, the Premier League clubs discussed Gartside's proposal. The league's chief executive Richard Scudamore emerged from the meeting with news of the vote – and the idea was dead in the water: 'As regards to Celtic and Rangers it's a non-starter. So we've made a clear and unequivocal statement. No means no. The clubs constitutionally voted to say we're not going to take this any further – Celtic and Rangers are not coming in.'

Also on this day

1998 After 34 years at the club, Roy Evans resigned from his job as joint-manager of Liverpool, leaving Gérard Houllier in sole charge.

1998 Peter Schmeichel announced that he would leave Manchester United at the end of the season.

2004 John Toshack was appointed manager of Wales.

2005 Michael Owen scored twice as England beat Argentina 3–2 in a friendly played in Geneva.

13 NOVEMBER
2004 – Spurs 4 Arsenal 5: the ice-hockey game

Martin Jol had just stepped up from assistant manager to replace the hapless Jacques Santini at White Hart Lane. Spurs had scored a paltry six league goals in the first 11 games of season 2004/05 under the Frenchman's management, and although they had scored two in Jol's first match as manager, they'd allowed Charlton to score three.

Despite a midweek League Cup win at Burnley, Tottenham seemed ill-equipped to welcome their greatest rivals to White

Hart Lane for the first north London derby of the season. Tottenham were 14th in the table, already 14 points adrift of their neighbours Arsenal.

Spurs took the lead when Noureddine Naybet connected with a Michael Carrick free-kick ten minutes before half-time. Theirry Henry equalized in first-half stoppage-time. All square at half-time, but the scoring had only just begun.

Early in the second half a catalogue of Tottenham errors led to Noé Pamarot fouling Freddie Ljungberg for a penalty that Lauren converted. Within a couple of minutes Patrick Vieira made it 3–1, only for Jermain Defoe to score for Spurs with a brilliant individual goal almost from the kick-off.

Half an hour to go and the game was shaping up to be a classic. Again the two sides traded quick-fire goals, first Ljungberg from a Fàbregas pass, then Ledley King with a touch on a free-kick. With 16 minutes left it was 4–3 to Arsenal.

With ten minutes to go, Robert Pirès scored from the narrowest of angles, but Spurs got yet another goal through Freddie Kanouté with two minutes to go. It finished Spurs 4 Arsenal 5.

Even in defeat Martin Jol took some pride, saying, 'We want to recreate a bit of our history, and that is all about attacking football.'

Chelsea were playing later in the day at Fulham. When their manager José Mourinho saw the result he sneered, 'That is not a proper football score; it is an ice-hockey result.'

Also on this day

1999 England won the first leg of the Euro 2000 qualification play-off against Scotland 2–0 at Hampden Park.

2002 Newcastle became the first team ever to qualify for the knockout stage of the Champions League having lost their first three games. Sir Bobby Robson's team lost 2–0 in Kiev, 1–0 at home to Feyenoord and 2–0 at Juventus before winning 1–0 at home to Juventus, 2–1 at home to Dynamo Kiev and 3–2 in Rotterdam against Feyenoord.

2006 Iain Dowie was sacked as Charlton manager after only 15 games and replaced by Les Reed.

14 NOVEMBER
1995 – Green light for the Stadium of Light

Sunderland had played at Roker Park for 99 years by the time they moved out in 1997. The old ground had been one of the venues for the 1966 World Cup Finals, hosting three group games and the quarter-final between the Soviet Union and Hungary.

Sunderland chairman Bob Murray had quickly realized that Roker Park could never be satisfactorily updated to meet the recommendations of the Taylor Report that followed the Hillsborough disaster, and began the search for a site for a new stadium as early as 1991.

Four years and a couple of false starts later, the club hit on the site of the old Wearmouth Colliery where generations of their fans had worked. In late 1995 permission was given to build a new 34,000 all-seated stadium at Wearmouth.

The 34,000 quickly became 40,000, and then 42,000 as the club responded to the enthusiasm for the development from its fan base.

Looking for a name that would cement the connection both the club and stadium had with the coal industry, Murray decided on the Stadium of Light, saying, 'The name is very much a symbOlić link to the thousands of miners and Sunderland supporters that emerged from the darkness and into the light every day when they returned to the surface after working in the mine.'

The link to one of the most famous stadiums in Europe, Benfica's Estádio da Luz in Lisbon, also gave the project an added sense of grandeur.

In 1997, playing in the second tier, Sunderland moved in and increased their average league attendance by 60 per cent in their first season to over 33,000. Following promotion to the Premier League, Sunderland expanded the stadium to hold 49,000 and averaged 45,069 per game in season 2000/01, the third highest average in the country that season.

The stadium is designed to be extended to hold 66,000 if necessary and remains one of the best in the country. Meanwhile, just over a mile away, Roker Park is now a housing estate – with roads named Goalmouth Close, Promotion Close and Midfield Drive.

Also on this day

1997 Ron Atkinson was given a short-term contract at Sheffield Wednesday, replacing David Pleat.

2002 Blackburn lost 2–0 at home to Celtic in the UEFA Cup, going out 3–0 on aggregate.

2003 Chelsea hammered Lazio 4–0 in Rome in the Champions League.

2009 The Republic of Ireland lost 1–0 to France in Dublin in the first leg of their World Cup qualifying play-off.

2012 Steven Gerrard won his 100th England cap in a 4–2 defeat to Sweden in Stockholm. The game featured a stupendous overhead-kick goal from Zlatan Ibrahimović, who scored all four Swedish goals.

15 NOVEMBER
2000 – Beckham takes the armband

When England captain Alan Shearer retired from international football after Euro 2000, manager Kevin Keegan restored the captain's armband to Tony Adams, who had previously been skipper under Terry Venables's management. But England's defeat at Wembley to Germany in October 2000 wasn't only the last game for the old stadium and Keegan – it was also Adams's last cap for his country.

Howard Wilkinson took charge of England's next game, in Finland, four days after the Wembley defeat and it was Martin Keown who led the team out as captain.

Leicester boss Peter Taylor, who had enjoyed a successful spell in charge of England's Under-21 team, was caretaker manager for the following match, a friendly in Turin against Italy. Taylor might only have been England manager for one game but he made his mark, naming David Beckham as captain for the first time.

Beckham wasn't Manchester United's captain, but at 25 he was approaching his prime and was certainly the most famous player in England and known all over the world.

Always charming with the press and public, always conscious of his responsibilities as captain, Beckham was kept on as skipper under Sven-Göran Eriksson and would end up captaining England in every game he played for the next six years.

His status as a player and his standing in the squad meant that, according to former England striker Ian Wright, 'Beckham only had to raise his eyebrows to put someone in their place.'

When Beckham stood down as captain in 2006, he said, 'On 15 November 2000 Peter Taylor gave me the greatest honour of my career in making me the captain of England, fulfilling my childhood dream. It has been an honour and a privilege to have captained our country.'

Also on this day

1994 Gerry Francis was appointed manager of Spurs.

1997 Rio Ferdinand won his first England cap in a 2–0 win over Cameroon.

2003 In the first legs of the Euro 2004 qualification play-offs, Scotland beat the Netherlands 1–0 at Hampden Park while Wales drew 0–0 in Russia.

2011 England beat Sweden 1–0, their first victory over the Swedes in 43 years. The match was watched by 48,876, a record low crowd for an England game at the new Wembley.

2011 The Republic of Ireland clinched their place at Euro 2012 with a 1–1 draw

at home to Estonia to win the tie 5–1 on aggregate.

2014 Wayne Rooney won his 100th England cap and scored his 44th international goal in a 3–1 win over Slovenia at Wembley.

16 NOVEMBER
1999 – Arsenal look to relocate

Arsenal's two-year experiment of playing Champions League home games at Wembley had been a financial success, if not quite a footballing one. Six attendances in excess of 70,000 had proved that Arsenal could attract huge crowds, now they wanted that revenue regularly but from a stadium they could call home.

In November 1999 the club announced that it had identified a site on which the new stadium would be built; it was Ashburton Grove, where a couple of streets converged, leading to some light industrial units and a recycling plant sandwiched between two railway lines. It was not much more than a long goal-kick from Highbury.

Arsenal's managing director Keith Edelman said, 'Our aim is to be a leading European club and, once we get into the new stadium, we will be in that position. The revenue from executive boxes and club level alone will be almost equivalent to the whole income at Highbury.'

Arsène Wenger said that apart from Arsenal's decision to appoint the revered Herbert Chapman as manager in 1925 it was 'the biggest decision in Arsenal's history'.

It was six-and-a-half years before Arsenal moved into their new home and the club put the cost of the move at £390m, some of which was offset by turning the old art-deco East and West Stands of Highbury into luxury apartments.

Nevertheless, the burden of financing the new stadium was cited as a reason why Arsenal found it difficult to prevent players like Nasri, van Persie and Fàbregas from leaving and the flow of trophies drying up.

In 2012 Wenger said, 'We want to pay the debt we owe from the stadium we built, that's around £15m per year. So it's normal that at the start, we have to make at least £15m or we lose money.'

Those financial restrictions seemed to be lifted when the club smashed its transfer record to sign Mesut Özil in 2013 for over £40m and the club won the FA Cup, its first trophy in nine years, the following May.

Also on this day

1994 Steve McManaman won his first England cap as a substitute in a 1–0 win against Nigeria.

1996 Everton's Gary Speed scored a hat-trick as they beat Southampton 7–1.

2002 Goal of the Season – Thierry Henry scored it for Arsenal against Spurs at Highbury.

2003 England were beaten 3–2 by Denmark at Old Trafford.

2009 George Burley was sacked by Scotland.

17 NOVEMBER
1993 – Wales so near and yet …

Wales qualified for the 1958 World Cup Finals and lost to Pelé's brilliance in the quarter-final. Managed by Terry Yorath, they came within an ace of reaching their second World Cup 35 years later.

With two teams to qualify from their group, Wales had begun their campaign with a crushing 5–1 defeat to Romania in Bucharest. The Welsh squad included Neville Southall, Gary Speed, Dean Saunders, Mark Hughes, Ian Rush and a young Ryan Giggs and they bounced back with wins over the Faroe Islands and Cyprus before losing in Belgium.

When Giggs and Rush scored to beat Belgium in Cardiff, it was clear that Wales were in with a chance of qualification.

Both games against Czechoslovakia were drawn and the last match saw Wales play Romania in Cardiff. Belgium and Romania topped the group on 13 points apiece, the Welsh and the Czechs had 12. Wales knew that if they won at Cardiff Arms Park, they were guaranteed a place at the World Cup.

Romania, only needing a draw, scored first when Gheorghe Hagi's shot squirmed under goalkeeper Neville Southall.

After an hour Wales equalized through Dean Saunders and within two minutes they were awarded a penalty when Dan Petrescu tripped Gary Speed.

Swindon's Paul Bodin stepped up to take the kick that could send Wales to the World Cup. Later he remembered, 'When the penalty was awarded, their goalkeeper grabbed the ball and gave it a good-luck kiss. I wiped it away, put the ball on the spot, and decided to put it in the top left-hand corner as powerfully as I could. I ran up and struck it cleanly. I watched it all the way and it looked good until it seemed to change trajectory at the last second. It crashed against the bar. Just two inches lower and we would have been winning.'

Late in the game Florin Răducioiu scored again for Romania. Wales, who had never come closer, were out again.

Also on this day

1993 England won 7–1 in San Marino having fallen behind to a goal from Davide Gualtieri after nine seconds, the fastest ever scored in international football. The result was not enough for England to qualify for the World Cup.

1993 The Republic of Ireland reached the 1994 World Cup with a 1–1 draw in Belfast against Northern Ireland.

1999 England qualified for the Euro 2000 Finals despite losing 1–0 to Scotland at Wembley in the second leg of their play-off.

2007 A disputed 88th-minute goal by Christian Panucci gave Italy a 2–1 win at Hampden Park and denied Scotland a place at Euro 2008.

2007 David Healy scored a record-breaking 13th goal in Northern Ireland's European Championship qualifying campaign as they beat Denmark 2–1 in Belfast.

18 NOVEMBER
2009 – The Hand of Henry

'Of course the fairest solution would be to replay the game, but it's not in my control.'

As Thierry Henry might have suspected, there would be no replay. France qualified for the 2010 World Cup Finals and the Republic of Ireland did not.

The French had won 1–0 in the first leg of their qualification play-off in Dublin. In the second leg in Paris, Robbie Keane

scored for Ireland to level the aggregate scores. With the game in extra-time, Henry clearly prevented a cross from going out of play with two touches of his left hand before passing for William Gallas to score the winning goal. Swedish referee Martin Hanson didn't see it, and wouldn't be persuaded by the Irish protests to disallow the goal. France won 2–1 on aggregate.

Managers and players were united in a call for video technology to be used to help referees. Arsène Wenger, who was at the game working for French TV, said, 'What is terrible for the referee is that he gave the goal knowing something was not regular, and yet he had no help. I saw him walk from the linesman to the middle of the park, thinking: "I have to give that goal," and knowing it is not a regular goal. That is where football is guilty.'

Speaking immediately after the game, Ireland's Robbie Keane said, 'He almost caught it and ran into the net with it so we're devastated. You wouldn't expect that from him, you wouldn't expect it from anyone.'

France's former *enfant terrible* Éric Cantona characteristically indicated that he would not have accepted it as 'one of those things'; the former Manchester United man said, 'What shocks me most is that this player [Henry], at the end of the game, went to sit next to an Ireland player to comfort him – when he had just screwed him. If I had been the Irishman he wouldn't have lasted three seconds.'

Six years later, with the FIFA corruption scandal gathering pace, the chief-executive of the Football Association of Ireland John Delaney claimed that the FAI were paid around €5m by FIFA to drop a legal case that argued that the result should not be allowed to stand. FIFA confirmed the payment, but said it was a loan to help with the construction costs of the now Aviva Stadium in Dublin.

Brilliant though Henry was, his handball will never be forgotten.

Also on this day

1995 Everton won at Liverpool 2–1, their first win at Anfield in eight years. Andrei Kanchelkis scored both, his first goals for the club.

2000 David Beckham won the first Manchester derby to be played in over four years, with a free-kick sealing a 1–0 win at Maine Road.

2005 Roy Keane left Old Trafford after more than 12 years at the club. His departure came only days after he criticized his teammates' performances in a 4–1 defeat at Middlesbrough in an interview for MUTV that was never broadcast.

19 NOVEMBER
1997 – Christian Gross arrives at Spurs

Foreign managers were rare in English football in the mid-1990s, but following the success of Arsène Wenger's first year at Arsenal, Tottenham widened their horizons when they were looking for a replacement for Gerry Francis.

They came up with Christian Gross, a 43-year-old Swiss who had already won two league titles with Grasshoppers Zürich. Like Wenger when he'd arrived in England, Gross was hardly a household name – unlike Wenger, he spoke only broken English. His strong Swiss/German accent soon made him a figure of fun in the tabloid press, drawing comparisons with the accents on the Second World War spoof 'Allo 'Allo, which had pulled in millions of viewers on TV.

When Gross arrived for his first day at White Hart Lane he waved a London Underground ticket over his head and said, 'I want this to become my ticket to dreams. I came by Underground because I wanted to know the way the fans feel coming to Spurs. I want to show that I am one of them.'

Spurs were a point above the relegation zone when Gross arrived, but within a month they'd lost 6–1 at home to Chelsea and 4–0 at Coventry. Even the return of Jürgen Klinsmann didn't make a huge difference; the German scored only three goals in his first four months back at the club.

In mid-April, Spurs went to fellow strugglers Barnsley and managed a draw. Then Klinsmann rediscovered his touch, scoring in a 2–0 win over Newcastle and getting four in the 6–2 win at Wimbledon that kept Spurs up.

When Spurs lost two of their first three games the following season, Gross was dismissed.

It's unusual for a sacked manager to give a press conference at all, but highly unusual to do it with the man who sacked him sitting alongside. But, as Gross insisted that his time had been a success, chairman Alan Sugar said, 'I think one has to say we were faced with an untenable situation created by the media, and we felt that Christian – no matter how professional or how good he is – had been destroyed by the media, it is as simple as that.'

Also on this day

2003 Scotland were hammered 6–0 by the Netherlands in Amsterdam in the second leg of their Euro 2004 play-off. On the same night Wales were knocked out by Russia, who won 1–0 in Cardiff.

2007 Steve Bruce left his job at Wigan to become manager of Birmingham.

2010 Blackburn Rovers were bought by the Rao family, owners of the Venky's poultry firm in India, in a £43m deal.

20 NOVEMBER
2010 – Spurs win at Arsenal at last

Spurs had played at Arsenal 19 times since a 3–1 victory at Highbury in an end of season match in 1993. Nineteen games, and they had failed to win any of them.

Arsenal had already knocked Spurs out of the League Cup with a 4–1 victory after extra-time at White Hart Lane. Another win would take them above Chelsea at the top of the Premier League, so Spurs had little to cling on to at half-time when they were 2–0 down to goals from Samir Nasri and Marouane Chamakh.

Harry Redknapp decided to take off Aaron Lennon and bring on Jermain Defoe at half-time, with the manager instructing his players to go out and attack. 'It was a gamble at half-time,' said Redknapp afterwards. 'We were either going to lose by five, or have a go to try to get back in the game. I decided to go for it, because that's in my nature.'

The gamble paid off almost immediately, Gareth Bale giving Spurs a lifeline with a clever finish. Spurs wiped out Arsenal's advantage with 25 minutes still to play – Cesc Fàbregas was guilty of handball and Rafael van der Vaart scored the resulting penalty.

At 2–2 it was anybody's game, but Spurs broke their Arsenal hoodoo four minutes from the end as Younès Kaboul headed van der Vaart's free-kick beyond Fabianksi for the winner.

On the touchline, Wenger picked up a bottle of water and threw it in frustration at the ground in front of him. 'It's difficult to understand how we lost this game,' said Wenger. 'It's painful, we lost our focus and made some basic mistakes and were punished. At 2–0 it looked too easy and we eased off a bit.'

Despite the win, Arsenal finished above Spurs at the end of the season, denying their rivals a place in the Champions League.

Also on this day

2006 **West Ham was bought by a consortium headed by Icelandic business executive Eggert Magnússon, who promised the club would be in the Champions League within five years.**

2008 **Arsenal's William Gallas gave an interview in which he criticized his teammates for a lack of courage and said that one (unnamed) player had insulted other members of the squad during a game. Two days later Gallas was stripped of the captaincy.**

21 NOVEMBER
2007 – England 2 Croatia 3: minging in the rain

It was a night on which the deficiencies of the Wembley roof were to be as exposed as the deficiencies of the England team.

Under Steve McLaren, England had struggled in a group from which his predecessor Sven-Göran Eriksson had predicted England would qualify 'quite easily'. There had been a draw at home to Macedonia, a horrible defeat in Croatia, a draw in Israel, defeat in Russia and even a woeful performance in Andorra. But even so, England only needed to draw at home to Croatia to make it to Euro 2008. A draw was a result that would suit Croatia too, and in Moscow the Russians feared a conspiracy between the English and Croatians to knock them out.

McLaren sprang a surprise before kick-off by picking 22-year-old Scott Carson in goal ahead of Paul Robinson. Carson was winning only his second cap and the Croatians sensed his nerves from the start.

In pouring rain England were 2–0 down inside 15 minutes. The first goal was a personal calamity for Carson. Niko Kranjčar took aim from 30 yards and Carson allowed the ball to spin over his left shoulder into the net. The second goal was neatly worked, leaving Ivica Olić to step round the goalkeeper and score into an empty net.

On the touchline McLaren stood holding a red and blue FA umbrella, which might have stopped him getting wet but didn't stop him floundering.

With Beckham and Defoe on at half-time England somehow clawed their way back into the game and seemed to have saved themselves when a fortunate

Frank Lampard penalty and a Peter Crouch goal made it 2–2 – the result the Russians feared.

But Croatia's coach, Slaven Bilic, wasn't content with that. He put on forward Mladen Petrić and continued to try to win. With a little over ten minutes to go, Petrić struck from distance and Carson was beaten again.

Russia joined Croatia at Euro 2008, the press dubbed McLaren 'The Wally with the brolly', and the FA sacked him the next day.

Also on this day

1993 Andy Cole scored a hat-trick as Newcastle beat Liverpool 3–0 at St James' Park.

1994 Everton's day in the Merseyside derby. Joe Royle's first game in charge ended in a 2–0 win for the Blues, with Duncan Ferguson scoring his first goal for the club and Neville Southall making a record-breaking 35th appearance in the fixture.

1998 Bottom of the table Blackburn sacked manager Roy Hodgson after a 2–0 defeat at home to Southampton.

2000 Leeds agreed a fee of £18m with West Ham for Rio Ferdinand.

2012 Chelsea sacked Roberto Di Matteo as manager and appointed Rafael Benítez until the end of the season.

22 NOVEMBER
2009 – Tottenham and Defoe run riot

Wigan had been beaten 5–0 at Manchester United, 4–0 at Arsenal and 4–0 at Portsmouth when they travelled to White Hart Lane to take on a Spurs side that had already scored five times in four matches that season.

A win for Spurs would hardly surprise anyone, nor would a big win for Spurs; but few would have envisaged that Tottenham would score nine to register their biggest ever top-flight victory.

Chris Kirkland was the unfortunate Wigan goalkeeper. At half-time Kirkland would have had no inkling of what was coming: he had only been beaten once, Peter Crouch scoring that goal after only nine minutes.

Jermain Defoe then scored three between the 51st minute and the 58th minute, the third fastest hat-trick in Premier League history. There had also been time for Paul Scharner to score at the other end, so with half an hour to play Spurs led 4–1.

Kirkland than made an extraordinary save to deny Crouch, before Aaron Lennon added a fifth and Defoe added another to his own tally to make it 6–1.

With three minutes to go the score was still 6–1, but Spurs scored three more. Defoe added his fifth of the game – a feat only previously matched in the Premier League by Andy Cole and Alan Shearer – a David Bentley free-kick hit the post and rebounded into the net off Kirkland, and Niko Kranjčar ensured that Spurs became only the second Premier League team ever to score nine in a match.

Afterwards Wigan manager Roberto Martínez said, 'We didn't help ourselves at all. The last three goals were unacceptable. We will learn from it and move on quickly. We lost one game and nothing else.'

Spurs finished the campaign in fourth, their highest place for 20 years. Wigan stayed up with a six-point cushion over the bottom three – despite losing 8–0 to Chelsea on the last day of the season.

Also on this day

1995 Blackburn lost 3–0 in the Champions League at Spartak Moscow. In a chaotic display, Graeme Le Saux and David Batty came close to fighting each other and Colin Hendry was sent off.

2001 Ipswich beat Inter Milan 1–0 at Portman Road in the UEFA Cup with Alun Armstrong scoring the only goal.

2007 After failing to qualify for Euro 2008 both Steve McLaren and his assistant Terry Venables were sacked.

2008 Goal of the Season – Glen Johnson scored it for Portsmouth against Hull City at Fratton Park.

2014 On his 400th game for the club, Leon Osman scored the winning goal for Everton against West Ham.

23 NOVEMBER
1996 – The Curious Incident of the Dia in the Saints Team

Ali Dia was a 31-year-old Senegalese striker, who had previously played in the lower leagues in France, Finland and then – most recently – for VfB Lübeck in the bottom reaches of German football. At least that's all probably true, but then nothing about Ali Dia turned out to be quite what it seemed.

Southampton manager Graeme Souness got a phone call from a man purporting to be the great Liberian former World Player of the Year, George Weah. 'Weah' told Souness that he had a cousin who had played in France for Paris Saint-Germain, who had 13 international caps, and who was looking for a club in England. His name was Ali Dia.

Souness invited Dia to Southampton's training ground and, after a kick-about in a five-a-side match, Souness decided to sign him on a one-month contract, presumably hoping that some of the Weah DNA might be in there somewhere.

The only problem was that Dia was actually in England having enrolled on a college course in Portsmouth, and the phone call was from Dia's friend and not from George Weah – who was not his cousin.

On 23 November 1996, Southampton were at home to Leeds. With the score at 0–0, Southampton's star man Matt Le Tissier pulled a muscle. Souness decided that Dia's big day had come, and put him on.

To his credit, Dia lasted 52 minutes before Souness took him off again, shortly after Leeds had scored their first goal in a 2–0 win. Le Tissier later remarked, 'His performance was almost comical. He kind of took my place, but he didn't really have a position. He was just wandering everywhere. I don't think he realized what position he was supposed to be in … it was embarrassing to watch.'

Not surprisingly Dia was released from his contract early and was reported to have played some matches for Gateshead while completing a business degree at Northumbria University.

Also on this day

1993 Following England's failure to qualify for the 1994 World Cup, Graham Taylor resigned as manager.

2000 Tore André Flo moved from Chelsea to Rangers for £12m.

2004 Sir Alex Ferguson celebrated his 1000th game in charge of

Manchester United with a 2–1 win over Olympique Lyonnais in the Champions League.

2007 Steve Bruce was appointed manager of Wigan.

2012 Mark Hughes was sacked by QPR.

2013 Crystal Palace appointed Tony Pulis as manager.

2014 England's women played at Wembley for the first time, losing 3–0 to Germany in front of a crowd of 45,619.

24 NOVEMBER
1998 – Newcastle buy Ferguson

Duncan Ferguson was most Everton fans' favourite player. The Scot had become a cult figure for his knack of scoring against the teams Everton loved to beat the most – Liverpool and Manchester United.

Ferguson was fantastic in the air, almost as good on the ground and a fearsome competitor. By 1998 he also seemed to have channelled his aggression to prevent any repeat of his notorious head-butt on Raith's John McStay that had led to a 44-day spell in Glasgow's Barlinnie jail for assault.

When Newcastle came to play Everton at Goodison Park in 1998, Ferguson was suspended. Everton won 1–0 with a goal from Michael Ball, and manager Walter Smith would have been smiling broadly as he headed for the dressing room on the final whistle.

That smile was about to be wiped from his face. What Smith didn't know was that, during the game, Everton's chairman Peter Johnson and his Newcastle counterpart Freddy Shepherd had been agreeing a deal to sell Ferguson to Newcastle for £7m.

The next day, when the news broke that Ferguson was leaving, Everton fans and their manager were furious – even more so when it became apparent that all of the money from the transfer would be used to reduce Everton's debt rather than find a replacement for the striker.

Smith threatened to resign unless Johnson publically admitted that he had done the deal without his knowledge. Eventually Johnson agreed, but things got worse for the chairman the following Saturday when Ferguson made his Newcastle debut, and scored twice against Wimbledon.

Meanwhile Everton fans who had travelled to watch their team at Charlton continued to protest against Johnson. The club's shareholders association threatened a vote of no confidence in him and, exactly a week after he'd sat over a table at Goodison Park with Freddy Shepherd and sold a legend, Johnson resigned.

Also on this day

1993 Gary Mabbutt suffered a broken cheekbone and eye socket after a challenge from Wimbledon's John Fashanu.

2001 At the sixth attempt, Southampton finally won their first game at their new St Mary's Stadium, 1–0 against Charlton.

2004 Harry Redknapp resigned as manager at Portsmouth.

2005 Alain Perrin was sacked by Portsmouth.

2012 Harry Redknapp was appointed manager of QPR.

25 NOVEMBER
2014 – City's Bayern comeback

Manchester City's billionaire owners didn't buy the club just to qualify for the Champions League, their aim was to win it. But City's Champions League credentials were poor going into the 2014/15 season.

Their first shot at the trophy, under Roberto Mancini in 2011/12, had been quite promising; they'd beaten Bayern Munich but narrowly failed to get out of the group stage.

Things got worse rather than better the following season when they took only three points and finished bottom in their group. Mancini was sacked at the end of the season.

Under their new manager Manuel Pellegrini, City won the Premier League again in 2013/14 and progressed past the group stage of the Champions League for the first time. City beat Bayern again as they joined the Germans in strolling through an easy group. Barcelona stopped them in their tracks in the first knockout round.

When City started the 2014/15 Champions League campaign in dismal fashion – and Chelsea looked like favourites for the Premier League – the pressure on Pellegrini was becoming intense.

Yet again, City had drawn Bayern Munich in their group, and lost 1–0 in Bavaria – no disgrace. Draws at home to Roma and at CSKA Moscow followed. But when CSKA won the return 2–1 in Manchester, and both Fernandinho and Yaya Touré were sent off, another group exit looked to be only a matter of time.

At home to Bayern Munich, City had to win to have any realistic hope of staying in the competition. Things looked good for Pellegrini when Bayern had Mehdi Benatia sent off after 20 minutes for a foul on Agüero, who scored the resulting penalty.

But even with ten men Bayern looked the more accomplished side and scored twice, through Xabi Alonso and Robert Lewandowski, late in the first half.

It was still 2–1 to Bayern with five minutes to go – enter Agüero again. First he pounced on a mistake by Alonso to make it 2–2, and then, in an echo of City's glorious last-gasp title win of 2012, dispossessed Jerome Boateng in injury-time to win the game 3–2.

A fortnight later City sealed their progress with a 2–0 win in Rome, only to be beaten by Barcelona again in the first knockout stage.

Also on this day

1994 **In a tearful confession, Arsenal's Paul Merson admitted to his gambling, alcohol and drug problems.**

1998 **Andy Cole scored twice and Dwight Yorke once as Manchester United drew 3–3 with Barcelona in the Nou Camp in their Champions League group game; the clubs had drawn by the same score at Old Trafford in their first meeting.**

2003 **Arsenal won 5–1 in the San Siro against Inter Milan in one of their best ever European displays.**

26 NOVEMBER
1992 – Eric the Red

Éric Cantona had scored 14 goals in 35 games for Leeds, playing his part in their title success of 1992, then scored a Wembley hat-trick in their Charity Shield

win over Liverpool and another in a 5–0 win over Spurs.

But Leeds manager Howard Wilkinson was not a huge fan of the Frenchman. 'Eric likes to do what he likes when he likes,' Wilkinson told the press. Despite going out of the Champions League to Rangers in early November of 1992 and their faltering form in the league, Cantona was spending a lot of time on the substitutes' bench.

Wilkinson had decided that his defence needed reinforcing, and Leeds chairman Bill Fotherby rang Manchester United about the possibility of signing their left back Denis Irwin.

Meanwhile, at Old Trafford, they needed a goalscorer. Dion Dublin had broken his leg, and they'd managed only 18 goals in the first 17 games of the season. Ferguson had tried, and failed, to sign Alan Shearer and David Hirst, and was considering a move for Mick Harford.

When the phone rang at Old Trafford a sequence of events began to unfold. Sir Alex Ferguson later recalled, 'The timing was weird, absolutely uncanny. Leeds came on the phone asking if we'd sell them Denis Irwin. It was a non-starter. But jokingly I suggested we'd swap him for Éric Cantona – and there was this pause at the other end …'

The deal was done quickly, United paying just £1.2m for the Frenchman – who left Elland Road with a parting shot to the manager: 'Wilkinson is just covering himself with these accusations. I was loved at Leeds. Now the fans smash windows and he does not know how to stop it, so he accuses me.'

Cantona went on to be one of Manchester United's greatest ever signings and Ferguson later said, 'If ever there was one player, anywhere in the world, who was made for Manchester United, it was Cantona. He swaggered in, stuck his chest out, raised his head and surveyed everything as though he were asking: "I'm Cantona. How big are you? Are you big enough for me?"'

Also on this day

2006 Frank Lampard was sent off as Phil Scolari's struggling Chelsea could only draw with Bordeaux in the Champions League.

2007 Derby County sacked manager Billy Davies after taking only six points from their first 14 games of the season. Davies was replaced by Paul Jewell, who couldn't halt their slide to relegation with Derby failing to win any of their remaining 24 games.

2014 Liverpool conceded an 88th-minute equalizer in a 2–2 draw with Bulgarian side Ludogorets in Sofia. It left their hopes of progression in the Champions League on a knife-edge.

27 NOVEMBER
2011 – The death of Gary Speed

The death of the Wales manager at the age of 42 left the football community in a state of shock and bewilderment. An inquest found that he had taken his own life, possibly accidentally. His death began a valuable debate about how depression can hit even those who appear to have everything going for them.

Speed was one of his country's great footballers, scoring seven goals in an international career that spanned 85 caps over 16 years; he was captain of Wales on 44 occasions. He became their manager in December 2010 and had led them to fine wins over Switzerland and Bulgaria in European Championship qualifying matches before beating Norway 4–1 in a friendly in what was to be his last match in charge.

His playing career took him from Leeds – where he won the title in 1992 – to Everton, the team he'd supported as a boy. From Goodison Park he moved to Newcastle, where he played in two FA Cup Finals and in a Champions League campaign, before three seasons at Bolton. Speed finished his playing career at Sheffield United, where he also took on a coaching role.

He played 841 club games in his career and scored 130 goals, netting at least one goal in 20 consecutive league seasons. In 2010 he was awarded an MBE.

On Speed's death, his former Welsh teammate Ryan Giggs said, 'I am totally devastated. Gary Speed was one of the nicest men in football and someone I am honoured to call a teammate and friend.'

Few players in the history of the Premier League have matched Gary Speed's achievements and few have been so respected by their peers.

Also on this day

2003 Manchester City were knocked out of the UEFA Cup by Polish minnows Groclin Dyskobolia.

2007 After narrowly failing to reach the finals of Euro 2008, Alex McLeish resigned as manager of Scotland.

2008 Portsmouth drew 2–2 with AC Milan at Fratton Park in the UEFA Cup.

2010 Dimitar Berbatov became the fourth player in Premier League history to score five goals in one game as Manchester United beat Blackburn 7–1.

2014 Tottenham's game against Partizan Belgrade in the Europa League was interrupted three times by 'sponsored' pitch invaders.

28 NOVEMBER
2009 – Bullard's penalty prank

When Hull City had been beaten 5–1 at Manchester City on Boxing Day 2008, their manager Phil Brown had famously given his half-time team talk on the pitch – wagging his finger at the players as they sat sheepishly on the turf in front of the travelling fans. Brown's team were 4–0 down at the time and he'd said, 'Our travelling fans deserved some kind of explanation for the first-half performance and it was difficult for me to do that from the confines of a changing room. We owed them an apology for the first-half performance.'

Some people thought it was a piece of managerial magic, others that he'd risked his own future by humiliating his players in public, but Brown's team went on to avoid relegation on the last day of the season.

Back at Manchester City the following November, Hull seemed to be in much better shape. They'd recovered from a 6–1 defeat at Liverpool to take 11 points from their next seven games. There was no need for any half-time apologies from Hull, even though they were behind, Shaun Wright-Phillips scoring the only goal with a deflected shot in stoppage-time.

Eight minutes from the end of the game, Hull were awarded a penalty when

Jan Vennegoor of Hesselink was fouled by Kolo Touré. Jimmy Bullard, who had just recovered from nine months out with a knee injury, came forward to take it in front of the Hull fans at the same end of the stadium as the infamous Brown team talk.

Bullard scored, and was immediately surrounded by his teammates, who sat in a circle around him while he wagged his finger in mock approbation. On the touchline, Brown saw the funny side, and later Bullard said, 'We decided to do it last night. We agreed that whoever scored an equalizer or winning goal had to be the one who did the pointing.'

The laughing stopped when Hull were relegated the following May.

Also on this day

1996 TV chef Delia Smith joined the board of directors at Norwich City.

2004 A late goal from youngster Neil Mellor secured a 2–1 win for Liverpool over Arsenal.

2007 Alex McLeish was appointed manager of Birmingham City.

2014 Roy Keane resigned from his job as assistant manager of Aston Villa.

29 NOVEMBER
1998 – Gerrard's Liverpool debut

Some of the crowd of just under 42,000 must have missed it. Liverpool were beating Blackburn 2–0 and anyone leaving early wouldn't have seen the 90th-minute substitution of Vegard Heggem. Liverpool's new Norwegian right back was replaced by 18-year-old Steven Gerrard, making his senior debut.

Liverpool had found Gerrard playing for Whiston Juniors when he was nine, and invited him to join their academy. Although he had trials at other clubs, including Manchester United, Gerrard has said that he'd only attended trials elsewhere in the hope of persuading Liverpool to offer him a youth contract.

When Gérard Houllier joined Liverpool at the start of the 1998/99 season he went to watch the Under-19 side play at the academy: 'I remember in the middle of the park there was this boy I didn't know at the time going box to box, shouting at people and already behaving like a leader. He was quick, he was tackling and could see a pass quickly. I wanted to have Stevie [with the first team]. At the time the coaches said we couldn't because he was always injured. I said, "I'm the boss, so he is coming with us".'

Gerrard spent some of his early matches playing at right back as injury kept Heggem on the sidelines. Soon an injury to Jamie Redknapp opened a door to the centre of Liverpool's midfield, where he thrived to such an extent that, in March 1999, Kevin Keegan invited him to gain some experience by training with the England squad.

At the end of his first season, in which he started five first-team games, the PFA's *Footballers' Factfile* described Gerrard as 'a youngster who might just go all the way'.

By the end of the following season Gerrard had his first goal (against Sheffield Wednesday), his first red card (against Everton), his first England cap (against Ukraine) and his first taste of senior tournament football as a substitute in the win over Germany at Euro 2000.

Also on this day

1993 After 20 years, Peter Swales stepped down as chairman of Manchester City.

2000 Liverpool won 8–0 at Stoke in the League Cup.

2001 Leeds signed Robbie Fowler from Liverpool for £11m.

2003 Blackburn manager Graeme Souness was sent off after accusing the referee of being a Tottenham fan. Blackburn beat Spurs 1–0.

2006 Fulham beat Arsenal for the first time in 40 years, 2–1 at Craven Cottage.

30 NOVEMBER
1999 – Manchester United: Intercontinental Champions

The Intercontinental Cup was designed to determine the best club side in the world – the champions of the South American Copa Libertadores competition taking on the winners of the European Cup. It was a tournament often dogged by foul play and the indifference of the European clubs that were due to take part.

In 1967 Celtic won the European Cup, and so became the first British side to play for the Intercontinental trophy. Playing against Argentina's Racing Club, Celtic won the first leg 1–0 in Glasgow only to lose the return in Argentina 2–1. With no away-goals rule, a play-off in Uruguay was arranged – a match that became known as 'The Battle of Montevideo'. Celtic lost 1–0 in a brutal game in which five players were sent off.

Manchester United represented Europe the following season, and lost to Estudiantes of Argentina 2–1 on aggregate. The following year the same Argentine club lost to AC Milan, but Milan's Argentine-born Néstor Combin was taken unconscious to hospital with a broken nose and cheekbone after being kicked and elbowed. Once in hospital he was arrested on charges of having avoided Argentine national service. Afterwards the Estudiantes goalkeeper Alberto Poletti was banned from football for life for kicking Combin in the face, Ramón Suárez was banned for 30 games and Eduardo Manera jailed for a month and banned for 20 games for their part in a disgraceful performance.

In both 1971 and 1973 European champions Ajax refused to play, with the beaten European Cup finalist taking their place. Bayern Munich followed suit in 1974, and in 1975 both the champions Bayern and runners-up Leeds declined to take part.

By the late 1970s when Liverpool (twice) and Nottingham Forest also refused to play, the competition seemed to have little future.

The cup was saved by the idea of playing a one-off match in neutral Japan. The first final in Tokyo saw Nottingham Forest lose to Nacional of Uruguay, in the second Liverpool were beaten by Brazil's Flamengo, in the third Aston Villa lost to Peñarol of Uruguay.

Liverpool's 1984 defeat to Argentina's Independiente was the last British involvement until 1999 when Roy Keane scored the only goal to win the cup for Manchester United against Palmeiras of Brazil.

United were the first and only British winners. The Intercontinental Cup was replaced, after 2004, by FIFA's Club World Cup.

Also on this day

1992 UEFA announce that England will host the 1996 European Championship.

1994 In his 600th game for Liverpool, Ian Rush scored a hat-trick in a 3–1 League Cup win at Blackburn.

2011 Steve Bruce was sacked by Sunderland.

December

1 DECEMBER
2002 – Shearer's Everton blast

If a player scores 409 senior goals for club and country, his best goal has to be something very special. Shearer himself rated the volley he scored at St James' Park against Everton in December 2002 as his best ever goal, and it was certainly special.

Newcastle had been beaten 5–3 by Manchester United the previous weekend and then lost 4–1 at Inter Milan in the Champions League. In contrast Everton, who were third in the table, had won their previous six Premier League matches, conceding only one goal in that time. They had also won at St James' in a thrilling League Cup tie that went to penalties after a 3–3 draw only three weeks earlier.

David Moyes's in-form side took the lead through Kevin Campbell, but were rocked when Joseph Yobo was sent off after only 20 minutes. Much of the next hour was spent with Newcastle hammering against a stubborn Everton wall of resistance. Their defence, marshalled by David Weir and Alan Stubbs, held firm until Shearer struck with six minutes to go.

The volley, from well outside the penalty area, was from a Shola Ameobi nod-down and ripped into the Everton net with such ferocity that Richard Wright had little chance to see it, let alone save it.

Asked to nominate his favourite goal, Shearer later said, 'I think that's the best in my career. I just remember a long ball and Shola heading it back to me. I could have taken another 500 of them in that position and not hit it as sweetly as that. I think 499 out of 500 might have gone into the top row of the Gallowgate End, but that day it went in the back of the net and it was a great feeling.'

Right arm raised in familiar celebration, Shearer sprinted away as St James' Park took a split second to register what he had just done before exploding into joy.

Two minutes from the end, Everton's Li Tie decided the game in Newcastle's favour, deflecting a Bellamy shot into his own net – but Shearer's goal had stolen the show.

Also on this day

1994 Vinnie Jones was called up by the country of his grandfather, Wales.

1995 James Wilson was born.

2013 Fulham sacked Martin Jol and appointed René Meulensteen as manager.

2 DECEMBER
2010 – The World Cup vote

The bidding process to host the 2018 World Cup Finals had formally begun early in 2009, with FIFA to announce the host nations of both the 2018 and 2022 Finals at the same congress in 2010.

Nine countries expressed an interest in hosting the 2018 Finals, but that quickly dwindled to four as it became clear that 2018 was destined for Europe and 2022 for either Asia, North America or Oceania. The four remaining 2018 candidates were England, Russia, a joint Netherlands/Belgium bid and another joint bid from Spain and Portugal.

After an internal bidding process, the FA identified 15 venues from which FIFA would select 12 host venues if England won the bid. Of these proposed venues, three were in London: Wembley, Arsenal's Emirates Stadium and either the Olympic Stadium or Tottenham's planned new ground. The other 12 were: Old Trafford, the City of Manchester Stadium, Elland Road, Hillsborough, the Stadium of Light, St James' Park, Villa Park, Anfield or Liverpool's proposed new ground in Stanley Park, Stadium MK in Milton Keynes, Home Park in Plymouth, and new builds in Bristol and Nottingham.

It was an ugly campaign tainted by accusations of corruption and vote-rigging. Two of the 24-person FIFA voting committee were suspended after being accused of offering their votes for sale.

Six months before the FIFA decision, the FA chairman and leader of the World Cup bid Lord Triesman resigned. He had been taped accusing Russia and Spain of plotting to bribe referees at the upcoming 2010 World Cup Finals.

Hoping to limit the damage, the bid team called on David Beckham, David Cameron and Prince William to charm and influence who they could.

After almost two years the furious lobbying, politicking, diplomacy, back-scratching and back-knifing neared its conclusion. In November, the leader of the Spain/Portugal bid, Miguel Ángel López, declared that he feared, 'All the fish is sold.' Nevertheless, the English bid-team travelled to Zürich hopeful of a positive outcome to show for a campaign that was estimated to have cost £19m.

Of the 22 votes, the FA's bid got 2 – one of them from Geoff Thompson, their own representative on the voting committee.

To some surprise, Russia won the right to host 2018. To most people's astonishment, 2022 went to Qatar. Doubts about the legitimacy of the process exploded in 2015 when senior FIFA officials were arrested as part of an FBI and Swiss police investigation into allegations of corruption.

Also on this day

2003 **Cesc Fàbregas became Arsenal's youngest ever scorer aged 16 years 212 days, beating a record set by Cliff**

Bastin. His goal came in Arsenal's 5–1 win over Wolves in the League Cup.

2004 Walter Smith was named as the new manager of Scotland.

2008 Manchester United's Cristiano Ronaldo followed in the footsteps of Denis Law, Bobby Charlton and George Best by winning the Ballon d'Or award as European Footballer of the Year.

3 DECEMBER
2005 – Redknapp quits Saints

Harry Redknapp once said, 'I didn't realize how much they dislike each other until I went there.' He was talking about Portsmouth and Southampton. Redknapp had been Portsmouth's manager between 2002 and 2004, successfully taking them into the Premier League for the first time in their history. Despite Redknapp's success, Portsmouth's owner Milan Mandarić wanted a director of football and appointed Croatian Velimir Zajec, ignoring Redknapp's objections.

True to his word, Redknapp resigned at the end of November and, despite assuring Portsmouth fans that they'd never see him 'down the road', he was appointed as struggling Southampton's manager two weeks later. The FA Cup tie between the two at the end of January was a heated affair, Redknapp's Southampton winning 2–1. Portsmouth got their revenge with a 4–1 win at Fratton Park in late April that helped to relegate Saints at the end of the season.

By now Redknapp knew all too well how much they disliked each other.

Back in the Championship for the 2005/06 season, Redknapp's Southampton had won only 5 of their first 20 games of the season. Meanwhile, under new manager Alain Perrin, Portsmouth had won only 2 of their first 13 in the Premier League.

The two club's fortunes were converging yet again.

Southampton chairman Rupert Lowe had taken the unusual step of appointing England's rugby union World Cup-winning coach Sir Clive Woodward as technical director. Redknapp insisted that he had no problem with that, but Woodward made no secret of his interest in becoming a football manager. Meanwhile, Portsmouth sacked Perrin.

When Portsmouth owner Milan Mandarić asked Southampton for permission to approach Redknapp about a return to Fratton Park, it was refused. But, just before a Southampton game against Burnley, Redknapp resigned. Four days later the managerial merry-go-round had him back at Portsmouth.

Redknapp said, 'It was a bad mistake to go to Southampton and that's not being disrespectful to them, but really I shouldn't have done it for the sake of the [Portsmouth] fans.'

Also on this day

1994 **A week after leaving Leicester to take over as manager of Aston Villa, Brian Little took his new club to play his old club at Filbert Street. Amid a chorus of boos, Little's side drew 1–1.**

2010 **Manchester City's Mario Balotelli and Jerome Boateng were photographed fighting during a training session.**

2011 **Martin O'Neill was appointed manager of Sunderland.**

4 DECEMBER
2013 – Sick as a canary

Norwich City must have felt they'd done something to upset Luis Suárez. Their first sight of the Uruguayan came at Anfield in October 2011, the game finished 1–1 and Suárez didn't have much influence – a good day all round for the Canaries.

The return game at Carrow Road in late April 2012 was different. Suárez scored all the goals in Liverpool's 3–0 win, the third a remarkable shot from only ten yards inside the Norwich half. It was his first hat-trick for Liverpool but, as Norwich would find out, there were more to come.

Suárez had started the 2012/13 season slowly, only three goals with the end of September in sight. A trip to Carrow Road got him going again. This time Liverpool won 5–2, Suárez scored three goals again and set up one for Nuri Şahin. Suárez only scored once in the next meeting, at Anfield in January 2013, but Liverpool still won 5–0.

In 2013/14 Suárez had nine goals from nine games when Norwich came to Anfield on 4 December. He made that 13 goals from ten games by scoring 4 in Liverpool's 5–1 win, taking his personal tally against Norwich to 11 goals in the last four games.

Norwich's manager Chris Hughton sounded like a master of understatement when he said, 'When he is on his day, Suárez is very difficult to handle. You just have to be very much on top of your own game and hope he doesn't have one of his better ones.'

Those four goals against Norwich sparked Suárez into a sensational run of form, scoring twice in each of Liverpool's next three games against West Ham, Spurs and Cardiff. Ten goals in four games – deciding who should be named the Premier League player of the month for December 2013 was not difficult.

Also on this day

1993 **Howard Kendall resigned to end his second spell in charge of Everton.**

1995 Dion Dublin scored a hat-trick for Coventry against Sheffield Wednesday, but finished on the losing side in a 4–3 defeat.

2000 Terry Venables was appointed as head coach at Middlesbrough to work alongside manager Bryan Robson.

2008 Roy Keane resigned as manager of Sunderland, leaving Ricky Sbragia to take charge.

2012 Manchester City's Champions League campaign finished with a defeat to Borussia Dortmund, leaving Roberto Mancini's side with only three points from six games.

5 DECEMBER
2000 – Eriksson 0 O'Leary 1

Lazio, who had won the European Cup Winners' Cup in 1999, had one of the most expensively assembled squads football had ever seen. Bankrolled by club president Sergio Cragnotti, Lazio had invested over £200m in new players in four seasons.

Managed by Sven-Göran Eriksson, who had just agreed to take over England at the end of the season, Lazio could call upon Marcelo Salas, Diego Simeone, Siniša Mihajlović, Pavel Nedvěd, Juan Sebastián Verón, Fernando Couto, Hernán Crespo and Fabrizio Ravanelli.

Their aim was to become Italian football's new powerhouse, breaking the cartel of Milan, Inter and Juventus.

Leeds were looking to do much the same in England. In a little over a season Leeds had signed Olivier Dacourt, Michael Bridges, Danny Mills, Darren Huckerby, Michael Duberry, Dominic Matteo, Jason Wilcox, Mark Viduka and Rio Ferdinand at a cost of around £60m.

With the two clubs seeming to have an almost unlimited supply of cash, it was not too fanciful to suggest that the Champions League meeting of Lazio and Leeds in Rome in December 2000 might be the first of many big clashes between two ambitious clubs.

Leeds played magnificently and refused to wilt, even though Lazio hit the bar and had another effort cleared off the line by Woodgate. Ten minutes from the end Mark Viduka back-heeled a pass to Alan Smith, who rifled home a winner.

After the game O'Leary proudly stressed his team's youthfulness: 'We rode our luck a little bit – but I thought overall we had the best chances and we took one of them. The team have got to learn: they are young people.'

Eriksson, whose team had already been beaten by Anderlecht in Brussels, found himself under intense pressure. When Lazio lost the Rome derby later in December the calls for Eriksson to leave became deafening. On 9 January

2001, he was released from his contract and replaced in Rome by Dino Zoff. The Swede started work at the FA the following day.

Also on this day

1993 Ross Barkley was born.

1996 Twenty-four hours after helping Rosenborg win 2–1 in the San Siro against AC Milan in the Champions League, Steffen Iversen signed for Spurs in a £2.5m deal.

2003 England, Wales and Northern Ireland were drawn together in the same qualifying group for the 2006 World Cup.

6 DECEMBER
1997 – Chelsea go with the Flo

Spurs had failed to beat Chelsea at White Hart Lane in over a decade, so this was always likely to be a tricky first home game in charge for Tottenham's new Swiss manager Christian Gross, but by the end of the game Gross must have been wondering what he'd let himself in for by moving to England.

With White Hart Lane being redeveloped, there were very few Chelsea fans in the crowd of 28,000. Gross came on the pitch and waved to the Tottenham fans before kick-off and then took his

place to watch an evenly matched first half. Chelsea's tall Norwegian striker Tore André Flo put Chelsea in front five minutes before half-time but Tottenham's defender and Gross's fellow-countryman Ramon Vega headed an equalizer just moments later.

To the manager's horror, Chelsea scored three goals in the first 20 minutes of the second half as the Spurs defence crumbled. Roberto Di Matteo's deflected effort had restored Chelsea's lead early in the second half before Dan Petrescu and Flo again made it 4–1 after an hour.

When Chelsea substitute Mark Nicholls scored his first ever goal to make it 5–1 with 12 minutes to go, Spurs fans started heading for the exits.

White Hart Lane was almost empty by the time Flo completed his hat-trick in the last minute with a delightful chip over Ian Walker.

It was Tottenham's heaviest home defeat since losing 6–0 to Arsenal in 1935, the first time Chelsea had ever scored six times against Spurs and Chelsea's biggest ever away win in a London derby.

Under Ruud Gullit's management Chelsea went on to win both the League Cup and Cup Winners' Cup that season. Spurs narrowly avoided relegation. Flo continued to be a regular scorer for Chelsea, despite never quite being a first-choice striker, until moving to Rangers in November 2000. His three goals at Spurs were his first, and only, Chelsea hat-trick.

Also on this day

1992 Éric Cantona made his Manchester United debut as a substitute in a 2–1 win over Manchester City at Old Trafford.

1999 Nottingham Forest were fined £25,000 by the FA for admitting illegal payments to players and staff between 1984 and 1993.

2010 Newcastle sacked Chris Hughton as manager.

2014 Arsenal fans shouted abuse at manager Arsène Wenger at Stoke railway station as the team travelled back to London after their 3–2 defeat at the Britannia Stadium.

7 DECEMBER
2013 – Misery for Moyes

David Moyes was the chosen one at Manchester United, picked by Sir Alex Ferguson to be his successor. Following in Ferguson's footsteps with a team that was past its best was never likely to be easy. After only four months it was looking virtually impossible.

Moyes had started well enough at United, winning the Community Shield and then trouncing Swansea 4–1 in South Wales in the opening game of the season. But an early defeat at Liverpool had been followed by a heavy loss against Manchester City, and by late September Moyes was already under pressure.

There had been some good days: a home win over Arsenal was swiftly followed by a 5–0 win in Germany against Bayer Leverkusen, but for every step forward there seemed to be two back.

Approaching the halfway point in the season United had dropped to ninth. Moyes must have been reeling when his former club Everton came to Old Trafford and won, something he had never achieved as Everton manager.

Four days later, on 7 December, Newcastle came to Old Trafford, where they had failed to win in over 40 years. The United boss went into the game aware that the club hadn't lost consecutive home games in 12 seasons.

Patrice Evra hit the post and Robin van Persie had a goal ruled out before Yohan Cabaye scored on the break for Newcastle, who won 1–0.

As he walked to the tunnel Moyes must have been impressed by the supportive reaction of the majority of United fans, but his belief that his side could still challenge for the Premier League title sounded hollow: 'I stand firm we will be very close. I hope we are in it at the end of the season.'

At the end of the season United were nowhere near retaining their title, and Moyes had already been sacked.

Also on this day

2002 Arsenal failed to score for the first time in 56 matches as they were beaten 2–0 at Manchester United.

2004 In his first season as Chelsea manager José Mourinho took his side to play his former club FC Porto in a Champions League group game – Porto won 2–1.

2005 Portsmouth confirmed Harry Redknapp as their new manager for his second spell at Fratton Park.

2011 Manchester United and Manchester City were both knocked out of the group stage of the Champions League. City went out despite a 2–0 home win over Bayern Munich, United were eliminated after losing 2–1 in Switzerland against FC Basel.

8 DECEMBER
2004 – Gerrard vs Olympiakos

'I don't want to wake up on Thursday morning in the UEFA Cup.'

So said Liverpool captain Steven Gerrard the day before their make-or-break final Champions League group game against Olympiakos.

Liverpool went into the last game in third place in the group, behind both Olympiakos and Monaco, both of whom had won their home games against Rafa Benítez's side. Liverpool had to win to go through, and they knew that if Olympiakos scored, they would have to win by two clear goals to finish above the Greeks.

Needing goals, but with striker Djibril Cissé out of action with a broken leg, Liverpool took a chance on the fitness of Milan Baroš, who had played only one game in over a month because of a hamstring injury. Liverpool's other strikers were 22-year-old Neil Mellor, who had just 14 first-team games and three goals on his Liverpool CV, or 20-year-old Florent Sinama Pongolle, who had three goals in 36 appearances, almost all as a substitute.

When Rivaldo fired home a free-kick after 26 minutes it seemed that being relegated to the UEFA Cup was exactly what was going to happen to Gerrard and Liverpool.

At half-time Benítez took off his left back Djimi Traoré and put on Sinama Pongolle. The young French striker scored within two minutes, tapping a Harry Kewell cross into the Olympiakos net at the Kop end and giving the home side hope.

Thirty minutes later Baroš finally ran out of energy. Needing two more goals, Liverpool had to replace their senior fit striker with Neil Mellor. Again the substitution worked almost immediately: Sinama Pongolle crossed, Antonio Núñez saw his header saved, but Mellor gleefully thumped home the rebound. Liverpool had ten minutes to score again.

With just four minutes left, and Liverpool pouring forward, Jamie Carragher crossed to Mellor standing with his back to goal on the edge of the Olympiakos penalty area. Mellor cushioned a header perfectly into the path of Steven Gerrard, who hit a half-volley that kept low and swerved away from the diving Nikopolidis into the corner of the net.

The next morning Gerrard woke up knowing that he'd kept Liverpool in the Champions League.

Also on this day

1993 Highbury was dropped as a venue for Euro 96 because the pitch was 4 metres too short. Nottingham Forest's City Ground was used instead.

1994 Raheem Sterling was born.

1996 Wimbledon defender John Scales had a last-minute change of heart and joined Liverpool rather than Leeds for £2m.

1998 David Batty signed for Leeds from Newcastle for £4.4m.

9 DECEMBER
1994 – Tottenham's spoonful of Sugar

In June 1994, having narrowly avoided relegation, Tottenham faced an FA commission charged with financial irregularities. These related to payments made to players before Alan Sugar had taken control at White Hart Lane.

Spurs had admitted that payments had been made to three players – Chris Fairclough, Paul Allen and Mitchell Thomas – before a transfer fee payable to the respective selling clubs had been fixed by a tribunal.

A transfer tribunal was used to establish a player's worth when the two clubs couldn't agree on a fee. A player's salary was a determining factor in establishing the size of the transfer fee, but Tottenham had kept these payments to players secret, so the tribunal was likely to have set a lower fee than might otherwise have been the case.

Tottenham pleaded guilty and hoped for leniency. They didn't get it. The FA fined them £600,000, banned them from the following season's FA Cup and deducted them 12 points – a move that it seemed might well condemn Tottenham to relegation the following season.

Chairman Alan Sugar accused the FA of having a personal vendetta against him because of his ongoing court battle with the England manager Terry Venables.

Midfielder David Howells described it as 'slow torture'.

Tottenham appealed on the grounds that the current owners were being punished for the previous regime's actions. In early July the points deduction was reduced from 12 to 6, but the fine was increased to £1.5m.

Encouraged, Alan Sugar decided to continue to fight the punishment. In December the investigating tribunal agreed that the deduction of points and FA Cup ban were unreasonably harsh. Sugar was the toast of Tottenham as both penalties were lifted completely.

Also on this day

2000 Tottenham's Ledley King scored the fastest ever goal in the Premier League, finding the net after 9.7 seconds of their 3–3 draw at Bradford City.

2003 Ruud van Nistelrooy equalled Denis Law's European goalscoring record for Manchester United, his 28th goal coming in a 2–0 win over Stuttgart.

2010 Alan Pardew was appointed the new manager of Newcastle United.

2012 Robin van Persie scored an injury-time winner for Manchester United in their 3–2 win at Manchester City, the club he had rejected in order to move to Old Trafford.

10 DECEMBER
2000 – The rise of Ipswich Town

Ipswich Town had produced two great England managers who, prior to leading their country in World Cups, had led the club to two memorable successes.

During his eight years at Portman Road, Sir Alf Ramsey's Ipswich were promoted to the top flight in 1961 and promptly crowned champions of England a year later. Sir Bobby Robson's reign at Ipswich lasted 13 years, during which time they won the 1978 FA Cup, the UEFA Cup in 1981 and twice finished as runners-up in the title race.

Ipswich hoped they had found another gem when George Burley was appointed manager in December 1994. But Burley had been unable to save the club from relegation out of the Premier League in 1995 and Ipswich spent the next five seasons trying to get back up to the top flight. They finally achieved promotion via the play-offs in 2000.

Their first season back was nothing short of sensational. It didn't start too well; Ipswich took only four points from their first five games. A 2–1 win at Leeds in mid-September started a six-game unbeaten run in the league, during which Arsenal were also defeated in the League Cup.

When Burley took his team to Anfield in December 2000, Ipswich were sixth in the table, one place behind Liverpool but only on goal difference.

Ipswich outplayed Gérard Houllier's side and thoroughly deserved their 1–0 win, secured by a brilliant goal from Marcus Stewart, his tenth of the season.

With Richard Wright in goal, the emerging Titus Bramble in defence alongside Hermann Hreidarsson, Matt Holland and Jim Magilton tireless in midfield and Stewart providing the cutting edge in attack, Ipswich left Anfield cock-a-hoop and with only Manchester United and Arsenal above them in the table.

'We were playing against one of the big teams with world-class players and we won because we had 100 per cent commitment,' said a delighted Burley.

Ipswich went on to finish fifth in the Premier League, only missing out on a Champions League place when they drew at Derby on the final day of the season. Nevertheless they had qualified for the UEFA Cup and also reached the semi-finals of the League Cup. Burley's stellar season was recognized by the League Managers' Association, who voted him Manager of the Year.

Also on this day

1994 Goal of the Season – Matt Le Tissier scored it for Southampton against Blackburn at Ewood Park.

2005 After taking just one point from their first seven home league games of the season, Birmingham City beat Fulham 1–0 at St Andrew's with a goal from Nicky Butt.

11 DECEMBER
2004 – Rafa's Goodison welcome

There's no doubt that Rafa Benítez would have been accustomed to some intense atmospheres during his management career in Spain. His old home stadium, Valencia's Mestalla, could be extremely hostile to the opposition and Benítez had run the gauntlet of both the Bernabéu and the Nou Camp. However, the noise of Goodison Park and the intensity of his first Merseyside derby seemed to take the new Liverpool boss by surprise.

The game came just three days after Liverpool's monumental efforts to beat Olympiakos in the Champions League, and three days before a home game against Portsmouth. A busy diary, certainly, but even so Benítez stunned Liverpool fans with his team selection – they feared he had misjudged the occasion by resting Xabi Alonso and Steve Finnan.

In a bear-pit of an atmosphere Evertonians licked their lips at the prospect of showing Benítez what the fixture was all about.

The first 20 minutes were frantic, aggressive and noisy; typical derby football. Tim Cahill missed the first big chance, a close-range header from Marcus Bent's cross. At the other end Nigel Martyn saved a Neil Mellor header from point-blank range.

The only goal came midway through the second half; Lee Carsley was the unlikely scorer, wrong-footing Liverpool goalkeeper Chris Kirkland from outside the box.

Kirkland, who had been battling with Jerzy Dudek to be Liverpool's first-choice goalkeeper, never played for Liverpool again.

It was David Moyes's first derby win and a first Everton win over Liverpool since 1999. The victory took Everton to second in the table, 12 points and five places above their neighbours.

Delighted Everton fans had a new name for Liverpool's Spanish manager – 'Rafa Beneath-us'.

Also on this day

2002 Bobby Robson took his Newcastle team to face his former club Barcelona in the Nou Camp; they were beaten 3–1 in the Champions League match.

2006 Alan Pardew was sacked by West Ham only months after leading them to the FA Cup Final.

2010 Having fallen out with Roberto Mancini, Carlos Tévez asked for a transfer from Manchester City.

2014 A 2–0 win in Rome secured Manchester City's place in the last 16 of the Champions League.

12 DECEMBER
2002 – Leeds ... over and out

Leeds United were one of the first successful English sides in Europe. Under Don Revie they embraced the challenge of playing on the continent, and their first three campaigns in Europe were all successful. Leeds were Fairs Cup semi-finalists in 1966, beaten finalists in 1967 and winners in 1968 (when they were the scourge of Scotland, beating Hibs, Rangers and Dundee in successive rounds).

Revie's side were then European Cup semi-finalists in 1970 – losing to Celtic – and Fairs Cup winners for the second time in 1971.

Two more European final defeats followed as Leeds became the 'nearly men' of the early and mid-1970s. They were beaten by AC Milan in the 1973 Cup Winners' Cup Final and by Bayern Munich in the 1975 European Cup Final.

At that match against Bayern in Paris, Leeds fans had rioted after a Peter Lorimer goal had been controversially ruled out.

The hooliganism that blighted the rest of the game earned Leeds a four-year European ban, reduced to two on appeal.

Huge investment in the club catapulted David O'Leary's Leeds side back to the forefront of Europe in the late 1990s. They were UEFA Cup semi-finalists in 2000 and reached the same stage of the Champions League the following season.

In 2002/03 Leeds, now managed by Terry Venables, were in the UEFA Cup and reached the third round, where they were drawn against Málaga. A 0–0 draw in Spain looked a good result for Leeds, but the second leg at Elland Road was to be memorable for all the wrong reasons.

First Michael Bridges ruptured his Achilles after only seven minutes. Then Málaga took the lead through their Panamanian Julio Dely Valdés.

Just moments later Lee Bowyer kicked out at Málaga's Gerardo and then stamped disgracefully on Gerardo's head when he was on the ground. The referee didn't see the stamp, and Bowyer was only booked.

Eirik Bakke equalized for Leeds, but the game descended into a bad-tempered scrap with both sides guilty of persistent fouling. With Leeds pushing for a second goal, Málaga sealed the tie when Dely Valdés scored again with ten minutes to go.

UEFA studied the video of Bowyer's stamp and banned him for six European matches. That ban never troubled Leeds, though. The match against Málaga was their 149th and, to date, last in European competition.

Also on this day

2001 The 20 Premier League chairmen voted unanimously against allowing Celtic and Rangers to join the Premier League. The issue was raised again, with the same result, eight years later.

2009 Goal of the Season – Maynor Figueroa scored it for Wigan against Stoke at the Britannia Stadium with a shot from a direct free-kick measured at 88 metres.

13 DECEMBER
2010 – Allardyce sacked, Kean in at Rovers

When Blackburn Rovers were bought in November 2010 by the Venky's Group, owned by brothers Balaji and Venkatesh Rao, Venky's chairman Anuradha J. Desai had said, 'We will absolutely respect the Jack Walker legacy and will be actively supporting the organization to ensure that Blackburn Rovers remains one of the best-run clubs within the Premier League.'

Desai had also stated her support for manager Sam Allardyce, saying at the end of November, 'We want results and

Sam has taken up the challenge. He deserves a chance.'

Unfortunately for Allardyce, Blackburn were beaten 7–1 at Manchester United the day after that rather half-hearted message. A win over Wolves and a narrow defeat at Bolton followed, leaving Blackburn 13th in the table, but only three points off 7th place. It was nowhere near enough for the ambitious Rao family, and Allardyce was sacked.

'We want good football and Blackburn to be fourth or fifth in the league or even better,' Desai told the *Lancashire Telegraph*. 'The fans should trust us because this is in the best interests of the club.'

Coach Steve Kean was put in charge, and soon Desai was talking about bringing in big names in the January transfer window. Ronaldinho was offered the chance to go to Ewood Park on a three-year deal worth £20m; David Beckham, said Desai, could join 'whenever he is ready to come'.

In reality Blackburn brought back their former striker Roque Santa Cruz on loan from Manchester City (he played nine times without scoring), Mauro Formica for £4m from Newell's Old Boys (deemed only to be good enough for the reserves until the following season), Rubén Rochina from Barcelona's B team (one start and three substitute appearances) and Jermaine Jones on loan from Schalke 04 (15 games and eight yellow cards).

Rovers won only 2 of their last 14 games, but avoided relegation on the last day of the season with a win at Wolves.

Twelve months later they were relegated, to a backdrop of bitter supporters' protests – losing eight of their last nine games in the Premier League.

Also on this day

1995 The Republic of Ireland failed to qualify for Euro 96 at the final hurdle, losing to the Netherlands in a play-off at Anfield. Patrick Kluivert scored both goals.

2006 Former West Ham player Alan Curbishley was appointed manager at Upton Park.

14 DECEMBER
2007 – Capello for England

When the FA were looking for a new England manager after the failure of Steve McLaren, they chose someone as little like his predecessor as possible.

McLaren had been English, relatively young, and a manager who enjoyed being on familiar terms with his squad. For McLaren John Terry was 'JT', Steven Gerrard was 'Stevie G', and Beckham 'Becks'. McLaren enjoyed being part of the dressing room, part of the banter.

Fabio Capello was Italian (and initially spoke very little English), he was 61 and he had no interest whatsoever in being the players' friend. Peter Crouch later said, 'He's got an aura about him. When he walks into a room everyone sits up and takes notice.'

Having managed at the top level in Italy and Spain, Capello certainly didn't sound in awe of the reputation of some of the English players he'd now be coaching. Asked to assess the qualities of England's team Capello said, 'This is my toughest job. Absolutely, I can't perform miracles. These are the players we have, and I can only call up the players we have.'

Capello, who said the England job would be his last before retirement, was taking a first step into international management but had a litany of titles from his club coaching career, which had taken him to AC Milan, Real Madrid, Roma and Juventus. He'd won the Champions League, the Italian league five times, the Spanish league twice and the Italian Cup three times.

Capello had to wait almost three months for his first match in charge of England. It was an anxious 2–1 win over Switzerland in a friendly at Wembley. Perhaps because of the manager's reputation as a disciplinarian, the England players seemed nervous of making mistakes. Asked about the England players' apparent fear of upsetting him, the steely-eyed Capello said, 'I never hit anyone, so I don't see why they should be scared.'

Also on this day

1996 Robbie Fowler scored four times in a 5–1 win against Middlesbrough, taking his Liverpool goal tally to 100 in 165 games, one game fewer than Ian Rush took to reach the same landmark.

2010 Gary Speed was appointed manager of Wales.

2013 Steve Clarke was sacked by West Bromwich Albion within hours of a 1–0 defeat at Cardiff City.

2013 Manchester City beat Arsenal 6–3 at the Etihad Stadium.

15 DECEMBER
1995 – Bosman's European win

Jean-Marc Bosman, a journeyman professional in Belgium and France, became one of the world's most famous players when he changed European football and its transfer system.

In June 1990 Bosman, on the fringes of the first team at FC Liège in Belgium, had the offer of a transfer to USL Dunkerque in France. Even though Bosman's contract had expired the Belgian club refused to let him leave without a transfer fee of £500,000, which Dunkerque couldn't afford to pay. When the deal collapsed Liège cut his wages by more than 50 per cent to £500 a month.

In August 1990, with no chance of playing for Liège but still unable to leave, Bosman decided to go to court to seek damages and the freedom to find himself a new club.

It took more than five years before the European Court of Justice found in his favour in December 1995. The ruling changed the landscape for all future transfers, allowing a player to run down his contract at one club and join another without a transfer fee being paid.

It's a ruling that has made some of the world's highest-profile footballers even richer, allowing them to demand higher signing-on fees and salaries from the clubs who are acquiring them. It hardly benefited Bosman at all.

In the five years that Bosman and the Belgian FA were battling in court, Bosman had played a few games in the French lower leagues but by 1995 his career was effectively over and he was bankrupt.

In 1998 Bosman was awarded around £300,000 in damages from the Belgian FA, but struggled to keep his life on track. In 2011, suffering from alcoholism and depression, he was sentenced to a year in jail for assault.

Also on this day

1999 West Ham beat Aston Villa 5–4 in a penalty shoot-out after a 2–2 draw in the League Cup quarter-final at Upton Park. The match was declared void because West Ham had brought on substitute Manny Omoyinmi with seven minutes to go. Omoyinmi hadn't told West Ham that he was ineligible, having played for Gillingham earlier in the competition. Aston Villa won the replayed game 3–1; Omoyinmi never played for West Ham again.

2005 Having left Manchester United, Roy Keane joined Celtic.

2011 Mario Balotelli was pictured appararently fighting with Micah Richards at Manchester City's training ground.

2012 Christian Benteke scored twice as Aston Villa won 3–1 at Liverpool.

16 DECEMBER
2000 – Di Canio's sporting chance

Paolo Di Canio was a player with a reputation. Extravagantly talented but temperamental, Di Canio had served an 11-game ban from football for pushing referee Paul Alcock when he was playing for Sheffield Wednesday.

Two years later, Di Canio was with West Ham. The Italian had become a firm favourite in east London with 18 goals in his first season, and looked on course to match that total in the following campaign. When West Ham travelled to Goodison Park in December, Di Canio was by far their top scorer on eight goals.

Everton took the lead with 15 minutes to go through Danny Cadamarteri, only for Freddie Kanouté to score a West Ham equalizer 8 minutes later.

With time running out, Everton's goalkeeper Paul Gerrard rushed from his goal intending to cut out a dangerous pass, only to crumple to the ground in agony. With the goalkeeper injured and out of his goal, the ball was crossed to Di Canio. He was standing on the edge of the penalty area with defenders rushing to block the Italian's route to goal. Those defenders were thanking him when, rather than attempt to score, Di Canio caught the ball and waved for the Everton physio to come on for the stricken Gerrard.

The response of the Everton crowd was to give Di Canio a standing ovation. Afterwards the West Ham striker said, 'I am not a saint, just like I wasn't a killer two years ago with the referee when I did something wrong. During the game, the opposition is my enemy. But when they are injured, they are my colleagues.'

The following week FIFA wrote to thank Di Canio, and in 2001 his action earned him their Fair Play Award with Sepp Blatter saying, 'Gestures like this are all too rare in football, especially at the professional level.'

West Ham would have gone into sixth place in the Premier League had Di Canio taken the opportunity to score. Afterwards his manager Harry Redknapp said, 'It was the most fantastic bit of sportsmanship I have ever seen, but I didn't know whether to laugh or cry.'

Also on this day

2008 Paul Ince was sacked as manager of Blackburn Rovers.

2012 Chelsea lost the final of the FIFA Club World Cup, 1–0 to Brazilian club Corinthians.

2013 Three days after losing 5–0 at home to Liverpool, André Villas-Boas was sacked by Tottenham Hotspur.

2014 Aged 37 and playing for New York Red Bulls, Thierry Henry announced his retirement from football.

17 DECEMBER
2001 – Michael Owen, Europe's best

Only five British players had ever been voted European Footballer of the Year: they were Stanley Matthews in 1956, Denis Law in 1964, Bobby Charlton in 1966, George Best in 1968 and Kevin Keegan in 1978 and 1979.

Kenny Dalglish (second to Michel Platini), Gary Lineker (to Igor Belanov) and David Beckham (to Rivaldo) had all been runners-up, but there had been no British winner in 22 years. Then, in 2001, just three days after his 22nd birthday, Michael Owen was voted Europe's best player.

2001, arguably Owen's finest calendar year, began in low-key circumstances. Working his way back' from injury, he was introduced as a substitute on New Year's Day as Liverpool narrowly beat Southampton at Anfield.

His first goals of the year didn't come until mid-February when he scored both in a 2–0 win over Roma in the UEFA Cup, but fitness worries meant he was only on the bench for the League Cup Final win over Birmingham City.

But Owen went on to score both goals against Arsenal as Liverpool won the 2001 FA Cup Final. Four days later he played as Liverpool won the UEFA Cup Final against Alavés. In August he scored in the Charity Shield win over Manchester United and in the European Super Cup win against Bayern Munich. He also scored 18 Premier League goals in the year as Liverpool qualified for the Champions League, and he added 6 England goals to his tally, including a stunning hat-trick against Germany in Munich.

When he won the award, with Raúl second and Oliver Kahn in third place, Owen said, 'I couldn't believe it when I was first told about it. I knew I was one of the players in question but it still seems unbelievable to me.'

Also on this day

1995 The draw for the group stages of the 1996 European Championship Finals as made in Birmingham. England were drawn in the same group as Scotland.

1999 Derby broke their transfer record with a £3m move for Branko Strupar from Genk.

2000 Manchester United lost a Premier League match at home for the first time in almost two years, Danny Murphy's free-kick giving Liverpool a 1–0 win.

2007 Despite both the England men's and women's teams qualifying, it was announced that Great Britain would not send football teams to compete at the Beijing Olympics.

2008 Sam Allardyce was appointed manager of Blackburn.

18 DECEMBER
2001 – Newcastle end their capital jinx

According to the AA, it's almost 300 miles from the Tyne Bridge to Trafalgar Square. From 29 November 1997 to 18 December 2001, Newcastle United played 29 games in London without ever having a win to celebrate on the long way home.

In those four years there were three defeats and a draw at Arsenal, three defeats and two draws at Chelsea, four defeats and one draw at Spurs, four defeats at West Ham, a defeat and two draws at Charlton, a defeat at Fulham, a defeat and two draws at Wimbledon

and a draw at Leyton Orient. They also lost three times at Wembley: first to Manchester United and Arsenal in successive FA Cup Finals, and then to Chelsea in an FA Cup semi-final.

The win at Crystal Palace back in 1997 must have seemed a long time ago when those faithful Geordie fans headed south again to watch their team play at Highbury in late 2001.

Newcastle fell behind to a Robert Pirès goal after 20 minutes and it seemed as though it would be business as usual for Newcastle in London, until Ray Parlour was sent off just before half-time.

Andy O'Brien scored an equalizer after an hour with a near-post header, but then Craig Bellamy got a red card from Graham Poll to even the numbers at ten men each.

With four minutes to go Sol Campbell brought down Laurent Robert and Alan Shearer kept his composure to score the penalty, his first ever goal at Highbury.

Robert broke clear in the last minute to seal the win and put Newcastle top of the Premier League. Six weeks later Newcastle won in London again, this time at Spurs. However, their defeat to Newcastle was the last league match Arsenal lost that season, and they won the title, with Newcastle finishing fourth.

Also on this day

1994 Scotland's hopes of qualifying for Euro 96 were damaged by a 1–0 defeat to Greece in Athens.

2000 After seeing his team held at home by Arsenal, Spurs chairman Alan Sugar confirmed his intention to sell the club, ending his ten years at the helm.

2005 Liverpool lost the final of the FIFA Club World Cup 1–0 to São Paulo, ending a club record run of 11 consecutive games without conceding a goal.

2014 Having failed to win at White Hart Lane for 14 years, West Ham completed their second win on Tottenham's ground in the space of ten weeks. Sam Allardyce's side, who had won a league game at Spurs 3–0 in October, won 2–1 in the League Cup quarter-final.

19 DECEMBER
2009 – Mancini in at City

Mark Hughes knew the morning papers were right. Manchester City had lost 3–0 at Spurs in midweek, and that had been the final straw. Roberto Mancini would be in the crowd at the Etihad Stadium that Saturday afternoon watching Manchester City take on Sunderland. Hughes knew that once the game was over, so was his time in charge.

The game was a thriller, City winning 4–3 after blowing both a 2–0 and 3–2 lead. Hughes's side had beaten Chelsea just two weeks before and were through to the semi-finals of the League Cup. His team had been together only a few weeks, with new faces Tévez, Lescott, Santa Cruz, Adebayor and Kolo Touré getting accustomed to their surroundings – record signing Robinho had hardly played after three months of injury.

But for City's Sheikh Mansour there were no excuses for a run of one win, eight draws and one defeat from ten games, which had seen them drop to sixth in the Premier League table.

At full-time, Mark Hughes hugged each of his players in turn and waved to the crowd. Two hours after the end of the game the club issued a statement saying, 'Manchester City Football Club can confirm the appointment, with immediate effect on a permanent contract, of Roberto Mancini … a hugely experienced manager with a proven track record of winning trophies and championships.'

Mancini, who had made four playing appearances for Leicester City in 2001, had eight years' experience managing in Italy with Fiorentina, Lazio and Inter

Milan, and there was no questioning his record of seven major domestic trophies.

There was a lot of sympathy for Hughes, who suspected that Mancini had been waiting in the wings for some weeks.

City's chief executive Garry Cook denied that, saying, 'It's important to know that Mancini was only offered the job after the Spurs game.' But Mancini himself let slip that, 'Two weeks before the Spurs game I had met chairman Khaldoon Al Mubarak ...'

The morning papers had been right.

Also on this day

1992 **Liverpool suffered their worst defeat for 16 years, losing 5–1 at Coventry.**

1992 **Éric Cantona scored his first Manchester United goal, in a 1–1 draw against Chelsea.**

1996 **Manager Frank Clark resigned at Nottingham Forest; 34-year-old Stuart Pearce became player/caretaker manager.**

20 DECEMBER
1996 – Middlesbrough caught cold

Bryan Robson's Middlesbrough were 16th in the Premier League and struggling. They'd just been beaten 5–1 at Liverpool, a match they'd played without the injured Juninho, Steve Vickers, Curtis Fleming, Nigel Pearson and Alan Moore.

When more of Robson's first-team squad starting calling in with flu, Robson reckoned he was without 23 players and Middlesbrough said they would not be travelling to play Blackburn the following day.

Blackburn's caretaker manager at the time was Tony Parkes, who later recalled, 'One of the players had gone home and he phoned me up and said he'd seen on Sky Sports that Middlesbrough weren't going to turn up because they had flu. I'd never heard of anything like that happening in football. I phoned the Premier League. They didn't believe me. They said they'll have to come, they'll bring the youth team. That was the first the Premier League had heard of it, too.'

But they didn't take a youth team – they called the game off, prompting a Premier League investigation. Middlesbrough's Fabrizio Ravanelli was asked by an Italian newspaper what he thought would happen. 'I reckon we will be relegated,' said the striker. 'I went to the training camp but everything was locked up. We have hardly any hope of salvation and they gave us three days off. The situation, I'm afraid, is truly tragic.'

Three weeks later the Premier League fined Middlesbrough £50,000 and docked them three points. By then Boro were already bottom of the table and they were suddenly four points behind the rest.

When the game was finally played, on 8 May 1997, Middlesbrough were one place off the bottom of the table and Blackburn were in 15th place. It was a 0–0 draw, which meant that with one game left to play Blackburn were safe, but Middlesbrough needed to win at Leeds in their last match to have any chance of staying up.

Middlesbrough drew at Leeds and were relegated. The points they were deducted would have been enough to keep them up.

Also on this day

1993 Fearing it might spark hooliganism, the German and English Football Associations reconsidered their plan to play a friendly in Hamburg on 20 April 1994 when they realized it was the anniversary of Adolf Hitler's birth.

2000 Leeds won the race to sign Robbie Keane on loan from Inter Milan with an option to buy the following season.

2007 Everton's 3–2 win at AZ Alkmaar in the UEFA Cup ended the Dutch club's 32-match unbeaten run on home soil.

2011 Luis Suárez was banned for eight games and fined £40,000 after being found guilty of racially abusing Patrice Evra.

21 DECEMBER
1995 – Farewell, Jack, a manager in a million

It wasn't the first time an Englishman had left a job as an international manager having failed to qualify for a major tournament, and it wasn't the last – but never before can a manager have left, after such a disappointment, with the plaudits and cheers of a nation ringing in his ears so loudly.

When Jack Charlton resigned as manager of the Republic of Ireland they had just lost to the Dutch in a play-off for the finals of Euro 96. It was his 93rd game in a reign lasting a decade.

'Big Jack' took over in December 1985. Ireland had produced some great players in the past – for example, Noel Cantwell, Johnny Giles, Liam Brady and Frank Stapleton – but they were a nation that had never seen their national team qualify for a major finals.

Charlton soon put that right, developing a strategy based on the athleticism and strength of the British leagues in which most of his squad played. Charlton also embraced those who, like Mick McCarthy, Ray Houghton, Chris Hughton and John Aldridge, qualified to play for Ireland through their parents and grandparents, successfully integrating them into his team.

The Irish not only qualified for the 1988 European Championship, they beat England in Stuttgart with a Ray

Houghton header. They were unfortunate not to reach the semi-finals after a narrow defeat to Netherlands.

Two years later in Italia 90 Charlton demonstrated that it was no fluke. Their opening game was against England again; it finished 1–1 in Cagliari. Further draws with Egypt and the Netherlands put them through to the last 16, where they beat Romania on penalties. After four games, and without winning any of them, Ireland played a World Cup quarter-final against the hosts Italy, only to lose 1–0 in Rome.

Revenge in the 1994 World Cup was sweet. Ray Houghton was the match-winner again as they beat Italy in New York. Their game in the last 16, against the Dutch in the heat of Orlando, proved a step too far.

In winning the World Cup with England, Charlton had achieved the ultimate prize as a player. As the manager of the Republic of Ireland, Charlton had surpassed all his predecessors and all expectations.

Louis Kilcoyne, president of the FAI, paid tribute: 'The people of Ireland owe Jack a huge debt of gratitude for all he has done for football and the country. Thanks, Jack, you have been a manager in a million.'

Also on this day

2001 Nicolas Anelka joined Liverpool on loan from Paris Saint-Germain.

2003 In the first ever Premier League south-coast derby, Southampton beat Portsmouth 3–0 at St Mary's.

2007 Lawrie Sanchez was sacked by Fulham.

2008 Manchester United became the first English winners of the FIFA Club World Cup with a 1–0 win over Ecuador's Liga de Quito, despite a red card for Nemanja Vidić.

22 DECEMBER
1997 – Klinsmann: take two

When Jürgen Klinsmann left Spurs for Bayern Munich after one gloriously eventful season, Spurs fans, and Tottenham's chairman Alan Sugar, were distraught. His 29 goals had taken Tottenham to the brink of the FA Cup Final and made them one of the teams to watch in 1994/95.

Claiming breach of contract, Sugar had unsuccessfully tried to get FIFA to prevent Klinsmann from playing for Bayern. The German hit back, saying, 'There is a big question over whether his heart is in the club and football. I wouldn't have wanted to leave Spurs if Sugar had shown more ambition.'

With Klinsmann in Germany, Sugar had to concede defeat – but not before having the final word. Brandishing a

Tottenham shirt signed by the German, he told a TV audience, 'He signed it, "To Alan, with a very special thank you". I'm bloody sure it was a special thank you, I'm the blooming mug that relaunched his career. I wouldn't wash my car with that shirt now.'

So it was something of a surprise when, in December 1997, Klinsmann returned to play for Sugar's Spurs, on a six-month contract, after a brief spell at Sampdoria.

With Christian Gross just a month into his spell as manager, Spurs were struggling. Introducing Klinsmann and Pleat to the press, Sugar was inevitably asked about his old row with the German striker: 'It was a long time ago and it's all water under the bridge now. It was all down to my naivety at the time. In other businesses we don't have contracts on things like that, we have handshakes. I was wrong but I can't keep continually eating humble pie.'

In his six months back at White Hart Lane, Klinsmann gave Spurs and Alan Sugar exactly what they wanted – nine goals in 18 games, which kept them up.

Also on this day

1996 Wimbledon, whose 14-match unbeaten run had taken them to third in the Premier League, were beaten 5–0 at Aston Villa.

1999 Newcastle beat Spurs 6–1 in an FA Cup third-round replay at St James' Park, Tottenham's heaviest ever FA Cup defeat.

2010 Caretaker boss Steve Kean was confirmed as Blackburn's full-time manager.

23 DECEMBER
2012 – A Bridge too far for Villa

Paul Lambert had just pulled off the two most significant results in his six months as manager of Aston Villa. First he had won 4–1 at his former club Norwich on his first return to Carrow Road since his bitter departure earlier in the year. That win had booked Villa a League Cup semi-final against Bradford City – a tie they would be red-hot favourites to win.

Then Lambert had taken his side to Anfield, where they beat Liverpool 3–1. After a rocky start it seemed that Villa were surging up the table and heading to Wembley. Unsurprisingly, Lambert picked the same Villa team that had won at Anfield to take on Rafa Benítez and Chelsea at Stamford Bridge.

The Blues had only just returned from losing the Club World Cup Final to Corinthians in Yokohama and Benítez, unpopular for his Liverpool connections and described as Chelsea's 'interim manager', was subject to weekly protests from his own fans. There was reason to believe that Villa might even repeat their Stamford Bridge win of almost exactly 12 months earlier.

In fact Chelsea ran riot. The suspicion that Benítez had the key to the enigma that was Fernando Torres was increased when the Spanish striker scored after three minutes, his seventh goal in nine games under Benítez. David Luiz and Branislav Ivanović added further goals before half-time.

Frank Lampard, starting a Premier League match for the 500th time, smashed in a fourth, Ramires a fifth and Oscar a sixth with a penalty.

Poor Villa, beaten 7–1 at the same stadium two years earlier, still had 11 minutes to play. Ramires added a seventh and, in added time, Eden Hazard made it 8–0.

'We got beaten up pretty badly all over the pitch,' said the honest Lambert.

It was only the second time in the Premier League that seven players had scored in the same match, and it was Aston Villa's heaviest defeat in their 138-year history. There was more misery ahead when they lost the League Cup tie to Bradford too.

Also on this day

1995 Newcastle beat Nottingham Forest 3–1, their tenth successive victory, to go ten points clear at the top of the Premier League.

1997 Coventry City broke their transfer record with a £3.25m deal for Romanian Viorel Moldovan from Grasshopper Zürich.

2009 Craig Levein was appointed manager of Scotland, replacing George Burley.

2013 After two games as caretaker manager, Tim Sherwood was named as manager of Spurs.

24 DECEMBER
2006 – Reed all about it

Charlton had become the model of a well-run medium-sized club, held up as an example to others of how to progress and build at a sustainable pace. They were an oasis of stability and common sense in the mad, ever-shifting world of Premier League football.

Alan Curbishley had made the leap from Charlton player to manager, initially with Steve Gritt alongside. In 15 years at the helm, Curbishley had helped lead them out of exile and back to the Valley Stadium, which had been closed for seven years. He had guided them into the Premier League, bounced back from relegation, and then stayed in the top flight for six seasons. Steadiness personified, Curbishley's side had finished no lower than 14th and no higher than 7th in those half-dozen years.

Inevitably, Curbishley had been linked with other jobs. He was shortlisted by the FA for the England manager's position in April 2006, and while waiting to see if he'd got the job, decided he wouldn't renew his contract at Charlton when it expired at the end of the season. 'This has nothing to do with England,' said Curbishley. 'It's a time of mixed emotions, but it is the right time for me and right for the club.'

Iain Dowie took over at Charlton in the summer of 2006, just as Steve McLaren – not Curbishley – was being appointed England manager.

Where Curbishley had lasted 15 years, Dowie lasted 12 league games – of which Charlton won 2. Panicking at the bottom of the table, Charlton sacked Dowie and appointed Les Reed, the former FA technical director, who had been Dowie's assistant.

Where Dowie had lasted 12 league games, Reed lasted 7, of which Charlton won one. When he was sacked on Christmas Eve 2006, Les Reed's time in charge was the shortest of any Premier League manager – just 41 days.

Alan Pardew took over as manager but wasn't able to save Charlton from relegation at the end of the season and, to date, they have never been back in the Premier League.

Also on this day

1993 The FA decided not to charge Wimbledon's John Fashanu for the challenge which left Spurs Gary Mabbutt with four fractures of the cheekbone and three of the eye socket.

1999 Bill Kenwright won control of Everton, buying out former chairman Peter Johnson for £20m.

2007 David Beckham revealed that he would be training with Arsenal during the MLS close season. Arsène Wenger insisted that it was not with a view to Beckham joining the club on loan.

25 DECEMBER
2002 – Ranieri's Christmas Day

Chelsea's Italian manager left nothing to chance. Ignoring the festive happiness around him, Ranieri dedicated his Christmas Day in 2002 to a study of every nuance of Southampton's tactics.

Ranieri admitted that his family was 'not too happy'. He might have wondered if it had all been worth it when the Boxing Day game finished goalless.

Christmas Day is probably the one day of the year when few of us would swap our routine with that of a professional footballer, for whom the training doesn't stop.

Former Arsenal defender Martin Keown remembers that, 'At Arsenal we'd train in the morning and then I'd race home to see the family for Christmas dinner. Then, just as everyone's settling in front of the TV, I'd hurry back to the club to travel to a hotel. The hotels were always dead, and if you were hungry you couldn't get any food. Arsène Wenger didn't like us having chocolates, but I used to sneak in a selection box! There was nothing worse than saying goodbye to the family, but it was better than being at home if you'd been dropped or were injured.'

Playing matches on Christmas Day, rather than just training, was once a British tradition. From the 1890s games, usually local derbies, were played – one on Christmas Day and the return fixture on Boxing Day.

They weren't always derbies though. Portsmouth drew 2–2 at Blackpool on Christmas Day 1954, a round trip of more than 500 miles, in the days before motorways. Portsmouth also figured in a memorable Christmas Day game in 1957 when 17-year-old Jimmy Greaves scored four times in a 7–4 win at Stamford Bridge, his first league hat-trick. Chelsea and Portsmouth also met on Christmas Day in 1946 – when Chelsea produced the first ever match programme, costing sixpence.

In 1886 in north Woolwich, a football club committee meeting was called for Christmas morning in the Royal Oak pub. When the members went into the pub their club was called Dial Square, when they came out it was called Royal Arsenal.

The last Christmas Day fixture in England was played in 1965; Blackpool beat Blackburn 4–2. The last played anywhere in Britain were in 1976, when Clydebank drew 2–2 with St Mirren and Alloa beat Cowdenbeath 2–1.

Also on this day

Footballers celebrating their birthdays on Christmas Day include Chris Kamara, Gary McAllister, Rob Edwards and Robbie Elliott.

26 DECEMBER
2006 – Evergreen Sheringham

Teddy Sheringham scored the first ever Premier League goal to be televised live, when the Sky Sports cameras captured his right-footed belter against Liverpool at the City Ground in August 1992. Fourteen years later Sheringham was still scoring goals in the top flight.

With 147 Premier League strikes, Sheringham stands with some of the best strikers ever to have played in the league – and he'd scored more than 100 goals for Millwall and Nottingham

Forest before the Premier League was even formed.

He joined Spurs soon after scoring that goal against Liverpool, and added 21 more league goals that season to become the new Premier League's top scorer in its first season. Playing for Spurs brought recognition and a place in the England team, but no trophies – they came in abundance in a four-season spell at Manchester United. At Old Trafford, Sheringham won the league title three times and in 1999 added both the FA Cup and Champions League, scoring in both finals against Newcastle and then Bayern Munich.

Another two-year spell at Tottenham was followed by a season at Portsmouth. Then, aged 38, he moved to West Ham in the second tier, and it seemed that his Premier League days were behind him. But his 21 goals in season 2004/05 helped West Ham earn promotion, and Sheringham found himself back in the top flight.

Sheringham was never quick, so getting older didn't impact on his greatest asset – his intelligence. He was not only a goalscorer, he was great at forming partnerships: with Tony Cascarino at Millwall, Jürgen Klinsmann at Spurs, Andy Cole at Manchester United and with Alan Shearer for England.

His goal for West Ham against Portsmouth on Boxing Day 2006 was his last in the Premier League, in what was to be his penultimate game at that level. It earned him the tag of the league's oldest scorer, aged 40 years and 268 days, and it came almost exactly 22 years after he'd made his debut.

Even then Sheringham wasn't finished, scoring four goals for Colchester in the Championship and playing his final game in April 2008, aged 42.

Also on this day

1999 Chelsea became the first club to select a starting 11 with no British players. Their team of de Goey, Ferrer, Leboeuf, Emerson Thome, Babayaro, Petrescu, Deschamps, Di Matteo, Ambrosini, Poyet and Flo beat Southampton 2–1. Jody Morris, from Hammersmith, came on as a substitute.

2002 Aged 16 years and 355 days, James Milner became the youngest player to score in the Premier League, 5 days younger than the previous record holder, Wayne Rooney. Milner's record was subsequently broken by James Vaughan.

27 DECEMBER
2013 – Tan sacks Mackay

Malky Mackay had been appointed manager of Cardiff City in 2011, and in his first season took them to the League

Cup Final, where they lost on penalties to Liverpool, and to the promotion play-offs.

Cardiff's owner was Vincent Tan, a Malaysian businessman who had bought the club in 2010 when it faced a winding-up order for unpaid taxes; Tan had subsequently paid off their £30m debt. In exchange Tan had insisted on the unpopular condition that his team change the colour of their kit from blue to his 'lucky' red.

The controversy over that switch was put to one side when Cardiff won the Championship title in 2013, to return to the top flight for the first time in 51 years.

Cardiff invested heavily in preparation for the Premier League, breaking their transfer record three times as first Andres Cornelius, then Steven Caulker and then Gary Medel joined the club.

By October Tan was unhappy with the return he was getting on those players, particularly Cornelius, who had cost almost £8m but who had played only twice. He blamed the head of recruitment Iain Moody, an old ally of Mackay's from their Watford days, whom Tan suspended.

Approaching Christmas 2013, with Cardiff a respectable 15th, Mackay started planning for further January signings. The day before they were due to play at Liverpool an email from Tan to Mackay became public. In it Cardiff's owner told

Mackay to resign or be sacked, claiming that Mackay had already overspent on his agreed budget.

Mackay defied Tan until he was sacked two days after Christmas. In May, with Ole Gunnar Solskjaer in charge, Cardiff were relegated.

Then in August – with Mackay on the verge of being appointed Crystal Palace manager by their sporting director, his old friend Iain Moody – Cardiff released a document outlining text messages exchanged by Mackay and Moody before they left Cardiff.

The texts, for which both men apologised contained racist, sexist and homophobic language. Moody resigned from Crystal Palace and Mackay had to look elsewhere for a job.

Also on this day

1993 Swindon lost 4–0 at home to Arsenal, leaving them bottom of the Premier League, one point and one place below Chelsea.

2003 Roman Abramovich was reported to have approached England manager Sven-Göran Eriksson about replacing manager Claudio Ranieri.

2007 Newcastle's Joey Barton was arrested on suspicion of assault in Liverpool city centre. He later pleaded guilty and was sentenced to six months in jail.

2014 Crystal Palace sacked manager Neil Warnock after exactly four months in charge.

28 DECEMBER
2013 – Anelka's quenelle

At 34 Nicolas Anelka might have been coming to the end of his career, but it was still quite a coup for West Bromwich Albion, his sixth Premier League club, when they signed him.

Anelka had played only one game for the club when it was reported that he had decided to retire following the death of his agent; in fact he took a week off on compassionate leave and returned to the side at the beginning of September.

He was still waiting for his first goal for the club when Albion went to West Ham at the end of December. It was a thrilling 3–3 draw, with Anelka scoring twice in the five minutes before half-time.

Nobody at the stadium mentioned his unusual goal celebration, his right arm stretched down with his left brought across his chest. But Premier League matches are beamed across the world and it certainly didn't go unnoticed in France, where they instantly recognized it as the highly controversial 'quenelle' gesture.

The quenelle was invented by the infamous French comedian, and friend of Anelka, Dieudonné. It has been described as an inverted Nazi salute, and the French Interior Minister Manuel Valls was in the process of attempting to ban Dieudonné's performances, saying he was 'no longer a comedian, but an anti-Semite and racist'.

Anelka defended himself, saying, 'The meaning of quenelle is anti-system. I do not know what religion has to do with this story.'

After taking advice, the FA charged Anelka with making a gesture that was 'abusive and/or indecent and/or insulting and/or improper', a charge that was denied by the player.

In February Anelka was found guilty, though the FA noted that, 'we did not find that Nicolas Anelka is an anti-Semite or that he intended to express or promote anti-Semitism by his use of the quenelle'.

He was banned for five matches and fined £80,000. In March Anelka, who had not played since late January, announced on Twitter that he had no intention of playing for West Brom again. Later the same day Albion announced that they had sacked him for gross misconduct.

Also on this day

1997 League leaders Manchester United lost 3–2 at Coventry.

2000 Chelsea signed Jesper Grønkjær from Ajax for £8m.

2007 Roy Hodgson was appointed manager of Fulham.

29 DECEMBER
2009 – Fernando's 50

In 2007 Liverpool had lost the Champions League Final to AC Milan, where they'd been unable to match the razor-sharp finishing of Pippo Inzaghi. Of their goalscorers only Peter Crouch with 18, Dirk Kuyt on 14 and Steven Gerrard with 11 had got into double figures that season – what Liverpool were lacking was a top-class centre forward who could provide a flood of goals, in the mould of Ian Rush, Robbie Fowler and Michael Owen at their peak. Fernando Torres was the answer.

The Spaniard's popularity at Anfield was guaranteed when his first goal for his new club came against rivals Chelsea on his home debut. Many players moving to a new country take a few months to settle into a new environment – not Torres. By the end of his first season Liverpool's number nine had 33 goals, 24 of them in the Premier League, including hat-tricks against Reading, Middlesbrough and West Ham. He had scored more goals in a season than any Liverpool player for a decade, more in a debut season than any foreign striker in the Premier League's history, and he'd scored in eight consecutive home games – equalling a Liverpool record set by Roger Hunt in 1961/62.

The only thing missing was a trophy, as Liverpool lost to Chelsea in the Champions League semi-final and finished fourth in the Premier League.

Injuries in the 2008/09 season limited Torres's tally of goals to 14 in the league and 17 in total. He had added another 11 Premier League goals by the time Liverpool played their final game of 2009 at Villa Park. Torres scored a 93rd-minute winner to reach 50 league goals for the club in his 72nd league game – 8 games faster than any player in Liverpool's history.

Also on this day

2001 After scoring 122 goals in five seasons at the club, Andy Cole moved from Manchester United to Blackburn for £8m.

2012 Theo Walcott scored a hat-trick for Arsenal as they beat Newcastle 7–3 at the Emirates Stadium.

2014 The managerial merry-go-round started to swing with Alan Pardew resigning from Newcastle in order to enter discussions with Crystal Palace and Alan Irvine being sacked at West Bromwich Albion.

30 DECEMBER
2009 – The League of Nations

When the first games in Premier League history had kicked off on 15 August 1992, almost 75 per cent of the players who started those matches qualified to play for England. Seventeen years later, at the very end of 2009, a landmark was set when Arsenal and Portsmouth kicked off at Fratton Park without an English player on the pitch.

The starting line-ups for Arsenal's 4–1 win were made up of seven Frenchmen, two Algerians, an Irishman, a Welshman, a Scot, a Bosnian, an Israeli, a South African, a Ghanaian, a Belgian, a Spaniard, a Russian, a Brazilian-born Croatian, a Cameroonian and an Icelander.

The influx of the best talent from around the world had added hugely to the appeal of the Premier League. The implications of that influx for the England national team have been less positive. In September 2013, in his first speech as chairman of the FA, Greg Dyke addressed what he called the 'frightening trend' of fewer and fewer players who were qualified to play for England actually playing in the Premier League.

While setting an ambitious target for the England team to reach the semi-finals of the European Championship in 2020 and win the World Cup in 2022, Dyke warned that unless the situation was addressed the national team would 'fail to compete seriously on the world stage'.

Dyke recalled the Professional Footballers' Association's 2007 claim that the Premier League had become 'a finishing school for the rest of the world, at the expense of our own players'.

Following the early exits of all English clubs from European competition, Dyke returned to his theme in March 2015, announcing that the FA would restrict entry of non-EU players to England. In future, he said, only 'outstanding talent' would be given work permits. The Premier League, he added, was in danger of 'having nothing to do with English people'.

England's manager Roy Hodgson had said, 'We have one of the lowest numbers of home-grown players and that must put us at a major disadvantage to other nations.'

Also on this day

1995 Blackburn's Alan Shearer became the first player to score 100 Premier League goals when he got their second goal in a 2–1 win over Spurs. Shearer scored 16 Premier League goals in 1992/93, 31 in 1993/94, 34 in 1994/95 and the goal against Spurs was his 19th of season 1995/96.

2006 Sheffield United beat Arsenal 1–0 at Bramall Lane, with defender Phil Jagielka in goal for the last 30 minutes after goalkeeper Paddy Kenny was forced off with a groin injury.

2009 Gary Megson was sacked as manager of Bolton Wanderers.

31 DECEMBER
1994 – John Jensen scores

A midfielder who shot to prominence with a terrific goal to help his country win the European Championship, John Jensen's next biggest claim to fame was his inability to score at all.

Jensen's Denmark had failed to qualify for the 1992 European Championship Finals, but were late replacements for Yugoslavia, who, with the Balkan War in progress, had been banned from participating by United Nations Security Council sanctions.

Denmark, runners-up to Yugoslavia in qualifying, then won the tournament, beating Germany 2–0 in the final in Gothenburg. Jensen's goal had been smashed right-footed from the edge of the penalty area past a startled Bodo Illgner in the German goal.

Jensen moved from Brøndby to Arsenal that summer, and Highbury fans licked their lips at the prospect of seeing his explosive shooting for themselves. Jensen certainly tried to give them what they wanted – his willingness to shoot was undimmed by his inability to score.

In his first season Jensen played in both the FA Cup Final and the replay as Arsenal beat Sheffield Wednesday. In 1993/94 he played in every match in Arsenal's successful European Cup Winners' Cup campaign except the final, which he missed due to injury.

Still without a goal, and having become a cult figure at Highbury, Jensen started his third season at the club with his place in the side under pressure from the emerging Ray Parlour.

The Dane had started only half of Arsenal's matches that season when they took on QPR at Highbury in his 98th game for the club. Arsenal were losing 1–0 when Jensen collected a pass on the edge of the penalty area and, in front of the North Bank, curled a brilliant shot beyond goalkeeper Tony Roberts and into the net.

It didn't help much, Arsenal lost 3–1, but before the next home game against Everton the stalls on the Avenell Road outside Highbury were selling T-shirts printed with 'I saw Jensen score!'

Jensen played another 40 games for Arsenal over the next 18 months – but never troubled the scoreboard again.

Also on this day

2005 After scoring seven goals in his first ten games for Newcastle, Michael Owen broke a metatarsal bone in his foot playing against Tottenham at White Hart Lane. It started a succession of injuries which limited him to 30 minutes of football in Newcastle's next 77 games.

2011 Robin van Persie beat Thierry Henry's Arsenal record for goals in one calendar year, scoring his 35th Premier League goal of 2011 in Arsenal's 1–0 win over QPR. Van Persie finished the year one goal short of Alan Shearer's Premier League record of 36, set in 1995.

Acknowledgements

I began my career in sports broadcasting in 1990, just as football became respectable again after years of hooliganism and tragedy. I consider myself extremely lucky to have worked throughout the era of the Premier League. In this book I've tried to include the stories, characters and matches that have made English football the most followed version of the world's game. To have been present for many of those occasions and to have met most of those characters is my very good fortune.

I am indebted to many people for this privilege. Thanks to Jonathan Pearce and Pete Simmons, who gave me an opportunity at Capital Radio. Thanks to Charles Runcie, who encouraged me to join the BBC, to Niall Sloane for introducing me to the world of television, and to Philip Bernie and Mark Cole for keeping me there.

Particular thanks should go to Andrew Clement, Paul Armstrong and Phil Bigwood at *Match of the Day*. I'm forever grateful for the early career advice and encouragement of John Motson and Barry Davies. Special thanks to Simon Brotherton for his friendship, and to all my fellow commentators on a wonderful programme, including the sadly missed Tony Gubba and David Oates. Thanks also to Nick Bushell and Phil Gibbens for staying cheerful throughout so many tournaments.

This book would not have come about without Daniel Mirzoeff at BBC Worldwide, Albert DePetrillo at Ebury Publishing, my editor Charlotte Macdonald and copy-editor Ian Allen.

Most of all thank you to my wife, Juliet, who has improved both this book and its author beyond measure.